Order this document
by MC88100UMAD/AD

MOTOROLA
SEMICONDUCTOR
TECHNICAL DATA

Errata to
MC88100 User's Manual Second Edition MC88100UM/AD REV 1

March 6, 1992

This errata applies to the *MC88100 User's Manual* Second Edition (MC88100UM/AD REV 1). The following pages have been amended.

Page:

1-1 The first bullet under **1.1 FEATURES** should read "Single-Clock Integer, Logical, Bit Field, and Branch Operations".

2-14 In the description of the SFD1 bit of the PSR, the following should be added at the end of the NOTE section. "Caution should be taken to avoid disabling the floating-point unit while there are still floating-point operations in the multiply pipeline or add pipeline. A trap-not-taken should be inserted before changing the processor status register to disable the floating-point unit."

3-17 In Table 3-1, the "<O5>" under the Abbreviation column should not have the brackets. It should be "O5".

3-62 For the **int** instruction, add "Floating-Point Inexact (if not masked)" to the Exceptions list.

3-67 In the first edition of the *MC88100 User's Manual*, the manual advised against using the **lda** instruction in the following formats:

lda (with and without size options) **r**D, **r**S1, **I**16
lda (with and without size options) **r**D, **r**S1, **r**S2
lda.b **r**D, **r**S1**[r**S2**]**

In the second edition of the *MC88100 User's Manual*, this information was deleted. Instead, the manual lists only three instruction options. To ensure future compatibility, the three instructions listed are the only permissible options for the **lda** instruction.

Also, the description section of the **lda** instruction should not make reference to the **.b**, or byte-size option. The second sentence of the second paragraph should be "The **.h** specifies half word (16 bits), and **.d** specifies double word (64 bits)." The fourth sentence of that paragraph should be "Operations that are half-word, word, and double word in size define scale factors of 2, 4, and 8, respectively."

3-74 For the **nint** instruction, add "Floating-Point Inexact (if not masked)" to the Exceptions list.

MOTOROLA

3-77 Add the following section after the Description section and before the Instruction Encoding section:

NOTE

It is necessary to precede every **rte** with an instruction that does not write into the register file (**stcr**, **st**, etc.) or the no-op instruction **or r0,r0,r0**."

3-90 For the **trnc** instruction, add "Floating-Point Inexact (if not masked)" to the Exceptions list.

3-92 The **xmem** instructions using the I16 addressing format should be deleted. There should be a note stating: "The first and second editions of the User's Manual presented the **xmem(.bu)** rD,rS1,**I16** as possible instruction options. However, these **xmem** instructions are not guaranteed in future 88000 parts. Therefore, to maintain future compatibility, these instructions must not be used."

4-1 The last sentence on this page reads "The data on this bus corresponds to addresses supplied by the data address bus." A better description is "The data on this bus corresponds to the contents of the addresses supplied by the data address bus."

4-2 In figure 4-1, the reset states of signals C31–C0 and CS/U are reversed. The reset state of C31–C0 should be "Input" while the reset state of CS/U should be "High Impedance".

5-9 Add the following at the end of the second paragraph:

"Table 5-1 shows the data P bus byte enable requirements for various operand sizes read while the MC88100 is in either big Endian or little Endian mode. DBE3–DBE0 on the P bus are driven identically to MBE3 MBE0 for the corresponding M bus transaction. In the table, bytes 0–3 correspond to the data bytes at memory address locations 0–3. Half-word 0 and half-word 1 correspond to the first two half-word operands in memory — namely those at address locations 0 and 2. Word reads are identical (all byte enables asserted) for both big Endian and little Endian modes. Double-word reads occur as two separate word read transactions. In big Endian mode, the most significant word is stored in lower memory. In little Endian mode, the least significant word is stored in lower memory."

5-10 Add the following at the end of the first paragraph:

"Table 5-2 shows the data P bus byte enable requirements for various operand sizes written while the MC88100 is in either big Endian or little Endian mode. DBE3–DBE0 on the P bus are driven identically to MBE3–MBE0 for the corresponding M bus transaction. The entire data bus is driven for byte and half-word writes. The byte strobes indicate which part of the bus is valid, depending on the byte-ordering mode of the processor. In the table, bytes 0–3 correspond to the data bytes at memory address locations 0–3. Half-word 0 and half-word 1 correspond to the first two half-word operands in memory — namely those at address locations 0 and 2. Word writes are identical (all byte enables asserted) for both big Endian and little Endian modes. Double-word writes occur as two separate word write transactions. In big Endian mode, the most significant word is stored in lower memory. In little Endian mode, the least significant word is stored in lower memory."

5-11 Insert Table 5-1 (attached) before Figure 5-11 and insert Table 5-2 (attached) after Figure 5-11.

6-8 In the middle of Figure 6-3 on Exception Recognition, there is a box that shows: TPSR ← PSR. TPSR should be EPSR.

6-15 In the last sentence of the first paragraph, the word "enable" should be "enabled".

6-15 Add the following at the end of the third paragraph: "It is necessary to precede every **rte** with an instruction that does not write into the register file (**stcr**, **st**, etc.) or the no-op instruction **or r0,r0,r0**."

there is a loss of accuracy, then the floating-point inexact exception must be signaled to the user exception handler, if there is one available. The exception handler checks the EFINX bit (bit 0) in the FPCR. If the EFINX bit is clear, then the AFINX bit is set and the valid result is written to the destination register. If the EFINX bit is set, then control passes to the user handler routine. Since the original exception taken by the hardware is a precise exception, the imprecise control registers are invalid. Therefore, the exception handler must model the information which is normally stored in those registers before passing control to the user handler routine. Note that the FIOV bit in the FPECR is set in this case, not the FINX bit.

If the exception handler determines that the floating-point number cannot be represented as a 32-bit integer, then the floating-point invalid exception must be signaled to the user exception handler, if there is one available. The exception handle checks the EFINV bit (bit 4) in the FPCR. If the EFINV bit is clear, then the AFINV bit is set in the FPSR and the largest, properly-signed integer is written to the destination register. If the EFINV bit is set, then control passes to the user handler routine. This exception, the floating-point reserved operand exception, and the floating-point divide-by-zero exception all use the same bit in the FPCR and FPSR to indicate an invalid operation; the bits in the FPECR can be used to determine which exception occurred.

Figure 6-8.5 (attached) illustrates the exception handling algorithm for the floating-point integer conversion overflow exception.

6-42 In **6.8.4.4 Floating Point Privilege Violation**, the second to the last sentence reads "When this exception occurs, the FPRV bit (bit 4) in the FPECR is set by hardware." The FPRV bit is bit 5, not bit 4.

6-42 The second paragraph of **6.8.4.5 FLOATING-POINT RESERVED OPERAND** should read:

This exception causes the FROP bit (bit 4) of the FPECR to be set by the hardware. The handling of this exception depends on the exact operands and operation. The default exception handler provides results for an operation on reserved operands (infinity, NaN, denorm) if the operation is not an exception as defined by the IEEE standard. If the operation is invalid according to the IEEE standard, and if the EFINV bit (bit 4) of the FPCR is set, then the user exception handler is invoked. If the EFINV bit of the FPCR is clear, then the AFINV bit (bit 4) of the FPSR is set by the default exception handler and a NaN is written to the destination.

6-42 **6.8.4.6 FLOATING-POINT DIVIDE-BY-ZERO** should read:

This exception occurs when division by zero is detected. When this exception occurs, the FDVZ bit (bit 3) of the FPECR is set by the hardware. The bits used in the FPCR and FPSR depend on the value of the divisor. If the divisor is zero (i.e., 0/0), and the EFINV bit (bit 4) of the FPCR is set, then the user exception handler is invoked (if supplied). If the EFINV bit is clear, then the AFINV bit (bit 4) of the FPSR is set by the default exception handler and a NaN is written to the destination. If the numerator is non-zero and the EFDVZ bit (bit 3) of the FPCR is set, then the user exception handler is invoked (if supplied). If the numerator is non-zero and the EFDVZ bit is clear, then the AFDVZ bit (bit 3) of the FPSR is set by the default exception handler and an infinity result is written to the destination.

6-43 The second paragraph of **6.8.5.1 FLOATING-POINT UNDERFLOW** should read:

How the exception handler processes the exception depends on the EFUNF bit (bit 2) in the FPCR. If the EFUNF bit is set, the software envelope passes control to the underflow user handler routine. If the EFUNF bit is not set (no user handler routine), then the default handler checks for loss of accuracy. Loss of accuracy occurs either when the hardware detects that significant bits were lost due to rounding (inexact result) or when the underflow default exception handler detects that significant bits were lost when the result was denormalized

(denormalization loss). If a loss of accuracy exists, the AFUNF bit (bit 2) is set, and the EFINX bit (bit 0) of the FPCR is checked. If the EFINX bit is set, then the user exception handler is invoked. If the EFINX bit is clear, the AFINX bit (bit 0) of the FPSR is set. Finally, if there is no underflow user exception handler and there is no loss of accuracy or if there is loss of accuracy but no inexact user exception handler, then the default exception handler completes the operation by writing the denormalized result to the destination register.

6-43 The second paragraph of **6.8.5.2 FLOATING-POINT OVERFLOW** should read:

How the exception handler processes this exception depends on the EFOVF bit (bit 1) in the FPCR. If the EFOVF bit of the FPCR is set, then the user exception handler is invoked. If the EFOVF bit is clear, the AFOVF bit (bit 1) of the FPSR is set by the default exception handler. The software envelope then checks if the EFINX bit (bit 0) in the FPCR is set. If the EFINX bit is set, the software envelope passes control to the user exception handler. If the EFINX bit is clear, then the AFINX bit (bit 0) of the FPSR is set and an infinity or the largest finite number is written to the destination.

6-44 Replace Figure 6-9 with the attached Figure 6-9.

6-45 Insert the following sentence after the second sentence of the first paragraph of **6.8.5.3 FLOATING-POINT INEXACT**: Note that the destination format could be either integer or floating-point.

6-45 The second paragraph of **6.8.5.3 FLOATING-POINT INEXACT** should read:

When this exception is signaled by the FPU, the processor sets the AFINX bit (bit 0) in the FPSR and checks the value of the EFINX bit (bit 0) in the FPCR. If the EFINX bit is set, then the floating-point imprecise exception is taken, and bit 0 of the FPECR is set by hardware. If the EFINX bit is clear, then exception processing does not occur. The EFINX bit is set or cleared by software, so the floating-point inexact exception can be enabled or disabled by software. This is the only floating-point exception that hardware sets the associated FPSR bit.

6-46 Replace Figure 6-10 with the attached Figure 6-10.

7-22 In Table 7-5, in the Trap instructions box, the asterisk next to the word Trap should be removed and instead placed next to the **tb0**, **tb1**, **tcnd**, and **rte** instructions.

8-16 In the last sentence of the second to the last paragraph the word "codes" should be replaced by the word "nodes".

8-18 **8.5 Serialized Operation** should be added. The SER bit of the Processor Status Register (PSR), is used to select between the serial and concurrent operating mode. When this bit is set, the processor is in serial mode, which results in each instruction completing its operation before the next instruction is issued. The processor still prefetches the next instruction, but goes no further in the instruction stream. This is identical to what happens when a **tb0**, **tb1**, **rte**, or **xmem** instruction is executed. The difference is that when the SER bit is set, all instructions execute in this manner. This is helpful in debugging because only one thing happens at a time.

Index-4 The PSR entry should point to page 2-12 instead of 2-11.

Table 5-1. Data Bus Requirements for Read Cycles

Big Endian

Transfer Size	Operand Address	DBE3	DBE2	DBE1	DBE0	Data D31:D24	Data D23:D16	Data D15:D8	Data D7:D0
Byte	0	1	0	0	0	Byte 0	x	x	x
	1	0	1	0	0	x	Byte 1	x	x
	2	0	0	1	0	x	x	Byte 2	x
	3	0	0	0	1	x	x	x	Byte 3
Half Word	0	1	1	0	0	(Half Word 0) MSB	LSB	x	x
	2	0	0	1	1	x	x	(Half Word 1) MSB	LSB
Word	0	1	1	1	1	MSB	(Word 0) HMB	LMB	LSB
Double Word	0	1	1	1	1	MSB	(Most Signficant Word) HMB	LMB	LSB
	4	1	1	1	1	MSB	(Least Signficant Word) HMB	LMB	LSB

Little Endian

Transfer Size	Operand Address	DBE3	DBE2	DBE1	DBE0	Data D31:D24	Data D23:D16	Data D15:D8	Data D7:D0
Byte	0	0	0	0	1	x	x	x	Byte 3
	1	0	0	1	0	x	x	Byte 2	x
	2	0	1	0	0	x	Byte 1	x	x
	3	1	0	0	0	Byte 0	x	x	x
Half Word	0	0	0	1	1	x	x	(Half Word 0) MSB	LSB
	2	1	1	0	0	(Half Word 1) MSB	LSB	x	x
Word	0	1	1	1	1	MSB	(Word 0) HMB	LMB	LSB
Double Word	0	1	1	1	1	MSB	(Least Signficant Word) HMB	LMB	LSB
	4	1	1	1	1	MSB	(Most Signficant Word) HMB	LMB	LSB

x = data and parity ignored

Table 5-2. Data Bus Requirements for Write Cycles

Big Endian

Transfer Size	Operand Address	DBE3	DBE2	DBE1	DBE0	Data D31:D24	Data D23:D16	Data D15:D8	Data D7:D0
Byte	0	1	0	0	0	**Byte***	Byte	Byte	Byte
	1	0	1	0	0	Byte	**Byte***	Byte	Byte
	2	0	0	1	0	Byte	Byte	**Byte***	Byte
	3	0	0	0	1	Byte	Byte	Byte	**Byte***
Half Word	0	1	1	0	0	**(Half Word)*** **MSB**	**LSB**	(Half Word) MSB	LSB
	2	0	0	1	1	(Half Word) MSB	LSB	**(Half Word)*** **MSB**	**LSB**
Word	0	1	1	1	1	MSB	(Word) HMB	LMB	LSB
Double Word	0	1	1	1	1	MSB	(Most Signficant Word) HMB	LMB	LSB
	4	1	1	1	1	MSB	(Least Signficant Word) HMB	LMB	LSB

Little Endian

Transfer Size	Operand Address	DBE3	DBE2	DBE1	DBE0	Data D31:D24	Data D23:D16	Data D15:D8	Data D7:D0
Byte	0	0	0	0	1	Byte	Byte	Byte	**Byte***
	1	0	0	1	0	Byte	Byte	**Byte***	Byte
	2	0	1	0	0	Byte	**Byte***	Byte	Byte
	3	1	0	0	0	**Byte***	Byte	Byte	Byte
Half Word	0	0	0	1	1	(Half Word) MSB	LSB	**(Half Word)*** **MSB**	**LSB**
	2	1	1	0	0	**(Half Word)*** **MSB**	**LSB**	(Half Word) MSB	LSB
Word	0	1	1	1	1	MSB	(Word) HMB	LMB	LSB
Double Word	0	1	1	1	1	MSB	(Most Signficant Word) HMB	LMB	LSB
	4	1	1	1	1	MSB	(Least Signficant Word) HMB	LMB	LSB

*On byte and half-word writes, the same byte or half-word is duplicated to fill the entire data bus.
The bold lettering denotes the location from where the data is latched.

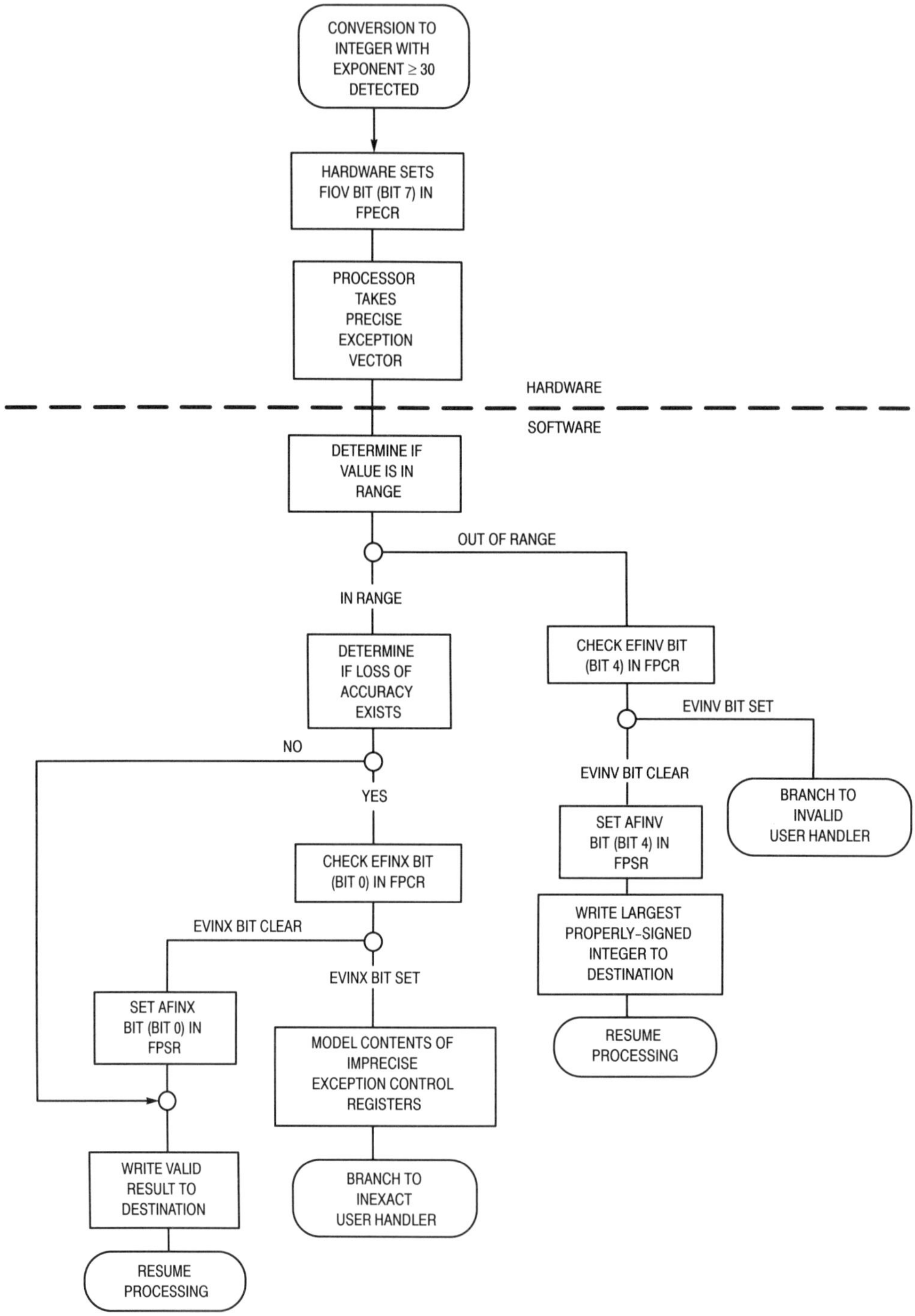

Figure 6-8.5. Floating-Point Conversion to Integer Overflow Exception Handling

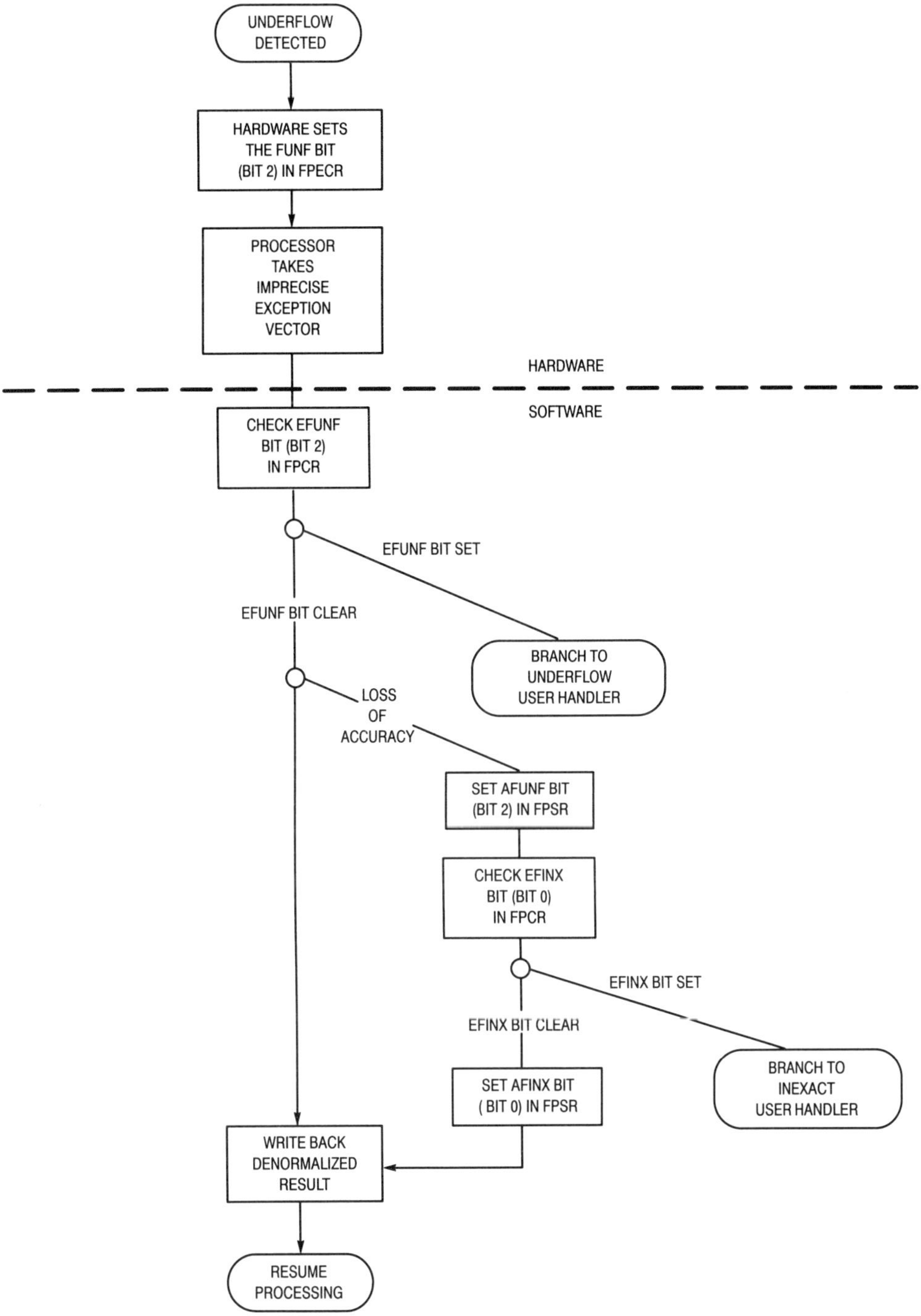

Figure 6-9. Floating-Point Underflow Algorithm

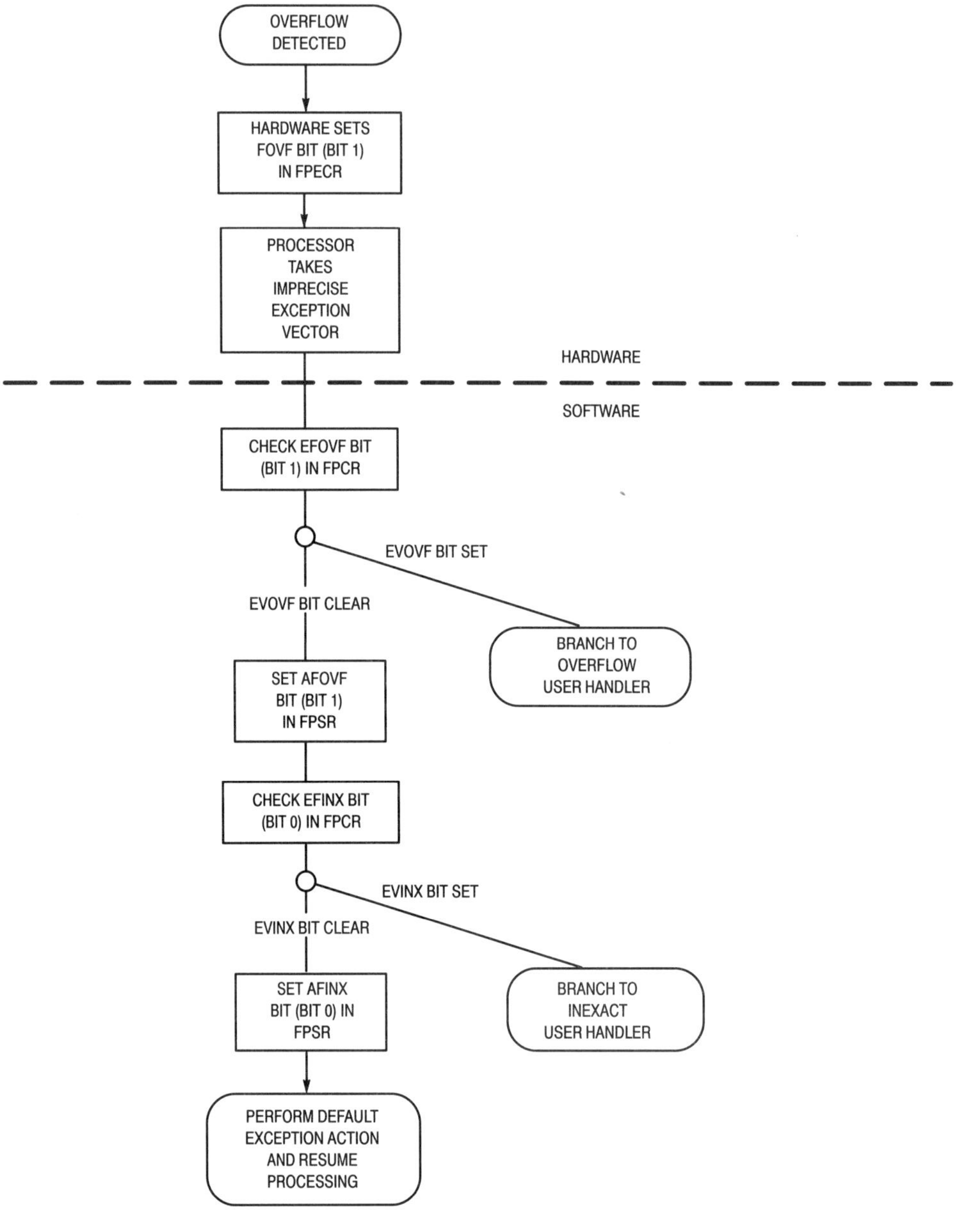

Figure 6-10. Floating-Point Overflow Exception Handling

Literature Distribution Centers:
USA: Motorola Literature Distribution; P.O. Box 20912; Phoenix, Arizona 85036.
EUROPE: Motorola Ltd.; European Literature Centre; 88 Tanners Drive, Blakelands, Milton Keynes, MK14 5BP, England.
JAPAN: Nippon Motorola Ltd.; 4-32-1, Nishi-Gotanda, Shinagawa-ku, Tokyo 141, Japan.
ASIA PACIFIC: Motorola Semiconductors H.K. Ltd.; Silicon Harbour Center, No. 2 Dai King Street, Tai Po Industrial Estate, Tai Po, N.T., Hong Kong.

MOTOROLA

MC88100UMAD/AD

◊

1ATX31054-0 PRINTED IN USA 4/92 IMPERIAL LITHO 85057 12,000 MPU YGABAA

MOTOROLA

MC88100

RISC MICROPROCESSOR USER'S MANUAL

second edition

PRENTICE HALL, Englewood Cliffs, New Jersey 07632

Motorola reserves the right to make changes without further notice to any products herein to improve reliability, function or design. Motorola does not assume any liability arising out of the application or use of any product or circuit described herein; neither does it convey any license under its patent rights nor the rights of others. Motorola products are not authorized for use as components in life support devices or systems intended for surgical implant into the body or intended to support or sustain life. Buyer agrees to notify Motorola of any such intended end use whereupon Motorola shall determine availability and suitability of its product or products for the use intended. Motorola and Ⓜ are registered trademarks of Motorola, Inc. Motorola, Inc. is an Equal Employment Opportunity/Affirmative Action Employer.

Printed in the United States of America

10 9 8 7 6 5 4 3 2 1

ISBN 0-13-567090-X

Prentice-Hall International (UK) Limited, *London*
Prentice-Hall of Australia Pty. Limited, *Sydney*
Prentice-Hall Canada Inc., *Toronto*
Prentice-Hall Hispanoamericana, S.A., *Mexico*
Prentice-Hall of India Private Limited, *New Delhi*
Prentice-Hall of Japan, Inc., *Tokyo*
Simon & Schuster Asia Pte. Ltd., *Singapore*
Editora Prentice-Hall do Brasil, Ltda., *Rio de Janeiro*

TABLE OF CONTENTS

Paragraph Number	Title	Page Number

Section 1
Introduction

Section 2
Programming Model

TABLE OF CONTENTS (Continued)

Section 3
Addressing Modes and Instruction Set

TABLE OF CONTENTS (Continued)

Section 4
Signal Description

TABLE OF CONTENTS (Continued)

Section 5
Bus Operation

TABLE OF CONTENTS (Continued)

Paragraph Number	Title	Page Number

Section 6
Exceptions

TABLE OF CONTENTS (Continued)

Section 7
Instruction Execution Timing

TABLE OF CONTENTS (Continued)

TABLE OF CONTENTS (Concluded)

LIST OF ILLUSTRATIONS

LIST OF ILLUSTRATIONS (Continued)

LIST OF TABLES

LIST OF TABLES (Continued)

SECTION 1
INTRODUCTION

The MC88100 is the first processor in the M88000 Family of reduced instruction set computer (RISC) microprocessors. Implemented with Motorola's high-density CMOS (HCMOS) technology, the MC88100 incorporates 32-bit registers, data paths, and addresses. The M88000 Family includes the MC88200 cache/memory management unit (CMMU), which adds high-speed memory caching, two-level demand-paged memory management, and support for shared-memory multiprocessing.

The MC88100 uses only simple instructions with extremely rapid execution times to yield maximum efficiency and throughput for M88000 systems. In addition, a full line of highly optimizing compilers, operating systems, boards, application programs, and development tools are available for the M88000. Instruction mnemonics used in this section can be identified by referring to **SECTION 3 ADDRESSING MODES AND INSTRUCTION SET**.

1.1 FEATURES

The MC88100 can execute a majority of the instructions in one machine cycle, or effective concurrent execution can be accomplished through internal pipelines in one machine cycle. Figure 1-1 shows a block diagram of the MC88100 and MC88200. Major features of the MC88100 are as follows:

- Single-Clock Integer, Logical Bit Field, Branch and Store Operations
- Fifty-One Instructions and Seven Operand Types
- Fine-Grain Parallelism:
  - — Four Fully Independent Execution Units with Five Concurrent Pipelines
  - — Execution Synchronized in Hardware by a Scoreboard Register
- Nondestructive Register and Condition Code Model Allowing Fast Operand Access and Operand Reuse
- Thirty-Two General-Purpose Registers
- Single- and Double-Precision IEEE 754 Floating-Point Compatibility (Up to One Operation per Clock Cycle)
- Full 32-Bit Combinatorial Multiplier
- Separate Data and Instruction Memory Ports (Harvard Bus Structure) Allowing Simultaneous Accesses:
  - — 30-Bit Data Address Bus (Byte Strobes Select Individual Bytes)
  - — 32-Bit Data Bus (32-Bit Word)

1

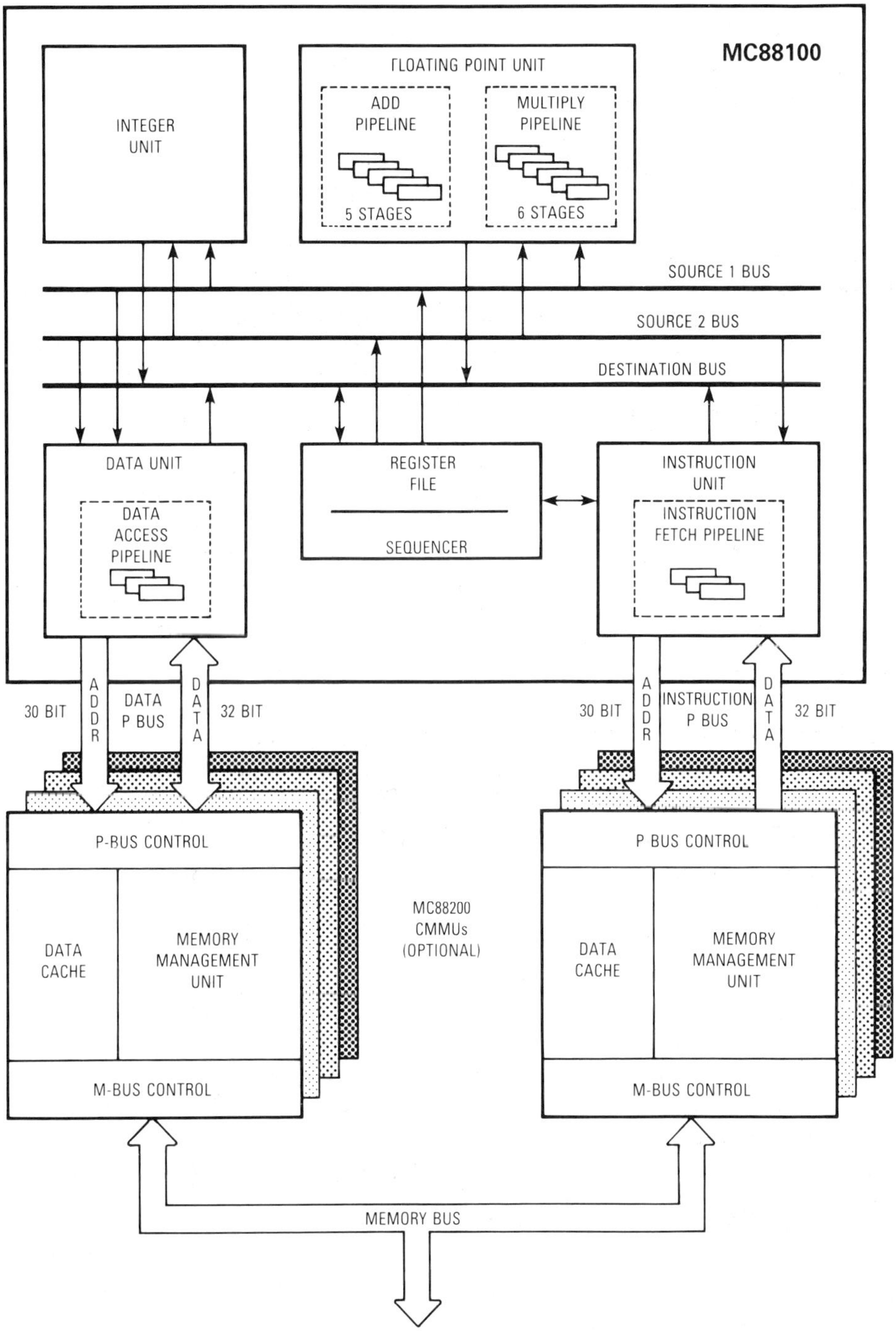

Figure 1-1. MC88100/MC88200 Block Diagram

— 30-Bit Instruction Address Bus (32-Bit Boundary Addressing)
— 32-Bit Instruction Bus (Fixed Instruction Length of 32 Bits)

- Pipelined Load and Store Operations (Up to 80 Mbytes/sec at 20 MHz)
- High-Speed Interrupt Processing with Minimal Interrupt Latency
- Functional Redundancy Fault Detection
- Selectable Big-Endian or Little-Endian Byte Ordering
- Interfaces Directly to Memory or to MC88200 CMMU
- Complex Instruction Sequences Easily Built from Simple Instructions by High-Level Language Compiler
- Extensible Architecture Facility through Special Function Units (SFUs)

1.2 OVERVIEW

The following paragraphs provide a brief overview of the architecture of the MC88100. Topics such as register-to-register operations, addressing modes, instruction formats, delayed branching, privileged levels, memory ports, and optimizing software are discussed.

1.2.1 Register-to-Register Architecture

The MC88100 provides register-to-register operation for all data manipulation instructions. Source operands are either located in source registers or provided as an immediate value embedded in the instruction. A separate destination register stores the results of an instruction, which allows source operand registers to be reused in subsequent instructions. Register contents are read from or written to memory only through **ld**, **st**, and **xmem** instructions. An **xmem** instruction provides an atomic load and store operation, which is useful for semaphore testing and multiprocessor synchronization.

1.2.2 Reduced Instruction Set

The MC88100 instruction set contains 51 instructions. All integer arithmetic, logical, bit-field, and certain flow-control instructions can execute in a single clock cycle. Memory-access and floating-point instructions are performed by dedicated execution units (see Figure 1-1), releasing other processor resources during multicycle instructions. The floating-point, data, and instruction units implement execution pipelines so one multicycle instruction can be started in each clock cycle. Although these individual instructions may take more than one cycle to complete, effective one-cycle execution can be accomplished. All instructions are implemented directly in hardware, precluding the need for microcoded operations. Complex operations are handled in software by using advances in operating system and optimizing compiler technology.

1

1.2.3 Simplified Addressing Modes

All data manipulation instructions are implemented as register-to-register or register-plus-immediate-value instructions, which eliminates memory-access delays in data manipulation instructions. In addition, there are a sufficient number of memory addressing modes: three addressing modes for data memory, four addressing modes for instruction memory, and three register addressing modes. Address calculations are simple and are implemented efficiently and execute quickly.

1.2.4 Instruction Formats

All instructions are implemented as single-word (32-bit) opcodes. The fixed instruction length eliminates the need for alignment circuitry, thereby decreasing instruction decode time. Formats are consistent across instructions, which allows for simplified, efficient decoding that occurs in parallel with operand accesses. Branch address calculations and register usage checking also operate in parallel with decoding. All instructions can be fetched in a single memory access.

1.2.5 Delayed Branching

The MC88100 incorporates delayed branching to reduce pipeline penalties associated with changes in program flow. In processors incorporating pipelined execution, changes in the program flow can reduce execution speed due to the time required to flush and refill the pipeline. However, the MC88100 takes advantage of delayed branching, which allows the instruction fetched after the branch instruction to be optionally executed, whether or not the branch is taken. Consequently, the pipeline continues to operate without unused cycles. The next instruction in the pipeline executes while the branch target instruction is prefetched from memory.

The execution of the instruction following the branch is under explicit software control through the value of a bit in the instruction encoding. When delayed branching is selected, the programmer or compiler picks a useful instruction to be executed before the change of flow and places the instruction after the branch in the instruction stream.

1.2.6 Levels of Privileges

The MC88100 defines two levels of privileges that allow memory accesses and control registers to be protected. The supervisor mode is the higher privileged level of execution; whereas, the user mode is the lower privileged level. Application software is typically processed in the user mode; resource access is limited to the user memory space, general-purpose registers, and certain internal registers in the execution units. The supervisor mode is typically used by operating systems and other system-level resources; memory and execution unit register access is unrestricted.

1

1.2.7 Multiple External Buses

The MC88100 uses a two-port nonmultiplexed memory access interface (Harvard architecture). Operand reads and writes from/to memory are performed through dedicated data address and data paths; instruction fetches also occur over dedicated instruction address and data paths. These ports operate concurrently, eliminating bus contention between data accesses and instruction fetches.

The memory buses are implemented through and controlled by the data unit and instruction unit. Each unit utilizes pipelined address calculation and data transfer/instruction fetch operations. The data unit executes all data memory access instructions. The instruction unit performs all instruction prefetches and executes all flow-control instructions. The MC88100 is capable of addressing 4 gigabytes of external data and of addressing over 1 gigaword of 32-bit instructions of program memory, in either supervisor or user memory spaces.

The MC88100 memory ports can interface directly to memory; however, most MC88100 designs incorporate at least two MC88200 CMMUs (one for data memory and one for instruction memory). The data unit and instruction unit use the separate processor buses (P buses) to interface these units to the respective MC88200s/memories. Two to eight CMMUs (see Figure 1-1) can be easily incorporated into an MC88100 system, by using up to four for the data memory space and up to four for the instruction memory space.

1.2.8 Optimizing Software

Optimizing compilers, linkers, and operating systems, which have been designed in conjunction with the design of the MC88100 architecture, are essential contributors to MC88100 performance. This software performs optimizations based on the concurrent execution pipelines; instructions are scheduled to avoid pipeline stalls due to data dependencies. Delayed branches are used a high percentage of the time. This software also makes efficient use of the MC88100 instruction set and register model.

A register usage convention has been established that supports the cross linking of procedures from various compilers and languages. With this convention, compilers and linkers allocate the general-purpose registers in a manner that minimizes data movement to and from memory, even during procedure calls. When a register save is necessary, it can be preformed in a single clock cycle due to the pipelined data unit.

1.3 EXECUTION UNITS AND REGISTER FILE

The MC88100 contains four execution units (see Figure 1-1) which operate independently and concurrently. Two of these units, the integer unit and the floating-point unit (FPU), execute all data manipulation instructions. Data memory accesses are performed by the data unit, and instruction prefetches are performed by the instruction unit. The integer unit

performs 32-bit arithmetic and logical operations and all bit-field operations. The FPU handles floating-point arithmetic (plus integer multiply and divide) in hardware, relieving the integer unit from more time-consuming floating-point calculations. The FPU implements two pipelines: one for multiply operations and one for all other floating-point instructions. In addition to these execution units, the MC88100 contains a register file/sequencer, which includes the general-purpose registers and performs many control functions. The MC88100 also has three internal buses; a source 1 bus (S1 bus), a source 2 bus (S2 bus), and one destination bus (D bus) that are used for passing operands between the register file and the different execution units.

1.3.1 Integer Unit

All integer, bit-field, and control register instructions are executed by the integer unit in one machine cycle. Integer multiply and divide are multicycle instructions executed by the FPU.

The integer unit contains 11 general control registers including four supervisor-only storage registers, a processor identification register (PID), and a processor status register (PSR). The function of the four storage registers is programmer defined. In addition, shadow and exception-time registers, copies of the instruction pointers, the scoreboard register, and PSR are maintained for exception recovery. The integer-unit control registers are accessed using the **ldcr**, **stcr**, and **xcr** instructions. Complete details on the registers are given in **SECTION 2 PROGRAMMING MODEL**.

1.3.2. Floating-Point Unit

The FPU executes the floating-point arithmetic instructions, integer/floating-point conversions, and integer multiply and divide instructions. Single-precision, double-precision, and mixed-mode arithmetic operations can be performed for floating-point instructions.

The FPU is implemented as two pipelines. Add, subtract, compare, divide, and convert instructions are executed by one pipeline; multiply instructions are executed by the other pipeline. The divide instruction is the only floating-point operation that is not completely pipelined. A divide instruction iterates through one execution stage once for each bit of accuracy required in the result. The free-running multiply pipeline operates independently.

The FPU contains 11 control registers. Nine of these registers are shadow registers containing status and intermediate results used for exception recovery; the other two registers are the floating-point status register and the floating-point control register. These two registers contain information on exception conditions (divide-by-zero, overflow, etc.) and control the floating-point rounding modes. All the FPU registers are privileged except the status and control registers. The FPU registers, which are accessed using the **fldcr**, **fstcr**, and **fxcr** instructions, are described in detail in **SECTION 6 EXCEPTIONS**.

The FPU requires more than one clock cycle per instruction. Floating-point instructions prevent subsequent instructions from using the results prematurely by setting a bit in the scoreboard register during their execution. For example, single-precision add, subtract, compare, and convert instructions require five cycles and the single-precision multiply instruction requires six cycles. However, due to the pipelined nature of the FPU, a new instruction can begin on each clock cycle.

1.3.3 Data Unit

The data unit executes the instructions that access data memory and controls the data memory interface portion of the data P bus. The data unit contains a dedicated calculation unit for address computation. Addresses are formed by adding the source 1 register operand specified by the instruction with either a source 2 register operand or a 16-bit immediate value embedded in the instruction placed on the S2 bus. This address is driven on the 30-bit data unit address bus. Refer to **SECTION 2 PROGRAMMING MODEL** for detailed information on the addressing capabilities of the MC88100. The instruction also selects the general-purpose register that provides the ultimate data source or destination.

Memory accesses are pipelined in the data unit. The memory access pipeline contains three stages. The pipelined nature of the P bus allows two data memory accesses to be active on the bus at the same time for two load/store operations. The following list identifies the three stages:

Stage 2 — Computes address.

Stage 1 — Drives the external data address bus; if the access is a store operation, fetches data from registers and drives the external data bus.

Stage 0 — Monitors the reply from the memory system; if the access is a load operation, reads the data bus and writes the load result to the general-purpose register.

The data unit maintains a total of nine data-unit general control registers that are used to reconstruct pending transactions after an exception condition has been corrected. The data-unit control registers are accessed as the integer-unit control registers with the **ldcr**, **stcr**, and **xcr** instructions.

The data-unit operations work concurrently with other MC88100 functions (instruction execution, etc.). The scoreboard register contains 32 bits; each bit corresponds to one of the general-purpose registers and indicates when one of the registers is awaiting the results of a memory access or is awaiting instruction completion. The scoreboard register prevents data that must be altered from being used by a subsequent instruction until it has been updated, therefore maintaining a sequential instruction execution model. Refer to **1.3.5.1 REGISTER FILE** for more information on the scoreboard register.

1.3.4 Instruction Unit

The instruction unit prefetches instructions from memory, performs the first steps of instruction decode, and provides instructions to the appropriate execution unit via encoded

internal control signals. The instructions prefetched from memory are dictated by program flow, which includes sequential accesses, execution of absolute jump, absolute and conditional branch instructions with displacement, and exception vectoring. Other tasks, such as partial instruction decoding and tasks related to subroutine returns and exception processing, are also performed. Registers are maintained that indicate the contents of the instruction pipeline at all times, providing history information for exception-condition recovery. In addition, a vector base register (VBR) is maintained that points to a memory page containing all of the exception vectors. The VBR is a general control register and is accessed with **ldcr**, **stcr**, and **xcr** instructions. Instruction prefetches from memory are performed on the instruction P bus.

The instruction unit maintains three instruction pointers that indicate the contents of the execution pipeline. The execute instruction pointer (XIP) points to the instruction currently executing in the integer unit, data unit, or FPU. The next instruction pointer (NIP) points to the instruction currently being accessed from memory and decoded for execution. The fetch instruction pointer (FIP) points to the memory location of the next instruction to be accessed.

The instruction unit identifies and saves the return pointer for **jsr** and **bsr** instructions to the register file. The return pointer is written to a specific general-purpose register. The return pointer is either the contents of the NIP or FIP at the time the **jsr** or **bsr** instruction begins execution, depending on whether or not delayed branching is used.

When an exception occurs, all memory accesses in progress are allowed to finish before the exception is processed. During exception processing, the processor context is frozen and the FPU is disabled. The instruction pipeline is then cleared, and the exception target address is computed. This address is written to the FIP so that the first instruction of the exception routine can be prefetched and normal execution can resume.

1.3.5 Register File/Sequencer

The MC88100 contains a register file/sequencer (see Figure 1-1) that contains the general-purpose registers and performs overall internal control functions. The following paragraphs briefly describe the register file/sequencer.

1.3.5.1 REGISTER FILE. The register file contains the 32 general-purpose registers, maintains concurrency control information, optimizes the operand/result internal bus utilization, and provides a means of separating instruction initiation from instruction completion.

The general-purpose registers provide operands for all integer and floating-point instructions, serve as the data source or destination for **st** and **ld** instructions, and provide addresses for branch and memory-access instructions. The register file has two output ports and one input/output port. The two output ports allow source operands (selected by the instruction unit) to be simultaneously placed on the S1 and S2 buses. The input/output

port is used to store results into destination registers. The **st** and **xmem** instructions use the D bus to transfer data from the register file unit to the data unit. General-purpose registers can be accessed via the D bus at the same time that source operands are being read.

Instruction execution begins sequentially but can finish in any order. All operands are read or written from/to registers or memory. The register file contains the scoreboard register, which maintains a bit for each of the general-purpose registers 'in use' except **r0** (**r0** contains the constant zero and cannot be modified). All instructions that take greater than one clock cycle to execute, cause the scoreboard bit(s) that correspond to the destination register(s) to be set. If an instruction requires a register that is to be read or written to, the scoreboard register is checked for the availability of that register. If the source and/or destination registers are flagged as 'in use' (defined as the destination register for a previous instruction still in execution), the execution of the requesting instruction is delayed until both the source and destination registers are flagged as available. The scoreboard register is checked on each clock cycle until the source and destination registers are available.

When an execution unit updates a general-purpose register, the updated data is placed on the D bus. When an execution unit reads a register, the register is read from either the S1 or S2 bus. To increase instruction throughput, the MC88100 incorporates a register feed-forward capability. Feed-forward gates the contents of the D bus onto the appropriate source bus so that, if an execution unit is waiting on the data, it receives the data at the same time that the register is updated. When both source registers required by an instruction are in use and may be modified by the previous instruction, both operands can be received by feed-forward. When the source operands are received, the destination register scoreboard bit(s) are set, and the instruction begins execution.

1.3.5.2 SEQUENCER. The sequencer performs the register writeback arbitration, performs exception arbitration, and generates control signals for the instruction unit and the internal buses.

When an execution unit has a result to write to a register, the execution unit requests a writeback slot granted by the writeback arbiter. If an exception is pending, the writeback arbiter prohibits register writeback grants except for memory-access results. If no exception is pending, the writeback arbiter generates a control signal that gates the data onto the D bus and into the selected register. If two or more execution units request a writeback slot, the writeback arbiter grants the writeback slot according to a defined priority scheme if no exceptions are pending. One-cycle instructions have the highest priority, followed by the FPU, then the data unit. If required, the sequencer also sends a control signal to the feed-forward logic to gate data from the D bus onto the selected source bus.

The exception arbiter controls exception recognition and resolves recognition of multiple exceptions by determining which exception the processor will recognize. The priority order of exceptions is precise exception, interrupt, and then imprecise exception. Exceptions are described fully in **SECTION 6 EXCEPTIONS**.

1

The flow-control circuitry in the sequencer monitors the scoreboard register, various signals from the instruction decode circuit, the branch unit (in the instruction unit), and the exception arbiter. This circuit also appropriately generates signals for the instruction prefetch mechanism in the instruction unit. These signals initiate operations such as clearing the execution pipeline and loading the branch target address.

1.3.6 Internal Buses

The MC88100 has one bidirectional and two unidirectional 32-bit register buses that perform all internal data transfers. The S1 and S2 buses carry source operands to the integer unit, data unit, instruction unit, and FPU. All source data comes from the general-purpose registers or from 16-bit immediate values embedded in the instruction. The bidirectional D bus transfers data from the execution units to the general-purpose registers. The D bus also transfers data to be stored from the register file to the data unit.

Arbitration for the internal buses is performed by the sequencer. The instruction unit selects the source registers for an instruction, which are gated onto the source buses under control of the sequencer. The destination register is selected by the writeback arbiter (part of the sequencer); the write request for the register file is generated by the appropriate execution unit.

1.3.7 Special-Function Units (SFUs)

A SFU executes instructions concurrently with other SFUs and with the integer, data, and instruction units. The SFUs are designed so that they can stand alone and can be added to or removed from a given implementation of the M88000 Family with no impact on the architecture. Multiple SFUs are connected to common buses and share data through general-purpose registers. The M88000 architecture allows up to seven SFUs per implementation. The MC88100 floating-point unit is implemented as SFU #1.

1.4 EXECUTION MODEL

The MC88100 obtains a high performance level through fine-grain parallelism and other advances in microprocessor architecture. The following paragraphs briefly describe the parallelism and advanced features incorporated in the MC88100.

1.4.1 Pipelining and Parallelism

The four execution units allow the MC88100 to perform up to five operations in parallel:

Access Program Memory
Execute an Arithmetic, Logical, or Bit-Field Instruction
Access Data Memory
Execute Floating-Point or Integer Divide Instructions
Execute Floating-Point or Integer Multiply Instructions

In addition, the floating-point, data, and instruction units themselves are pipelined and can complete an operation in every clock cycle:

- Up to Five Floating-Point Add, Subtract, Compare, or Convert Instructions Can Execute Simultaneously
- Up to Six Floating-Point or Four Integer Multiply Instructions Execute Simultaneously
- Up to Three Data Memory Accesses Can Be in Progress Simultaneously
  - Two Memory Accesses on the External Bus
  - One Address Calculation
- Up to Two Instruction Fetches Can Be in Progress Simultaneously

The instruction unit pipeline supplies the appropriate execution unit with instructions that are to be executed by a concurrent pipeline. Data memory access instructions are dispatched to the data unit; whereas, floating-point, integer multiply, and integer divide instructions are dispatched to the FPU. The FPU contains two pipelines, one handling floating-point and integer multiplication, the other handling floating-point add, subtract, compare and conversions between integer and floating-point, as well as integer and floating-point divide instructions. All other instructions are executed by the integer unit (or instruction unit for branches) in one machine cycle.

1.4.2 Fine-Grain Parallelism

All MC88100 execution units contain an additional level of fine-grain parallelism. Instruction decode and source operand fetches from the registers are performed simultaneously. Branch instruction decode and branch target address calculation are performed in parallel with the next sequential instruction fetch. The three internal register buses allow three simultaneous register accesses, eliminating internal bus contention by the concurrent execution pipelines. The MC88100 also supports concurrent register writes and reads. One execution unit can write a result to the destination register while another unit fetches the source operands from other registers (or possibly the same register).

1.4.3 Register Set

The MC88100 has two programming models corresponding to the supervisor and user modes of operation. As shown in Figure 1-2, the MC88100 contains three types of registers that provide data and execution information to the execution units. Most control registers can be accessed only in supervisor mode. The following list briefly describes the three types of registers:

1. General-purpose registers (**r31**–**r0**) located in the register file/sequencer contain program data (source operands and instruction results). All of these registers, with the exception of **r0** (constant zero), have read/write access. Register **r0** contains the constant zero and a write operation to **r0** has no effect.

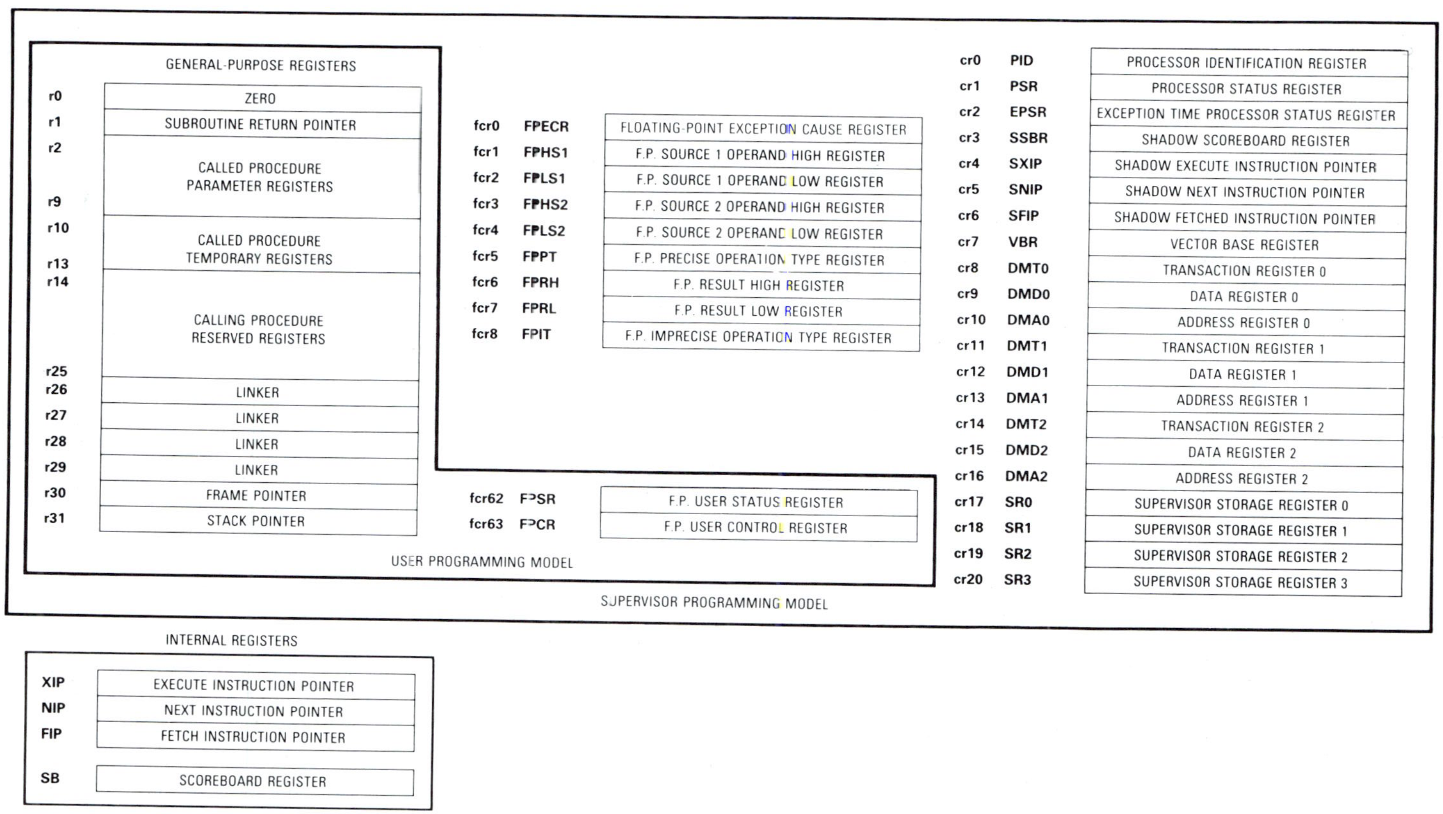

Figure 1-2. Programming Model

2. Control registers in the various execution units contain status, execution control, and exception processing information. Some of these registers have read/write access; others are read only.

3. Internal registers located in the register file/sequencer and instruction unit control instruction execution and data availability. These registers are not explicitly accessible to the programmer.

1.4.4 Condition Computations

Conditional test results are generated in a manner that complements concurrent operations and parallel execution. Conditions are computed at the explicit request of the programmer using compare instructions. Conditional test results are loaded into any specified general-purpose register instead of into a dedicated condition code register, eliminating contention between concurrent execution units accessing a dedicated condition code register. Since conditions are computed by explicit instructions, optimizing compilers can reorder the execution sequence of instructions to obtain maximum efficiency. The MC88100 also provides dedicated branch and trap instructions that combine an explicit compare with conditional branching into a single, fast operation.

1.4.5 Operand Types and Addressing Modes

The MC88100 supports seven operand types grouped into three categories. The categories are integer, floating-point, and bit fields, as shown in Table 1-1. Additional data types may be included in future members of the M88000 Family through inclusion of additional SFUs.

The MC88100 provides three methods of addressing the data memory space and four methods of addressing the instruction memory space. The following list identifies the three data addressing modes:

Register Indirect with Unsigned Immediate Index

Register Indirect with Register Index

Register Indirect with Scaled Register Index

Table 1-1. Operand Types

Operand Type	Expressed As
Integer	Signed and Unsigned Byte (8 Bits) Signed and Unsigned Half Word (16 Bits) Signed and Unsigned Word (32 Bits) Signed and Unsigned Double Word (64 Bits)
Floating Point	IEEE 754 Single Precision (32 Bits) IEEE 754 Double Precision (64 Bits)
Bit Fields	Signed and Unsigned Bit Fields from 1 to 32 Bits

1

The following list identifies the four instruction addressing modes:
Register with 9-Bit Vector Number
Register with 16-Bit Signed Displacement
Instruction Pointer Relative (26-Bit Signed Displacement)
Register Direct

Refer to **SECTION 2 PROGRAMMING MODEL** for more detailed information on the operation of the addressing modes.

1.4.6 Instruction Set

The MC88100 instruction set is divided into six categories: integer arithmetic, floating-point arithmetic, logical, bit field, load/store/exchange, and flow control. The MC88100 instruction set is summarized in Table 1-2.

Table 1-2. Instruction Summary

Integer Arithmetic Instructions

Mnemonic	Description
add	Add
addu	Add Unsigned
cmp	Compare
div	Divide
divu	Divide Unsigned
mul	Multiply
sub	Subtract
subu	Subtract Unsigned

Floating-Point Arithmetic Instructions

Mnemonic	Description
fadd	Floating-Point Add
fcmp	Floating-Point Compare
fdiv	Floating-Point Divide
fldcr	Load from Floating-Point Control Register
flt	Convert Integer to Floating Point
fmul	Floating-Point Multiply
fstcr	Store to Floating-Point Control Register
fsub	Floating-Point Subtract
fxcr	Exchange Floating-Point Control Register
int	Round Floating Point to Integer
nint	Round Floating Point to Nearest Integer
trnc	Truncate Floating Point to Integer

Logical Instructions

Mnemonic	Description
and	AND
mask	Logical Mask Immediate
or	OR
xor	Exclusive OR

Load/Store/Exchange Instructions

Mnemonic	Description
ld	Load Register from Memory
lda	Load Address
ldcr	Load from Control Register
st	Store Register to Memory
stcr	Store to Control Register
xcr	Exchange Control Register
xmem	Exchange Register with Memory

Flow-Control Instructions

Mnemonic	Description
bb0	Branch on Bit Clear
bb1	Branch on Bit Set
bcnd	Conditional Branch
br	Unconditional Branch
bsr	Branch to Subroutine
jmp	Unconditional Jump
jsr	Jump to Subroutine
rte	Return from Exception
tb0	Trap on Bit Clear
tb1	Trap on Bit Set
tbnd	Trap on Bounds Check
tcnd	Conditional Trap

Bit-Field Instructions

Mnemonic	Description
clr	Clear Bit Field
ext	Extract Signed Bit Field
extu	Extract Unsigned Bit Field
ff0	Find First Bit Clear
ff1	Find First Bit Set
mak	Make Bit Field
rot	Rotate Register
set	Set Bit Field

SECTION 2
PROGRAMMING MODEL

2

This section briefly describes the MC88100 processor states, operand conventions, registers, and floating-point implementation. These aspects affect all operations such as instruction execution and memory accesses. Exceptions are briefly described in this section, but the details of individual exceptions (including exception recovery) are given in **SECTION 6 EXCEPTIONS**. Instruction mnemonics used in this section can be identified by referring to **SECTION 3 ADDRESSING MODES AND INSTRUCTION SET**.

2.1 PROCESSOR STATES

The MC88100 is always in one of three states: normal instruction execution, exception, or reset. The reset state is entered when the reset ($\overline{\text{RST}}$) signal is asserted. The exception state is entered under two types of conditions. One condition is caused when the program encounters certain unusual or erroneous conditions. The other type of exception occurs when the program requires a resource administered by system software executing at a higher level of privilege or an external interrupt is detected. The following paragraphs describe the three states of the MC88100.

2.1.1 Reset State

When $\overline{\text{RST}}$ is asserted, all current processor operations abort. When $\overline{\text{RST}}$ is negated, the processor restarts instruction execution in a defined sequence. The control registers are initialized as appropriate, external signals are placed in the high-impedance state, and when $\overline{\text{RST}}$ is negated the processor begins instruction execution at a defined address in physical memory (defined by the reset vector). Refer to **SECTION 5 BUS OPERATIONS** and **SECTION 6 EXCEPTIONS** for more information on the effects of reset.

2.1.2 Instruction Execution

During normal instruction execution, the MC88100 operates at either the supervisor or user level of privilege. These levels define which memory space is accessed during external bus transactions and which registers are available to the programmer. The level of privilege is determined by the MODE bit in the processor status register (PSR). The following paragraphs describe the levels of privilege.

2

2.1.2.1 SUPERVISOR LEVEL OF PRIVILEGE. The supervisor mode is the highest level of privilege. The processor operates in the supervisor mode when the MODE bit is set. When operating in the supervisor mode, memory accesses reference the supervisor address space in data (data supervisor/user select (DS/$\overline{U}$) asserted) or instruction (code supervisor/user select (CS/$\overline{U}$) asserted) memory. The programmer can specify the **[.usr]** option for memory-access instructions to force access to the user data address space while operating at the supervisor mode. The supervisor mode allows execution of all instructions and allows access to all control registers and general-purpose registers.

Operating system software typically executes in the supervisor mode. Among the operating system services provided are resource allocation (memory and peripherals), exception handling, and software execution control (task initiation, scheduling, etc.). Execution control normally includes control of the user programs and protecting the system from accidental or malicious corruption by a user program.

The MODE bit is set automatically when an exception is recognized so that the exception handler executes in supervisor mode. All bus transactions performed during exception processing reference the supervisor memory spaces. Reset also causes the MODE bit to be set, placing the processor into supervisor mode.

2.1.2.2 USER LEVEL OF PRIVILEGE. The processor operates at the user level of privilege when the MODE bit in the PSR is clear. For memory accesses, the DS/$\overline{U}$ and CS/$\overline{U}$ signals are negated, causing the user data and user instruction memory to be referenced. Control register access is restricted at the user level of privilege. The only control registers accessible are the floating-point control and status registers. Using other control registers in the user privilege mode causes an exception.

2.1.2.3 CHANGING LEVELS OF PRIVILEGE. The user mode changes to the supervisor mode under four conditions:

1. An exception occurs. An exception places the processor into the exception processing state, which includes the switch to the supervisor mode.
2. A reset is signaled, which is a special form of exception processing.
3. A user program executes a trap instruction.
4. An interrupt or memory access fault occurs.

When the processor switches to supervisor mode, the MODE bit is set in the PSR, and all memory accesses default to supervisor memory. Therefore, the **.usr** option must be specified for **ld**, **st**, and **xmem** instructions to access user memory. All control registers are accessible to the supervisor software.

The supervisor mode changes to the user mode under two conditions:

1. The processor executes an **rte** instruction to restore the processor context in effect before a trap instruction or exception occurs as part of its execution. The **rte** instruction restores the PSR, which returns the processor to user mode when the mode bit of the restored PSR is clear.

2. A **stcr** or **xcr** instruction explicitly clears the MODE bit in the PSR. Since the FIP and NIP registers are not changed, this method of clearing the MODE bit usually causes undesired program execution results.

2

2.1.3 Exception State

Exceptions are conditions that cause the processor to suspend execution of the current instruction stream and perform exception processing. Exception processing provides an efficient context switch so that system software can handle the exception condition while maintaining the integrity of the hardware and other software. Exceptions include:

Interrupts, which are Signaled Externally via the Interrupt Input
Externally Signaled Errors, such as a Memory Access Fault
Internally Recognized Errors, such as Divide-by-Zero
Trap Instructions

Exceptions can occur at any time during normal instruction execution. Exceptions are recognized internally when the processor is between instructions (the previous instruction has been executed or dispatched, and the next instruction has not begun). When an exception is recognized, the processor freezes the execution context in shadow and exception-time registers (which precludes other exceptions from occurring), explicitly disables interrupts, and enters the supervisor mode. In addition, the floating-point unit (FPU) is disabled and the data unit is allowed to complete all pending accesses. Instruction execution transfers in an orderly manner to the appropriate exception handler routine. The exception handler routine is the software that processes the exception condition and restores the processor to normal operation.

To provide the necessary information to recover from an exception, the MC88100 maintains copies of certain internal registers and the PSR. Shadowing is used for tracking these internal registers at each stage of instruction execution. When shadowing is enabled, copies of these registers are written to corresponding general control and FPU control shadow registers on each machine cycle. The registers that are shadowed are the three instruction pointers, the scoreboard register, the data-unit pipeline registers, and the FPU source operand, result, precise operands, and imprecise operation type registers. These shadow registers maintain a copy of the instruction pipeline, the memory-access pipeline, and the floating-point source operands at the end of each cycle. The PSR has a corresponding exception-time register. The exception-time register is only updated at the time an exception is recognized (not on each machine cycle). The exception-time PSR and shadow registers should be explicity modified by software only when shadowing is disabled.

2

When an exception occurs, the shadow registers and exception-time PSR contain the processor context at the time of the exception (instruction pointers, status, etc.). The exception handler routine uses this saved context to determine the exact cause of the exception and to take corrective action. For example, when an integer divide exception occurs, the shadow execute instruction pointer (SXIP) points to the instruction that caused the exception. When a trap instruction is executed, the shadow registers are used to restore the processor context after the trap is handled. (The trap may be a request for operating system services or another operation performed at the supervisor level.) At the end of an exception handler routine, an **rte** instruction is usually executed. This instruction restores the context saved in the control registers to the corresponding internal registers. Refer to **SECTION 6 EXCEPTIONS** for detailed information on registers, priorities, and exception handling.

2.2 OPERAND CONVENTIONS

The following paragraphs describe how the various data types are represented in the MC88100, both in registers and in memory.

2.2.1 Operand Types

The MC88100 supports seven operand types. The following list defines the different operand types:

Byte — 8 Bits
Half Word — 16 Bits (two bytes)
Word — 32 Bits (four bytes)
Double Word — 64 Bits (eight bytes)
Single-Precision Floating Point — 32 Bits (four bytes)
Double-Precision Floating Point — 64 Bits (eight bytes)
Bit Field — 1 to 32 Bits in a 32-Bit Register

The operand size for each instruction is either explicitly encoded in the instruction or implicitly defined by the instruction operation. Bit fields are explicitly defined by the instruction or by a source register specified in the instruction.

2.2.2 Data Organization in Registers

The general-purpose registers contain operands of all seven types. Refer to Figure 2-1 for a description of the data organization in registers.

Since the memory interface supports operand types other than 32-bit words, the MC88100 incorporates rules for placing memory data into registers or extracting data from registers (for storing to memory). Byte operands are always loaded or extracted from the lower eight bits of a register, but when an **ld** instruction loads a byte into a register, it either sign

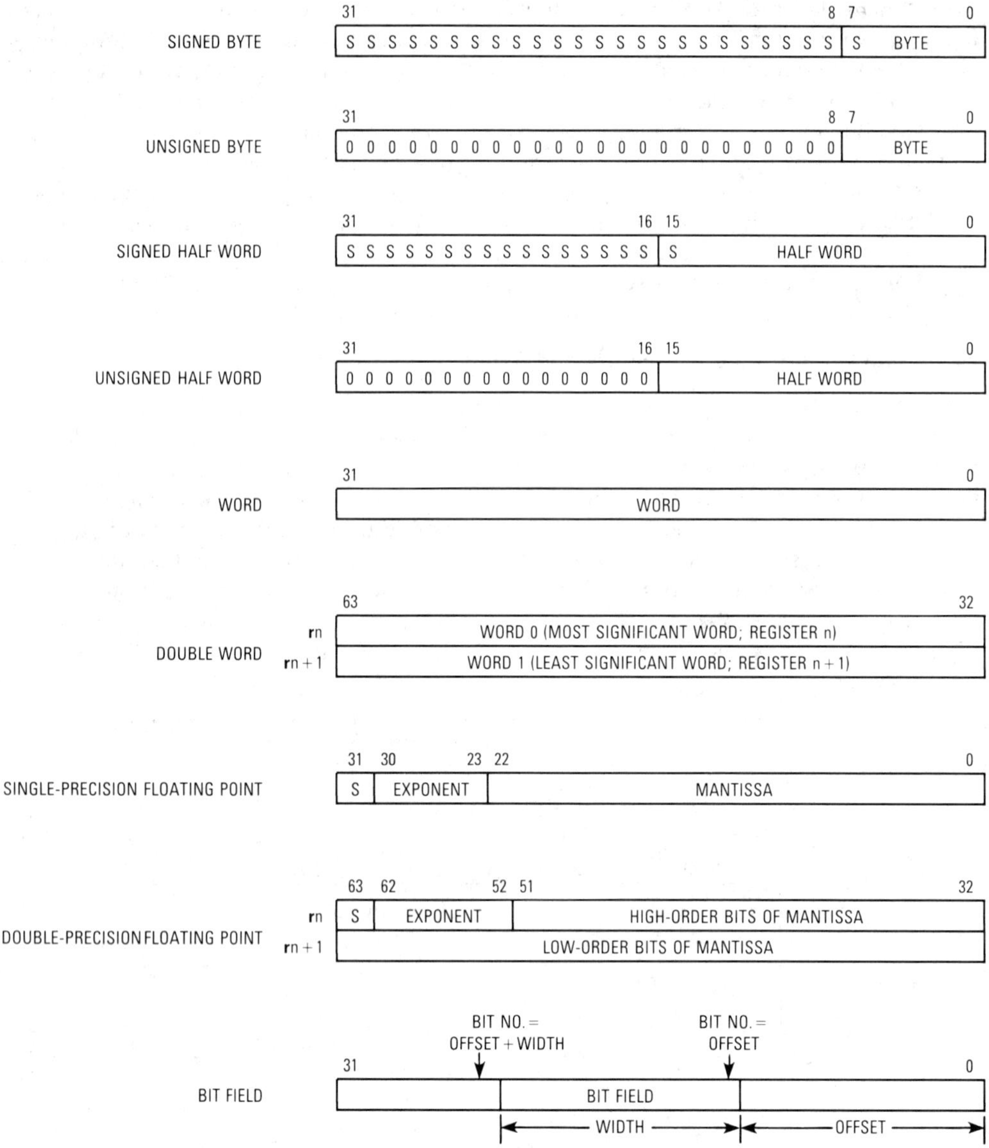

Figure 2-1. Data Organization in Registers

extends or zero extends bits 31 through 8. Half words are always loaded or extracted from the lower 16 bits of a register, except the **ld** instruction either sign extends or zero extends bits 31 through 16. Word operands load or store the entire 32 bits to/from memory; double-word operands load and store two adjacent registers (**rn** and **rn** + 1) with **rn** always containing the higher order word. For single-precision floating-point operands, bit 31 contains

the sign bit, bits 30–23 contain the exponent, and the remaining bits comprise the mantissa. For double-precision floating-point operands, the upper order register (**rn**) contains the sign bit, an exponent field, and the upper 20 bits of the mantissa. The lower order register (**rn**+1) contains the remaining bits of the mantissa. Double-word operands and double-precision floating-point operands can be specified as beginning with **r31**, in which case **r0** contains the lower order word. However, **r0** may never be modified (writes to **r0** are ignored). Bit-field operands are specified by an offset and a width. The most significant bit (MSB) of the bit field is closest to bit 31 of the register and the least significant bit (LSB) is closest to bit 0 of the register. The value of the offset equals the bit number of the LSB of the bit field and the offset+width −1 equals the bit number of the MSB of the bit field.

2.2.3 Data Organization in Memory and Byte Ordering

The organization of data in memory is similar to the register organization, except that bit fields are represented as part of bytes, half words, and words. In addition, the MC88100 supports two byte-ordering configurations for operands in memory. In the "Big-Endian" byte-ordering configuration, the lower addresses correspond to higher order bytes. The address n (modulo 4 address) of a word corresponds to the most significant byte of the word. The least significant byte corresponds to address n+3. In the "Little-Endian" byte-ordering configuration, the less significant bytes, half-words, and words reside at the lowest addresses (see Figure 2-2). In effect, the byte ordering, is controlled by the byte-ordering (BO) bit in the PSR. The BO bit is cleared, enabling "Big-Endian" byte ordering after a processor reset.

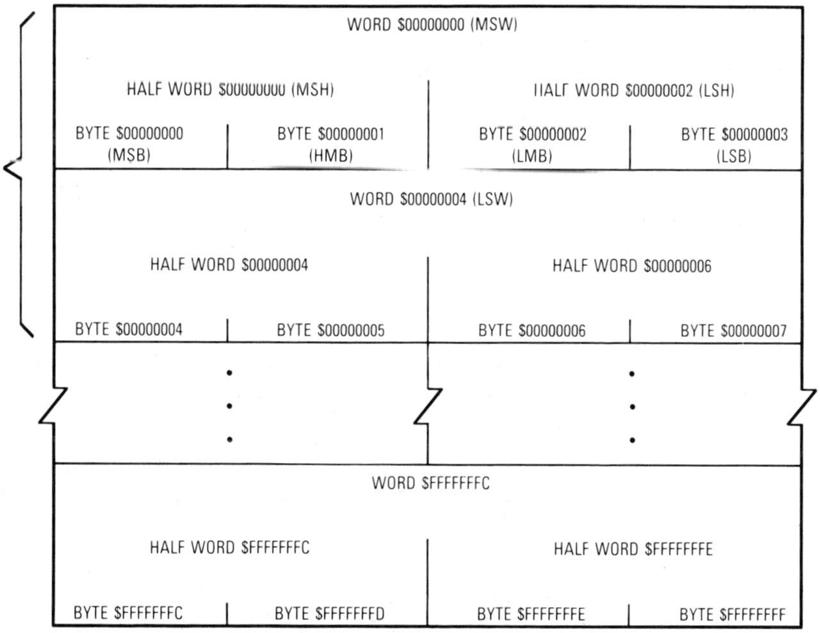

BIG-ENDIAN BYTE ORDERING

Figure 2-2. Byte-Ordering Configuration in Memory (Sheet 1 of 2)

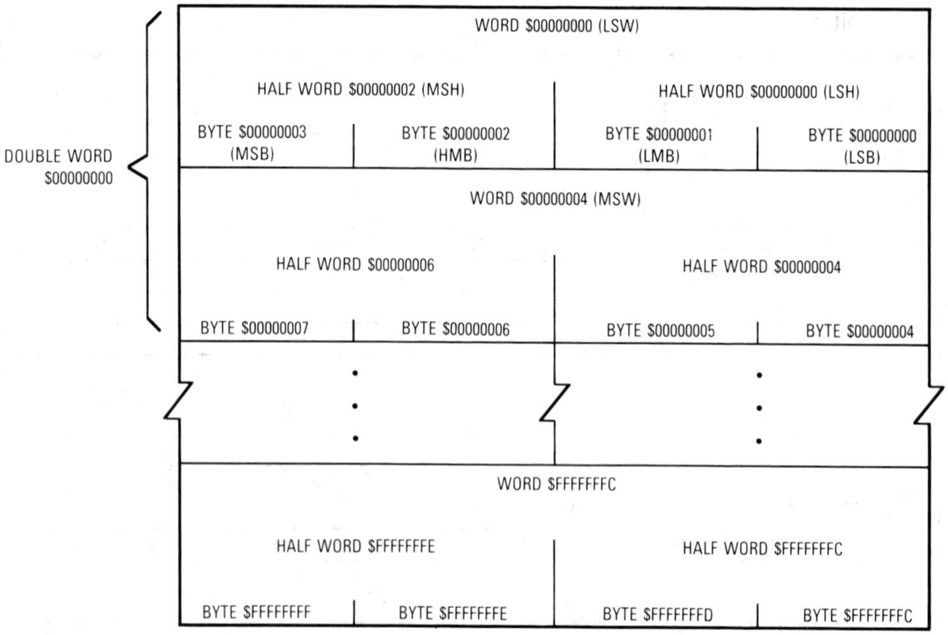

LITTLE-ENDIAN BYTE ORDERING

LEGEND:
MSB – Most Significant Byte
HMB – Higher Middle Byte
LMB – Lower Middle Byte
LSB – Least Significant Byte
LSH – Least Significant Half Word
MSH – Most Significant Half Word
MSW – Most Significant Word
LSW – Least Significant Word

Figure 2-2. Byte-Ordering Configuration in Memory (Sheet 2 of 2)

The relationship between the way data is stored in memory and the way it is loaded into registers is shown in Figure 2-3. This figure shows the results of a **ld** instruction for byte, half-word, word, and double-word operands. In each example, the "Big-Endian" configuration is shown first, and the "Little-Endian" is shown second. Word loads are the same for either byte-ordering configuration. For any operand size, the same value is placed in the register for both configurations; the only difference is the address of each value in memory. For example, Figure 2-3 shows how the lower middle byte (LMB) is loaded into a register in each configuration. The byte address is different for the "Big-Endian" and the "Little-Endian" configurations for an LMB load; the address is one less for the "Little-Endian" configuration.

The store operations work the same as load operations, except the direction of the transfer between the register and memory is reversed.

NOTE

All data in memory must be aligned to the appropriate address boundary. Half words are aligned on modulo two boundaries, words are aligned on modulo four

2

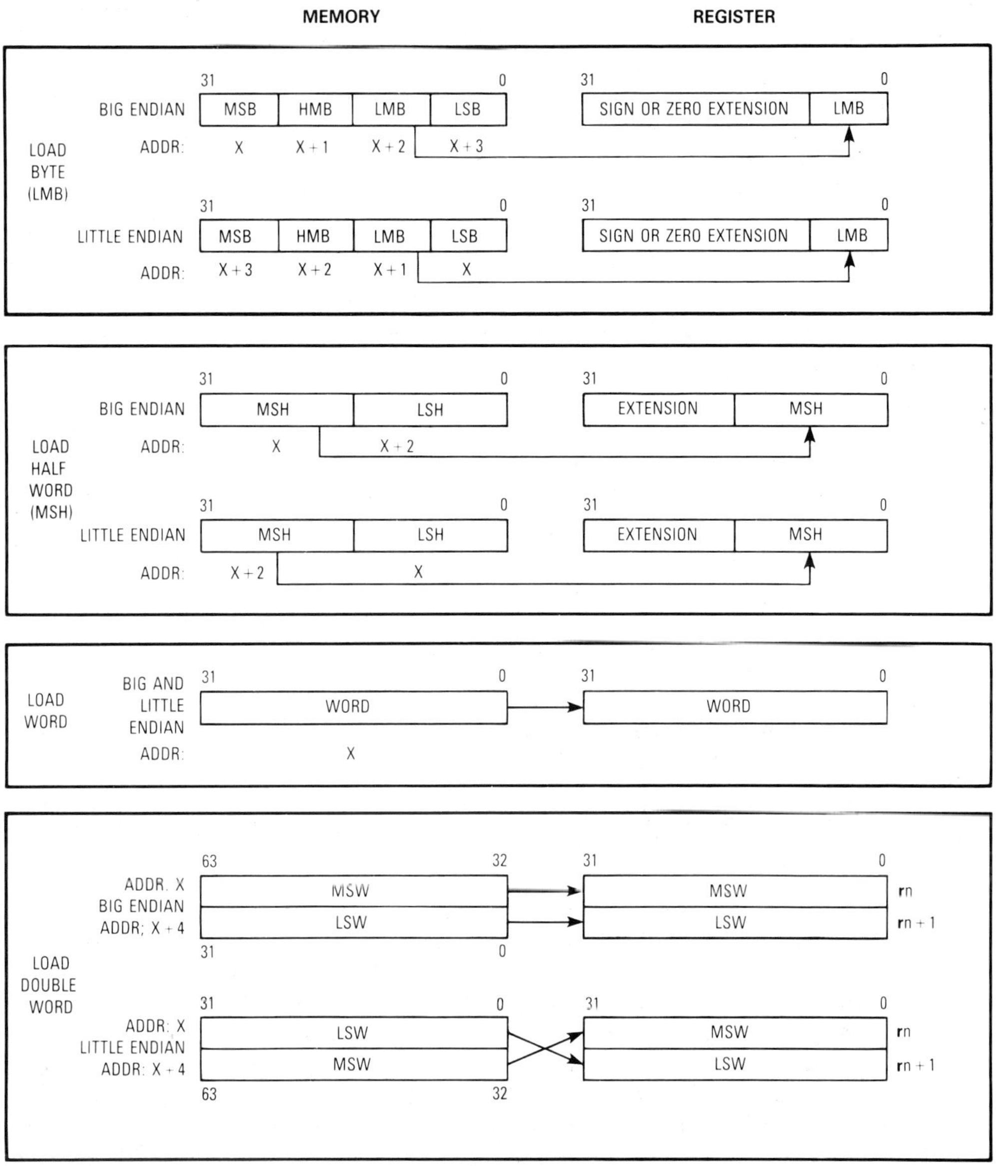

LEGEND: MSB – Most Significant Byte; HMB – Higher Middle Byte; LMB – Lower Middle Byte; LSB – Least Significant Byte; LSH – Least Significant Half Word; MSH – Most Significant Half Word; MSW – Most Significant Word; LSW – Least Significant Word

Figure 2-3. Operand Loads for Different Byte-Ordering Configurations

boundaries, and double words are aligned on modulo eight boundaries. An attempt to perform a misaligned access causes an exception if misaligned exceptions are enabled in the PSR. Otherwise, an attempt to perform a misaligned access causes the address to be truncated to a proper boundary.

2.3 REGISTER DESCRIPTION

The MC88100 contains three types of registers which provide data and execution information to the execution units and to software. Register access rights depend on the register type and current level of privilege. The following paragraphs describe the programmer's view of some of the MC88100 general-purpose, control, and internal registers. Refer to **SECTION 6 EXCEPTIONS** for more information on floating-point and exception control registers.

2.3.1 Supervisor/User Programming Model

The supervisor programming model includes all general-purpose and control registers. The general-purpose registers (**r31–r0**) provide data and address information for instruction execution. The general control registers (**cr20–cr0**) provide exception recovery and status information for the integer unit, data unit, and instruction unit. The general control registers are copied to and from the general-purpose registers using the **ldcr**, **stcr**, and **xcr** instructions. These instructions restrict access of the general control registers to only the supervisor software. The FPU control registers (**fcr8–fcr0**) provide exception recovery and status and control information for the FPU. These registers are copied to and from the general-purpose registers using the **fldcr**, **fstcr**, and **fxcr** instructions. Refer to **SECTION 6 EXCEPTIONS** for the full description of these registers. Refer to Figure 1-2 for an illustration of the programming model.

In user mode, all of the general-purpose registers can be accessed. However, the only control registers accessible in the user mode are the floating-point control register **(fcr63)** and floating-point status register **(fcr62)**.

2.3.2 General-Purpose Registers

There are 32 general-purpose registers, each 32 bits wide. These registers contain instruction operands and results, and provide address and bit-field information. In addition, the general-purpose registers have hardware and software usage conventions. Hardware conventions are strictly enforced by the MC88100. Although the software conventions are not enforced, they should be observed to guarantee compatibility with future hardware and software. Table 2-1 shows the organization of the general-purpose registers.

Double-word and double-precision floating-point operands can be read from and written to any two adjacent registers. However, the conventions listed below should be considered when defining double words.

2

Table 2-1. General-Purpose Registers

Register Number	Name
r0	Zero
r1	Subroutine Return Pointer
r2 • • **r9**	Called Procedure Parameter Registers
r10 • • **r13**	Called Procedure Temporary Registers
r14 • • **r25**	Calling Procedure Reserved Registers
r26	Linker
r27	Linker
r28	Linker
r29	Linker
r30	Frame Pointer
r31	Stack Pointer

The register conventions are as follows:

1. Register **r0** always contains zero, which is used in instructions requiring the constant zero as an operand (for example, compare to zero). This is a hardware convention; the software can write to **r0** but this operation has no effect (i.e., writes are ignored).

2. Register **r1** contains the return pointer generated by **bsr** or **jsr** to subroutine instructions. This is a hardware convention; both of these instructions overwrite the data in **r1** when they execute. However, this register is not protected, software can read or overwrite the return pointer (or any other data) contained in **r1**.

3. Registers **r9** through **r2** are used for passing parameters to a called routine. These registers can be overwritten by the called routine. This is a software convention.

4. Register **r13** through **r10** are used as temporary storage. They can be overwritten by a called routine but do not contain parameters for the called routine. This is a software convention.

5. Registers **r25** through **r14** are used as data storage for the current routine. A called routine must ensure that the data in these registers is returned without modification when it finishes execution. These registers must be preserved for the calling routine. This is a software convention.

6. Registers **r29** through **r26** are reserved for use by the linker, which is a software convention.

7. Register **r30** is reserved for use as a software frame pointer, which is a software convention.

8. Register **r31** is reserved for use as a software stack pointer, which is a software convention.

2.3.3 General Control Registers

The MC88100 contains 21 general control registers accessible only in supervisor mode. Fourteen of these registers provide exception information for integer-unit and data-unit exceptions. The remaining registers provide status information, the base address of the exception vector table, and general-purpose storage. Table 2-2 shows all the general control and floating-point control registers. When a control register is read, reserved bits are returned as zeros in the current implementation. Writes to reserved bits are ignored. The following paragraphs describe the processor identification register (PID), the PSR, and the supervisor storage registers. Refer to **SECTION 6 EXCEPTIONS** for more detailed information on the other control registers.

2.3.3.1 PROCESSOR IDENTIFICATION REGISTER (PID). This register contains the architectural revision number, the processor version number, and a bit that indicates whether the processor is in master or checker mode. This register is read only.

	31–16	15–8	7–1	0
cr0	0 0 0 0 0 0 0 0 0 0 0 0 0 0 0 0	ARCH REVISION	VERSION #	M/C

Bits 31–16 — Reserved

Read as zero; not guaranteed to be zero in future implementations.

ARCH REVISION — Architectural Revision Number

Identifies the particular processor (MC88100 future-generation, special-purpose processors). The revision number changes when a major architectural change is made that warrants a new part number. The revision number for MC88100 is zero.

VERSION # — Version Number

Identifies the particular mask version of the MC88100 processor. The version number is changed by Motorola when mask changes are made that affect the functionality of the device.

M/C — Master/Checker

The M/C bit reflects the inverted value of the $\overline{\text{PCE}}$ input signal. When this bit is set, the MC88100 operates in its normal fashion. When this bit is clear, the MC88100 operates in checker mode as described in **SECTION 8 APPLICATIONS INFORMATION**.

1 – Master Mode

0 – Checker Mode

2

Table 2-2. Control Registers

Register Number	Acronym	Name
cr0	PID	Processor Identification Register
cr1	PSR	Processor Status Register
cr2	EPSR	Exception-Time Processor Status Register
cr3	SSBR	Shadow Scoreboard Register
cr4	SXIP	Shadow Execute Instruction Pointer
cr5	SNIP	Shadow Next Instruction Pointer
cr6	SFIP	Shadow Fetched Instruction Pointer
cr7	VBR	Vector Base Register
cr8	DMT0	Transaction Register 0
cr9	DMD0	Data Register 0
cr10	DMA0	Address Register 0
cr11	DMT1	Transaction Register 1
cr12	DMD1	Data Register 1
cr13	DMA1	Address Register 1
cr14	DMT2	Transaction Register 2
cr15	DMD2	Data Register 2
cr16	DMA2	Address Register 2
cr17	SR0	Supervisor Storage Register 0
cr18	SR1	Supervisor Storage Register 1
cr19	SR2	Supervisor Storage Register 2
cr20	SR3	Supervisor Storage Register 3
fcr0	FPECR	Floating-Point Exception Cause Register
fcr1	FPHS1	Floating-Point Source 1 Operand High Register
fcr2	FPLS1	Floating-Point Source 1 Operand Low Register
fcr3	FPHS2	Floating-Point Source 2 Operand High Register
fcr4	FPLS2	Floating-Point Source 2 Operand Low Register
fcr5	FPPT	Floating-Point Precise Operation Type Register
fcr6	FPRH	Floating Point Result High Register
fcr7	FPRL	Floating-Point Result Low Register
fcr8	FPIT	Floating-Point Imprecise Operation Type Register
fcr62	FPSR	Floating-Point User Status Register
fcr63	FPCR	Floating-Point User Control Register

2.3.3.2 PROCESSOR STATUS REGISTER (PSR). The PSR contains information about the current operations of the processor. These bits are set by hardware or software to report the status of processor operations or to control processor operations. The operation of various bits in the PSR depends on the value of the shadow freeze bit (SFRZ, bit 0) in the PSR. For detailed information on the implications and effects of the SFRZ bit, refer to

SECTION 6 EXCEPTIONS. This register has read/write access. Only bits 31–28 and 3–0 can be modified by an **stcr** or **xcr** instruction.

	31	30	29	28	27 ... 10	9 ... 4	3	2	1	0
cr1	MODE	BO	SER	C	0 0 0 0 0 0 0 0 0 0 0 0 0 0 0 0 0 0	1 1 1 1 1 1	SFD1	MXM	IND	SFRZ

MODE — Supervisor/User Mode

This bit is set by hardware when the processor changes to the supervisor mode (due to an exception condition or trap instruction); it may be cleared by software to return the MC88100 to operating in the user mode. Refer to **2.1.2.3 CHANGING LEVELS OF PRIVILEGE** for more information related to the MODE bit.

0 – User Mode
1 – Supervisor Mode

NOTE

The MODE bit should only be cleared by an **rte** instruction. When the MODE bit is cleared by a control register instruction (load or exchange), two problems can occur. First, the privilege check on the next instruction may not be correct and second, the next instruction may have been fetched from the incorrect (user or supervisor) memory space.

BO — Byte Ordering

This bit is set by an **stcr** or **xcr** instruction to indicate the current byte ordering. See **2.2.3 Data Organization in Memory and Byte Ordering** for a full description of byte ordering.

0 – Big-Endian Byte Ordering
1 – Little-Endian Byte Ordering

SER — Serial Mode

The serial mode is generally used for debugging purposes since it significantly reduces machine throughput. Refer to **SECTION 8 APPLICATIONS INFORMATION** for more information on serializing the processor. This bit is set by software as appropriate.

0 – Concurrent Operation Allowed
1 – Serial Mode

C — Carry

This bit is modified by hardware according to the results of an add or subtract instruction. It is only modified when the instruction explicitly requests the use of the carry bit.

0 – Carry Was Not Generated by an Add or Subtract Instruction
1 – Carry Was Generated by an Add or Subtract Instruction

Bit 27–10 —Reserved

Always read as zero but are not guaranteed in future implementations; writes are ignored.

2

Bits 9–4 — SFU Disable

These bits will be used to enable additional SFUs in future versions of the MC88100. These bits are hardwired to "one" since the MC88100 contains only one special function unit (SFU1), the FPU. An attempt to execute an instruction that selects an unimplemented SFU causes a precise exception for that SFU.

1 – Unimplemented SFUs Always Disabled

SFD1 — SFU1 Disable

This bit is automatically set by hardware when an exception or reset occurs. This bit can also be set or cleared explicitly by load or exchange control register instructions.

0 – SFU1 Enabled

1 – SFU1 Disabled

NOTE

Initiating a floating-point instruction or an integer multiply or divide instruction while this bit is set causes a floating-point unimplemented precise exception.

MXM — Misaligned Access Enable

This bit is set by software to disable the misaligned access exception. When this bit is set and a misaligned access is attempted, the processor truncates the address to a consistent boundary. See **6.5.2 Misaligned Access Exception** for more information.

0 – Misaligned Data Access Causes an Exception

1 – Misaligned Data Access Does Not Cause an Exception

IND — Interrupt Disable

This bit is automatically set by hardware to disable interrupts when an exception occurs. This bit can also be set or cleared explicitly by **stcr** or **xcr** instructions to specifically disable/enable interrupts. Interrupts must be disabled when shadowing is frozen to avoid an error exception.

0 – Interrupt Enabled

1 – Interrupt Disabled

SFRZ — Shadow Freeze

This bit is set by hardware when an exception occurs to preserve the processor context for the exception. This bit can also be set or cleared explicitly by **stcr** or **xcr** instructions or implicitly by an **rte**. If this bit is set and any exception occurs, the MC88100 takes the error exception. Setting the SFRZ bit in the PSR with an **stcr** or **xcr** instruction does not cause the SFRZ bit to be set in the EPSR. The EPSR contains the value of the PSR before the **stcr** or **xcr** instruction is executed.

0 – Shadow Registers Enabled

1 – Shadow Registers Frozen

2.3.3.3 SUPERVISOR STORAGE REGISTERS. The integer unit contains four 32-bit supervisor storage registers. These registers provide high-speed storage for supervisor software to store data and pointers, which are protected from user-mode access. Their use and

contents are determined by software. These registers have read/write access through the **ldcr**, **stcr**, and **xcr** instructions.

2.3.4 Internal Registers

2

The internal registers of the MC88100 are the registers that the processor uses to track instruction execution and register dependencies. These include the three instruction pointers and the scoreboard register. The internal registers are not available in any of the register models; they can only be modified and used indirectly. There are additional internal registers in the MC88100, but these are not visible to the programmer. Refer to **SECTION 6 EXCEPTIONS** for information on the shadow registers.

1. The execute instruction pointer (XIP) register contains the address of the instruction that is currently being executed by the integer unit or that was just issued to the FPU or data unit (depending on the instruction).
2. The next instruction pointer (NIP) register contains the address of the instruction that is currently being received from memory and decoded by the instruction unit (next instruction to execute).
3. The fetch instruction pointer (FIP) points to the memory location of the next accessed instruction; this address is being driven to memory for the instruction prefetch. For sequential execution, the fetched instruction is read from the address of the next instruction to execute plus four bytes (FIP = NIP + 4). Jump target addresses are received on the source 2 bus from the operand specified in the jump instruction. Unconditional branch addresses are computed from the XIP plus the signed 26-bit word displacement included in the branch instruction (FIP = XIP + d26). Conditional branch addresses for the branch taken case are calculated as FIP = XIP + d16.
4. The scoreboard (SB) register contains a bit corresponding to each general-purpose register (**r31** through **r1**). If a bit is set, the corresponding register is currently in use (specified as a destination) by a previous instruction. Scoreboarding is discussed in detail in **SECTION 3 ADDRESSING MODES AND INSTRUCTION SET** and **SECTION 7 INSTRUCTION SET TIMING**.

2.4 FLOATING-POINT IMPLEMENTATION

The following paragraphs summarize the MC88100 floating-point implementation and how it conforms to ANSI/IEEE Standard 754-1985. Numeric representations, operations, and handling of exception are discussed.

NOTE

The MC88100 implements ANSI/IEEE Standard 754-1985 functionality. Although the information presented in the following paragraphs will aid in understanding the MC88100 floating-point implementation, they are not intended as a complete definition of the ANSI/IEEE floating-point functionality. The ANSI/IEEE standard is the governing document for this information.

2.4.1 Numeric Formats

The MC88100 supports two floating-point formats: single and double precision. Single-precision floating-point numbers are represented in 32 bits; double-percision numbers are represented in 64 bits. Figure 2-4 shows the two floating-point formats. In each case, the numbers are encoded as three fields:

1. Sign — A one-bit field which is 0 (clear) for positive numbers and 1 (set) for negative numbers. For an add or subtract operation, the sign bit reflects the sign of the result unless the operation is $x + (-x)$. In the $x + (-x)$ case, the sign bit is set if the rounding mode is round-toward-negative-infinity or else it is cleared. For a multiplication or division operation, the sign bit is the exclusive-OR of the signs of the operands. The **fcmp** instruction does not consider the sign bit for zero (i.e., $+0 = -0$).
2. Exponent — A bit field which represents the exponent of the floating-point number. The exponent is eight bits for single-precision numbers and 11 bits for double-precision numbers. The exponent is represented in excess 127 notation for single-precision numbers and in excess 1023 notation for double-precision numbers.
3. Mantissa — A bit field which represents the fractional binary portion of the normalized floating-point number. The mantissa is 23 bits for single-precision numbers and 52 bits for double-precision numbers.

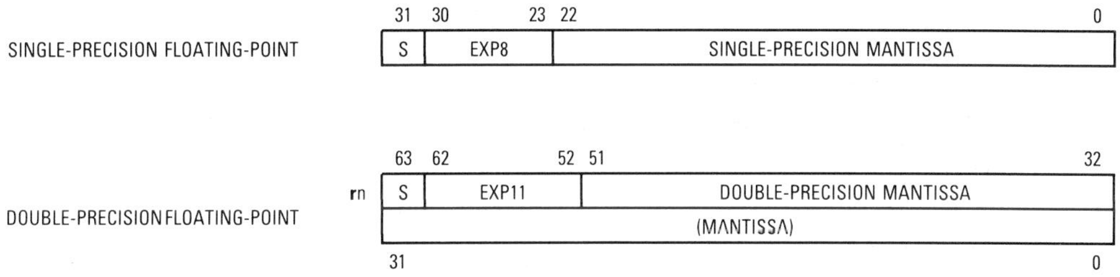

Figure 2-4. Floating-Point Formats

Exponents are biased so that positive and negative exponents do not require sign bits or complementary arithmetic. Two exponent values are reserved for special representations. One representation, an exponent value of zero, indicates a denormalized number (mantissa nonzero) or zero (mantissa zero). The other representation is an exponent value of all ones (binary) which indicates infinity (mantissa zero) or a not-a-number (NAN, mantissa nonzero). Exponents are adjusted so that the mantissa is always normalized. Table 2-3 summarizes the exponent values; Table 2-4 summarizes the representation of floating-point numbers. The biasing and special representations are consistent with the IEEE standard.

Since all normalized, real floating-point numbers have an integer part of one, the IEEE standard does not represent the one in the mantissa. This bit is implied in all normalized, real floating-point numbers and is referred to as the "hidden" bit. The bits contained in

2

Table 2-3. Exponent Values Summary

Exponent	Single-Precision	Double-Precision
Maximum Exponent (Unbiased)	+127	+1023
Minimum Exponent (Unbiased)	−126	−1022
Exponent Bias	+127	+1023
Width	8 Bits	11 Bits

Table 2-4. Floating-Point Number Representation

Sign Bit	Exponent (Biased)	Mantissa	Result
0	Maximum	Nonzero	+NAN
0	Maximum	Zero	+Infinity
0	0<Exponent<Max	Nonzero	+Real
0	0	Nonzero	+Denormalized
0	0	Zero	+0
1	0	Zero	−0
1	0	Nonzero	−Denormalized
1	0<Exponent<Max	Nonzero	−Real
1	Maximum	Zero	−Infinity
1	Maximum	Nonzero	−NAN

the mantissa represent only the binary fraction of the floating-point number. Figure 2-5 illustrates the normalized representation of the number 1.0_{10} in single-precision format and the function of the hidden bit.

Floating-point numbers are normalized to the format of

1. <binary fraction>

   The 1 (represented by the hidden bit) is followed by the binary point (the binary equivalent of the decimal point) then followed by the binary fraction. The following is an example of the normalization process for the number 1/8 (.125):

   $.125_{10} = .001_2 = (1.0*2^{-3})$

   In single-precision format:

   Sign bit = 0
   Biased Exponent = +124(−3+127)
   Hidden Bit = 1
   Mantissa = 0

2.4.2 Denormalized Numbers

Denormalization occurs when a number is too small or too large to be represented as a normalized number in the result format. For example, the smallest single-precision number

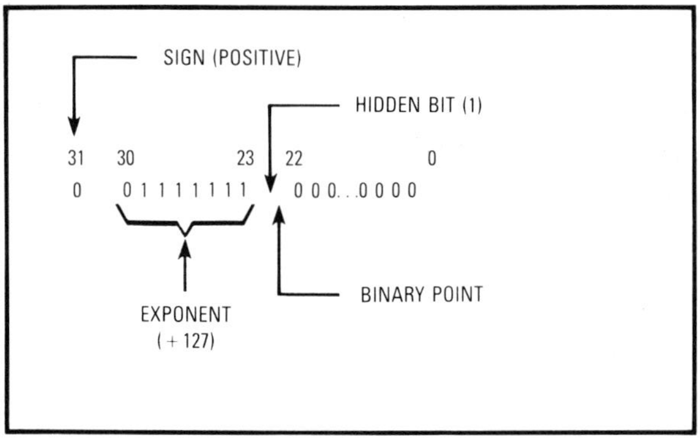

Exponent (biased) =	+127
Minus bias	−127
True Exponent =	0
Mantissa =	1.0
Value =	$1.0 * 2^0$
=	$1.0_2 = 1.0_{10}$

Figure 2-5. Floating-Point Representation of 1.0 (Single Precision)

that can be represented is $(1.0*2^{-126})$. If this number is divided by four, the result cannot be represented as a single-precision normalized number:

$$(1.0*2^{-126}) \div (1.0*2^2) = (1.0*2^{-128})$$

In this case, the denormalized result is represented with a sign bit of zero (positive), an exponent of zero (denormalized number), and a mantissa having the second bit from the left set. Since the mantissa is 2^{-2} ($.01_2$), the format indicates that the desired result was 2^{-128}.

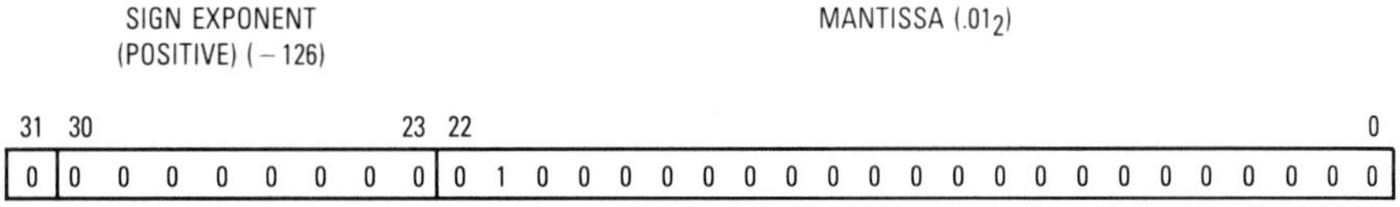

When a denormalization occurs, a floating-point exception occurs (in this case, a floating-point underflow exception). The MC88100 adjusts the result so that the exception handler can determine the actual value of the result and take corrective actions. Refer to **SECTION 6 EXCEPTIONS** for detailed information on exceptions.

2.4.3 Not-a-Numbers (NANs)

The IEEE standard includes representations for not-a-numbers (NANs). There are two types of NANs, signaling and nonsignaling. Both NANs cause a reserved operand exception; the signaling NAN causes the user exception handler to be invoked when available (see **SECTION 6 EXCEPTIONS**). A signaling NAN is useful for flagging uninitialized variables and uninitialized memory. A signaling NAN is a NAN representation with bit 22 clear. A nonsignaling NAN is useful for representing the results of invalid operations such as 0/0. A nonsignaling NAN is a NAN representation with bit 22 set.

2

2.4.4 Rounding

The MC88100 supports four rounding modes. These rounding modes use three added bits of precision associated with the result of a floating-point operation. The rounding modes and extra precision bits are consistent with the IEEE standard; the rounding mode is selected by loading bits 15 and 14 in the floating-point control register (FPCR). The four rounding modes are listed in Table 2-5.

Table 2-5. Rounding Modes

FPCR Bits		Rounding Modes
15	14	
0	0	Round-to-Nearest Results rounded down toward closest number.
0	1	Round-Toward-Zero Extra bits of precision are truncated.
1	0	Round-Toward-Negative-Infinity Results are rounded towards the more negative number.
1	1	Round-Toward-Positive-Infinity Results are rounded towards the more positive number.

The three extra bits of precision are:

1. Guard Bit (G) — This bit represents the bit immediately to the right of the least significant bit (LSB).
2. Round Bit (R) — This bit represents the bit immediately to the right of the guard bit. Although not necessary for all rounding, certain floating-point operations extend the precision by one bit before normalization. The round bit represents this bit.
3. Sticky Bit (S) — This bit represents all bits immediately to the right of the round bit. The value of the sticky bit is determined by taking the logical OR of all the bits that would be in the result if the result was infinitely precise. For example, a single-precision multiply instruction might generate 24 extra bits of precision in the product. The first bit of extra precision (to the right of bit zero) would be the guard bit and the next bit would be the round bit. The remaining 22 bits would be logically ORed to produce the sticky bit.

Figure 2-6 illustrates the guard, round, and sticky bits for the previous example.

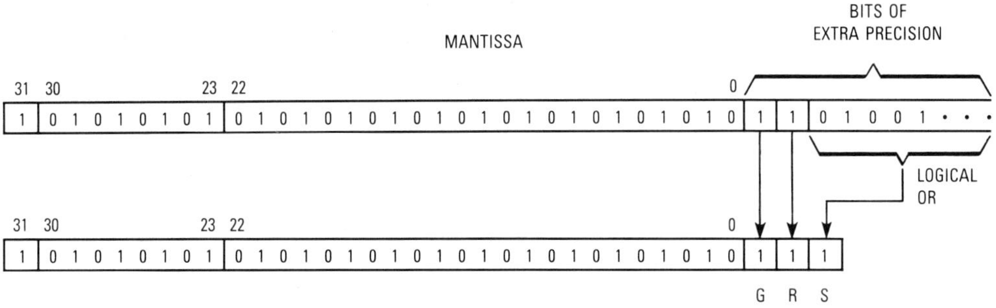

Figure 2-6. Guard, Round, and Sticky Bits

2.4.4.1 ROUND-TO-NEAREST. Rounding to the nearest number is the default rounding mode of the MC88100 processor. In this mode, numbers are rounded up when the guard, round, and sticky bits make a result closer to the higher number. However, a "tie" situation occurs when the guard bit is one and the other bits are zero. In the case of a tie, the number is rounded up if the higher number is even and is not rounded if the higher number is odd.

Figure 2-7 illustrates the round-to-nearest rounding method for the numbers "00", "01", and "10". When the guard bit is one and the round and sticky bits are both zero, then the rounding depends on thc LSB. When the LSB is one, the number is not rounded (00). When the LSB is one, the number is round (10). The following logic statements summarize this rounding method.

If G=0	Do Not Round
If G=1 and (R=1 or S=1)	Round Up
If G=1, R=0, and S=0	
If LSB=0	Do Not Round
If LSB=1	Round Up

2.4.4.2 ROUND-TO-ZERO. When round-to-zero is selected, the guard, round, and sticky bits are ignored (i.e., no rounding is performed).

2.4.4.3 ROUND-TOWARD-POSITIVE-INFINITY. When round-toward-positive-infinity is selected, the number is rounded to the next higher number when any of the extra precision bits are set. In the case of positive numbers, a one is added to the mantissa to make the number more positive and with negative numbers, nothing is added to the result. Then

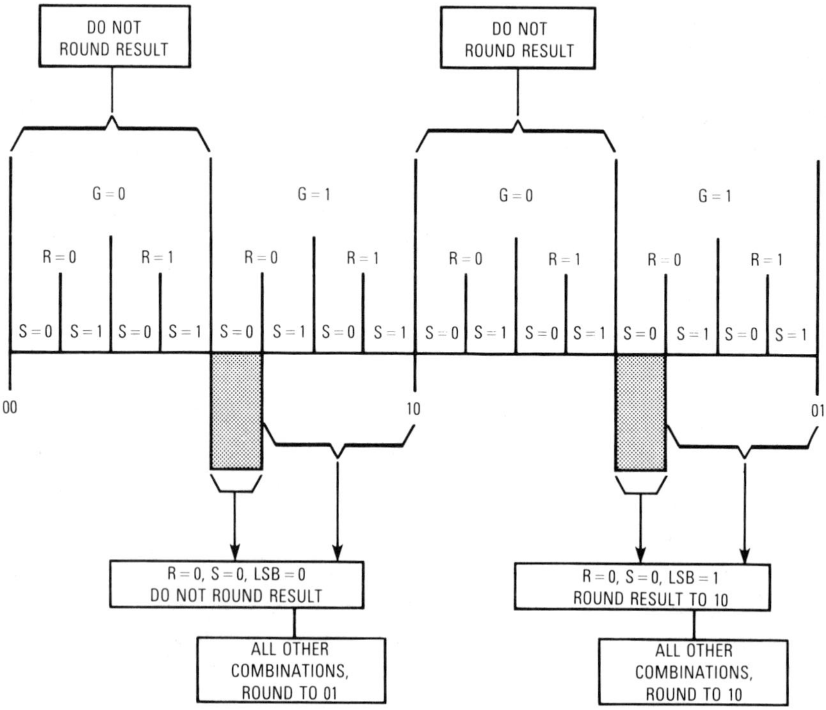

Figure 2-7. Round-to-Nearest Rounding Method

the guard, round, and sticky bits are discarded. In other words, if (G = 1 or R = 1 or S = 1) a positive number is rounded up and a negative number is not changed.

2.4.4.4 ROUND-TOWARD-NEGATIVE-INFINITY. When round-toward-negative-infinity is selected, the number is rounded down to the next lower number when any of the extra precision bits are set. In the case of positive numbers, nothing is subtracted from the result, but with negative numbers, a one is added to the mantissa to make the number more negative. Then the guard, round, and sticky bits are discarded. In other words, if (G = 1 or R = 1 or S = 1) a negative number is rounded down and a positive number is not changed.

2.4.5 IEEE Exceptions Conformance

The IEEE standard defines five exceptions that are supported by the MC88100. The following paragraphs briefly describe these exceptions. In addition to these five exceptions, the MC88100 implements other exceptions such as the privilege-violation exception. Further

information on exceptions (such as exception handling information) can be found in **SECTION 6 EXCEPTIONS**.

2

Whenever an exception occurs, the MC88100 traps to an exception handler routine. Default exception handler routines are available from Motorola that perform the actions described in the following paragraphs, and user exception handler routines can be incorporated into software to perform other processing. When the user exception handlers are available (installed and enabled), then they are executed when the appropriate IEEE exceptions occur. When they are not available, the default handlers are executed. The actions performed by the default routines are consistent with the IEEE standard.

2.4.5.1 INVALID FLOATING-POINT OPERATION EXCEPTION. This exception is signaled when the MC88100 hardware determines that the operand is invalid for the operation being performed. This does not mean that the operation is in error. Only certain conditions are considered an exception according to the IEEE standard. The other conditions cannot be handled by the MC88100 hardware and must be completed by software. When the operation is not an exception according to the standard, the software provides the proper result. When the operation results in a true exception, then the appropriate bit(s) are set in the floating-point exception cause register (FPECR), and either the user exception handlers are called or the default action is performed. When an exception occurs and no user handler is available, then the appropriate bit is set in the floating-point status register (FPSR) and the default action is performed. Specifically:

1. **Operations on NANs.** If a signaling NAN is detected, bit 4 (AFINV) in the FPSR is set, and a nonsignaling NAN is written to the destination. If a nonsignaling NAN is detected, a nonsignaling NAN is written to the destination, but the FPSR is not modified.
2. **Operations on Infinities.** If one operand is infinity and the other a real number, then the properly signed infinity is written to the destination. If the operation is the magnitude subtraction of infinities $((+\infty)+(-\infty))$, ∞/∞ or $0*\infty$, then bit 4 in the FPSR is set, and a nonsignaling NAN is written to the destination.
3. **Operations on Denormalized Numbers.** Operations on denormalized numbers are always completed. The result, which may or may not be a denormalized number, is written to the specified destination.
4. **Zero-Divide-By-Zero (0/0).** Bit 4 in the FPSR is set, and a nonsignaling NAN is written to the destination.
5. **Conversion to Integer Overflow.** Bit 4 in the FPSR is set, and a nonsignaling NAN is written to the destination.

2.4.5.2 FLOATING-POINT DIVIDE-BY-ZERO EXCEPTION. This exception is signaled for all divide-by-zero operations. The supervisor exception code first checks if the operation is divide-by-zero. If the operation is considered an invalid operation by the IEEE standard, then the appropriate invalid operation handler is called. Otherwise, the result is infinity

with the appropriate sign: $+\text{finite}/+0 = +\infty$, $+\text{finite}/-0 = -\infty$, $-\text{finite}/+0 = -\infty$, $-\text{finite}/-0 = +\infty$.

2.4.5.3 OVERFLOW EXCEPTION. This exception is signaled when a floating-point operation produces an exponent that is too large to be represented in the result format. The overflow exception is caused when the exponent is greater than +127 for single-precision results and greater than +1023 for double-precision results. When this exception occurs, the MC88100 normally executes the user overflow exception handler. If that is not available, then the user inexact exception handler is executed. When neither exception handler is available, then the default exception handler formulates the result according to the rounding mode in effect as listed in Table 2-6.

2

Table 2-6. Overflow Rounding Effects

FPCR Bits		Rounding Effects
15	14	
0	0	For the round-to-nearest case, the result is set of ∞ with the appropriate sign.
0	1	For the round-to-zero case, the result is set to the format's largest value with the appropriate sign.
1	0	For round to $-\infty$, the result depends on whether it is positive or negative. A positive result is set to the format's largest positive value; whereas, a negative result is set to $-\infty$.
1	1	For round to $+\infty$, the result depends on whether it is positive or negative. A positive result is set to $+\infty$; whereas, a negative result is set to the format's largest (most negative) negative value.

When the user overflow exception handler is enabled, the result passed to the handler is the intermediate result (inifinitely precise) divided by 2^a, where 'a' (bias adjust) is +192 for single-precision numbers and +1536 for double-precision numbers.

2.4.5.4 UNDERFLOW EXCEPTION. This exception can be signaled under two conditions. First, this exception can occur when an operation produces an exponent smaller (more negative) than can be represented in the result format. (The IEEE standard refers to this condition as "tinniness", and allows tinniness to be determined either before or after any appropriate rounding is performed.) The MC88100 determines this condition after rounding. The second cause is the loss of precision during normalization or rounding (inexactness). The MC88100 software can execute a user exception handler when only tinniness is detected. The result passed to the handler is the intermediate result (infinitely precise) multiplexed by 2^a, where 'a' (bias adjust) is +192 for single-precision number and +1536 for double-precision numbers. If the exception handler is not available, then the default exception handler writes the denormalized result to the destination register (specified by the instruction). Both tinniness and loss of accuracy must be detected (i.e., bit 2 (AFUNF) set in the FPSR) for this exception to occur when the exception handler is not available.

2

2.4.5.5 INEXACT EXCEPTION. This exception occurs when rounding causes a loss of accuracy, or when an overflow occurs and the overflow exception handler is not available. For loss of accuracy, bit 0 (EFINX) in the FPCR is checked. If this bit is set (user handler available), then the exception is taken. The control registers contain the result of the operation, the guard, round, and sticky bits, and whether or not the result was rounded by adding one. If the user handler is not available, the hardware writes the rounded result to the destination register.

For overflow, the inexact exception handler is taken if there is no exception handler for overflow. First, bit 0 (AFINX) in the FPSR is set. Then, if there is a user handler for the inexact exception, that user handler is taken. Otherwise, the result is the properly signed largest finite number or infinity, depending on the rounding mode in effect. This exception is the only exception that can be masked by hardware. If the MC88100 sets bit 0 (EFINX) in the FPCR, then this exception is not signaled.

SECTION 3
ADDRESSING MODES AND INSTRUCTION SET

This section describes the various instruction types and categories and the corresponding addressing modes available in the MC88100. The complete instruction set, an opcode summary, and programming tips are listed.

3

3.1 INSTRUCTION TYPES AND ADDRESSING MODES

All instructions are one word (32 bits) in length. Immediate operands and displacements are encoded in the instruction word. All other operands are located in registers which can be moved to and from memory with load and store instructions.

The MC88100 executes three types of instructions: flow-control, data memory access, and register-to-register instructions. Flow-control instructions alter the sequential flow of instructions through the processor. Data memory access instructions load data into the general-purpose registers, store data to memory, exchange a memory location with a general-purpose register, or can compute effective addresses. Register-to-register instructions manipulate data stored in the general-purpose registers.

Each instruction type has unique addressing capabilities. Flow-control instructions reference those sections of memory that contain instructions; these references are made by the instruction unit. Data memory access instructions address those sections of memory that contain program data. These references are made by the data unit. Register-to-register instructions are confined to accessing only the general-purpose registers, or in certain cases, the control registers.

The following paragraphs describe the operations of the three instruction types showing the instruction formats for each addressing mode.

3.1.1 Register-to-Register Instructions

The MC88100 supports four addressing modes for its register-to-register instructions. The following paragraphs describe these addressing modes.

3.1.1.1 TRIADIC REGISTER ADDRESSING MODE. Triadic register addressing uses three 5-bit fields encoded in the instruction to specify two source registers and a destination register (**r**D). This addressing mode is common to all data manipulation instructions. Some instructions do not use all three register selection fields (unused fields should be zero).

For arithmetic and logical instructions, the data in the source 1 (**r**S1) and source 2 (**r**S2) registers is processed by the integer unit or floating-point unit (FPU) as directed by the top six bits and the subopcode, and the result is placed in the destination register (**r**D). These instructions include **add**, **addu**, **and**, **cmp**, **div**, **divu**, **fadd**, **fcmp**, **fdiv**, **fmul**, **fsub**, **mul**, **or**, **sub**, **subu**, and **xor**. In addition, the **int**, **nint**, **flt**, and **trnc** instructions use this form of addressing, although the source 1 register (**r**S1) is unused.

3

Bit-field instructions can use this addressing mode such that the lower ten bits of the source 2 register (**r**S2) comprise two 5-bit fields that specify a bit-field operand in **r**S1. One of the 5-bit values specifies the offset of the bit field in **r**S1, and the other specifies the width of the bit field. The upper 22 bits of **r**S2 are ignored. The specified bit field is appropriately processed by the integer unit (set bit field, clear bit field, etc.), and the result is placed in **r**D. The width and offset values can also be specified as immediate operands, as described in **3.1.1.2 REGISTER WITH 10-BIT IMMEDIATE ADDRESSING**. The bit-field instructions include **clr**, **ext**, **extu**, **mak**, **rot**, and **set**.

For bit scan instructions (**ff0** and **ff1**), the operand in **r**S2 is searched by the integer unit to find either the first bit set or the first bit clear. The register is scanned from most significant bit (bit 31) to least significant bit (bit 0). The result is returned in **r**D. The S1 field is ignored.

The **rte** instruction uses a variation of triadic addressing in which no operands are specified. When this instruction executes, the exception-time and shadow registers are loaded into the run-time registers. Program execution resumes in the context saved in the exception-time and shadow registers.

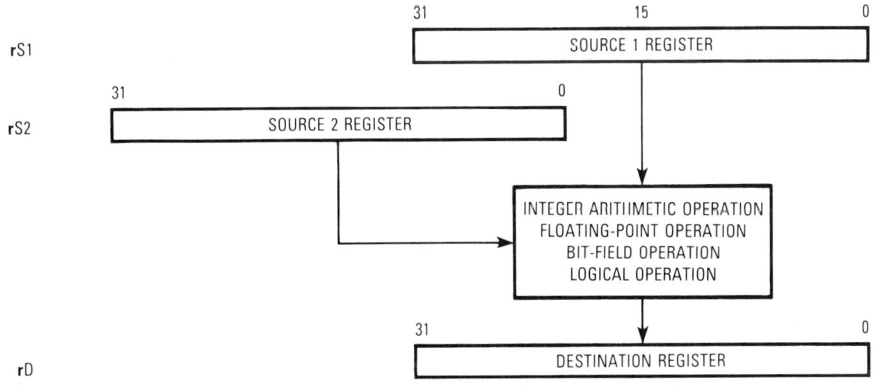

Instruction Format (Floating-Point)

31–26	25–21	20–16	15–5	4–0
1 0 0 0 0 1	D	S1	SUBOPCODE	S2

D — The D field specifies the destination register which receives the result of the operation.

S1 — The S1 field specifies the source 1 operand register. For the **int**, **nint**, **flt**, and **trnc** instructions, S1 must be zero.

SUBOPCODE — This field identifies the floating-point instruction (**fadd**, **fcmp**, **fdiv**, **fmul**, **fsub**, **int**, **nint**, **flt**, and **trnc**).

S2 — The S2 field specifies the source 2 operand register.

Instruction Format (Nonfloating-Point)

31–26	25–21	20–16	15–5	4–0
1 1 1 1 0 1	D	S1	SUBOPCODE	S2

D — The D field specifies the destination register which receives the result of the operation. This field is ignored for instructions that do not generate results.

S1 — The S1 field specifies the source 1 operand register. For bit scan and the **rte** instructions, this field is ignored.

SUBOPCODE — This field identifies the nonfloating-point instruction (**add**, **addu**, **and**, **cmp**, **div**, **divu**, **ext**, **extu**, **ff0**, **ff1**, **mak**, **mul**, **or**, **rot**, **rte**, **set**, **sub**, **subu**, **trnc**, and **xor**).

S2 — The S2 field specifies the source 2 operand register. For the **rte** instruction this field is ignored.

3.1.1.2 REGISTER WITH 10-BIT IMMEDIATE ADDRESSING. This mode of addressing is used in bit-field instructions (**clr**, **ext**, **extu**, **mak**, **rot**, **set**).

The appropriate data in the register specified by the S1 field is processed by the integer unit, and the result is placed in **rD**. The 10-bit immediate field serves as two 5-bit fields that specify the width and offset of the S1 operand field.

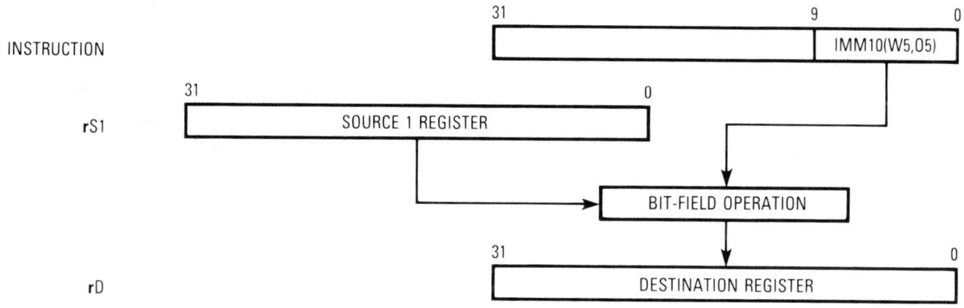

Instruction Format

31–26	25–21	20–16	15–10	9–0
1 1 1 1 0 0	D	S1	SUBOPCODE	IMM10 (W5, 05)

D — Instructions write the result to the destination register specified by the D field.

S1 — The S1 field specifies the source 1 operand register.

SUBOPCODE — This field identifies the particular instruction (**clr**, **ext**, **extu**, **mak**, **rot**, **set**).

IMM10 — This field contains the 10-bit immediate value which represents a 5-bit width and a 5-bit offset.
Bits 9–5 — 5-bit width
Bits 4–0 — 5-bit offset

3.1.1.3 REGISTER WITH 16-BIT IMMEDIATE ADDRESSING. This form of addressing is used by arithmetic and logical instructions requiring an immediate source value. The data in the **r**S1 and the 16-bit immediate operand are processed by the integer unit or FPU, and the result is placed in **r**D. The instructions that use this mode include **add**, **addu**, **and**, **cmp**, **div**, **divu**, **mask**, **mul**, **or**, **sub**, **subu**, and **xor**.

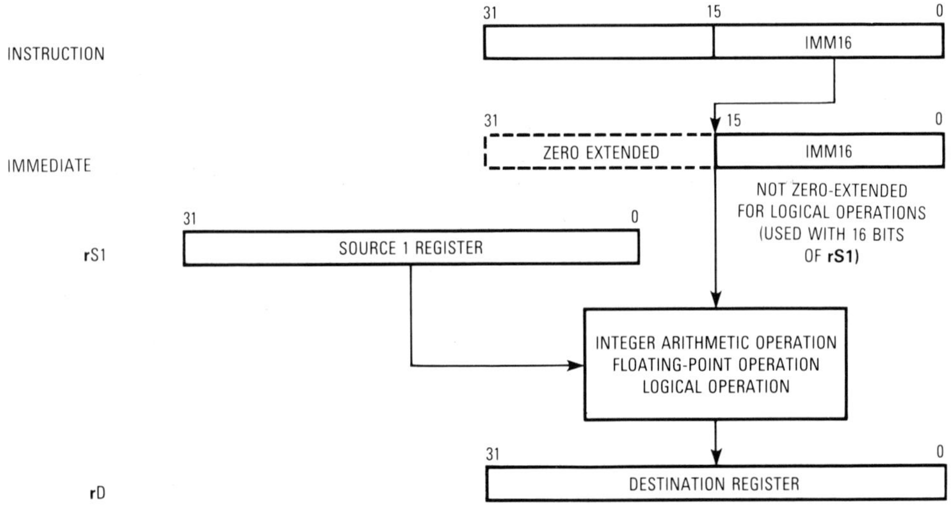

Instruction Format

31–26	25–21	20–16	15–0
OPCODE	D	S1	IMM16

OPCODE — This field identifies the particular instruction (**add**, **addu**, **and**, **cmp**, **div**, **divu**, **mask**, **mul**, **or**, **sub**, **subu**, **xor**).

D — Operations write the result to the destination register specified by the D field.

S1 — The S1 field specifies the source 1 operand register.

IMM16 — This field contains the unsigned immediate value.

3.1.1.4 CONTROL REGISTER ADDRESSING. Control register addressing is used to reference the general control and FPU control registers. General-purpose registers are loaded from, stored to, or exchanged with the control registers. This addressing mode applies to both the user and supervisor programming modes. The instructions that use this mode include **ldcr**, **stcr**, **xcr**, **fldcr**, **fstcr**, and **fxcr**.

Instruction Format

31–26	25–21	20–16	15–14	13–11	10–5	4–0
1 0 0 0 0 0	D	S1	OP	SFU	CRS/CRD	S2

D — For load and exchange instructions, the D field specifies the general-purpose register that is loaded with the contents of the selected control register. For store instructions, the D field is ignored.

S1 — For store and exchange instructions, the S1 field specifies the general-purpose register containing the data to be transferred to the selected control register. For load instructions, the S1 field is ignored.

OP — This field identifies the particular instruction (**ldcr**, **stcr**, **xcr**, **fldcr**, **fstcr**, **fxcr**).

SFU — This field specifies the special function unit (SFU) accessed by the instruction. The value zero specifies the integer unit control registers; the value one specifies the floating-point unit control registers. Other values (2–7) cause an SFU precise exception for the addressed SFU.

CRS/CRD — This field specifies the control register. In the case of a load instruction, the control register is the source; in the case of a store instruction, the control register is the destination.

S2 — The S2 field must contain the same value as the S1 field (for decoding purposes) and serves the same purpose as the S1 field.

3.1.2 Data Memory Access Instructions

The MC88100 supports three addressing modes for accessing the data memory space. All of these addressing modes can be used by the **ld**, **st**, **xmem**, and **lda** instructions to access data in memory or to generate a memory address. The addressing modes used are the same as the triadic register and register with 16-bit immediate (see **3.1.1 Register-to-Register Instructions**).

Address calculations are performed using unsigned arithmetic. Overflows are not detected; results are truncated to the number of available bits.

3.1.2.1 REGISTER INDIRECT WITH ZERO-EXTENDED IMMEDIATE INDEX.

The contents of **r**S1 are added to the 16-bit zero-extended immediate index contained in the I16 field of the instruction. The result is a data memory address used to load or store data via the data processor bus (P bus). For a load instruction, the memory data is loaded into the register specified by the D field. For a store or exchange memory instruction, the data in the register specified by the D field is stored to memory. For the **lda** instruction, the calculated address is loaded into the specified destination register.

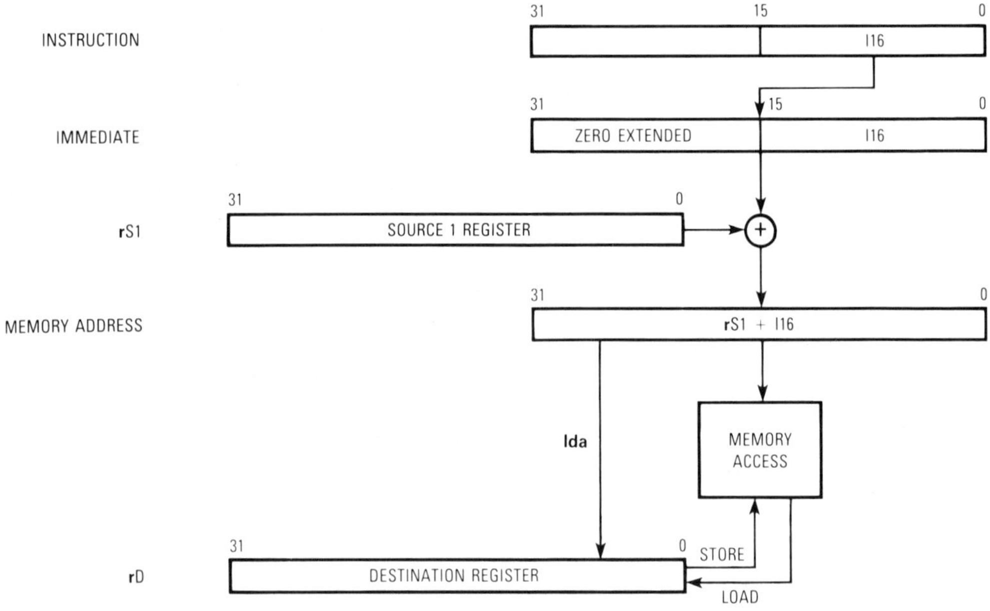

Instruction Format

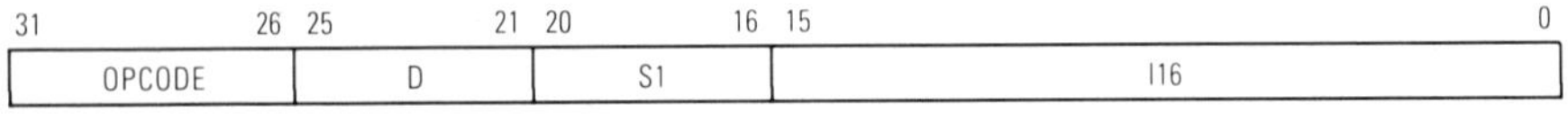

OPCODE — This field identifies the particular instruction (**ld**, **st**, **xmem**, and **lda**).

D — The D field specifies the destination register for a load instruction. In the case of a store or exchange memory instruction, the D field specifies the source register for the data. (The D field specifies the register that is stored since the internal D bus is used for accessing the source register).

S1 — The S1 field specifies the source 1 operand register used in the address calculation.

I16 — This field contains a 16-bit immediate index.

3.1.2.2 REGISTER INDIRECT WITH INDEX. The contents of **r**S1 is added to the contents of **r**S2. The result is a data memory address used to load or store data via the data P bus. For a load instruction, the memory data is loaded into the register specified by the D field. For a store or exchange memory instruction, the data in the register specified by the D field is stored to memory. For the **lda** instruction, the calculated address is loaded into the specified destination register.

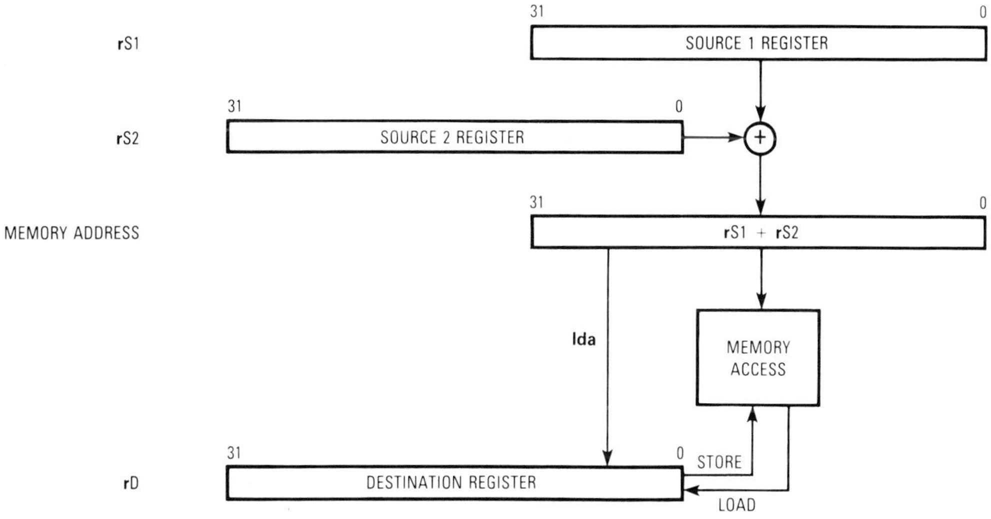

Instruction Format

31–26	25–21	20–16	15–5	4–0
1 1 1 1 0 1	D	S1	SUBOPCODE	S2

D — The D field specifies the destination register for a load instruction. For the store or exchange memory instructions, the D field specifies the source register for the data. (The D field specifies the register that is stored since the internal D bus is used to access the source register).

S1 — The S1 field specifies the source 1 operand register used in the address calculation.

SUBOPCODE — This field identifies the particular instruction (**ld**, **st**, **xmem**, or **lda**).

S2 — The S2 field specifies the source 2 operand register used in the address calculation.

3.1.2.3 REGISTER INDIRECT WITH SCALED INDEX. The contents of **r**S2 is scaled by the size of the access and then added to the contents of **r**S1. The result is a data memory address used to load or store data via the data P bus. For a load instruction, the memory data is loaded into the register specified by the D field of the instruction. For a store or exchange memory instruction, the data in the register specified by the D field is stored to memory. For the **lda** instruction, the calculated address is loaded into the specified destination register.

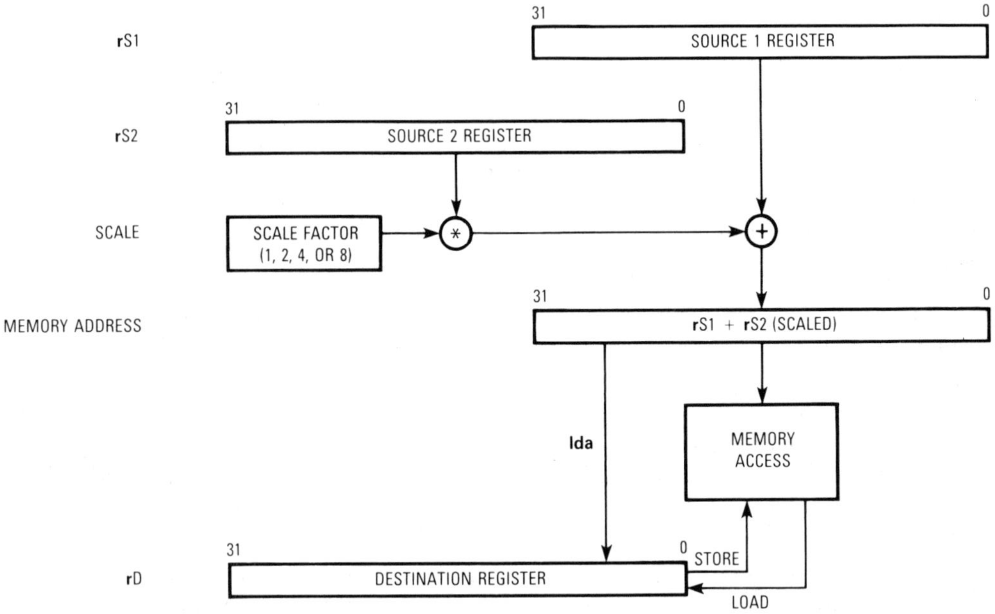

Instruction Format

31–26	25–21	20–16	15–5	4–0
1 1 1 1 0 1	D	S1	SUBOPCODE	S2

D — The D field specifies the destination register for a load instruction. For the store or exchange memory instruction, the D field specifies the source register for the data. (The D field specifies the register that is stored since the internal D bus is used to access the source register.)

S1 — The S1 field specifies the source 1 operand register used in the address calculation.

SUBOPCODE — This field identifies the particular instruction (**ld**, **st**, **xmem**, **lda**), including the scaling factor for the memory data. When the source 2 operand is scaled, it is shifted by 0, 1, 2, or 3 bits (multiplied by scale factor 1, 2, 4, or 8) for byte, half-word, word, or double-word accesses, respectively. For byte accesses, the SUBOPCODE field is distinctly different from the register indirect with index (unscaled) cases but the result is identical.

S2 — The S2 field specifies the source 2 operand register used in the address calculation.

3.1.3 Flow-Control Instructions

Flow-control instructions address or reference instruction memory using four different addressing modes. The following paragraphs describe the flow-control instructions and addressing modes, showing the instruction format and a flow diagram of the instruction. The triadic register addressing mode uses the same instruction format as the register-to-register instructions.

Address calculations are performed using signed arithmetic. Overflows are not detected; results are truncated to the number of available bits.

3.1.3.1 TRIADIC REGISTER ADDRESSING. This form of addressing is used to specify the target of a jump instruction or the operands of a trap-on-bound instruction. These instructions have the same format as the register-to-register instructions. Like the register-to-register instructions, all three of the specified registers do not have to be used.

3.1.3.1.1 Jump Instructions (jmp, jsr). The contents of the **r**S2 is placed in the fetch instruction pointer (FIP), causing program execution to be transferred to that address. The lower two bits of S2 are ignored so that FIP contains a word address. The S1 and D fields are not used and are ignored by the processor.

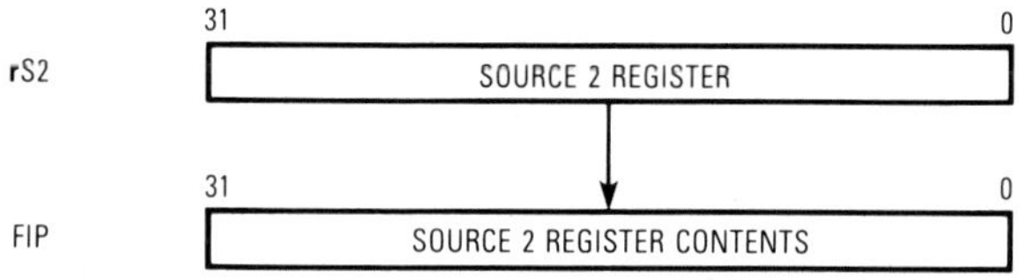

Instruction Format

31–26	25–21	20–16	15–5	4–0
1 1 1 1 0 1	D	S1	SUBOPCODE	S2

D — This field is ignored.

S1 — This field is ignored.

SUBOPCODE This field identifies the particular instruction (**jmp**, **jmp.n**, **jsr**, **jsr.n**).

S2 The S2 field specifies the source 2 register.

3.1.3.1.2 Trap-Generating Bounds-Check Instruction (tbnd). The data in **r**S1 and **r**S2 is compared, and a trap is taken if the source 1 data is greater than the source 2 data (unsigned). The D field is not used and is ignored by the processor. If the trap is taken, execution transfers to the bounds check exception vector as follows: the 20-bit address in the vector base register (VBR) is concatenated with the bounds check exception vector and three trailing zeros to form the 30-bit instruction address. The result is placed in the FIP, and program execution begins from that address.

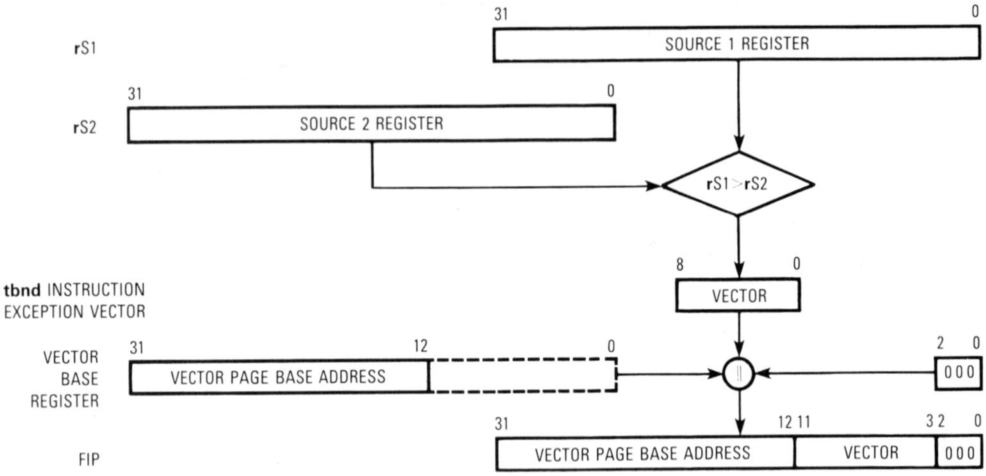

Instruction Format

31 26	25 21	20 16	15 5	4 0
1 1 1 1 0 1	D	S1	SUBOPCODE	S2

D This field is ignored.

S1 The S1 field specifies the source 1 operand register.

SUBOPCODE This field identifies the particular instruction (**tbnd**).

S2 The S2 field specifies the source 2 register.

3.1.3.2 REGISTER WITH 9-BIT VECTOR TABLE INDEX. This addressing method is used by the **tb0**, **tb1**, and **tcnd** (trap-generating) instructions.

For bit-test trap instructions, the bit in **rS1** specified by the B5 field is tested for either a set or clear condition. For conditional trap instructions, the source 1 register is tested for the condition(s) specified in the M5 field. In either case, if the test condition is true, the 20-bit address in the vector base register (VBR) is concatenated with the VEC9 field of the instruction and three trailing zeros to form the 30-bit instruction address. Exception processing begins, and the vector is fetched from the resulting address.

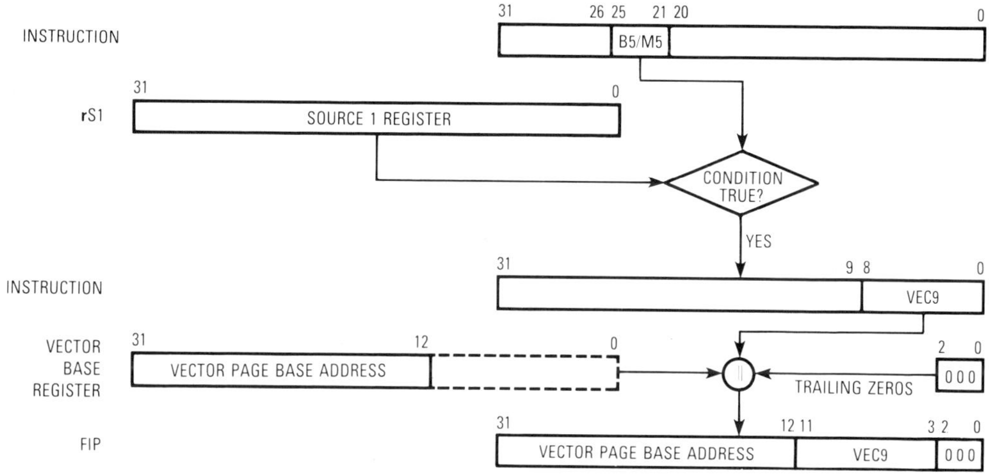

Instruction Format

31–26	25–21	20–16	15–9	8–0
1 1 1 1 0 0	B5/M5	S1	SUBOPCODE	VEC9

B5/M5 — For bit test, the B5 field specifies the bit to be tested in the register specified by the S1 field. For conditional tests, bits 25–21 of the M5 field specify which conditions to test out of four possible conditions:

- Bit 25: Reserved, unused by the branch selection logic (must be zero for future compatibility).
- Bit 24: Maximum negative number [Sign and Zero]
- Bit 23: Less than zero [Sign and (not Zero)]
- Bit 22: Equal to zero [(not Sign) and Zero]
- Bit 21: Greater than zero [(not Sign) and (not Zero)]

Multiple conditions can be specified by setting more than one bit in this field. These conditions are shown in the following table.

Bit:	25	24	23	22	21
eq0 (equals zero)	0	0	0	1	0
ne0 (not equal to zero)	0	1	1	0	1
gt0 (greater than zero)	0	0	0	0	1
lt0 (less than zero)	0	1	1	0	0
ge0 (greater than/equals zero)	0	0	0	1	1
le0 (less than/equals zero)	0	1	1	1	0

S1 — The S1 field specifies the source 1 operand register.

SUBOPCODE — This field identifies the particular instruction (**tb0**, **tb1**, **tcnd**).

VEC9 — This field contains the 9-bit vector number.

3

3.1.3.3 REGISTER WITH 16-BIT DISPLACEMENT/IMMEDIATE. This form of addressing is used by branch and trap instructions for target address and test condition generation.

3.1.3.3.1 Bit-Test Branch Instructions (bb0, bb1, bcnd). For bit-test branch instructions, the bit in **r**S1 is specified by the B5 field is tested for either a set or clear condition. For condition-test branch instructions, **r**S1 is tested for the condition(s) specified in the M5 field. In either case, if the test condition is true, the 16-bit displacement specified in the instruction is shifted left two positions and sign extended to 32 bits. The two least significant bits are cleared to force word alignment. This value is added to the execute instruction pointer (XIP), and the result is loaded into the FIP. Program execution is transferred to that address.

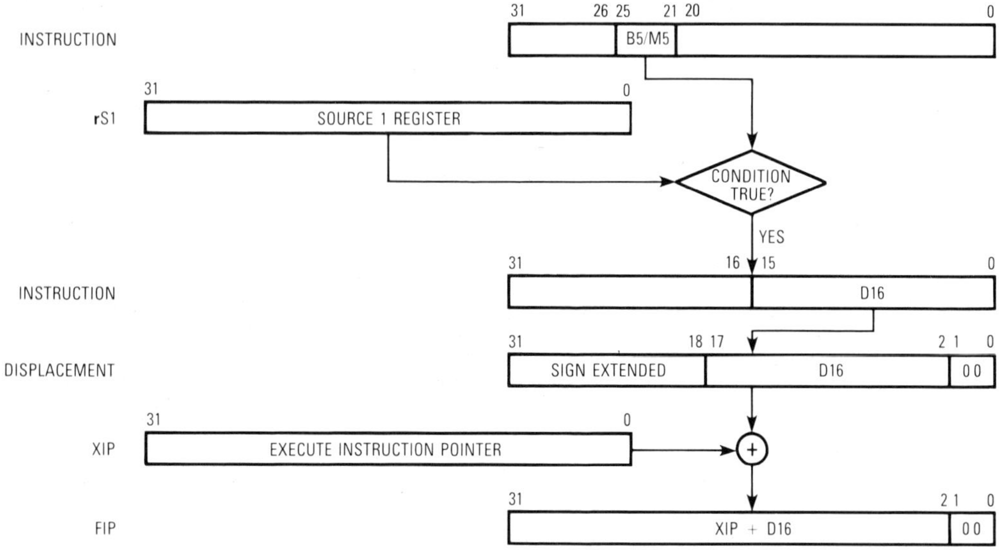

Instruction Format

31–26	25–21	20–16	15–0
OPCODE	B5/M5	S1	D16

OPCODE — This field identifies the particular instruction (**bb0**, **bb0.n**, **bb1**, **bb1.n**, **bcnd**, **bcnd.n**).

B5/M5 — For bit test, the B5 field specifies the bit to be tested in the register specified by the S1 field. For conditional tests, bits 25–21 of the M5 field specify which conditions to test out of four possible conditions:

Bit 25: Reserved, unused by the branch selection logic (must be zero for future compatibility).
Bit 24: Maximum negative number [Sign and Zero]
Bit 23: Less than zero [Sign and (not Zero)]
Bit 22: Equal to zero [(not Sign) and Zero]
Bit 21: Greater than zero [(not Sign) and (not Zero)]

Multiple conditions can be specified by setting more than one bit in this field. These conditions are:

Bit:	25	24	23	22	21
eq0 (equals zero)	0	0	0	1	0
ne0 (not equal to zero)	0	1	1	0	1
gt0 (greater than zero)	0	0	0	0	1
lt0 (less than zero)	0	1	1	0	0
ge0 (greater than/equals zero)	0	0	0	1	1
le0 (less than/equals zero)	0	1	1	1	0

S1 — The S1 field specifies the source 1 operand register.

D16 — This field specifies a signed 16-bit displacement.

3.1.3.3.2 Trap-Generating Bounds-Check Instruction (tbnd). The data in **rS1** is compared to the specified immediate operand, and a trap is taken if the register data is greater than the immediate operand (unsigned). If the trap is taken, the bounds check vector number is combined with the VBR, and the result is concatenated with three trailing zeros and loaded into the FIP. Exception processing begins for the bounds check exception.

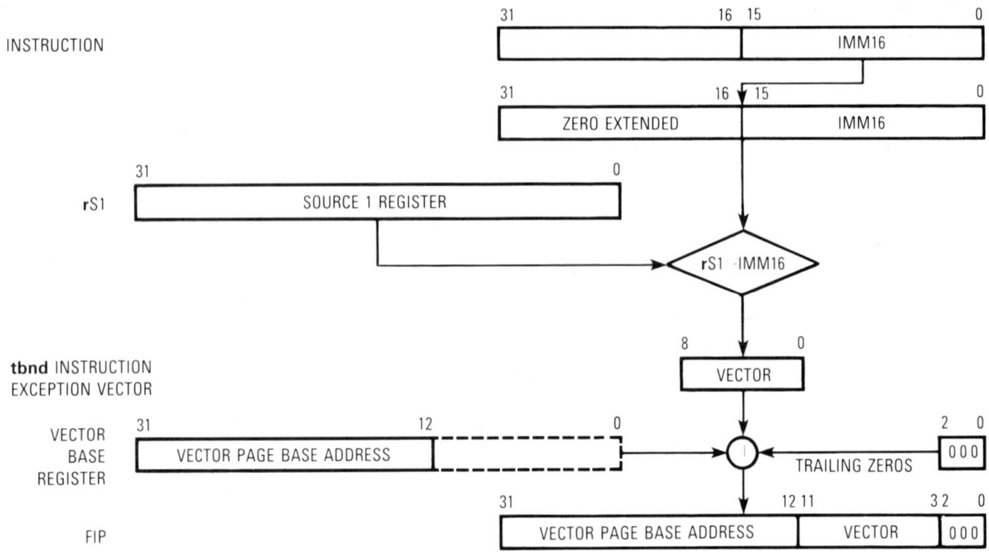

Instruction Format

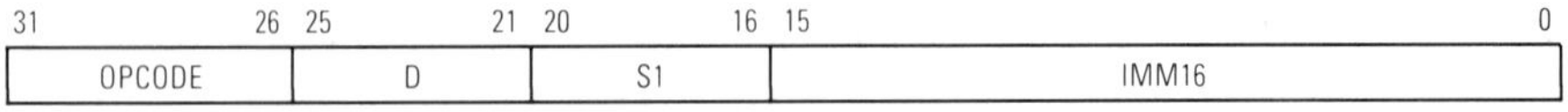

OPCODE This field identifies the particular instruction (**bb0**, **bb0.n**, **bb1**, **bb1.n**, **bcnd**, **bcnd.n**, **tbnd**).

D Unused — should be zero for future compatibility.

S1 The S1 field specifies the source 1 operand register.

IMM16 This field specifies a 16-bit immediate operand for the **tbnd** instruction.

3.1.3.4 26-BIT BRANCH DISPLACEMENT. This form of addressing is used to specify the branch target instruction in unconditional branch instructions (**br**, **bsr**).

Unconditional branch instructions use a sign-extended 26-bit displacement to calculate the location of a new target instruction. The displacement is shifted left by two bits and sign extended to 32 bits. The two least significant bits are cleared to force word alignment. This value is then added to the XIP to form the address of the target instruction. The computed address is placed in the FIP, causing program execution to be transferred to that address.

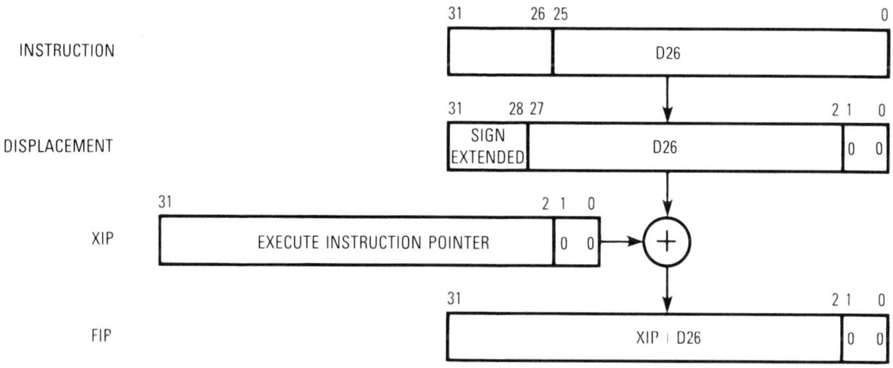

Instruction Format

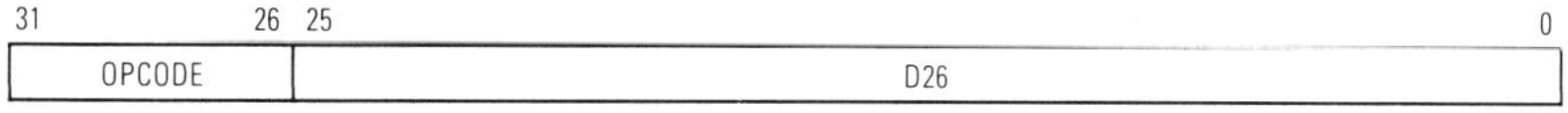

OPCODE This field identifies the particular instruction (**br**, **br.n**, **bsr**, **bsr.n**).

D26 This field specifies the displacement to the target instruction.

3.2 INSTRUCTION CATEGORIES

The instructions used in the MC88100 fall into six categories: logical, integer arithmetic, floating point, bit field, load/store/exchange, and flow control. The following paragraphs describe the different categories along with the operand syntax and the operation performed. Table 3-1 provides the identification of abbreviations and symbols used in the instruction tables and instruction set.

Table 3-1. Instruction Description Notations

Abbreviation	Description
r1	General-Purpose Register 1
rS1	Source 1 Register — register containing the first source operand
rS2	Source 2 Register — register containing the second source operand
rD	Destination Register — register destination that will be modified by the operation (source of data on a store operation)
crS	Source Control Register
crD	Destination Control Register
crS/D	Source and Destination Control Register (for **xcr** instruction)
fcrS	Source Floating-Point Control Register
fcrD	Destination Floating-Point Control Register
fcrS/D	Floating-Point Source and Destination Control Register (for **fxcr** instruction)
D16, D26	16- and 26-Bit Signed Instruction Address Displacement
IMM16	Unsigned 16-Bit Immediate Operand
I16	Unsigned 16-Bit Immediate Index
VEC9	Offset from the page address contained in the Vector Base Register
M5	5-Bit Condition Match Field — the bits indicate the following conditions: Bit 25: Reserved Bit 24: S and Z Bit 23: S and (not Z) Bit 22: (not S) and Z Bit 21: (not S) and (not Z) S: Sign bit (bit 31 of the tested register) Z: Zero bit (logical NOR of bits 30 through 0 of the tested register)
B5	Unsigned 5-Bit Integer denoting a bit number within a word
<O5>	Unsigned 5-Bit Integer denoting a bit-field offset within a word
W5	Unsigned 5-Bit Integer denoting a bit-field width within a word, with 0 denoting a width of 32
{**.n**}	Delay Branch Option — if specified, execute the next sequential instruction before the branch target instruction

—Continued —

Table 3-1. Instruction Description Notations — Continued

<table>
<tr><th>Abbreviation</th><th>Description</th></tr>
<tr><td>{.c}</td><td>Complement Option — if specified, the second operand is ones complemented before it is used in the operation</td></tr>
<tr><td>{.u}</td><td>Upper Half-Word Option — if specified, the 16-bit logical operation is performed with the upper 16 bits of the source register</td></tr>
<tr><td>{.car}
.ci
.co

.cio</td><td>Carry
'Carry In' Option — if specified, include the PSR carry bit in the arithmetic operation
'Carry Out' Option — if specified, set or clear the PSR carry bit based on the result of the arithmetic operation
'Carry In/Carry Out' Option — if specified, include the PSR carry bit in the arithmetic operation and set or clear the carry bit based on the result</td></tr>
<tr><td>.sz
.b
.bu
.h
.hu
.s
.d</td><td>Memory Size: default = word
Byte (8 bits)
Unsigned Byte (8 bits)
Half Word (16 bits)
Unsigned Half Word (16 bits)
Single Word (32 bits)
Double Word (64 bits)</td></tr>
<tr><td>.fsz

.s
.d</td><td>Floating-Point Operand Size — The .fsz is a three-letter designator that corresponds to the sizes of the D, S1, and S2 operands, respectively (two-letter designator for D and S2 operands for the conversion instructions). Floating-point operations support mixed operand sizes; two or three register operands can use two or three of the ".s" or ".d" qualifiers in any combination to support the operand size mix. For example:
fadd.dds r3,r5,r9; r3 and r5 are double precision, r9 is single precision
Single Precision
Double Precision</td></tr>
<tr><td>{.usr}</td><td>User memory option. This option pertains to memory access instructions, allowing the user memory space to be accessed while in the supervisor mode.</td></tr>
<tr><td>[rS2]</td><td>Scaled Index</td></tr>
<tr><td>X</td><td>"Don't Care" Bit</td></tr>
<tr><td>+</td><td>Add</td></tr>
<tr><td>−</td><td>Subtract</td></tr>
<tr><td>×</td><td>Multiply</td></tr>
<tr><td>::</td><td>Compare</td></tr>
<tr><td>/</td><td>Divide</td></tr>
<tr><td>V</td><td>OR</td></tr>
<tr><td>||</td><td>Concatenate</td></tr>
<tr><td><<</td><td>Shift Left</td></tr>
<tr><td>←</td><td>Replaced By</td></tr>
<tr><td>Λ</td><td>AND</td></tr>
<tr><td>⊕</td><td>Exclusive OR</td></tr>
<tr><td><</td><td>Relational test, true if left operand is less than right operand</td></tr>
<tr><td>></td><td>Relational test, true if left operand is greater than right operand</td></tr>
<tr><td>{ }</td><td>Optional</td></tr>
</table>

3.2.1 Logical Instructions

The logical instructions provide three common logical operations: AND, OR, and exclusive OR. An immediate mask instruction is also provided. These instructions operate on the entire source 1 operand (when triadic addressing is used) or can operate only on the lower or upper half-word of the source 2 operand (when register with 16-bit immediate addressing is used). In addition, when triadic addressing is used, the logical instructions can optionally complement the source 2 operand before the operation occurs. Table 3-2 lists the logical instructions.

Table 3-2. Logical Instructions

Instruction	Name	Operand Syntax	Operation
and{.u}	Logical AND	rD,rS1,IMM16	rD ◆ **rS1** (lower or upper 16 bits) \ IMM16; remaining 16 bits of **rS1** are copied to **rD**.
and{.c}		rD,rS1,rS2	rD ◆ **rS1** \ **rS2** (normal or complemented).
mask{.u}	Logical Mask Immediate	rD,rS1,IMM16	rD (lower or upper 16 bits) ◆ **rS1** (lower or upper 16 bits) \ IMM16. Remaining bits ◆ zero.
or{.u}	Logical OR	rD,rS1,IMM16	rD ◆ **rS1** (lower or upper 16 bits) V IMM16; remaining 16 bits of **rS1** or copied to **rD**.
or{.c}		rD,rS1,rS2	rD ◆ **rS1** V **rS2** (normal or complemented).
xor{.u}	Logical Exclusive OR	rD,rS1,IMM16	rD ◆ **rS1** (lower or upper 16 bits) + IMM16; remaining 16 bits of **rS1** are copied to **rD**.
xor{.c}		rD,rS1,rS2	rD ◆ **rS1** + **rS2** (normal or complemented)

3.2.2 Integer Arithmetic Instructions

These instructions provide the standard arithmetic operations and an integer compare operation. For add, subtract, and divide operations, both a signed and an unsigned instruction are available in the instruction set. Various combinations of carry bits can be optionally specified for the add and subtract instructions. Table 3-3 lists the integer arithmetic instructions.

Table 3-3. Integer Arithmetic Instructions

Instruction	Name	Operand Syntax	Operation
add **add**{.car}	Integer Add	rD,rS1,IMM16 rD,rS1,rS2	rD ◆ rS1 + IMM16 rD ◆ rS1 + rS2
addu{.car}	Unsigned Integer Add	rD,rS1,IMM16 rD,rS1,rS2	rD ◆ rS1 + IMM16 rD ◆ rS1 + rS2
cmp	Integer Compare	rD,rS1,IMM16 rD,rS1,rS2	rD ◆ rS1 :: IMM16 rD ◆ rS1 :: rS2
div	Integer Divide	rD,rS1,IMM16 rD,rS1,rS2	rD ◆ rS1/IMM16 rD ◆ rS1/rS2
divu	Unsigned Integer Divide	rD,rS1,IMM16 rD,rS1,rS2	rD ◆ rS1/IMM16 rD ◆ rS1/rS2
mul	Integer Multiply	rD,rS1,IMM16 rD,rS1,rS2	rD ◆ rS1 × IMM16 rD ◆ rS1 × rS2
sub **sub**{.car}	Integer Subtract	rD,rS1,IMM16 rD,rS1,rS2	rD ◆ rS1 − IMM16 rD ◆ rS1 − rS2
subu **subu**{.car}	Unsigned Integer Subtract	rD,rS1,IMM16 rD,rS1,rS2	rD ◆ rS1 − IMM16 rD ◆ rS1 − rS2

NOTE: Although the **div**, **divu**, and **mul** instructions are classified as integer instructions, these instructions are executed by the floating-point unit.

3.2.3 Floating-Point Instructions

The floating-point instructions provide ANSI-IEEE 754-1985 (*IEEE Standard for Binary Floating-Point Arithmetic*) standard floating-point arithmetic and integer/floating-point conversions for various operand sizes (single- and double-precision). This instruction category also includes the instructions that access the floating-point control registers. Table 3-4 lists the floating-point instructions.

Table 3-4. Floating-Point Instructions

Instruction	Name	Operand Syntax	Operation
fadd.fsz	Floating-Point Add	rD,rS1,rS2	rD ← rS1 + rS2
fcmp.fsz	Floating-Point Compare	rD,rS1,rS2	rD ← rS1 :: rS2
fdiv.fsz	Floating-Point Divide	rD,rS1,rS2	rD ← rS1/rS2
fldcr	Load From Floating-Point Control Register	rD,**fcrS**	rD ← **fcrS**
flt.fsz	Convert Integer to Floating Point	rD,rS2	rD ← float(rS2)
fmul.fsz	Floating-Point Multiply	rD,rS1,rS2	rD ← rS1 × rS2
fstcr	Store to Floating-Point Control Register	rD,**fcrD**	**fcrD** ← rD
fsub.fsz	Floating-Point Subtract	rD,rS1,rS2	rD ← rS1 − rS2
fxcr	Exchange Floating-Point Control Register	rD,rS,**fcrS**/D	rD ← **fcrS**/D, temp ← rS **fcrS**/D ← temp
int.fsz	Round Floating Point to Integer	rD,rS2	rD ← round(rS2)
nint.fsz	Round Floating Point to Nearest Integer	rD,rS2	rD ← round_nearest(rS2)
trnc.fsz	Truncate Floating Point	rD,rS2	rD ← trunc(rS2)

NOTE: If general-purpose register **r0** is specified as the destination register for any floating-point instruction except **fstcr**, **fldcr**, and **fxcr**, the MC88100 takes a floating-point unimplemented opcode exception as described in **SECTION 6 EXCEPTIONS**.

3.2.4 Bit-Field Instructions

The bit-field instructions set, clear, make, extract, rotate, and find bit fields in the source operand. Bit fields are specified by a width and an offset field in the instruction, or by the lower ten bits of the **rS2** operand. These lower ten bits are treated as two 5-bit fields, with bits 4–0 specifying the offset (<O5>) from the source 1 operand bit 0 position and with bits 9–5 specifying the width of the field (W5). Bit-field instructions also perform left and right shift operations. A width of zero specifies all 32 bits. Table 3-5 lists the bit-field instructions.

Table 3-5. Bit-Field Instructions

Instruction	Name	Operand Syntax	Operation
clr	Clear Bit Field	**rD**,**rS1**,W5<O5> **rD**,**rS1**,**rS2**	**rD** ← **rS1** with bit field clear. Bit field is O5 bits from bit zero, W5 bits wide.
ext	Extract Bit Field	**rD**,**rS1**,W5<O5> **rD**,**rS1**,**rS2**	**rD** ← **rS1** bit field. **rS1** bit field is O5 bits from bit zero, W5 bits wide, sign extended. The resulting bit field is placed in **rD** starting at bit 0.
extu	Extract Bit Field Unsigned	**rD**,**r**,S1,W5<O5> **rD**,**rS1**,**rS2**	**rD** ← **rS1** bit field. **rS1** bit field is O5 bits from bit zero, W5 bits wide, zero extended. The resulting bit field is placed in **rD** starting at bit 0.
ff0	Find First Bit Clear	**rD**,**rS2**	**rD** ← position of **rS2** first zero bit (32 if none found). The search begins at bit 31 of **rS2** (the most significant bit).
ff1	Find First Bit Set	**rD**,**rS2**	**rD** ← position of **rS2** first one bit (32 if none found). The search begins at bit 31 of **rS2** (the most significant bit).
mak	Make Bit Field	**rD**,**rS1**,W5<O5> **rD**,**rS1**,**rS2**	**rS1** bit field is W5 bits wide starting at bit zero. **rD** ← **rS1** bit field shifted left by offset O5. Remaining **rD** bits cleared.
rot	Rotate Register	**rD**,**rS1**,<O5> **rD**,**rS1**,**rS2**	**rD** ← **rS1** rotated right by O5 bits.
set	Set Bit Field	**rD**,**rS1**,W5<O5> **rD**,**rS1**,**rS2**	**rD** ← **rS1** with bit field set. Bit field is O5 bits from bit zero, W5 bits wide.

3.2.5 Load/Store/Exchange Instructions

These instructions perform the memory accesses that move data of various sizes between memory and general-purpose registers. Also, this category includes the instructions that access the integer unit control registers. Table 3-6 lists the load/store/exchange instructions.

Table 3-6. Load/Store/Exchange Instructions

Instruction	Name	Operand Syntax	Operation
ld {.sz} **ld** {.sz}{**.usr**}	Load Register from Memory	rD,rS1,I16 rD,rS1,rS2 rD,rS1,[rS2]	rD ← contents of memory location. Memory address is rS1 + I16, rS1 + rS2, or rS1 + (rS2<<scale). Scale factor = 0, 1, 2, or 3 for byte, half word, word, or double word, respectively.
lda {.sz}	Load Address	rD,rS1,I16 rD,rS1,rS2 rD,rS1,[rS2]	rD ← rS1 + I16, rS1 + rS2, or rS1 + (rS2<<scale). Scale factor = 0, 1, 2, or 3 for byte, half word, word, or double word, respectively.
ldcr	Load from Control Register	rD,crS	rD ← crS
st {.sz} **st** {.sz}{**.usr**}	Store Register to Memory	rD,rS1,I16 rD,rS1,rS2 rD,rS1,[rS2]	Contents of memory location ← rD. Memory address is rS1 + I16, rS1 + rS2, or rS1 + (rS2<<scale). Scale factor = 0, 1, 2, or 3 for byte, half word, word, or double word, respectively.
stcr	Store to Control Register	rD,crD	crD ← rD
xmem.bu **xmem.bu**{**.usr**} **xmem**{**.usr**}	Exchange Register with Memory	rD,rS1,I16 rD,rS1,rS2 rD,rS1,[rS2]	rD ← contents of memory location. Contents of memory location ← rD. Memory address is rS1 + I16, rS1 + rS2, or rS1 + (rS2<<scale). Scale factor = 0 or 2 for byte or word, respectively.
xcr	Exchange Control Register	rD,rS,crS/D	temp ← rS; rD ← crS/D; crS/D ← temp

3.2.6 Flow-Control Instructions

The flow-control instructions alter the sequential execution stream. These instructions include jump, branch, and trap instructions. Table 3-7 lists the flow-control instructions.

Table 3-7. Flow-Control Instructions

Instruction	Name	Operand Syntax	Operation
jmp {**.n**}	Unconditional Jump	**r**S2	FIP ← **r**S2
jsr {**.n**}	Jump to Subroutine	**r**S2	FIP ← **r**S2 With **.n** option, **r1** ← NIP + 4; without **.n** option **r1** ← NIP
bb0 {**.n**}	Branch on Bit Clear	B5,**r**S1,D16	If bit B5 of register **r**S1 clear, FIP ← XIP + D16
bb1 {**.n**}	Branch on Bit Set	B5,**r**S1,D16	If bit B5 of register **r**S1 set, FIP ← XIP + D16
bcnd {**.n**}	Conditional Branch	M5,**r**S1,D16	If **r**S1 meets condition(s) M5, FIP ← XIP + D16
br {**.n**}	Unconditional Branch	D26	FIP ← XIP + D26
bsr {**.n**}	Branch to Subroutine	D26	FIP ← XIP + D26 With **.n** option, **r1** ← NIP + 4; without **.n** option **r1** ← NIP
tb0	Trap on Bit Clear	B5,**r**S1,VEC9	If bit B5 of register **r**S1 clear, save execution context; FIP ← VBR ‖ VEC9 ‖ 3 trailing zeros
tb1	Trap on Bit Set	B5,**r**S1,VEC9	If bit B5 of register **r**S1 set, save execution context, FIP ← VBR ‖ VEC9 ‖ 3 trailing zeros
tbnd	Trap on Bounds Check	**r**S1,IMM16 **r**S1,**r**S2	If **r**S1 > IMM16 or **r**S1 > **r**S2(unsigned comparison), save execution context FIP ← VBR ‖ bounds check vector ‖ 3 trailing zeros
tcnd	Conditional Trap	M5,**r**S1,VEC9	If **r**S1 meets condition(s) M5, save execution context, FIP ← VBR ‖ VEC9 ‖ 3 trailing zeros
rte	Return from Exception	(none)	Restore saved context

3.3 PROGRAMMING TIPS

The following paragraphs provide information to the programmer on shift instructions, delayed branching, and condition computations.

3.3.1 Shift Instructions

Shift functions are easily performed through MC88100 bit-field instructions. The following paragraphs list common shift functions and the instructions used to perform them. Refer to **3.4 INSTRUCTION SET** for more detailed information on how the shift functions are invoked.

3.3.1.1 SHIFT RIGHT ARITHMETIC. When the W5 field of an **ext** (extract signed bit field) instruction contains all zeros (specifying a width of 32 bits), the instruction operates as an arithmetic shift right instruction. The offset specifies the number of positions to shift. The high-order bits are sign filled in the destination register. The following illustration shows the shift usage of the **ext** instruction:

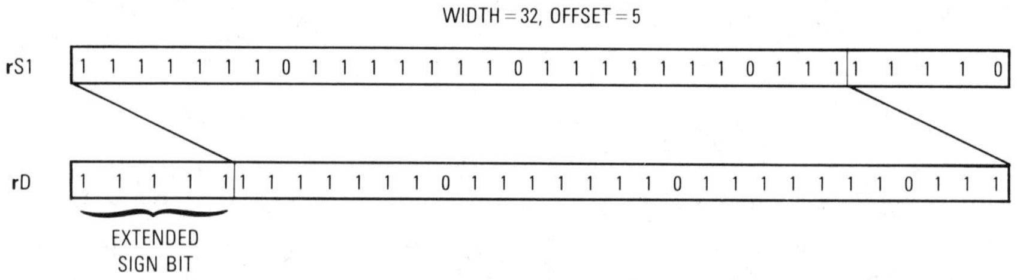

3.3.1.2 SHIFT RIGHT LOGICAL. When the W5 field of an **extu** instruction contains all zeros (specifying a width of 32 bits), this instruction operates as a logical shift right instruction. The offset specifies the number of positions to shift. The high-order bits are zero filled in the destination register. The following illustration shows the shift usage of the **extu** instruction:

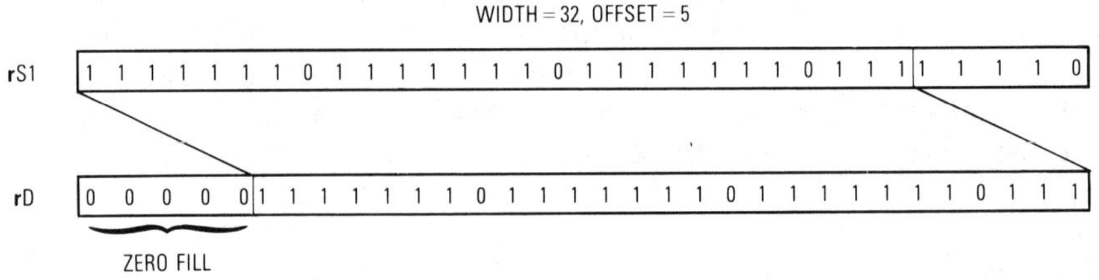

3.3.1.3 SHIFT LEFT. When the W5 field of a **mak** instruction contains all zeros (specifying a width of 32 bits), the instruction operates as a shift left instruction. That is, the width field selects the entire register; the offset specifies the number of positions to shift. The low-order bits are zero filled in the destination register. The following illustration shows the shift usage of the **mak** instruction:

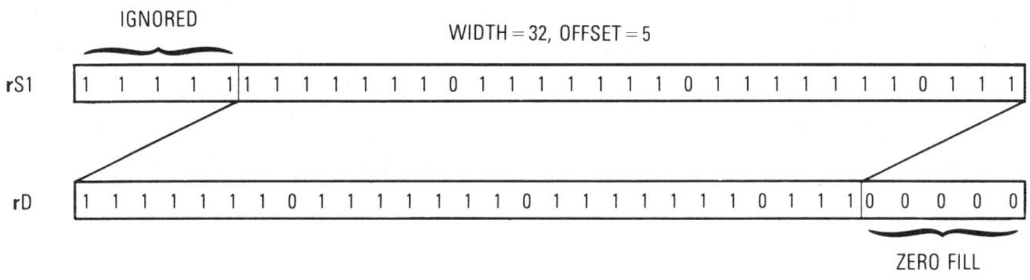

3.3.1.4 SHIFT CIRCULAR. The **rot** (rotate register) instruction rotates the bits in **r**S1 to the right by the number of bits specified in the O5 field. The result is placed in **r**D. For triadic register addressing, the five low-order bits of the data contained in **r**S2 are used as the O5 field. Bits 9–5 in **r**S2 must be zero; the other bits are ignored.

3.3.2 Delayed Branching

The branch and jump instructions have a delayed branch option (**.n**) that can be specified so that the next sequential instruction is executed before the branch instruction (regardless of the branch condition). This provides an efficient use of processor resources when branches are taken because the time required to prefetch the target instruction is overlapped with useful instruction execution.

The programmer can take advantage of the delayed branching feature for unconditional branch or jump instructions by intentionally placing an instruction that normally resides before the branch so that it physically follows the branch (in the delay slot) and specifying the **.n** option for the branch. Alternately, the first instruction from the target can be copied from the target address to fill the delay slot. For conditional branch or jump instructions, the delay slot can also be filled with an instruction from before the branch (if it does not affect the execution of the branch instruction). The delay slot can also be filled with an instruction from the target address, provided that program execution is not adversely affected by the extra execution of that instruction in the case of the branch not taken.

3.3.3 Condition Computation

The MC88100 architecture requires that condition bits be evaluated explicitly when they are needed. Therefore, looping structures in the MC88100 are most efficiently implemented

by branch instructions that count down to zero (rather than counting up to the loop count) because the compare and branch function can be easily implemented with one instruction (**bcnd**). If the **bcnd** instruction is used, no other conditions must be evaluated for the branch, and an extra comparison instruction is not required.

Other conditions can be evaluated by executing a compare instruction (**cmp** or **fcmp**) followed by an extract bit-field instruction. An unsigned extract (**extu**) of the appropriate condition bit in the destination register for the **cmp** creates a Boolean variable with the values 0 and 1. A signed extract (**ext**) of the appropriate condition bit creates a Boolean variable with the values 0 and −1. If the condition does not need to be assigned, a branch-on-bit instruction efficiently branches on any condition generated by the compare instruction.

3.4 INSTRUCTION SET

These paragraphs provide detailed descriptions of each instruction in the MC88100 instruction set. The instructions are arranged in alphabetical order with the instruction mnemonic in large bold type for easy reference.

Each instruction description provides a complete discussion of the instruction operation, the assembler syntax, and the instruction encoding. The assembler syntax is supported by the Motorola MC88100 assembler. Figure 3-1 illustrates how the information is presented for each instruction.

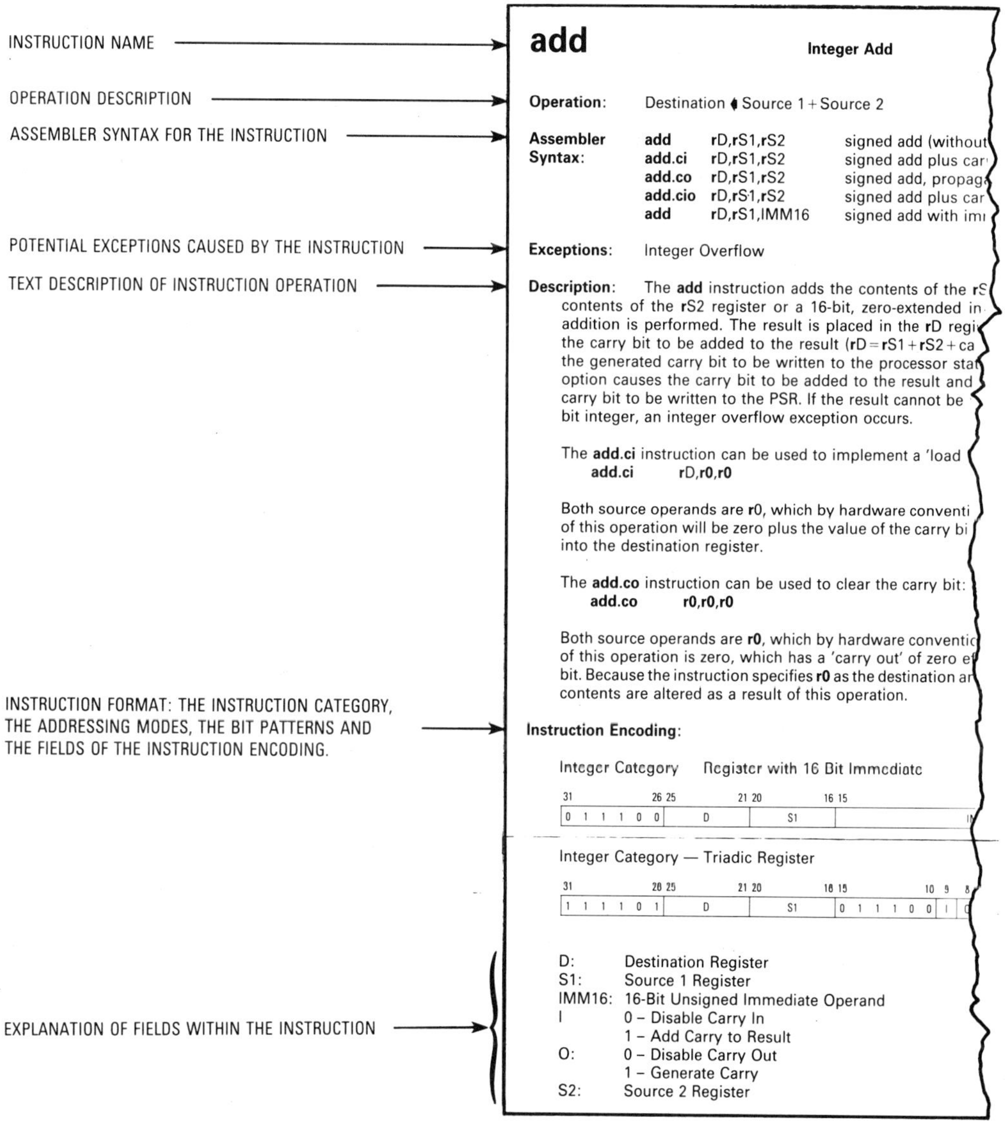

Figure 3-1. Instruction Description Format

Operation: Destination ← Source 1 + Source 2

Assembler Syntax:

add	rD,**r**S1,**r**S2	signed add (without carry)
add.ci	rD,**r**S1,**r**S2	signed add plus carry
add.co	rD,**r**S1,**r**S2	signed add, propagate carry out
add.cio	rD,**r**S1,**r**S2	signed add plus carry, propagate carry out
add	rD,**r**S1,IMM16	signed add with immediate (without carry)

Exceptions: Integer Overflow

Description: The **add** instruction adds the contents of the **r**S1 register with either the contents of the **r**S2 register or a 16-bit, zero-extended immediate operand. Binary addition is performed. The result is placed in the **r**D register. The **.ci** option causes the carry bit from the PSR to be added to the result (**r**D = **r**S1 + **r**S2 + carry); the **.co** option causes the generated carry bit to be written to the processor status register (PSR). The **.cio** option causes the carry bit to be added to the result and also causes the generated carry bit to be written to the PSR. If the result cannot be represented as a signed 32-bit integer, an integer overflow exception occurs.

The **add.ci** instruction can be used to implement a 'load carry bit' operation:

add.ci rD,**r0**,**r0**

Both source operands are **r**0, which by hardware convention contains zero. The result of this operation will be zero plus the value of the carry bit; i.e., the carry bit is loaded into **r**D.

The **add.co** instruction can be used to clear the carry bit:

add.co **r0**,**r0**,**r0**

Both source operands are **r0**, which by hardware convention contains zero. The result of this operation is zero, which has a 'carry out' of zero effectively clearing the carry bit. Because the instruction specifies **r0** as the destination and it is read only, no register contents are altered as a result of this operation.

add — Integer Add — add

Instruction Encoding:

Integer Category — Register with 16-Bit Immediate

31–26	25–21	20–16	15–0
0 1 1 1 0 0	D	S1	IMM16

Integer Category — Triadic Register

31–26	25–21	20–16	15–10	9	8	7–5	4–0
1 1 1 1 0 1	D	S1	0 1 1 1 0 0	I	O	0 0 0	S2

D:	Destination Register
S1:	Source 1 Register
IMM16:	16-Bit Unsigned Immediate Operand
I	0 – Disable Carry In
	1 – Add Carry to Result
O:	0 – Disable Carry Out
	1 – Generate Carry
S2:	Source 2 Register

addu — Unsigned Integer Add — addu

Operation: Destination ← Source 1 + Source 2

Assembler Syntax:

addu	rD,rS1,rS2	unsigned add (without carry)
addu.ci	rD,rS1,rS2	unsigned add plus carry
addu.co	rD,rS1,rS2	unsigned add, propagate carry out
addu.cio	rD,rS1,rS2	unsigned add plus carry, propagate carry out
addu	rD,rS1,IMM16	unsigned add with immediate (without carry)

Exceptions: None

Description: The **addu** instruction adds the contents of the **rS1** register with either the contents of the **rS2** register or a 16-bit, zero-extended immediate operand. Binary addition is performed. The result is placed in the **rD** register. The **.ci** option causes the carry bit to be added to the result (**rD**=**rS1**+**rS2**+carry). The **.co** option causes the generated carry bit to be written to the PSR. The **.cio** option causes the carry bit to be added to the result and also causes the generated carry bit to be written to the PSR.

The **addu** instruction does not cause an overflow exception when the sum of the operands cannot be represented as an unsigned 32-bit integer (see the **add** instruction).

Instruction Encoding:

Integer Category — Register with 16-Bit Immediate

31–26	25–21	20–16	15–0
0 1 1 0 0 0	D	S1	IMM16

Integer Category — Triadic Register

31–26	25–21	20–16	15–10	9	8	7–5	4–0
1 1 1 1 0 1	D	S1	0 1 1 0 0 0	I	O	0 0 0	S2

D: Destination Register
S1: Source 1 Register
IMM16: 16-Bit Unsigned Immediate Operand
I: 0 – Disable Carry In
1 – Add Carry to Result
O: 0 – Disable Carry Out
1 – Generate Carry
S2: Source 2 Register

Operation: Destination $\leftarrow$ Source 1 $\wedge$ Source 2

Assembler Syntax:

and rD,rS1,rS2
and.c rD,rS1,rS2
and rD,rS1,IMM16
and.u rD,rS1,IMM16

Exceptions: None

Description: For triadic register addressing, the data contained in the **r**S1 and **r**S2 registers is logically ANDed. The result is stored into the **r**D register. If the **.c** (complement) option is specified, the source 2 operand is complemented before being ANDed.

For register with immediate addressing, the lower 16 bits of the **r**S1 register and the 16-bit unsigned immediate operand encoded in the instruction are logically ANDed. The upper 16 bits of **r**S1 are copied unchanged into **r**D. If the **.u** (upper word) option is specified, the upper 16 bits of the source 1 operand are ANDed with the immediate operand, and the lower 16 bits of **r**S1 are copied unchanged into **r**D. The result is stored into the **r**D register.

Instruction Encoding:

Logical Category — Register with 16-Bit Immediate

31–27	26	25–21	20–16	15–0
0 1 0 0 0	U	D	S1	IMM16

Logical Category — Triadic Register

31–26	25–21	20–16	15–11	10	9–5	5–0
1 1 1 1 0 1	D	S1	0 1 0 0 0	C	0 0 0 0 0	S2

U: 0 – AND IMM16 to bits 15–0 of S1
   1 – AND IMM16 to bits 31–16 of S1
D: Destination Register
S1: Source 1 Register
IMM16: 16-Bit Unsigned Immediate Operand
C: 0 – Second operand not complemented before the operation
   1 – Second operand complemented before the operation
S2: Source 2 Register

Operation: If bit clear: $FIP \leftarrow XIP + D16 \ll 2$

Assembler Syntax:
bb0 B5, **r**S1, D16
bb0.n B5, **r**S1, D16

Exceptions: None

Description: The **bb0** instruction examines the bit of the **r**S1 register specified by the B5 field. If the bit is clear, the branch is taken. The 16-bit displacement is sign extended and shifted left two bits to form a word displacement; the branch target address is formed by adding this displacement to the address of the **bb0** instruction. The **.n** (delayed branch) option causes the instruction following the **bb0** instruction to be executed before the branch target instruction is executed.

To ensure future compatibility, the instruction following a **bb0.n** instruction should not be a trap, jump, branch, or any other instruction that modifies the instruction pointer. This programming error is not detected.

Instruction Encoding:

Flow-Control Category — Register with 16-Bit Displacement

31–27	26	25–21	20–16	15–0
1 1 0 1 0	N	B5	S1	D16

N: 0 – Next sequential instruction suppressed
1 – Next sequential instruction executed before branch is taken
B5: 5-Bit Unsigned Integer denoting a bit number in the S1 operand
S1: Source 1 Register
D16: 16-Bit Sign-Extended Displacement

bb1 — Branch On Bit Set — bb1

Operation: If bit set: FIP ← XIP+D16<<2

Assembler Syntax:
bb1 B5, **r**S1, D16
bb1.n B5, **r**S1, D16

Exceptions: None

Description: The **bb1** instruction examines the bit of the **r**S1 register specified by the B5 field. If the bit is set, a branch is taken. The 16-bit displacement is sign extended and shifted left two bits to form a word displacement; the branch target address is formed by adding this displacement to the address of the **bb1** instruction. The **.n** (delayed branch) option causes the instruction following the **bb1** instruction to be executed before the branch target instruction.

To ensure future compatibility, the instruction following a **bb1.n** instruction should not be a trap, jump, branch, or any other instruction that modifies the instruction pointer. This programming error is not detected.

Instruction Encoding:

Flow-Control Category — Register with 16-Bit Displacement

31–27	26	25–21	20–16	15–0
1 1 0 1 1	N	B5	S1	D16

N: 0 – Next sequential instruction suppressed
1 – Next sequential instruction executed before branch is taken
B5: 5-Bit Integer denoting a bit number in the S1 operand
S1: Source 1 Register
D16: 16-Bit Sign-Extended Displacement

bcnd — Conditional Branch — bcnd

Operation: If condition true: FIP ← XIP + D16<<2

Assembler Syntax:

bcnd **eq0**,**r**S1,D16	**bcnd.n** **eq0**,**r**S1,D16
bcnd **ne0**,**r**S1,D16	**bcnd.n** **ne0**,**r**S1,D16
bcnd **gt0**,**r**S1,D16	**bcnd.n** **gt0**,**r**S1,D16
bcnd **lt0**,**r**S1,D16	**bcnd.n** **lt0**,**r**S1,D16
bcnd **ge0**,**r**S1,D16	**bcnd.n** **ge0**,**r**S1,D16
bcnd **le0**,**r**S1,D16	**bcnd.n** **le0**,**r**S1,D16
bcnd M5,**r**S1,D16	**bcnd.n** M5,**r**S1,D16

Exceptions: None

Description: The **bcnd** instruction compares the data contained in the **r**S1 register to zero and branches if the value in the register meets the condition specified in the instruction (**eq0** for equals zero, etc.). The condition of the **r**S1 register is determined by the value of two bits: 1) the sign bit (most significant bit) and 2) the zero bit (logical NORing of the 31 low-order operand bits). These two bits are concatenated to form an index into the M5 field of the instruction (see the instruction encoding below). If the indexed bit is set, the branch is taken. This allows branching on conditions such as zero, negative, positive, greater than or equal to zero, and less than or equal to zero without preceding the branch instruction with a compare instruction. The 16-bit displacement is sign extended and shifted left two bits to form a word displacement; the branch target address is formed by adding this displacement to the address of the **bcnd** instruction. The **.n** (delayed branch) option causes the instruction following the **bcnd.n** instruction to be executed before the branch target instruction.

The Motorola MC88100 assembler provides mnemonics for commonly used comparison conditions. The following chart lists these mnemonics and their corresponding bit values for the M5 field. The M5 field may also be indicated explicitly by a literal value.

Bit:	25	24	23	22	21
eq0 (equals zero)	0	0	0	1	0
ne0 (not equal to zero)	0	1	1	0	1
gt0 (greater than zero)	0	0	0	0	1
lt0 (less than zero)	0	1	1	0	0
ge0 (greater than/equals zero)	0	0	0	1	1
le0 (less than/equals zero)	0	1	1	1	0

To ensure future compatibility, the instruction following a **bcnd.n** instruction should not be a trap, jump, branch, or any other instruction that modifies the instruction pointer. This programming error is not detected.

bcnd Conditional Branch bcnd

Instruction Encoding:

Flow-Control Category — Register with 16-Bit Displacement

31 – 27	26	25 – 21	20 – 16	15 – 0
1 1 1 0 1	N	M5	S1	D16

N: 0 – Next sequential instruction suppressed
1 – Next sequential instruction executed before branch is taken

M5: 5-Bit Condition Match Field:

- bit 25: reserved, unused by the branch selection logic (must be zero for future compatibility)
- bit 24: maximum negative number [Sign and Zero]
- bit 23: less than zero [Sign and (not Zero)]
- bit 22: equal to zero [(not Sign) and Zero]
- bit 21: greater than zero [(not Sign) and (not Zero)]

S1: Source 1 Register

D16: 16-Bit Signed-Extended Displacement

br — Unconditional Branch — br

Operation: $FIP \leftarrow XIP + D26 << 2$

Assembler Syntax:
br D26
br.n D26

Exceptions: None

Description: The **br** instruction causes an unconditional transfer of program flow to the address formed by adding the 26-bit, sign-extended word displacement (shifted left two bits) to the address of the branch instruction. The **.n** (delayed branch) option causes the instruction following the **br.n** instruction to be executed before the branch target instruction.

To ensure future compatibility, the instruction following a **br.n** instruction should not be a trap, jump, branch, or any other instruction that modifies the instruction pointer. This programming error is not detected.

Instruction Encoding:

Flow-Control Category — 26-Bit Displacement

31–27	26	25–0
1 1 0 0 0	N	D26

N: 0 – Next sequential instruction suppressed
1 – Next sequential instruction executed before branch is taken

D26: 26-Bit Sign-Extended Displacement

Operation: FIP ← XIP + D26<<2
r1 ← NIP (+4 if **.n** option)

Assembler Syntax:
bsr D26
bsr.n D26

Exceptions: None

Description: The **bsr** instruction causes an unconditional transfer of program flow to the target address and the return address is saved in register **r1**. The branch target address is formed by adding the 26-bit, sign-extended word displacement (shifted left two bits) to the address of this instruction (value of XIP). If the **.n** option is not specified, the return address is the address of the instruction following the **bsr** instruction (value of NIP). The **.n** (delayed branch) option causes the instruction following the **bsr.n** instruction to be executed before the branch target instruction. When the **.n** option is specified, the return address is the address of the second instruction following the **bsr.n** instruction (value of NIP+4).

To ensure future compatibility, the instruction following a **bsr.n** instruction should not be a trap, jump, branch, or any other instruction that modifies the instruction pointer. This programming error is not detected.

The **bsr** instruction can be used to implement a 'load instruction pointer' operation:

```
        bsr     label
label:
```

This instruction branches to the instruction identified by **label**, which is also the next instruction in the instruction stream . The return address (instruction following the **bsr** instruction) identified by **label** is stored in register **r1**. Therefore, **r1** contains the value of the XIP.

Instruction Encoding:

Flow-Control Category — 26-Bit Displacement

31–27	26	25–0
1 1 0 0 1	N	D26

N: 0 – Next sequential instruction suppressed
1 – Next sequential instruction executed before branch is taken

D26: 26-Bit Sign-Extended Displacement

Operation: Destination ← (Source 1 ∧ (Bit-Field of 0s))

Assembler Syntax:
clr rD,rS1, W5<O5>
clr rD,rS1,rS2
clr rD,rS1,[<]05[>]

Exceptions: None

Description: The **clr** instruction copies the contents of the **rS1** register into the **rD** register and inserts a field of zeros, of width W5, into the data. The field is offset from bit zero of the **rS1** register by the number of bits specified in the O5 field. For example, if W5 contains 5 and O5 contains 16, a field of 5 zeros is placed in bits 16 through 20 of the **rS1** operand. For triadic register addressing, bits 9–5 and bits 4–0 of the **rS2** register are used as the W5 and O5 fields, respectively, and the rest of the **rS2** register is ignored. If the specified field extends beyond bit 31, those bits are ignored.

The following illustration shows the operation of the **clr rD**, **rS1**, 5<16> instruction.

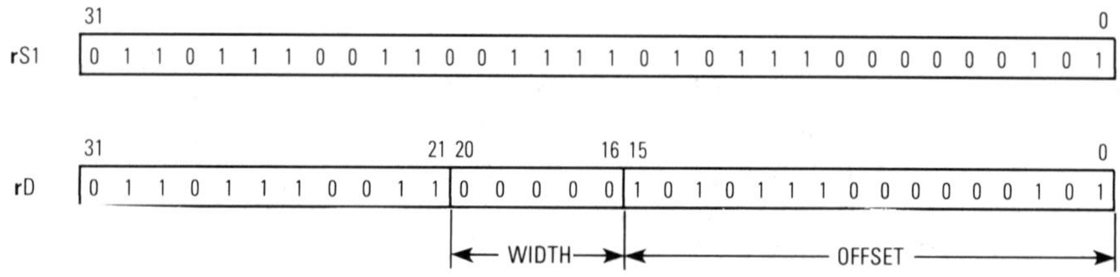

Instruction Encoding:

Bit-Field Category — Register with 10-Bit Immediate

31–26	25–21	20–16	15–10	9–5	4–0
1 1 1 1 0 0	D	S1	1 0 0 0 0 0	W5	05

Bit-Field Category — Triadic Register

31–26	25–21	20–16	15–5	4–0
1 1 1 1 0 1	D	S1	1 0 0 0 0 0 0 0 0 0 0	S2

D: Destination Register
S1: Source 1 Register
W5: 5-Bit Unsigned Integer denoting a Bit-Field Width (0 denotes 32 bits)
O5: 5-Bit Unsigned Integer denoting a Bit-Field Offset
S2: Source 2 Register

3

Operation: Destination ← Source 1 :: Source 2

Assembler Syntax:
cmp rD,rS1,rS2
cmp rD,rS1,IMM16

Exceptions: None

Description: The **cmp** instruction compares the data contained in the **r**S1 register with either the data in the **r**S2 register or with the specified, zero-extended 16-bit immediate operand. The instruction returns the evaluated conditions as a bit string in the destination register. The format and interpretation of the returned bit string in the **r**D register is given below:

Returned String:

31–12	11	10	9	8	7	6	5	4	3	2	1–0
0 0 0 0 0 0 0 0 0 0 0 0 0 0 0 0 0 0 0 0*	hs	lo	ls	hi	ge	lt	le	gt	ne	eq	0 0*

*Bits 31–12 and 1–0 are not guaranteed to be zeros in future implementations.

hs: true (1) if and only if S1 U≥S2 (unsigned greater than or equal)
lo: true (1) if and only if S1 U<S2 (unsigned less than)
ls: true (1) if and only if S1 U≤S2 (unsigned less than or equal)
hi: true (1) if and only if S1 U>S2 (unsigned greater than)
ge: true (1) if and only if S1≥S2 (signed greater than or equal)
lt: true (1) if and only if S1<S2 (signed less than)
le: true (1) if and only if S1≤S2 (signed less than or equal)
gt: true (1) if and only if S1>S2 (signed greater than)
ne: true (1) if and only if S1≠S2 (not equal)
eq: true (1) if and only if S1=S2 (equal)

The results of the comparison can be used by branch on bit instructions (**bb0** and **bb1**) to synthesize 'compare and branch on condition' operations. The results can also be used by trap on bit instructions (**tb0** and **tb1**). Note that the trap-on bounds-check (**tbnd**) instruction is more efficient for out-of-bounds array access checking.

Instruction Encoding:

Integer Category — Register with 16-Bit Immediate

31–26	25–21	20–16	15–0
0 1 1 1 1 1	D	S1	IMM16

cmp Integer Compare cmp

Integer Category — Triadic Register

31–26	25–21	20–16	15–10	9–8	7–5	4–0
1 1 1 1 0 1	D	S1	0 1 1 1 1 1	0 0*	0 0 0	S2

*The MC88100 does not decode these bits; however, assemble as shown to guarantee compatibility with future implementations.

D: Destination Register
S1: Source 1 Register
IMM16: 16-Bit Unsigned Immediate Operand
S2: Source 2 Register

div — Signed Integer Divide — div

Operation: Destination ← Source 1/Source 2

Assembler Syntax:
div rD,rS1,rS2
div rD,rS1,IMM16

Exceptions:
Integer Divide
Floating-Point Unimplemented (only if FPU disabled)

Description: The data contained in the **r**S1 register is divided by either the data in the **r**S2 register or by the zero-extended 16-bit immediate operand specified in the instruction. A 32-bit twos complement binary division is performed. The quotient is stored in the **r**D register.

If the divisor is zero or either operand is negative, an integer divide exception is generated, and program control is transferred to the integer divide exception handler. A floating-point unimplemented exception is taken if execution of the **div** is attempted while the FPU is disabled.

Instruction Encoding:

Integer Category — Register with 16-Bit Immediate

31–26	25–21	20–16	15–0
0 1 1 1 1 0	D	S1	IMM16

Integer Category — Triadic Register

31–26	25–21	20–16	15–10	9	8	7–5	4–0
1 1 1 1 0 1	D	S1	0 1 1 1 1 0	0	0*	0 0 0	S2

*The MC88100 does not decode these bits; however, assemble as shown to guarantee compatibility with future implementations.

D: Destination Register
S1: Source 1 Register
IMM16: 16-Bit Zero-Extended Immediate Operand
S2: Source 2 Register

divu — Unsigned Integer Divide — divu

Operation: Destination ← Source 1/Source 2

Assembler Syntax:
divu rD,**r**S1,**r**S2
divu rD,**r**S1,IMM16

Exceptions: Integer Divide
Floating-Point Unimplemented (only if FPU is disabled)

Description: The data contained in the **r**S1 register is divided by either the data in the **r**S2 register or by the zero-extended 16-bit immediate operand specified in the instruction. A 32-bit twos complement binary division is performed. The quotient is stored in the **r**D register.

If the divisor is zero, an integer divide exception is generated and program control is transferred to the integer divide exception handler. A floating-point unimplemented exception is taken if execution of **divu** is attempted while FPU is disabled.

Instruction Encoding:

Integer Category — Register with 16-Bit Immediate

31–26	25–21	20–16	15–0
0 1 1 0 1 0	D	S1	IMM16

Integer Category — Triadic Register

31–26	25–21	20–16	15–10	9–8	7–5	4–0
1 1 1 1 0 1	D	S1	0 1 1 0 1 0	0 0*	0 0 0	S2

*The MC88100 does not decode these bits; however, assemble as shown to guarantee compatibility with future implementations.

D: Destination Register
S1: Source 1 Register
IMM16: 16-Bit Zero-Extended Immediate Operand
S2: Source 2 Register

Operation: Destination ⧫ (sign-extended bit field) of Source 1

Assembler Syntax:
ext rD,rS1,W5<O5>
ext rD,rS1,rS2
ext rD,rS1,[<]05[>]

3

Exceptions: None

Description: The **ext** instruction extracts a bit field from the **r**S1 register. The bit-field width is specified by the W5 field, and the offset from the least significant bit is specified by the O5 field. The extracted bit field is sign extended to 32 bits and placed in the **r**D register. For triadic register addressing, bits 9–5 and 4–0 of the **r**S2 register are used for the W5 and O5 fields, respectively, and the rest of the **r**S2 register is ignored. If the bit field extends beyond bit 31, then bit 31 is used as the sign bit and is extended in the destination register. The following illustration shows the operation of the **ext** instruction.

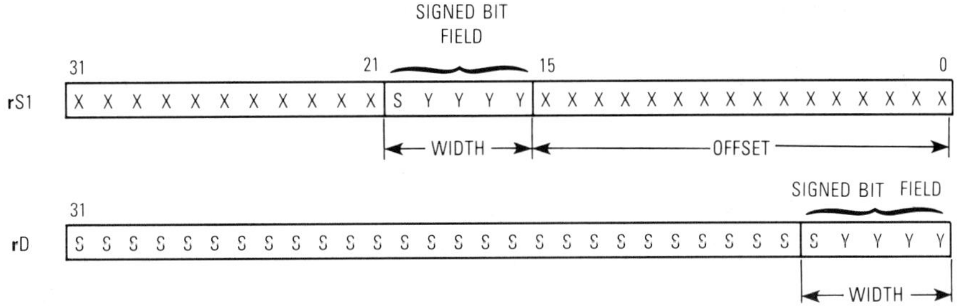

When the W5 field contains all zeros (specifying a width of 32 bits), this instruction operates as an arithmetic shift right instruction. The offset specifies the number of positions to shift. The high-order bits are sign filled in the destination register. The following illustration shows an example of a shift operation with the **ext** instruction:

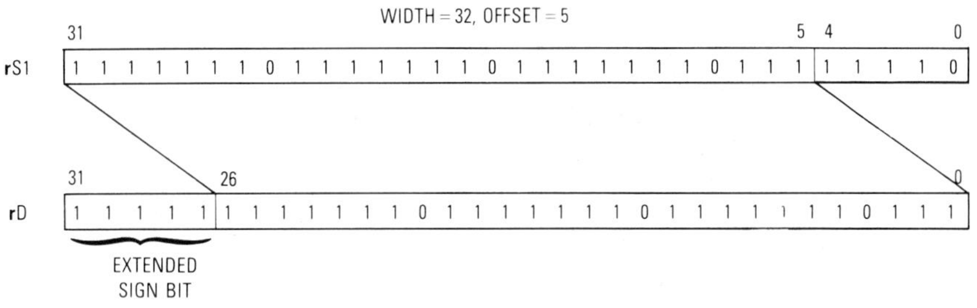

Instruction Encoding:

Bit-Field Category — Register with 10-Bit Immediate

31 26	25 21	20 16	15 10	9 5	4 0
1 1 1 1 0 0	D	S1	1 0 0 1 0 0	W5	O5

Bit-Field Category — Triadic Register

31 26	25 21	20 16	15 5	4 0
1 1 1 1 0 1	D	S1	1 0 0 1 0 0 0 0 0 0 0	S2

D: Destination Register
S1: Source 1 Register
W5: 5-Bit Unsigned Integer denoting a Bit-Field Width (0 denotes 32 bits)
O5: 5-Bit Unsigned Integer denoting a Bit-Field Offset
S2: Source 2 Register

extu — Extract Unsigned Bit Field

Operation: Destination ← (zero-extended bit field) of Source 1

Assembler Syntax:
extu rD,rS1,W5<O5>
extu rD,rS1,rS2
extu rD,rS1,[<]O5[>]

Exceptions: None

Description: The **extu** instruction extracts a bit field from the **r**S1 register. The bit-field width is specified by the W5 field, and the offset from the least significant bit is specified by the O5 field. The extracted bit field is zero extended to 32 bits and placed in the **r**D register. For triadic register addressing, bits 9–5 and 4–0 of the register specified by the **r**S2 field are used for the W5 and O5 fields, respectively, and the rest of **r**S2 is ignored. If the field extends beyond bit 31, then the result is zero extended in the destination register. The following illustration shows the operation of the **extu** instruction.

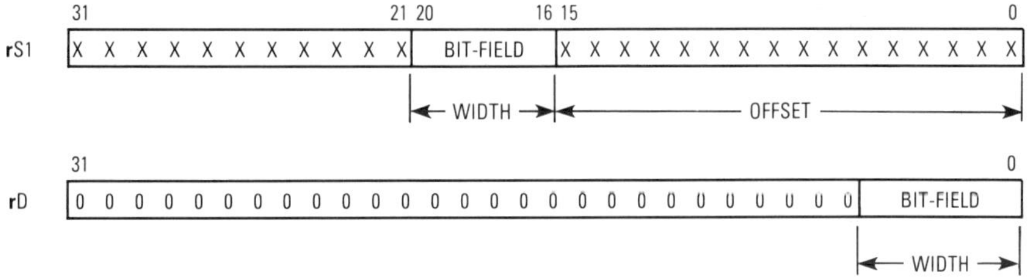

When the W5 field contains all zeros (specifying a width of 32 bits), this instruction operates as a logical shift right instruction. The offset specifies the number of positions to shift. The high-order bits are zero filled in the destination register. The following illustration shows an example of a shift operand with the **extu** instruction:

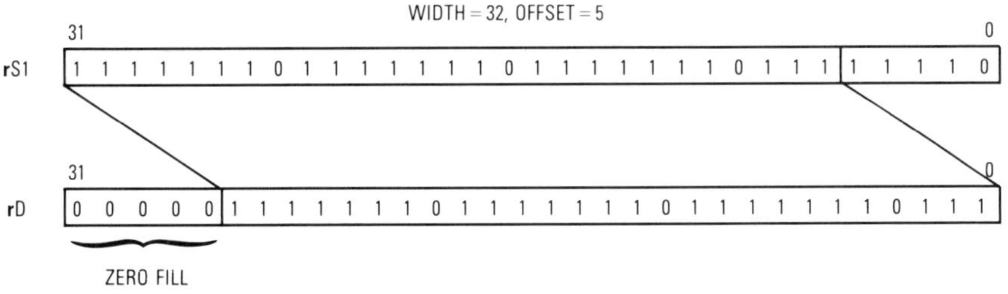

Instruction Encoding:

Bit-Field Category — Register with 10-Bit Immediate

31–26	25–21	20–16	15–10	9–5	4–0
1 1 1 1 0 0	D	S1	1 0 0 1 1 0	W5	O5

Bit-Field Category — Triadic Register

31–26	25–21	20–16	15–5	4–0
1 1 1 1 0 1	D	S1	1 0 0 1 1 0 0 0 0 0 0	S2

D:	Destination Register
S1:	Source 1 Register
W5:	5-Bit Unsigned Integer denoting a Bit-Field Width (0 denotes 32 bits)
O5:	5-Bit Unsigned Integer denoting a Bit-Field Offset
S2:	Source 2 Register

Operation: Destination ← Source 1 + Source 2

Assembler Syntax:

fadd.sss rD,rS1,rS2
fadd.ssd rD,rS1,rS2
fadd.sds rD,rS1,rS2
fadd.sdd rD,rS1,rS2
fadd.dss rD,rS1,rS2
fadd.dsd rD,rS1,rS2
fadd.dds rD,rS1,rS2
fadd.ddd rD,rS1,rS2

Exceptions:

Floating-Point Reserved Operand
Floating-Point Overflow
Floating-Point Underflow
Floating-Point Inexact (if not masked)
Floating-Point Unimplemented

Description: The **fadd** instruction checks the data in the **r**S1 and **r**S2 registers for reserved operands. If no reserved operands are found, the **r**S1 and **r**S2 operands are added according to the IEEE 754 standard, and the result is placed in the **r**D register. If reserved operands are found, a floating-point reserved operand exception is taken. The other exception conditions occur when an overflow, underflow, or inexact result is detected. Any combination of single- and double-precision operands can be specified. If **r0** is specified as the destination register or if execution of **fadd** is attempted while the FPU is disabled, a floating-point unimplemented exception is taken.

SECTION 6 EXCEPTIONS contains more information on the floating-point implementation.

Instruction Encoding:

Floating-Point Category — Triadic Register

31–26	25–21	20–16	15–11	10–9	8–7	6–5	4–0
1 0 0 0 0 1	D	S1	0 0 1 0 1	T1	T2	TD	S2

D: Destintion Register (**r0** not allowed)
S1: Source 1 Register
T1: Source 1 Operand Size
T2: Source 2 Operand Size
TD: Destination Operand Size
Note: For the T1, T2, and TD Fields:
00 – Single Precision
01 – Double Precision
S2: Source 2 Register

Operation: Destination ◆ Source 1 :: Source 2

Assembler Syntax:

fcmp.sss rD,rS1,rS2
fcmp.ssd rD,rS1,rS2
fcmp.sds rD,rS1,rS2
fcmp.sdd rD,rS1,rS2

Exceptions: Floating-Point Reserved Operand
Floating-Point Unimplemented

Description: The **fcmp** instruction checks the contents of the **r**S1 and **r**S2 registers for reserved operands. If reserved operands are found, a floating-point reserved operand exception is taken. If no reserved operands are found, the instruction subtracts the **r**S2 operand from **r**S1 and evaluates a number of conditions according to the IEEE 754 standard. The evaluation results are returned as a bit string in the **r**D register and the subtraction result is discarded. A comparison to zero and a comparison with bound is also initiated by this instruction, returning bits that correspond to the following conditions: ou (out of range), ib (in range or on boundary), in (in range), or ob (out of range or on boundary). The range is between zero and the value in the **r**S2 register. If the **r**S2 operand is negative, ou, ib, in, and ob are all zero. Any combination of single- and double-precision source operands can be specified. If **r0** is specified as the destination register or if execution of **fcmp** is attempted while the FPU is disabled, a floating-point unimplemented exception is taken.

The returned comparison results can be used by branch on bit instructions (**bb0**, **bb1**) to synthesize 'conditional branch on comparison' operations (branch equal, branch high, etc).

The reserved operand exception handler can complete some operations in software when an exception occurs. For example, comparison of denormalized numbers can be performed in software. The exception handler can then generate a return string, setting the appropriate bits from the comparison.

SECTION 6 EXCEPTIONS contains more information on the floating-point exceptions.

Result String:

31 ... 12	11	10	9	8	7	6	5	4	3	2	1	0
0 0 0 0 0 0 0 0 0 0 0 0 0 0 0 0 0 0 0 0*	ob	in	ib	ou	ge	lt	le	gt	ne	eq	cp	nc

*Bits 31–12 are not guaranteed to be zeros in future implementations.

ob: out of range or on boundary 

in: in range 

ib: in range or on boundary 

ou: out of range 

ge: true (1) if and only if (**rS1**)≥(**rS2**) (signed greater than or equal)
lt: true (1) if and only if (**rS1**)<(**rS2**) (signed less than)
le: true (1) if and only if (**rS1**)≤(**rS2**) (signed less than or equal)
gt: true (1) if and only if (**rS1**)>(**rS2**) (signed greater than)
ne: true (1) if and only if (**rS1**)≠(**rS2**) (not equal)
eq: true (1) if and only if (**rS1**)=(**rS2**) (equal)
cp: true (1) if and only if the two operands are comparable (i.e., the two operands are ordered as specified by IEEE standard 754-1985)
nc: true (1) if, and only if, the two operands are not comparable (i.e., the two operands are unordered as specified by IEEE standard 754-1985)

Instruction Encoding:

Floating-Point Category — Triadic Register

31–26	25–21	20–16	15–11	10–9	8–7	6–5	4–0
1 0 0 0 0 1	D	S1	0 0 1 1 1	T1	T2	0 0	S2

D: Destination Register (**r0** not allowed)
S1: Source 1 Register
T1: Source 1 Operand Size
T2: Source 2 Operand Size
Note: For the T1 and T2 Fields:
00 – Single Precision
01 – Double Precision
S2: Source 2 Register

Operation: Destination ← Source 1/Source 2

Assembler Syntax:

fdiv.sss rD,rS1,rS2
fdiv.ssd rD,rS1,rS2
fdiv.sds rD,rS1,rS2
fdiv.sdd rD,rS1,rS2
fdiv.dss rD,rS1,rS2
fdiv.dsd rD,rS1,rS2
fdiv.dds rD,rS1,rS2
fdiv.ddd rD,rS1,rS2

Exceptions:

Floating-Point Reserved Operand
Floating-Point Divide by Zero
Floating-Point Overflow
Floating-Point Underflow
Floating-Point Inexact (if not masked)
Floating-Point Unimplemented

Description: The contents of the **r**S1 and **r**S2 registers are checked for reserved operands. If no reserved operands are found, the **r**S1 operand is divided by the **r**S2 operand according to the IEEE 754. The result is placed in the **r**D register. Any combination of single- and double-precision operands can be specified. An attempt to divide by zero causes a floating-point divide by zero exception. If reserved operands are found, a floating-point reserved operand exception is taken. The other exception conditions occur when an overflow, underflow, or inexact result is detected. If **r0** is specified as the destination register or if execution of **fdiv** is attempted while FPU is disabled, a floating-point unimplemented exception is taken.

SECTION 6 EXCEPTIONS contains more information on the floating-point exceptions.

Instruction Encoding:

Floating-Point Category — Triadic Register

31 26	25 21	20 16	15 11	10 9	8 7	6 5	4 0
1 0 0 0 0 1	D	S1	0 1 1 1 0	T1	T2	TD	S2

D: Destintion Register (**r0** not allowed)
S1: Source 1 Register
T1: Source 1 Operand Size
T2: Source 2 Operand Size
TD: Destination Operand Size
Note: For the T1, T2, and TD Fields:
00 – Single Precision
01 – Double Precision
S2: Source 2 Register

Operation: Destination ◄ (bit number) of Source 2 Scanned for First Bit Clear

Assembler Syntax: **ff0** rD,rS2

Exceptions: None

Description: This instruction scans the **r**S2 register from the most significant bit to the least significant bit. The destination register is loaded with the bit number of the first bit that was found clear: zero for the least significant bit and 31 for the most significant bit. If no bits are found clear, the destination register is loaded with 32.

Instruction Encoding:

Bit-Field Category — Triadic Register

31–26	25–21	20–16	15–5	4–0
1 1 1 1 0 1	D	0 0 0 0 0*	1 1 1 0 1 1 0 0 0 0 0	S2

*The MC88100 does not decode these bits; however, they should be assembled as shown to guarantee compatibility with future implementations.

D: Destination Register
S2: Source 2 Register

Operation: Destination ← (bit number) of Source 2 Scanned for First Bit Set

Assembler Syntax: **ff1** **r**D,**r**S2

Exceptions: None

Description: This instruction scans the **r**S2 register from the most significant bit to the least significant bit. The destination register is loaded with the bit number of the first bit that was found set, zero for the least significant bit and 31 for the most significant bit. If no bits are found set, the destination register is loaded with 32.

Instruction Encoding:

Bit-Field Category — Triadic Register

31 26	25 21	20 16	15 5	4 0
1 1 1 1 0 1	D	0 0 0 0 0*	1 1 1 0 1 0 0 0 0 0 0	S2

*The MC88100 does not decode these bits; however, they should be assembled as shown to guarantee compatibility with future implementations.

D: Destination Register
S2: Source 2 Register

fldcr — Load from Floating-Point Control Register

Operation: Destination ← Floating-Point Control Register

Assembler Syntax: **fldcr** **r**D,**fcr**S

Exceptions: Floating-Point Privilege Violation

Description: The contents of the floating-point unit control register specified by the FCRS field is loaded in the general-purpose register specified by the D field. Floating-point control registers **fcr8–fcr0** are privileged registers and can only be accessed in the supervisor mode. Registers **fcr63** and **fcr62** are the floating-point control and status registers, respectively, and can be accessed in either the supervisor or user mode.

Registers **fcr61–fcr9** are currently unimplemented but are privileged. A load from these registers returns zeros to **r**D when executed in the supervisor mode in the current implementation, and causes a floating-point privilege violation exception when executed in the user mode.

Refer to **SECTION 6 EXCEPTIONS** for more information on FPU control registers.

Instruction Encoding:

Floating-Point Category — Control Register

31–26	25–21	20–16	15–11	10–5	4–0
1 0 0 0 0 0	D	0 0 0 0 0*	0 1 0 0 1	FCRS	0 0 0 0 0*

*The MC88100 does not decode these bits; however, they should be assembled as shown to guarantee compatibility with future implementations.

D: Destination Register
FCRS: Floating-Point Control Register Source

Operation: Destination ← Float (Source 2)

Assembler Syntax:
flt.ss rD,rS2
flt.ds rD,rS2

Exceptions:
Floating-Point Inexact (if not masked)
Floating-Point Unimplemented

Description: The signed integer number contained in the **r**S2 register is converted to floating-point representation. The result is placed in the **r**D register. The **r**S2 can only be specified as single precision because it is an integer, but the destination register can be single or double precision (not **r0**). If **r0** is specified as the destination register or if execution of **flt** is attempted while the FPU is disabled, a floating-point unimplemented exception is taken.

SECTION 2 PROGRAMMING MODEL and **SECTION 6 EXCEPTIONS** contain more information on the floating-point implementation.

Instruction Encoding:

Floating-Point Category — Triadic Register

31–26	25–21	20–7	6–5	4–0
1 0 0 0 0 1	D	0 0 0 0 0 0 0 1 0 0 0 0 0 0	TD	S2

D: Destination Register (**r0** not allowed)
TD: Destination Operand Size
Note: For the TD Field:
00 – Single Precision
01 – Double Precision
S2: Source 2 Register

fmul — Floating-Point Multiply — fmul

Operation: Destination ← Source 1 × Source 2

Assembler Syntax:

fmul.sss rD,rS1,rS2
fmul.ssd rD,rS1,rS2
fmul.sds rD,rS1,rS2
fmul.sdd rD,rS1,rS2
fmul.dss rD,rS1,rS2
fmul.dsd rD,rS1,rS2
fmul.dds rD,rS1,rS2
fmul.ddd rD,rS1,rS2

Exceptions:

Floating-Point Reserved Operand
Floating-Point Overflow
Floating-Point Underflow
Floating-Point Inexact (if not masked)
Floating-Point Unimplemented

Description: The contents of the **r**S1 and **r**S2 registers are checked for reserved operands. If no reserved operands are found, the **r**S1 and **r**S2 operands are multiplied according to the IEEE 754. The result is placed in the **r**D register. Any combination of single- and double-precision operands can be specified. If reserved operands are found, a floating-point reserved operand exception is taken. The other exception conditions occur when an overflow, underflow, or inexact result is detected. If **r0** is specified as the destination register or if execution of **fmul** is attempted while the FPU is disabled, a floating-point unimplemented exception is taken.

Instruction Encoding:

Floating-Point Category — Triadic Register

31–26	25–21	20–16	15–11	10–9	8–7	6–5	4–0
1 0 0 0 0 1	D	S1	0 0 0 0 0	T1	T2	TD	S2

D: Destination Register (**r0** not allowed)
S1: Source 1 Register
T1: Source 1 Operand Size
T2: Source 2 Operand Size
TD: Destination Operand Size
Note: For the T1, T2, and TD Fields:
00 – Single Precision
01 – Double Precision
S2: Source 2 Register

Operation: Floating-Point Control Register ← Destination

Assembler Syntax: **fstcr** rS1,**fcr**D

Exceptions: Floating-Point Privilege Violation

Description: The contents of the general-purpose register specified by the S1 field is stored to the FPU control register specified by the FCRD field. Floating-point control registers **fcr8–fcr0** are privileged registers and can only be accessed in the supervisor mode. Registers **fcr63** and **fcr62** are the floating-point control and status registers, respectively, and can be accessed in either the supervisor or user mode. Registers **fcr8–fcr1** are readonly, and an **fstcr** instruction addressing these registers performs a null operation.

Registers **fcr61–fcr9** are currently unimplemented but are privileged. An **fstcr** instruction to any of these registers performs a null operation in supervisor mode and causes a floating-point privilege violation exception in user mode.

Instruction Encoding:

Floating-Point Category — Control Register

31 26	25 21	20 16	15 11	10 5	4 0
1 0 0 0 0 0	0 0 0 0 0*	S1	1 0 0 0 1	FCRD	S2

*The MC88100 does not decode these bits; however, they should be assembled as shown to guarantee compatibility with future implementations.

S1: Source 1 Register
FCRD: Floating-Point Control Destination Register
S2: Source 2 Register
Note: S1 and S2 fields must contain the same value.

fsub — Floating-Point Subtract — fsub

Operation: Destination ← Source 1 − Source 2

Assembler Syntax:

fsub.sss rD,rS1,rS2
fsub.ssd rD,rS1,rS2
fsub.sds rD,rS1,rS2
fsub.sdd rD,rS1,rS2
fsub.dss rD,rS1,rS2
fsub.dsd rD,rS1,rS2
fsub.dds rD,rS1,rS2
fsub.ddd rD,rS1,rS2

Exceptions:

Floating-Point Reserved Operand
Floating-Point Overflow
Floating-Point Underflow
Floating-Point Inexact (if not masked)
Floating-Point Unimplemented

Description: The contents of the **r**S1 and **r**S2 registers are checked for reserved operands. If no reserved operands are found, the source 2 operand is subtracted from the source 1 operand according to the IEEE 754 standard. The result is placed in the destination register. Any combination of single- and double-precision operands can be specified. If invalid operands are found, a floating-point reserved operand exception is taken. The other exception conditions occur when an overflow, underflow, or inexact result is detected. If **r0** is specified as the destination register or if execution of **fsub** is attempted while the FPU is disabled, a floating-point unimplemented exception is taken.

Instruction Encoding:

Floating-Point Category — Triadic Register

31–26	25–21	20–16	15–11	10–9	8–7	6–5	4–0
1 0 0 0 0 1	D	S1	0 0 1 1 0	T1	T2	TD	S2

D: Destintion Register (**r0** not allowed)
S1: Source 1 Register
T1: Source 1 Operand Size
T2: Source 2 Operand Size
TD: Destination Operand Size
Note: For the T1, T2, and TD Fields:
00 – Single Precision
01 – Double Precision
S2: Source 2 Register

Operation: Destination ◆ Floating-Point Control Register
Floating-Point Control Register ◆ Source 1

Assembler Syntax: **fxcr** rD,rS1,**fcr**S/D

Exceptions: Floating-Point Privilege Violation

Description: The contents of the general-purpose register specified by the S1 field are transferred to the FPU control register specified by the FCRS/D field, and the contents of the **fcr**S/D register are transferred to the **r**D register. Floating-point control registers **fcr8–fcr0** are privileged registers and can only be accessed in the supervisor mode. Registers **fcr63** and **fcr62** are the floating-point control and status registers, respectively, and can be accessed in either the supervisor or the user mode. Register **fcr8–fcr1** are readonly, and an **fxcr** instruction addressing these registers performs a load into the general-purpose destination registers only.

Registers **fcr61–fcr9** are currently unimplemented but are privileged. An **fxcr** instruction to any of these registers performs a load of all zeros into **r**D when executed in the supervisor mode, and causes a floating-point privilege violation exception in user mode.

Instruction Encoding:

Floating-Point Category — Control Register

31–26	25–21	20–16	15–11	10–5	4–0
1 0 0 0 0 0	D	S1	1 1 0 0 1	FCRS/D	S2

D: Destination Register
S1: Source 1 Register
FCRS/D: Floating-Point Control Register Source/Destination
S2: Source 2 Register
Note: S1 and S2 fields must contain the same value.

int — Round Floating Point to Integer

Operation: Destination ← Round (Source 2)

Assembler Syntax:
int.ss rD,rS2
int.sd rD,rS2

Exceptions:
Floating-Point Reserved Operand
Floating-Point Integer Conversion Overflow
Floating-Point Unimplemented

Description: The single- or double-precision floating-point number contained in the **r**S2 register is converted to a 32-bit integer using the rounding mode specified in the floating-point control register (FPCR). The result is placed in the **r**D register. If the **r**S2 operand exponent is greater than or equal to 30, then the floating-point integer conversion overflow exception is taken. If invalid operands are found, a floating-point reserved operand exception is taken. If **r0** is specified as the destination register or if execution of **int** is attempted while the FPU is disabled, a floating-point unimplemented exception is taken.

Instruction Encoding:

Floating-Point Category — Triadic Register

31–26	25–21	20–9	8–7	6–5	4–0
1 0 0 0 0 1	D	0 0 0 0 0 0 1 0 0 1 0 0	T2	0 0	S2

D: Destination Register (**r0** not allowed)
T2: Source 2 Operand Size
Note: For the T2 Field:
00 – Single Precision
01 – Double Precision
S2: Source 2 Register

Operation: Fetch Instruction Pointer ← Source 2

Assembler Syntax:
jmp rS2
jmp.n rS2

Exceptions: None

Description: This instruction performs an unconditional transfer of program flow to the absolute address contained in the **r**S2 register. The two least significant bits of that register are masked to force the FIP to an instruction (word) boundary. The **.n** (delayed branch) option causes the instruction following the **jmp.n** instruction to execute before the target instruction.

To ensure future compatibility, the instruction following a **jmp.n** instruction should not be a trap, jump, branch, or any other instruction that modifies the instruction pointers. This programming error is not detected.

The **jmp** instruction can be used to return from subroutines as in the following example:

jmp r1

The **bsr** and **jsr** instructions place the return address in register **r1** as a hardware convention. The **jmp** instruction above jumps to this return address.

Instruction Encoding:

Flow-Control Category — Triadic Register

31 – 26	25 – 16	16 – 11	10	9 – 5	4 – 0
1 1 1 1 0 1	0 0 0 0 0 0 0 0 0 0*	1 1 0 0 0	N	0 0 0 0 0	S2

*The MC88100 does not decode these bits; however, they should be assembled as shown to guarantee compatibility with future implementations.

N: 0 – Next sequential instruction suppressed
1 – Next sequential instruction executed before branch is taken

S2: Source 2 Register

jsr — Jump to Subroutine

Operation: Fetch Instruction Pointer ◆ Source 2
r1 ◆ Next Instruction Pointer (+4 if **.n** specified)

Assembler Syntax:
jsr rS2
jsr.n rS2

Exceptions: None

Description: This instruction performs an unconditional transfer of program control and saves the return address in register **r1**. The **jsr** target address is contained in the **r**S2 register. The two least significant bits of that register are masked, forcing the FIP to an instruction (word) boundary. The return address is the address of the instruction following the **jsr** instruction (value of NIP). The **.n** (delayed branch) option causes the instruction following the **jsr.n** instruction to execute before the jump target instruction. When the **.n** option is specified, the return address is the address of the second instruction following the **jsr.n** instruction (value of NIP+4).

To ensure future compatibility, the instruction following a **jsr.n** instruction should not be a trap, jump, branch, or any other instruction that modifies the instruction pointers. This programming error is not detected.

Instruction Encoding:

Flow-Control Category — Triadic Register

31–26	25–16	16–11	10	9–5	4–0
1 1 1 1 0 1	0 0 0 0 0 0 0 0 0 0*	1 1 0 0 1	N	0 0 0 0 0	S2

*The MC88100 does not decode these bits; however, they should be assembled as shown to guarantee compatibility with future implementations.

N: 0 – Next sequential instruction suppressed
1 – Next sequential instruction executed before branch is taken

S2: Source 2 Register

Operation: Destination Register ◆ Source Data

Assembler Syntax:

UNSCALED		UNSCALED		SCALED	
ld.b	rD,rS1,IMM16	**ld.b**	rD,rS1,rS2	**ld.b**	rD,rS1[rS2]
ld.bu	rD,rS1,IMM16	**ld.bu**	rD,rS1,rS2	**ld.bu**	rD,rS1[rS2]
ld.h	rD,rS1,IMM16	**ld.h**	rD,rS1,rS2	**ld.h**	rD,rS1[rS2]
ld.hu	rD,rS1,IMM16	**ld.hu**	rD,rS1,rS2	**ld.hu**	rD,rS1[rS2]
ld	rD,rS1,IMM16	**ld**	rD,rS1,rS2	**ld**	rD,rS1[rS2]
ld.d	rD,rS1,IMM16	**ld.d**	rD,rS1,rS2	**ld.d**	rD,rS1[rS2]
		ld.b.usr	rD,rS1,rS2	**ld.b.usr**	rD,rS1[rS2]
		ld.bu.usr	rD,rS1,rS2	**ld.bu.usr**	rD,rS1[rS2]
		ld.h.usr	rD,rS1,rS2	**ld.h.usr**	rD,rS1[rS2]
		ld.hu.usr	rD,rS1,rS2	**ld.hu.usr**	rD,rS1[rS2]
		ld.usr	rD,rS1,rS2	**ld.usr**	rD,rS1[rS2]
		ld.d.usr	rD,rS1,rS2	**ld.d.usr**	rD,rS1[rS2]

Exceptions: Data Access Exception
Misaligned Access Exception (if not masked)
Privilege Violation (**.usr** option only)

Description: This instruction reads data from the specified memory location and loads it into the destination register. The memory base address is contained in the **r**S1 register. Added to this base is either a zero-extended 16-bit immediate index or an unsigned 32-bit word index contained in the **r**S2 register. The index in the **r**S2 register can be scaled or unscaled. The destination register is marked 'in use' (in the scoreboard register) until the memory fetch completes.

Exceptions are recognized between any two memory transactions on the P bus. Therefore, the double-word load (**ld.d**) can encounter a data access exception between word accesses. Also, if the destination register is **r31** for the **ld.d** instruction, the most significant word of the data is placed in **r31**. The least significant word is read from memory but is not written into **r0**; **r0** always contains zero (due to hardware convention). The two bus transactions required for a double-word load do not lock the P bus. Therefore, in a system that interfaces the data P bus to CMMUs, the double-word load to memory may be interrupted by an alternate memory bus master.

The **ld** instruction with no options specifies a 32-bit operation. The **.b** option specifies signed byte (8 bits), **.bu** specifies unsigned byte (8 bits), **.h** specifies signed half word (16 bits), **.hu** specifies unsigned half word (16 bits), and **.d** specifies double word (64 bits). For the scaled index modes, the scale factor is determined by the size option of the instruction. Operations that are byte, half word, word, and double word in size define scale factors of 1, 2, 4, and 8, respectively, when the **r**S2 field is specified within square brackets **[ ]**.

When the MODE bit of the PSR is set, the memory address is normally to supervisor memory space; when MODE is clear, the memory address is normally to user memory space, and the value of the MODE bit is reflected on the DS/$\overline{\text{U}}$ P bus signal. The **.usr** option specifies that the memory access must be to the user address space regardless of the mode bit (user or supervisor) in the PSR. The **.usr** option is privileged and only available in supervisor mode.

Instruction Encoding:

Load/Store/Exchange Category — Register Indirect with Zero-Extended Immediate Index

31 30	29 28	27 26	25 ... 21	20 ... 16	15 ... 0
0 0	P	TY	D	S1	I16

Load/Store/Exchange Category — Register Indirect with Index

31 ... 26	25 ... 21	20 ... 16	15 14	13 12	11 10	9	8	7 ... 5	4 ... 0
1 1 1 1 0 1	D	S1	0 0	P	TY	0	U	0 0 0	S2

Load/Store/Exchange Category — Register Indirect with Scaled Index

31 ... 26	25 ... 21	20 ... 16	15 14	13 12	11 10	9	8	7 ... 5	4 ... 0
1 1 1 1 0 1	D	S1	0 0	P	TY	1	U	0 0 0	S2

P: 00 – Load Unsigned (half-word and byte operation only)
01 – Load Signed

TY: 00 – Double Word
01 – Word
10 – Half Word
11 – Byte

D: Destination Register

S1: Source 1 Register

I16: 16-Bit Immediate Index

U: 0 – Access per User/Supervisor Bit in PSR (normal mode)
1 – Access User Space Regardless of PSR

S2: Source 2 Register

lda Load Address lda

Operation: Destination ⧫ Source 1 + Source 2

Assembler Syntax:

lda.h	**r**D,**r**S1[**r**S2]
lda	**r**D,**r**S1[**r**S2]
lda.d	**r**D,**r**S1[**r**S2]

Exceptions: None

Description: This instruction creates a memory address from the specified operands. The memory base address is contained in the **r**S1 register. Added to this base is either a zero-extended 16-bit immediate index or an unsigned 32-bit word index contained in the **r**S2 register. The index in the **r**S2 register can be scaled or unscaled. The resulting address is placed in the destination register. The address calculated by this instruction is not checked for alignment relative to the operation type.

The **lda** instruction with no options specifies a 32-bit operation. The **.b** option specifies byte (8 bits), **.h** specifies half word (16 bits), and **.d** specifies double word (64 bits). For the scaled index modes, the scale factor is determined by the size option of the instruction. Operations that are byte, half word, word, and double word in size define scale factors of 1, 2, 4, and 8, respectively, when the **r**S2 field is specified within square brackets [ ].

Instruction Encoding:

Load/Store/Exchange Category — Register Indirect with Zero-Extended Immediate Index

31–28	27 26	25–21	20–16	15–0
0 0 1 1	TY	D	S1	I16

Load/Store/Exchange Category — Register Indirect with Index

31–26	25–21	20–16	15–12	11–10	9	8	7–5	4–0
1 1 1 1 0 1	D	S1	0 0 1 1	TY	0	0*	0 0 0	S2

*If set and the instruction attempted in user mode, a privilege violation exception occurs.

Load/Store/Exchange Category — Register Indirect with Scaled Index

31–26	25–21	20–16	15–12	11–10	9	8	7–5	4–0
1 1 1 1 0 1	D	S1	0 0 1 1	TY	1	0*	0 0 0	S2

*If set and the instruction is attempted in user mode, a privilege violation exception occurs.

TY: 00 – Double Word
01 – Word
10 – Half Word
11 – Byte

D: Destination Register

S1: Source 1 Register

S2: Source 2 Register

I16: 16-Bit Immediate Index

Load from Control Register (Privileged Instruction)

ldcr

Operation: Destination Register ◆ Control Register

Assembler Syntax: **ldcr** **r**D,**cr**S

Exceptions: Privilege Violation

Description: The data contained in the integer-unit control register specified by the CRS field of the instruction is loaded to the general-purpose register specified by the destination field. Integer-unit control registers may only be accessed in the supervisor mode; otherwise, a privilege violation occurs.

Instruction Encoding:

Load/Store/Exchange Category — Control Register

31–26	25–21	20–16	15–11	10–5	4–0
1 0 0 0 0 0	D	0 0 0 0 0*	0 1 0 0 0	CRS	0 0 0 0 0*

*The MC88100 does not decode these bits; however, they should be assembled as shown to guarantee compatibility with future implementations.

D: Destination Register
CRS: Control Register Source

mak — Make Bit Field

Operation: (bit field) Destination ← (bit field) of Source 1

Assembler Syntax:
mak rD,rS1,W5<O5>
mak rD,rS1,rS2
mak rD,rS1,[<]O5[>]

Exceptions: None

Description: The **mak** instruction extracts a bit field from the **r**S1 register. The bit field, whose width is specified by the W5 field, begins with the least significant bit of the **r**S1 register. The extracted field is placed in the **r**D register, offset from the least significant bit by the O5 field. Any bits outside of the field are cleared to zero. For triadic register addressing, bits 9–5 and bits 4–0 of the **r**S2 register are used for the W5 and O5 fields, respectively, and the rest of **r**S2 is ignored. If the W5 field specifies bits outside of the destination register, those bits are ignored.

The following illustration shows the operation of the **mak** instruction.

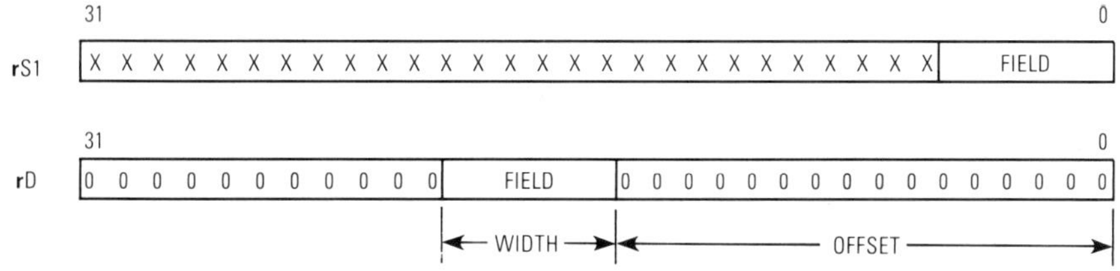

When the W5 field contains all zeros (specifying a width of 32 bits), this instruction operates as a shift left instruction. That is, the width field selects the entire register; the offset specifies the number of positions to shift. The low-order bits are zero-filled in the destination register. The following illustration shows an example of a shift left operation with the **mak r**D, **r**S1, 0<5> instruction:

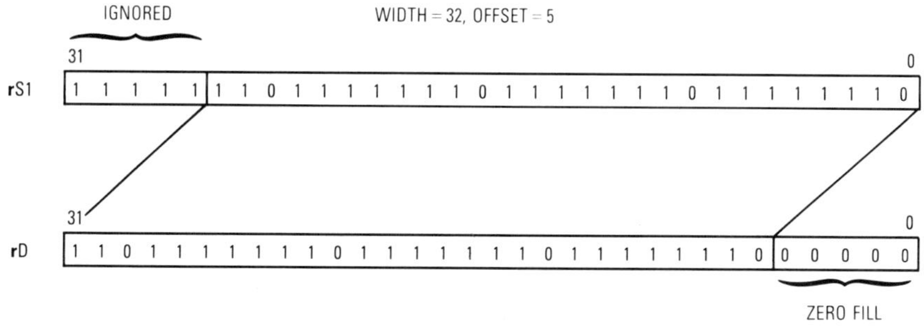

mak — Make Bit Field — mak

Instruction Encoding:

Bit-Field Category — Register with 10-Bit Immediate

31–26	25–21	20–16	15–10	9–5	4–0
1 1 1 1 0 0	D	S1	1 0 1 0 0 0	W5	O5

Bit-Field Category — Triadic Register

31–26	25–21	20–16	15–5	4–0
1 1 1 1 0 1	D	S1	1 0 1 0 0 0 0 0 0 0 0	S2

D: Destination Register
S1: Source 1 Register
W5: 5-Bit Unsigned Integer denoting a Bit-Field Width (0 denotes 32 bits)
O5: 5-Bit Unsigned Integer denoting a Bit-Field Offset
S2: Source 2 Register

Operation: Destination ← Source 1 ∧ IMM16

Assembler Syntax:
mask rD,**r**S1,IMM16
mask.u rD,**r**S1,IMM16

Exceptions: None

Description: The lower 16 bits of the **r**S1 register are logically ANDed with the unsigned 16-bit immediate value, and the upper 16 bits of the destination register are cleared. If the **.u** (upper word) option is specified, the upper 16 bits of the **r**S1 register are ANDed, and the lower 16 bits of the destination register are cleared. The result is stored in the **r**D register.

Instruction Encoding:

Logical Category — Register with 16-Bit Immediate

31–27	26	25–21	20–16	15–0
0 1 0 0 1	U	D	S1	IMM16

U: 0 – Apply IMM16 to bits 15–0 of S1
1 – Apply IMM16 to bits 31–16 of S1
D: Destination Register
S1: Source 1 Register
IMM16: 16-Bit Unsigned Immediate Operand

Operation: Destination ← Source 1 × Source 2

Assembler Syntax:
mul rD,rS1,rS2
mul rD,rS1,IMM16

Exceptions: Floating-Point Unimplemented (if FPU is disabled)

Description: The data in the **r**S1 register is multiplied by either the data in the **r**S2 register or by the unsigned, zero-extended 16-bit immediate value. The least significant 32 bits of the product are stored into the **r**D register. If **mul** instruction execution is attempted while the FPU is disabled, a floating-point unimplemented exception is taken.

Instruction Encoding:

Integer Category — Register with 16-Bit Immediate

31–26	25–21	20–16	15–0
0 1 1 0 1 1	D	S1	IMM16

Integer Category — Triadic Register

31–26	25–21	20–16	15–10	9–8	7–5	4–0
1 1 1 1 0 1	D	S1	0 1 1 0 1 1	0 0*	0 0 0	S2

*The MC88100 does not decode these bits; however, they should be assembled as shown to guarantee compatibility with future implementations.

D: Destination Register
S1: Source 1 Register
IMM16: 16-Bit Zero-Extended Immediate Operand
S2: Source 2 Register

nint — Floating-Point Round to Nearest Integer — nint

Operation: Destination ← Round-Nearest (Source 2)

Assembler Syntax:
nint.ss rD,rS2
nint.sd rD,rS2

Exceptions:
Floating-Point Reserved Operand
Floating-Point Integer Conversion Overflow
Floating-Point Unimplemented

Description: This instruction converts the floating-point number contained in the **r**S2 register to an integer using the IEEE 754 round-to-nearest rounding method, and delivers the result to the **r**D register. The **r**S2 operand can be either single or double precision. If the **r**S2 operand exponent is greater than or equal to 30, a floating-point integer conversion overflow exception is taken. If reserved operands are found, a floating-point reserved operand exception is taken. If **r0** is specified as the destination register or if execution of the **nint** instruction is attempted while the FPU is disabled, a floating-point unimplemented exception is taken.

Instruction Encoding:

Floating-Point Category — Triadic Register

31–26	25–21	20–9	8–7	6–5	4–0
1 0 0 0 0 1	D	0 0 0 0 0 0 1 0 1 0 0 0	T2	0 0	S2

D: Destination Register (**r0** not allowed)
T2: Source 2 Operand Size
- 00 – Single Precision
- 01 – Double Precision

S2: Source 2 Register

or — Logical OR — or

Operation: Destination ← Source 1 V Source 2

Assembler Syntax:

or rD,rS1,rS2
or.c rD,rS1,rS2
or rD,rS1,IMM16
or.u rD,rS1,IMM16

Exceptions: None

Description: For triadic register addressing, the contents of the **rS1** register is logically ORed with the contents of the **rS2** register. The result is stored into the **rD** register. If the **.c** (complement) option is specified, the source 2 operand is complemented before being ORed.

For register with immediate addressing, the contents of the **rS1** register is ORed with the unsigned 16-bit immediate operand, and the upper 16 bits of **rS1** are copied unchanged to **rD**. If the **.u** (upper word) option is specified, the upper 16 bits of the source 1 operand are ORed with the immediate operand, and the lower 16 bits of **rS1** are copied unchanged to **rD**. The result is stored into the **rD** register.

Instruction Encoding:

Logical Category — Register with 16-Bit Immediate

31 27	26	25 21	20 16	15 0
0 1 0 1 1	U	D	S1	IMM16

Logical Category — Triadic Register

31 26	25 21	20 16	15 11	10	9 5	4 0
1 1 1 1 0 1	D	S1	0 1 0 1 1	C	0 0 0 0 0	S2

U:	0 – OR IMM16 to Bits 15–0 of S1
	1 – OR IMM16 to Bits 31–16 of S1
D:	Destination Register
S1:	Source 1 Register
IMM16:	16-bit Unsigned Immediate Operand
C:	0 – Second operand not complemented before the operation
	1 – Second operand complemented before the operation
S2:	Source 2 Register

Operation: Destination $\leftarrow$ Source 1 rotated by O5

Assembler Syntax:
rot rD,rS1,<O5>
rot rD,rS1,rS2

Exceptions: None

Description: The **rot** instruction rotates the bits in the **r**S1 register to the right by the number of bits specified in the O5 field. The result is placed in the **r**D register. For triadic register addressing, the five low-order bits of the data contained in the **r**S2 register are used as the O5 field. Bits 5 through 9 in the **r**S2 register should be zero to guarantee future compatibility; the other bits are ignored.

Instruction Encoding:

Bit-Field Category — Register with 10-Bit Immediate

31 26	25 21	20 16	15 10	9 5	4 0
1 1 1 1 0 0	D	S1	1 0 1 0 1 0	0 0 0 0 0*	O5

*The MC88100 does not decode these bits; however, they should be assembled as shown to guarantee compatibility with future implementations.

Bit-Field Category — Triadic Register

31 26	25 21	20 16	15 5	4 0
1 1 1 1 0 1	D	S1	1 0 1 0 1 0 0 0 0 0 0	S2

D: Destination Register
S1: Source 1 Register
O5: 5-Bit Unsigned Integer denoting a Bit-Field Offset
S2 Source 2 Register

rte — Return from Exception (Privileged Instruction)

rte

Operation: PSR ← EPSR
NIP ← SNIP
FIP ← SFIP
SB ← SSBR

Assembler Syntax: **rte**

Exceptions: Privilege Violation

Description: This instruction provides an orderly termination of exception processing. It causes the exception time and shadow registers to be restored into the appropriate execution units and pipelines. Instruction execution resumes in the context defined by the SNIP, SFIP, EPSR, and SSBR registers. An **rte** instruction executed in the user mode causes a privilege violation.

Execution of the **rte** instruction synchronizes the MC88100 in that all previous operations are allowed to complete (effectively clearing the scoreboard register and data-unit pipeline) before the **rte** executes.

See **SECTION 6 EXCEPTIONS** for more information on exceptions and the side effects of executing an **rte** instruction. Refer to **SECTION 8 APPLICATIONS INFORMATION** for information on serialization.

Instruction Encoding:

Flow-Control Catageory — Triadic Register

31 … 26	25 … 16	15 … 5	4 … 0
1 1 1 1 0 1	0 0 0 0 0 0 0 0 0 0*	1 1 1 1 1 1 0 0 0 0 0	0 0 0 0 0*

*The MC88100 does not decode these bits; however, they should be assembled as shown to guarantee compatibility with future implementations.

set — Set Bit Field

Operation: Destination ← (Source 1 ∨ (Bit Field of 1's))

Assembler Syntax:
set rD,**r**S1,W5<O5>
set rD,**r**S1,**r**S2
set rD,**r**S1,[<]O5[>]

3

Exceptions: None

Description: The **set** instruction reads the **r**S1 register and inserts a field of ones, of width W5, into the data. The offset from bit zero is specified (in bits) by the O5 field. The result is placed in the **r**D register. For example, when W5 contains 5 and O5 contains 16, the destination register will contain the **r**S1 operand with a field of five ones in bit 16 through bit 20. For triadic register addressing, bits 9–5 and bits 4–0 of the **r**S2 register are used for the W5 and O5 fields, respectively. If the W5 field specifies bits outside of the destination register, those bits are ignored.

The following illustration shows the operation of the **set r**D,**r**S1,5<16> instruction.

	31 … 0
rS1	1 1 1 0 0 1 0 1 1 1 1 0 0 0 1 0 1 1 1 0 0 0 1 1 1 1 1 1 1 0 0 1

	31		0
rD	1 1 1 0 0 1 0 1 1 1	1 1 1 1 1	0 1 1 1 0 0 0 1 1 1 1 1 1 1 0 0 1
		← WIDTH →	← OFFSET →

Instruction Encoding:

Bit-Field Category — Register with 10-Bit Immediate

31–26	25–21	20–16	15–10	9–5	4–0
1 1 1 1 0 0	D	S1	1 0 0 0 1 0	W5	O5

Bit-Field Category — Triadic Register

31–26	25–21	20–16	15–5	4–0
1 1 1 1 0 1	D	S1	1 0 0 0 1 0 0 0 0 0 0	S2

D: Destination Register
S1: Source 1 Register
W5: Unsigned 5-Bit Integer denoting a Bit-Field Width (0 denotes 32 bits)
O5: Unsigned 5-Bit Integer denoting a Bit-Field Offset
S2: Source 2 Register

Operation: Memory Location ◀ Source Register (specified as **r**D)

Assembler Syntax:

UNSCALED		UNSCALED		SCALED	
st.b	**r**D,**r**S1,IMM16	**st.b**	**r**D,**r**S1,**r**S2	**st.b**	**r**D,**r**S1[**r**S2]
st.h	**r**D,**r**S1,IMM16	**st.h**	**r**D,**r**S1,**r**S2	**st.h**	**r**D,**r**S1[**r**S2]
st	**r**D,**r**S1,IMM16	**st**	**r**D,**r**S1,**r**S2	**st**	**r**D,**r**S1[**r**S2]
st.d	**r**D,**r**S1,IMM16	**st.d**	**r**D,**r**S1,**r**S2	**st.d**	**r**D,**r**S1[**r**S2]
		st.b.usr	**r**D,**r**S1,**r**S2	**st.b.usr**	**r**D,**r**S1[**r**S2]
		st.h.usr	**r**D,**r**S1,**r**S2	**st.h.usr**	**r**D,**r**S1[**r**S2]
		st.usr	**r**D,**r**S1,**r**S2	**st.usr**	**r**D,**r**S1[**r**S2]
		st.d.usr	**r**D,**r**S1,**r**S2	**st.d.usr**	**r**D,**r**S1[**r**S2]

Exceptions: Data Access Exception
Misaligned Access Exception (if not masked)
Privilege Violation (**.usr** option only)

Description: This instruction writes the contents of the specified register to the specified memory location. The **r**D field is used to specify the register data that will be stored in memory. The memory base address is contained in the **r**S1 register. Added to this base is either a zero-extended 16-bit immediate index or the signed 32-bit word index contained in the **r**S2 register. The index in the **r**S2 register can be scaled or unscaled.

Exceptions are recognized between any two memory transactions on the P bus. Therefore, the double-word instruction (**st.d**) can encounter a data access exception between word accesses. Also, if the source register is **r31** for the **st.d** instruction, the data is taken from **r31** and **r0**. The two bus transactions required for a double-word store do not lock the P bus. Therefore, in a system that interfaces the data P bus to CMMUs, the double-word store to memory may be interrupted by an alternate memory bus master.

The **st** instruction with no options specifies a 32-bit operation. The **.b** option specifies byte (8 bits), **.h** specifies half word (16 bits), and **.d** specifies double word (64 bits, registers **r**D and **r**D + 1). For the scaled index modes, the scale factor is determined by the size option of the instruction. Operations that are byte, half word, word, and double word in size define scale factors of 1, 2, 4, and 8, respectively, when the **r**S2 field is specified within square brackets **[ ]**.

When the MODE bit of the PSR is set, the memory address is normally to supervisor memory space; when MODE is clear, the memory address is normally to user memory space, and the value of the MODE bit is reflected on the DS/$\overline{U}$ P bus signal. The **.usr** option specifies that the memory access must be to the user address space regardless of the mode bit (user or supervisor) in the PSR. The **.usr** option is privileged and only available in supervisor mode.

Instruction Encoding:

Load/Store/Exchange Category — Register Indirect with Zero-Extended Immediate Index

31 28	27 26	25 21	20 16	15 0
0 0 1 0	TY	D	S1	I16

Load/Store/Exchange Category — Register Indirect with Index

31 26	25 21	20 16	15 12	11 10	9	8	7 5	4 0
1 1 1 1 0 1	D	S1	0 0 1 0	TY	0	U	0 0 0	S2

Load/Store/Exchange Category — Register Indirect with Scaled Index

31 26	25 21	20 16	15 12	11 10	9	8	7 5	4 0
1 1 1 1 0 1	D	S1	0 0 1 0	TY	1	U	0 0 0	S2

D: For the store instruction, this destination field actually specifies the data (source) that is stored

TY: 00 – Double Word
01 – Word
10 – Half Word
11 – Byte

S1: Source 1 Register

I16: 16-Bit Immediate Index

U: 0 – Access per User/Supervisor Bit in PSR (normal mode)
1 – Access User Space Regardless of PSR

S2: Source 2 Register

Store to Control Register (Privileged Instruction)

stcr

Operation: Control Register ← Source Register

Assembler Syntax: **stcr** rS1,crD

Exceptions: Privilege Violation

Description: The data contained in the general-purpose register specified by the S1 field of the instruction is stored to the integer-unit control register specified by the CRD field. The integer-unit control registers can only be accessed in supervisor mode.

Instruction Encoding:

Load/Store/Exchange Category — Control Register

31–26	25–21	20–16	15–11	10–5	4–0
1 0 0 0 0 0	0 0 0 0 0*	S1	1 0 0 0 0	CRD	S2

*The MC88100 does not decode these bits; however, they should be assembled as shown to guarantee compatibility with future implementations.

S1: Source 1 Register
CRD: Control Register Destination
S2: Source 2 Register
Note: The S1 and S2 fields must contain the same register number.

sub — Integer Subtract — sub

Operation: Destination ← Source 1 − Source 2

Assembler Syntax:

sub	rD,rS1,rS2	subtract (without borrow)
sub.ci	rD,rS1,rS2	subtract and use borrow in
sub.co	rD,rS1,rS2	subtract and propagate borrow out
sub.cio	rD,rS1,rS2	subtract and propagate borrow in and out
sub	rD,rS1,IMM16	subtract immediate (without borrow)

Exceptions: Integer Overflow

Description: The data contained in the **r**S2 register is subtracted from the data contained in the **r**S1 register, or an unsigned zero-extended 16-bit immediate operand is subtracted from the **r**S1 register. The result is placed in the **r**D register. The carry bit can optionally be used to perform subtract with borrow operations. A cleared carry bit indicates a borrow, and a set carry bit indicates no borrow. (Effectively, borrow for subtraction is the opposite of carry for addition.) If the results cannot be reported as a signed 32-bit integer, an integer overflow exception occurs.

Subtraction is performed by adding the ones complement of the source 2 operand and either a constant one or the carry bit to the source 1 operand. All 32 bits of the operand participate in the addition. The generated carry bit can optionally be written to the PSR. If the carry out of the sign bit position and the carry into the sign bit are not the same, an overflow exception occurs.

The **sub.co** instruction can be used to implement a "set carry bit" operation:

sub.co r0,r0,r0

The instruction subtracts zero from zero (**r0** contains zero by hardware convention), resulting in a one carry bit. Because the instruction specifies **r0** as the destination and it is read-only, no register contents are altered as a result of this operation.

Instruction Encoding:

Integer Category — Register with 16-Bit Immediate

31–26	25–21	20–16	15–0
0 1 1 1 0 1	D	S1	IMM16

sub — Integer Subtract

Integer Category — Triadic Register

31–26	25–21	20–16	15–10	9	8	7–5	4–0
1 1 1 1 0 1	D	S1	0 1 1 1 0 1	I	O	0 0 0	S2

D: Destination Register
S1: Source 1 Register
IMM16: 16-Bit Zero-Extended Immediate Operand
I: 0 – Disable Carry In
1 – Enable Carry In
O: 0 – Disable Carry Out
1 – Enable Carry Out
S2: Source 2 Register

subu — Unsigned Integer Subtract — subu

Operation: Destination ← Source 1 − Source 2

Assembler Syntax:

subu	rD,rS1,rS2
subu.ci	rD,rS1,rS2
subu.co	rD,rS1,rS2
subu.cio	rD,rS1,rS2
subu	rD,rS1,IMM16

Exceptions: None

Description: The data contained in the **r**S2 register is subtracted from the data contained in the **r**S1 register, or an unsigned zero-extended 16-bit immediate operand is subtracted from the **r**S1 register. The result is placed in the **r**D register. The carry bit can optionally be used to perform subtract with borrow operations.

Subtraction is performed by adding the ones complement of the source 2 operand and either a constant one or the carry bit to the source 1 operand. All 32 bits of the operand participate in the addition. The generated carry bit can optionally be written to the PSR.

Instruction Encoding:

Integer Category   Register with 16-Bit Immediate

31–26	25–21	20–16	15–0
0 1 1 0 0 1	D	S1	IMM16

Integer Category — Triadic Register

31–26	25–21	20–16	15–10	9	8	7–5	4–0
1 1 1 1 0 1	D	S1	0 1 1 0 0 1	I	O	0 0 0	S2

D: Destination Register
S1: Source 1 Register
IMM16: 16-Bit Zero-Extended Immediate Operand
I: 0 – Disable Carry In
   1 – Enable Carry In
O: 0 – Disable Carry Out
   1 – Enable Carry Out
S2: Source 2 Register

Operation: If Bit B5 Clear: Trap VEC9

Assembler Syntax: **tb0** B5,**r**S1,VEC9

Exceptions: Trap VEC9
Privilege Violation

Description: The **tb0** instruction examines the bit in the **r**S1 register specified by the B5 field. If that bit is clear, exception processing is initiated. The exception vector address is formed by concatenating the upper 20 bits of the vector base register with the 9-bit VEC9 field, followed by a 3-bit field of zeros.

Execution of the **tb0** instruction synchronizes the MC88100 in that all previous operations are allowed to complete (effectively clearing the scoreboard register and data unit pipeline) before the **tb0** executes.

When executed in user mode, a trap to a hardware vector (vectors 0 through 127) causes a privilege violation exception whether or not the trap condition is met.

Instruction Encoding:

Flow-Control Category — 9-Bit Vector Table Address

31–26	25–21	20–16	15–9	8–0
1 1 1 1 0 0	B5	S1	1 1 0 1 0 0 0	VEC9

B5: 5-Bit Unsigned Integer denoting a Bit Number
S1: Source 1 Register
VEC9: Vector Number from the start of the Page Address in the Vector Base Register

Operation: If Bit B5 Set: Trap VEC9

Assembler Syntax: **tb1** B5,**r**S1,VEC9

3

Exceptions: Trap VEC9
Privilege Violation

Description: The **tb1** instruction examines the bit in the **r**S1 register specified by the B5 field. If that bit is set, exception processing is initiated. The exception vector address is formed by concatenating the upper 20 bits of the vector base register with the 9-bit VEC9 field followed by a 3-bit field of zeros.

Execution of the **tb1** instruction synchronizes the MC88100 in that all previous operations are allowed to complete (effectively clearing the scoreboard register and data unit pipeline) before the **tb1** executes.

When in the user mode, a trap to a hardware vector (vectors 0 through 127) causes a privilege violation exception whether or not the trap condition is met.

Instruction Encoding:

Flow-Control Category — 9-Bit Vector Table Address

31–26	25–21	20–16	15–9	8–0
1 1 1 1 0 0	B5	S1	1 1 0 1 1 0 0	VEC9

B5: 5-Bit Unsigned Integer denoting a Bit Number
S1: Source 1 Register
VEC9: Vector Number from the start of the Page Address in the Vector Base Register

tbnd — Trap On Bounds Check — tbnd

Operation: If unsigned(S1)>unsigned(S2): Trap (bounds check vector)
If unsigned(S1)>unsigned (IMM16): Trap (bounds check vector)

Assembler Syntax:
tbnd rS1,rS2
tbnd rS1,IMM16

Exceptions: Bounds Check

Description: The data contained in the **r**S1 register is compared either to the data contained in the **r**S2 register or to the zero-extended 16-bit immediate operand using unsigned arithmetic. If the source 1 operand is larger (out of bounds), a bounds check trap is taken and exception processing is initiated.

Although this instruction is a conditional trap instruction, it does not synchronize the processor before it executes.

Instruction Encoding:

Flow-Control Category — Register with 16-Bit Immediate

31 … 26	25 … 21	20 … 16	15 … 0
1 1 1 1 1 0	0 0 0 0 0*	S1	IMM16

*The MC88100 does not decode these bits; however, they should be assembled as shown to guarantee compatibility with future implementations.

Flow-Control Category — Triadic Register

31 … 26	25 … 21	20 … 16	15 … 5	4 … 0
1 1 1 1 0 1	0 0 0 0 0*	S1	1 1 1 1 1 0 0 0 0 0 0	S2

*The MC88100 does not decode these bits; however, they should be assembled as shown to guarantee compatibility with future implementations.

S1: Source 1 Register
IMM16: 16-Bit Zero-Extended Immediate Operand
S2: Source 2 Register

3

Operation: If Condition True: Trap

Assembler Syntax:

tcnd **eq0**,**r**S1,VEC9
tcnd **ne0**,**r**S1,VEC9
tcnd **gt0**,**r**S1,VEC9
tcnd **lt0**,**r**S1,VEC9
tcnd **ge0**,**r**S1,VEC9
tcnd **le0**,**r**S1,VEC9
tcnd M5,**r**S1,VEC9

Exceptions: Trap VEC9
Privilege Violation

Description: The **tcnd** instruction examines the data contained in the **r**S1 register to determine the value of two bits: 1) the sign bit (most significant bit) and 2) the zero bit (logical NORing of the 31 low-order operand bits). These two bits are concatenated to form an index into the M5 field of the instruction. If the indexed bit is one, then exception processing is initiated. This allows traps on conditions such as zero, negative, positive, greater than or equal to zero, and less than or equal to zero, without preceding the trap instruction by a compare instruction. The exception vector address is formed by concatenating the upper 20 bits of the vector base register with the 9-bit VEC9 field followed by a 3-bit field of zeros.

The Motorola MC88100 assembler provides mnemonics for commonly used comparison conditions. The following chart lists these mnemonics and their corresponding bit values for the M5 field. The M5 field may also be indicated explicitly by a literal value.

Bit:	25	24	23	22	21
eq0 (equals zero)	0	0	0	1	0
ne0 (not equal to zero)	0	1	1	0	1
gt0 (greater than zero)	0	0	0	0	1
lt0 (less than zero)	0	1	1	0	0
ge0 (greater than/equal zero)	0	0	0	1	1
le0 (less than/equals zero)	0	1	1	1	0

Execution of the **tcnd** instruction synchronizes the MC88100 in that all previous operations are allowed to complete (effectively clearing the scoreboard register and data unit pipeline) before the **tcnd** executes.

In the user mode, a trap to a hardware vector (vectors 0 through 127) causes a privilege violation exception whether or not the trap condition is met.

tcnd — Conditional Trap — tcnd

Instruction Encoding:

Flow-Control Category — 9-Bit Vector Table Address

31–26	25–21	20–16	15–9	8–0
1 1 1 1 0 0	M5	S1	1 1 1 0 1 0 0	VEC9

M5: 5-Bit Condition Match Field

- bit 25: reserved, unused by the branch selection logic
- bit 24: maximum negative number [Sign and Zero]
- bit 23: less than zero [Sign and (not Zero)]
- bit 22: equal to zero [(not Sign) and Zero]
- bit 21: greater than zero [(not Sign) and (not Zero)]

S1: Source 1 Register

VEC9: Vector Number from the start of the Page Address in the Vector Base Register

trnc — Truncate Floating-Point to Integer — trnc

Operation: Destination ← Truncate(Source 2)

Assembler Syntax:
trnc.ss rD,rS2
trnc.sd rD,rS2

Exceptions:
Floating-Point Reserved Operand
Floating-Point Integer Conversion Overflow
Floating-Point Unimplemented

Description: The single- or double-precision number specified by the **r**S2 register is converted to a 32-bit integer using the IEEE 754 round-to-zero rounding method. The result is placed in the **r**D register. If the **r**S2 operand exponent is greater than or equal to 30, the floating-point integer conversion overflow exception is taken. If reserved operands are found, a floating-point reserved operand exception is taken. If **r0** is specified as the destination register or if execution of the **trnc** instruction is attempted while the FPU is disabled, a floating-point unimplemented exception is taken.

Instruction Encoding:

Floating-Point Category — Triadic Register

31 26	25 21	20 16	15 9	8 7	6 5	4 0
1 0 0 0 0 1	D	0 0 0 0 0	0 1 0 1 1 0 0	T2	0 0	S2

D: Destination Register (**r0** not allowed)
T2: Source 2 Operand Size
 00 – Single Precision
 01 – Double Precision
S2: Source 2 Register

Exchange Control Register
(Privileged Instruction)

Operation: (temp) ← Source 1
Destination Register ← Control Register
Control Register ← (temp)

Assembler Syntax: **xcr** rD,**r**S1,**cr**S/D

Exceptions: Privilege Violation

Description: The data contained in the general-purpose register specified by the source 1 field of the instruction is copied into the control register specified by the CRS/D field, while the contents of the specified control register are loaded into the general-purpose register specified by the D field.

Instruction Encoding:

Load/Store/Exchange Category — Control Register

31–26	25–21	20–16	15–11	10–5	4–0
1 0 0 0 0 0	D	S1	1 1 0 0 0	CRS/D	S2

D: Destination Register
S1: Source 1 Register
CRS/D: Control Register Source and Destination
S2: Source 2 Register
Note: S1 and S2 fields must contain the same register number.

Operation:

(temp) ← Source Register
Source Register ← Destination
Destination ← (temp)

Assembler Syntax:

UNSCALED		UNSCALED	
xmem.bu	rD,rS1,IMM16	**xmem.bu**	rD,rS1,rS2
xmem	rD,rS1,IMM16	**xmem**	rD,rS1,rS2
		xmem.bu.usr	rD,rS1,rS2
		xmem.usr	rD,rS1,rS2

SCALED	
xmem.bu	rD,rS1[rS2]
xmem	rD,rS1[rS2]
xmem.bu.usr	rD,rS1[rS2]
xmem.usr	rD,rS1[rS2]

Exceptions:

Data Access Exception
Misaligned Access Exception (if not masked)
Privilege Violation (**.usr** option only)

Description: The **xmem** instruction exchanges the contents of the destination register with a memory location. The memory base address is contained in the **r**S1 register. Added to this base is either a zero-extended 16-bit immediate index or the unsigned 32-bit word index contained in the **r**S2 register. The index in the **r**S2 register can be scaled or unscaled. If the instruction does not cause a priviledge exception, the contents of the **r**D register are exchanged (load and store) with the memory location. The destination register is marked 'in use' (in the scoreboard register) until the memory fetch completes.

The memory accesses generated for the load and store are indivisible; that is, the instruction cannot be interrupted by external interrupts, bus arbitration, or imprecise exceptions. The only potential interruption occurs if the store causes a data access exception after the load has already been performed. After the software handles the exception, the **xmem** instruction must be executed again to ensure operand consistency.

Execution of the **xmem** instruction synchronizes the MC88100 in that all previous operations are allowed to complete (effectively clearing the scoreboard register and data unit pipeline) before the **xmem** executes.

The **xmem** instruction with no options specifies a 32-bit operation. The **.bu** option specifies an unsigned byte (8 bits).

For the scaled index modes, the scale factor is determined by the size option of the instruction. Operations that are byte and word in size define scale factors of one and four respectively, when the **r**S2 field is specified within square [ ].

The current memory space is defined by the value of bit 31 (MODE) in the PSR. When MODE is set, the memory address is normally to supervisor memory space; when MODE is clear, the memory address is to user memory space, and the value of the MODE bit is reflected on the DS/$\overline{\text{U}}$ P bus signal. The **.usr** option specifies that the memory access must be to the user address space regardless of the mode bit (user or supervisor) in the PSR. The **.usr** option is privileged and only available in supervisor mode.

The **xmem** instruction asserts the $\overline{\text{DLOCK}}$ (bus lock) signal on the P bus to prevent the memory accesses from being interrupted. Bus locking with the **xmem** instruction is intended for semaphore operations and can have side effects on the on-chip cache of an MC88200 (CMMU). Refer to **SECTION 8 APPLICATIONS INFORMATION** for more information on synchronization operations.

Instruction Encoding:

Load/Store/Exchange Category — Register Indirect with Zero-Extended Immediate Index

31–28	27–26	25–21	20–16	15–0
0 0 0 0	TY	D	S1	IMM16

Load/Store/Exchange Category — Register Indirect with Index

31–26	25–21	20–16	15–12	11–10	9	8	7–5	4–0
1 1 1 1 0 1	D	S1	0 0 0 0	TY	0	U	0 0 0	S2

Load/Store/Exchange Category — Register Indirect with Scaled Index

31–26	25–21	20–16	15–12	11–10	9	8	7–5	4–0
1 1 1 1 0 1	D	S1	0 0 0 0	TY	1	U	0 0 0	S2

TY: 00 – Byte
01 – Word
D: Destination Register
S1: Source 1 Register
IMM16: 16-Bit Immediate Index
S2: Source 2 Register
U: 0 – Access per User/Supervisor Bit in PSR (normal mode)
1 – Access User Space Regardless of PSR

3

Operation: Destination ← Source 1 ⊕ Source 2

Assembler Syntax:

xor	r**D**,**rS1**,**rS2**
xor.c	r**D**,**rS1**,**rS2**
xor	r**D**,**rS1**,IMM16
xor.u	r**D**,**rS1**,IMM16

Exceptions: None

Description: For triadic register addressing, the contents of the **rS1** register are exclusive XORed with the contents of the **rS2** register. The result is stored into the **rD** register. If the **.c** (complement) option is specified, the source 2 operand is complemented before being XORed.

For register with immediate addressing, the contents of the **rS1** register are logically XORed with the unsigned 16-bit immediate operand, and the upper 16 bits of **rS1** are copied unchanged to **rD**. If the **.u** (upper word) option is specified, the upper 16 bits of the source 1 operand are XORed, and the lower 16 bits of **rS1** are copied unchanged to **rD**. The result is stored into the **rD** register.

Instruction Encoding:

Logical Category — Register with 16-Bit Immediate

31–27	26	25–21	20–16	15–0
0 1 0 1 0	U	D	S1	IMM16

Logical Category — Triadic Register

31–26	25–21	20–16	15–11	10	9–5	4–0
1 1 1 1 0 1	D	S1	0 1 0 1 0	C	0 0 0 0 0	S2

U:	0 – XOR IMM16 with Bits 15–0 of S1 1 – XOR IMM16 with Bits 31–16 of S1
D:	Destination Register
S1:	Source 1 Register
IMM16:	16-bit Unsigned Immediate Operand
C:	0 – Second operand not complemented before the operation 1 – Second operand complemented before the operation
S2:	Source 2 Register

3.5 OPCODE SUMMARY

The following paragraphs present two maps of the MC88100 instruction encodings. The paragraphs are organized by instruction category, and provide definitions for all of the instruction fields. See **3.5.7 Instruction Encodings In Numeric Order** for a list of instructions in ascending order by opcode.

3.5.1 Logical Instructions

Table 3-8 lists the opcode map for the logical instructions category.

Table 3-8. Logical Instructions

Mnemonic	31				27	26	25–21	20–16	15–0
and	0	1	0	0	0	U	D	S1	IMM16
mask	0	1	0	0	1	U	D	S1	IMM16
xor	0	1	0	1	0	U	D	S1	IMM16
or	0	1	0	1	1	U	D	S1	IMM16

Mnemonic	31					26	25–21	20–16	15				11	10	9				5	4–0
and	1	1	1	1	0	1	D	S1	0	1	0	0	0	C	0	0	0	0	0	S2
xor	1	1	1	1	0	1	D	S1	0	1	0	1	0	C	0	0	0	0	0	S2
or	1	1	1	1	0	1	D	S1	0	1	0	1	1	C	0	0	0	0	0	S2

U: 0 – Apply IMM16 to Bits 15–0 of S1
1 – Apply IMM16 to Bits 31–16 of S1
D: Destination Register
S1: Source 1 Register
IMM16: 16-bit Unsigned Immediate Operand
C: 0 – Second operand not complemented before the operation
1 – Second operand complemented before the operation
S2: Source 2 Register

3.5.2 Integer Arithmetic Instructions

Table 3-9 lists the opcode map for the integer arithmetic instructions category.

Table 3-9. Integer Arithmetic Instructions

Mnemonic	31–26	25–21	20–16	15–0
addu	0 1 1 0 0 0	D	S1	IMM16
subu	0 1 1 0 0 1	D	S1	IMM16
divu	0 1 1 0 1 0	D	S1	IMM16
mul	0 1 1 0 1 1	D	S1	IMM16
add	0 1 1 1 0 0	D	S1	IMM16
sub	0 1 1 1 0 1	D	S1	IMM16
div	0 1 1 1 1 0	D	S1	IMM16
cmp	0 1 1 1 1 1	D	S1	IMM16

Mnemonic	31–26	25–21	20–16	15–10	9	8	7–5	4–0
addu	1 1 1 1 0 1	D	S1	0 1 1 0 0 0	I	O	0 0 0	S2
subu	1 1 1 1 0 1	D	S1	0 1 1 0 0 1	I	O	0 0 0	S2
divu	1 1 1 1 0 1	D	S1	0 1 1 0 1 0	0	0*	0 0 0	S2
mul	1 1 1 1 0 1	D	S1	0 1 1 0 1 1	0	0*	0 0 0	S2
add	1 1 1 1 0 1	D	S1	0 1 1 1 0 0	I	O	0 0 0	S2
sub	1 1 1 1 0 1	D	S1	0 1 1 1 0 1	I	O	0 0 0	S2
div	1 1 1 1 0 1	D	S1	0 1 1 1 1 0	0	0*	0 0 0	S2
cmp	1 1 1 1 0 1	D	S1	0 1 1 1 1 1	0	0*	0 0 0	S2

D: Destination Register
S1: Source 1 Register
IMM16: 16-bit Unsigned Immediate Operand
I: 0 – Disable Carry In 1 – Add Carry to Result
O: 0 – Disable Carry Out 1 – Generate Carry
S2: Source 2 Register
*: The MC88100 does not decode these bits; however, assemble as shown to guarantee compatibility with future implementations.

3.5.3 Special-Function Unit (SFU) Instructions

The general opcode map for instructions executed by an SFU is identified below:

31–29	28–26	25–21	20–16	15–7	6–5	4–0
1 0 0	SFU ID	D	S1	SUB OPCODE	TD	S2

The SFU ID field (bits 28–26) identifies which SFU is specified. If SFU ID = 0 0 1, the floating-point unit is specified. If SFU ID = 0 0 0, the instruction is an SFU control register instruction as shown below:

31 29	28 26	25 21	20 16	15 14	13 11	10 5	4 0
1 0 0	0 0 0	D	S1	DIR	SFU #	SFU CR	S2

The SFU # field (bits 13–11) identifies which SFU is specified. The encoding of SFU # field = 0 0 0 is used for general control register instructions. If SFU # = 0 0 1, the floating-point unit control registers are specified.

In the current implementation, an attempt to execute an instruction that specifies SFU2 through SFU7 causes an SFU precise exception for that particular SFU. However, all encodings that correspond to SFU2 through SFU7 are reserved for future definition by Motorola. Table 3-10 lists the opcode map for the floating-point instruction category:

Table 3-10. Floating-Point Instructions

Mnemonic	31 26	25 21	20 16	15 11	10 9	8 7	6 5	4 0
fmul	1 0 0 0 0 1	D	S1	0 0 0 0 0	T1	T2	TD	S2
flt	1 0 0 0 0 1	D	0 0 0 0 0	0 0 1 0 0	0 0	0 0	TD	S2
fadd	1 0 0 0 0 1	D	S1	0 0 1 0 1	T1	T2	TD	S2
fsub	1 0 0 0 0 1	D	S1	0 0 1 1 0	T1	T2	TD	S2
fcmp	1 0 0 0 0 1	D	S1	0 0 1 1 1	T1	T2	0 0	S2
int	1 0 0 0 0 1	D	0 0 0 0 0	0 1 0 0 1	0 0	T2	0 0	S2
nint	1 0 0 0 0 1	D	0 0 0 0 0	0 1 0 1 0	0 0	T2	0 0	S2
trnc	1 0 0 0 0 1	D	0 0 0 0 0	0 1 0 1 1	0 0	T2	0 0	S2
fdiv	1 0 0 0 0 1	D	S1	0 1 1 1 0	T1	T2	TD	S2

Mnemonic	31 26	25 21	20 16	15 11	10 5	4 0
fldcr	1 0 0 0 0 0	D	0 0 0 0 0*	0 1 0 0 1	FCRS	0 0 0 0 0*
fstcr	1 0 0 0 0 0	0 0 0 0 0*	S1	1 0 0 0 1	FCRD	S2
fxcr	1 0 0 0 0 0	D	S1	1 1 0 0 1	FCRS/D	S2

D: Destination Register (**r0** allowed for **fldcr**, **fstcr**, and **fxcr** only)
S1: Source 1 Register
T1: Source 1 Operand Size
T2: Source 2 Operand Size
TD: Destination Operand Size
Note: For the T1, T2, and TD Fields:
00 – Single Precision
01 – Double Precision
S2: Source 2 Register
FCRS: Floating-Point Control Register Source
FCRD: Floating-Point Control Destination Register
FCRS/D: Floating-Point Control Source/Destination
*: The MC88100 does not decode these bits; however, assemble as shown to guarantee compatibility with future implementation.

3.5.4 Bit-Field Instructions

Table 3-11 lists the opcode map for the bit-field instruction category.

Table 3-11. Bit-Field Instructions

Mnemonic	Encoding					
	31 26	25 21	20 16	15 10	9 5	4 0
clr	1 1 1 1 0 0	D	S1	1 0 0 0 0 0	W5	O5
set	1 1 1 1 0 0	D	S1	1 0 0 0 1 0	W5	O5
ext	1 1 1 1 0 0	D	S1	1 0 0 1 0 0	W5	O5
extu	1 1 1 1 0 0	D	S1	1 0 0 1 1 0	W5	O5
mak	1 1 1 1 0 0	D	S1	1 0 1 0 0 0	W5	O5
rot	1 1 1 1 0 0	D	S1	1 0 1 0 1 0	0 0 0 0 0*	O5
	31 26	25 21	20 16	15	5	4 0
clr	1 1 1 1 0 1	D	S1	1 0 0 0 0 0	0 0 0 0 0	S2
set	1 1 1 1 0 1	D	S1	1 0 0 0 1 0	0 0 0 0 0	S2
ext	1 1 1 1 0 1	D	S1	1 0 0 1 0 0	0 0 0 0 0	S2
extu	1 1 1 1 0 1	D	S1	1 0 0 1 1 0	0 0 0 0 0	S2
mak	1 1 1 1 0 1	D	S1	1 0 1 0 0 0	0 0 0 0 0	S2
rot	1 1 1 1 0 1	D	S1	1 0 1 0 1 0	0 0 0 0 0	S2
	31 26	25 21	20 16	15	5	4 0
ff1	1 1 1 1 0 1	D	0 0 0 0 0*	1 1 1 0 1 0	0 0 0 0 0	S2
ff0	1 1 1 1 0 1	D	0 0 0 0 0*	1 1 1 0 1 1	0 0 0 0 0	S2

D: Destination Register
S1: Source 1 Register
W5: 5-Bit Unsigned Integer Denoting a Bit-Field Width (0 denotes 32 bits)
O5: 5-Bit Unsigned Integer Denoting a Bit-Field Offset
S2: Source 2 Register
*: The MC88100 does not decode these bits; however, assemble as shown to guarantee compatibility with future implementation.

3.5.5 Load/Store/Exchange Instructions

Table 3-12 lists the opcode map for the load/store/exchange instruction category.

Table 3-12. Load/Store/Exchange Instructions

Mnemonic	31	30	29	28	27–26	25–21	20–16	15–0
xmem (imm)	0	0	0	0	TY	D	S1	I16
ld (imm)	0	0	P		TY	D	S1	I16
st (imm)	0	0	1	0	TY	D	S1	I16
lda (imm)	0	0	1	1	TY	D	S1	I16

Mnemonic	31–26	25–21	20–16	15–11	10–5	4–0
ldcr	1 0 0 0 0 0	D	0 0 0 0 0*	0 1 0 0 0	CRS	0 0 0 0 0*
stcr	1 0 0 0 0 0	0 0 0 0 0*	S1	1 0 0 0 0	CRD	S2
xcr	1 0 0 0 0 0	D	S1	1 1 0 0 0	CRS/CRD	S2

Mnemonic	31–26	25–21	20–16	15–14	13–12	11–10	9	8	7–5	4–0
ld (uns)	1 1 1 1 0 1	D	S1	0 0	P	TY	0	U	0 0 0	S2
ld (scl)	1 1 1 1 0 1	D	S1	0 0	P	TY	1	U	0 0 0	S2

Mnemonic	31–26	25–21	20–16	15–12	11–10	9	8	7–5	4–0
xmem (uns)	1 1 1 1 0 1	D	S1	0 0 0 0	TY	0	U	0 0 0	S2
xmen (scl)	1 1 1 1 0 1	D	S1	0 0 0 0	TY	1	U	0 0 0	S2
st (uns)	1 1 1 1 0 1	D	S1	0 0 1 0	TY	0	U	0 0 0	S2
st (scl)	1 1 1 1 0 1	D	S1	0 0 1 0	TY	1	U	0 0 0	S2
lda (uns)	1 1 1 1 0 1	D	S1	0 0 1 1	TY	0	0†	0 0 0	S2
lda (scl)	1 1 1 1 0 1	D	S1	0 0 1 1	TY	1	0†	0 0 0	S2

P: 00 – Load Unsigned (byte and half-word only)
01 – Load Signed
TY: 00 – Double Word
01 – Word
10 – Half Word
00 – Byte
D: Destination Register (Source for Store Operations)
S1: Source 1 Register
I16: 16-Bit Immediate Index
U: 0 – Access per User/Supervisor Bit in PSR (normal mode)
1 – Access User Space Regardless of PSR
S2: Source 2 Register
CRS: Control Register Source
CRD: Control Register Destination
†: Causes privilege violation exception if bit is set and instruction is executed in user mode.
*: The MC88100 does not decode these bits; however, assemble as shown to guarantee compatibility with future implementation.

3.5.6 Flow-Control Instructions

Table 3-13 lists the opcode map for the flow-control instruction category.

Table 3-13. Flow-Control Instructions

Mnemonic	Encoding					
	31 27	26	25 0			
br	1 1 0 0 0	N	D26			
bsr	1 1 0 0 1	N	D26			
	31 27	26	25 21	20 16	15 0	
bb0	1 1 0 1 0	N	B5	S1	D16	
bb1	1 1 0 1 1	N	B5	S1	D16	
bcnd	1 1 1 0 1	N	M5	S1	D16	
	31 26	25 21	20 16	15 9	8 0	
tb0	1 1 1 1 0 0	B5	S1	1 1 0 1 0 0 0	VEC9	
tb1	1 1 1 1 0 0	B5	S1	1 1 0 1 1 0 0	VEC9	
tcnd	1 1 1 1 0 0	M5	S1	1 1 1 0 1 0 0	VEC9	
	31 26	25 16	15 11	10	9 5	4 0
jmp	1 1 1 1 0 1	0 0 0 0 0 0 0 0 0 0*	1 1 0 0 0	N	0 0 0 0 0	S2
jsr	1 1 1 1 0 1	0 0 0 0 0 0 0 0 0 0*	1 1 0 0 1	N	0 0 0 0 0	S2
	31 26	25 16	15 0			
rte	1 1 1 1 0 1	0 0 0 0 0 0 0 0 0 0*	1 1 1 1 1 1 0 0 0 0 0 0 0 0 0 0			
	31 26	25 21	20 16	15 0		
tbnd	1 1 1 1 1 0	0 0 0 0 0*	S1	IMM16		
tbnd	1 1 1 1 0 1	0 0 0 0 0*	S1	1 1 1 1 1 0 0 0 0 0 0	S2	

N: 0 – Next sequential instruction suppressed
1 – Next sequential instruction executed before branch is taken
B5: 5-Bit Integer Denoting a Bit Number in the S1 Operand
S1: Source 1 Register
D16: 16-Bit Sign-Extended Displacement
M5: 5-Bit Condition Match Field:
Bit 25: reserved, unused by the branch selection logic
Bit 24: maximum negative number [Sign and Zero]
Bit 23: less than zero [Sign and (not Zero)]
Bit 22: equal to zero [(not Sign) and Zero]
Bit 21: greater than zero [(not Sign) and (not Zero)]
D26: 26-bit Sign-Extended Displacement
S2: Source 2 Register
VEC9: Vector number from the start of the page address in the vector base register
*: The MC88100 does not decode these bits; however, assemble as shown to guarantee compatibility with future implementation.

3.5.7 Instruction Encodings In Numeric Order

Table 3-14 lists the opcode map for the MC88100 instruction set in ascending order.

Table 3-14. Instruction Numeric Listing (Sheet 1 of 3)

Mnemonic	31	30	29	28	27	26	25–21	20–16	15–0
xmem (imm)	0	0	0	0	TY		D	S1	IMM16
ld (imm)	0	0	P		TY		D	S1	IMM16
st (imm)	0	0	1	0	TY		D	S1	IMM16
lda (imm)	0	0	1	1	TY		D	S1	IMM16
and	0	1	0	0	0	U	D	S1	IMM16
mask	0	1	0	0	1	U	D	S1	IMM16
xor	0	1	0	1	0	U	D	S1	IMM16
or	0	1	0	1	1	U	D	S1	IMM16
addu	0	1	1	0	0	0	D	S1	IMM16
subu	0	1	1	0	0	1	D	S1	IMM16
divu	0	1	1	0	1	0	D	S1	IMM16
mul	0	1	1	0	1	1	D	S1	IMM16
add	0	1	1	1	0	0	D	S1	IMM16
sub	0	1	1	1	0	1	D	S1	IMM16
div	0	1	1	1	1	0	D	S1	IMM16
cmp	0	1	1	1	1	1	D	S1	IMM16

Mnemonic	31–26	25–21	20–16	15–11	10–5	4–0
ldcr	1 0 0 0 0 0	D	0 0 0 0 0*	0 1 0 0 0	CRS	0 0 0 0 0*
fldcr	1 0 0 0 0 0	D	0 0 0 0 0*	0 1 0 0 1	FCRS	0 0 0 0 0*
stcr	1 0 0 0 0 0	0 0 0 0 0*	S1	1 0 0 0 0	CRD	S2
fstcr	1 0 0 0 0 0	0 0 0 0 0*	S1	1 0 0 0 1	FCRD	S2
xcr	1 0 0 0 0 0	D	S1	1 1 0 0 0	CRS/CRD	S2
fxcr	1 0 0 0 0 0	D	S1	1 1 0 0 1	FCRS/D	S2

Mnemonic	31–26	25–21	20–16	15–11	10 9	8 7	6 5	4–0
fmul	1 0 0 0 0 1	D	S1	0 0 0 0 0	T1	T2	TD	S2
flt	1 0 0 0 0 1	D	0 0 0 0 0	0 0 1 0 0	0 0	0 0	TD	S2
fadd	1 0 0 0 0 1	D	S1	0 0 1 0 1	T1	T2	TD	S2
fsub	1 0 0 0 0 1	D	S1	0 0 1 1 0	T1	T2	TD	S2
fcmp	1 0 0 0 0 1	D	S1	0 0 1 1 1	T1	T2	0 0	S2
int	1 0 0 0 0 1	D	0 0 0 0 0	0 1 0 0 1	0 0	T2	0 0	S2
nint	1 0 0 0 0 1	D	0 0 0 0 0	0 1 0 1 0	0 0	T2	0 0	S2
trnc	1 0 0 0 0 1	D	0 0 0 0 0	0 1 0 1 1	0 0	T2	0 0	S2
fdiv	1 0 0 0 0 1	D	S1	0 1 1 1 0	T1	T2	TD	S2

Mnemonic	31–27	26	25–0
br	1 1 0 0 0	N	D26
bsr	1 1 0 0 1	N	D26

* The MC88100 does not decode these bits; however, assemble as shown to guarantee compatibility with future implementation.

Table 3-14. Instruction Numeric Listing (Sheet 2 of 3)

Mnemonic	31–27	26	25–21	20–16	15–0
bb0	1 1 0 1 0	N	B5	S1	D16
bb1	1 1 0 1 1	N	B5	S1	D16
bcnd	1 1 1 0 1	N	M5	S1	D16

Mnemonic	31–26	25–21	20–16	15–10	9–5	4–0
clr	1 1 1 1 0 0	D	S1	1 0 0 0 0 0	W5	O5
set	1 1 1 1 0 0	D	S1	1 0 0 0 1 0	W5	O5
ext	1 1 1 1 0 0	D	S1	1 0 0 1 0 0	W5	O5
extu	1 1 1 1 0 0	D	S1	1 0 0 1 1 0	W5	O5
mak	1 1 1 1 0 0	D	S1	1 0 1 0 0 0	W5	O5
rot	1 1 1 1 0 0	D	S1	1 0 1 0 1 0	0 0 0 0 0*	O5

Mnemonic	31–26	25–21	20–16	15–9	8–0
tb0	1 1 1 1 0 0	B5	S1	1 1 0 1 0 0 0	VEC9
tb1	1 1 1 1 0 0	B5	S1	1 1 0 1 1 0 0	VEC9
tcnd	1 1 1 1 0 0	M5	S1	1 1 1 0 1 0 0	VEC9

Mnemonic	31–26	25–21	20–16	15–12	11–10	9	8	7–5	4–0
xmem (uns)	1 1 1 1 0 1	D	S1	0 0 0 0	TY	0	U	0 0 0	S2
xmem (scl)	1 1 1 1 0 1	D	S1	0 0 0 0	TY	1	U	0 0 0	S2
ld (uns)	1 1 1 1 0 1	D	S1	0 0 P	TY	0	U	0 0 0	S2
ld (scl)	1 1 1 1 0 1	D	S1	0 0 P	TY	1	U	0 0 0	S2
st (uns)	1 1 1 1 0 1	D	S1	0 0 1 0	TY	0	U	0 0 0	S2
st (scl)	1 1 1 1 0 1	D	S1	0 0 1 0	TY	1	U	0 0 0	S2
lda (uns)	1 1 1 1 0 1	D	S1	0 0 1 1	TY	0	0‡	0 0 0	S2
lda (scl)	1 1 1 1 0 1	D	S1	0 0 1 1	TY	1	0‡	0 0 0	S2

Mnemonic	31–26	25–21	20–16	15–11	10	9–5	4–0
and	1 1 1 1 0 1	D	S1	0 1 0 0 0	C	0 0 0 0 0	S2
xor	1 1 1 1 0 1	D	S1	0 1 0 1 0	C	0 0 0 0 0	S2
or	1 1 1 1 0 1	D	S1	0 1 0 1 1	C	0 0 0 0 0	S2

Mnemonic	31–26	25–21	20–16	15–10	9	8	7–5	4–0
addu	1 1 1 1 0 1	D	S1	0 1 1 0 0 0	I	O	0 0 0	S2
subu	1 1 1 1 0 1	D	S1	0 1 1 0 0 1	I	O	0 0 0	S2
divu	1 1 1 1 0 1	D	S1	0 1 1 0 1 0	0	0*	0 0 0	S2
mul	1 1 1 1 0 1	D	S1	0 1 1 0 1 1	0	0*	0 0 0	S2
add	1 1 1 1 0 1	D	S1	0 1 1 1 0 0	I	O	0 0 0	S2
sub	1 1 1 1 0 1	D	S1	0 1 1 1 0 1	I	O	0 0 0	S2
div	1 1 1 1 0 1	D	S1	0 1 1 1 1 0	0	0*	0 0 0	S2
cmp	1 1 1 1 0 1	D	S1	0 1 1 1 1 1	0	0*	0 0 0	S2

* The MC88100 does not decode these bits; however, assemble as shown to guarantee compatibility with future implementation.

‡ Causes privilege violation exception if bit is set and instruction is executed in user mode.

Table 3-14. Instruction Numeric Listing (Sheet 3 of 3)

Mnemonic	31–26	25–21	20–16	15–5	4–0
clr	1 1 1 1 0 1	D	S1	1 0 0 0 0 0 0 0 0 0 0	S2
set	1 1 1 1 0 1	D	S1	1 0 0 0 1 0 0 0 0 0 0	S2
ext	1 1 1 1 0 1	D	S1	1 0 0 1 0 0 0 0 0 0 0	S2
extu	1 1 1 1 0 1	D	S1	1 0 0 1 1 0 0 0 0 0 0	S2
mak	1 1 1 1 0 1	D	S1	1 0 1 0 0 0 0 0 0 0 0	S2
rot	1 1 1 1 0 1	D	S1	1 0 1 0 1 0 0 0 0 0 0	S2

Mnemonic	31–26	25–16	15–11	10	9–5	4–0
jmp	1 1 1 1 0 1	0 0 0 0 0 0 0 0 0 0*	1 1 0 0 0	N	0 0 0 0 0	S2
jsr	1 1 1 1 0 1	0 0 0 0 0 0 0 0 0 0*	1 1 0 0 1	N	0 0 0 0 0	S2

Mnemonic	31–26	25–21	20–16	15–5	4–0
ff1	1 1 1 1 0 1	D	0 0 0 0 0*	1 1 1 0 1 0 0 0 0 0 0	S2
ff0	1 1 1 1 0 1	D	0 0 0 0 0*	1 1 1 0 1 1 0 0 0 0 0	S2
tbnd	1 1 1 1 0 1	0 0 0 0 0*	S1	1 1 1 1 1 0 0 0 0 0 0	S2
rte	1 1 1 1 0 1	0 0 0 0 0	0 0 0 0 0*	1 1 1 1 1 1 0 0 0 0 0	0 0 0 0 0*
tbnd	1 1 1 1 1 0	0 0 0 0 0*	S1	IMM16	

* The MC88100 does not decode these bits; however, assemble as shown to guarantee compatibility with future implementation.

3

SECTION 4
SIGNAL DESCRIPTION

This section supplies information about the external signals of the MC88100. Figure 4-1 shows the functional organization of the signals by function, type, active state, pin count, and mnemonic name. Following the figure are paragraphs describing each signal or group of signals. Refer to **SECTION 5 BUS OPERATION** for more information on the data processor bus (P bus) and instruction P bus operation. Instruction mnemonics used in this section can be identified by referring to **SECTION 3 ADDRESSING MODES AND INSTRUCTION SET**.

4

All output signals, except the error (ERR) signal, are placed in the high-impedance state when the P bus checker enable (PCE) signal is asserted.

NOTE

The terms assert and negate are used extensively in this manual to avoid confusion between active-high and active-low signals. **Assert** or **assertion** indicates that a signal is active or true, regardless of whether the signal is active high or active low. **Negate** or **negation** indicates that the signal is inactive or false.

4.1 DATA PROCESSOR BUS SIGNALS

The following paragraphs describe the signals that interface the data unit to external memory or cache memory management units (CMMUs) across the data P bus.

4.1.1 Data Address Bus (DA31–DA2)

The data address bus provides the 30-bit word address to the data memory space. An entire data word (32 bits) is always addressed; individual bytes or half words are selected by the data byte enable (DBE3–DBE0) signals.

4.1.2 Data Bus (D31–D0)

D31–D0 are the 32 bidirectional data bus signals that interface the MC88100 to the data memory space. The data on this bus corresponds to addresses supplied by the data address bus.

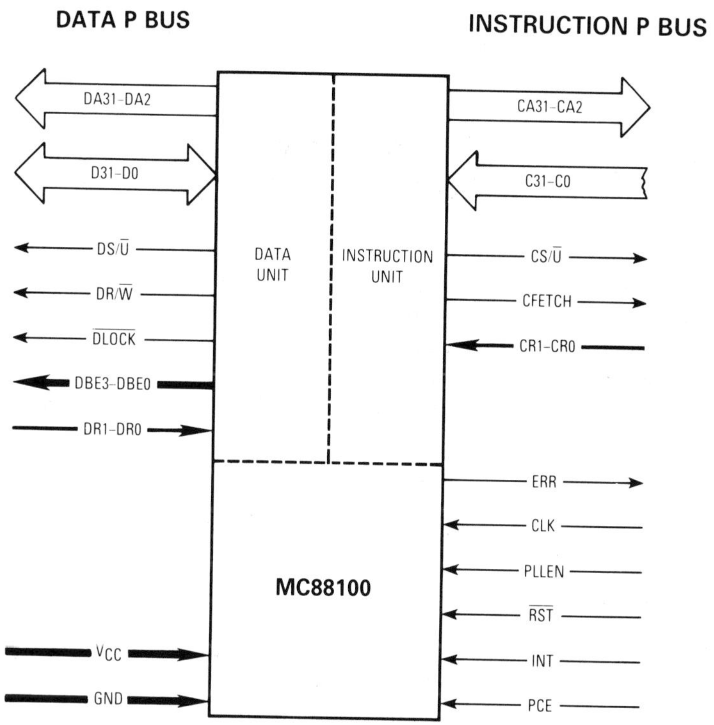

Function	Mnemonic	Type	Active	Count	Reset
Data Address	DA31–DA2	Output	—	30	High Impedance*
Data	D31–D0	I O	—	32	High Impedance*
Data Supervisor User Select	DS $\overline{\text{U}}$	Output	—	1	High Impedance*
Data Read Write	DR $\overline{\text{W}}$	Output	—	1	High Impedance*
Data Bus Lock	$\overline{\text{DLOCK}}$	Output	Low	1	High Impedance*
Data Byte Enable	DBE3–DBE0	Output	High	4	High Impedance*
Data Reply	DR1–DR0	Input	—	2	Input
Code Address	CA31–CA2	Output	—	30	High Impedance*
Code	C31–C0	Input	—	32	High Impedance*
Code Supervisor User Select	CS $\overline{\text{U}}$	Output	—	1	Input
Code Fetch	CFETCH	Output	High	1	High Impedance*
Code Reply	CR1–CR0	Input	—	2	Input
Error	ERR	Output	High	1	Low
Reset	$\overline{\text{RST}}$	Input	Low	1	Input
Interrupt	INT	Input	High	1	Input
P Bus Checker Enable	PCE	Input	High	1	Input
Clock	CLK	Input	High	1	Input
Phase Lock Enable	PLLEN	Input	High	1	Input
Power	V_{CC}	—	—	18	—
Ground	GND	—	—	18	—

*These signals remain in the high-impedance state for one clock cycle after the $\overline{\text{RST}}$ signal is recognized as negated (high).

Figure 4-1. Functional Diagram of MC88100 Signals

4.1.3 Data Supervisor/User Select (DS/$\overline{\text{U}}$)

The DS/$\overline{\text{U}}$ signal selects between the user and supervisor data memory spaces. The high level selects supervisor memory, and the low level selects user memory. The level on this signal for a given access is determined by the value of the MODE bit in the processor status register (PSR) or by the {**.usr**} (user memory) option of the **ld** and **st** instructions.

4.1.4 Data Read/Write (DR/$\overline{\text{W}}$)

The DR/$\overline{\text{W}}$ signal indicates whether the memory transaction is a read (DR/$\overline{\text{W}}$ = high level) or a write (DR/$\overline{\text{W}}$ = low level).

4.1.5 Data Bus Lock ($\overline{\text{DLOCK}}$)

The $\overline{\text{DLOCK}}$ signal is a memory lock signal used by the **xmem** instruction in conjunction with the MC88200 CMMU. When $\overline{\text{DLOCK}}$ is asserted, the CMMU does not allow the system memory to be accessed by any other bus master between the two **xmem** accesses. Refer to **SECTION 8 APPLICATIONS INFORMATION** for more information on memory locking and memory access synchronization.

4.1.6 Data Byte Enable (DBE3–DBE0)

The data byte enable signals are used during data memory accesses to the MC88200 CMMU (or memory). Table 4-1 lists the signals and indicates which bytes are accessed at the addressed location.

Table 4-1. Data Byte Enable Signals

Signal	Data Bits
DBE3	D31–D24
DBE2	D23–D16
DBE1	D15–D8
DBE0	D7–D0

DBE3–DBE0 are valid during the address phase of memory write transactions and indicate which byte(s) in memory should be modified. A memory read can be four bytes wide, and the processor uses the enable signals to extract the required data. Therefore, during a **ld** instruction, the memory system can drive all 32 data signals, regardless of whether one, two, or four byte enable signals are asserted.

When the byte enable signals are all negated, the pending transaction (address phase) is a null transaction; otherwise, the transaction is a valid load or store operation.

4.1.7 Data Reply (DR1–DR0)

The data reply input signals indicate the status of a memory access during the reply phase of a bus transaction. Table 4-2 lists the different encodings for the data reply signals.

Table 4-2. Data Reply Encodings

DR1	DR0	Transaction
0	0	Reserved
1	0	Successful Memory Transaction
0	1	Memory Wait
1	1	Transaction Fault

The addition of an external pullup resistor is recommended on each reply signal so that, if no external device responds to a transaction, a fault is indicated.

4.2 INSTRUCTION PROCESSOR BUS SIGNALS

The following paragraphs describe the signals that interface the instruction unit to external memory or CMMUs.

4.2.1 Code Address Bus (CA31–CA2)

The code address lines provide the 30-bit word address to the instruction memory space. All instructions are 32 bits wide and are aligned on 32 bit boundaries; therefore, the lower two bits of the address space are not required and are implied to be zero.

4.2.2 Code Bus (C31–C0)

C31–C0 are the 32 signals that interface the MC88100 to the instruction memory space. Instructions are always 32 bits wide. The code bus is a unidirectional, read-only bus.

4.2.3 Code Supervisor/User Select (CS/$\overline{\text{U}}$)

The CS/$\overline{\text{U}}$ output signal selects between the user and supervisor instruction memory spaces. A high level selects supervisor memory, and a low level selects user memory. The level on the CS/$\overline{\text{U}}$ signal is determined by the value of the MODE bit in the PSR.

4.2.4 Code Fetch (CFETCH)

The CFETCH output signals when an instruction fetch is in progress. When CFETCH is asserted during the address phase of a bus transaction, an instruction fetch is beginning. A negated signal indicates that a null transaction is beginning.

4.2.5 Code Reply (CR0–CR1)

The code reply input signals indicate the status of an instruction memory access during the reply phase of a bus transaction. Table 4-3 lists the encodings for the code reply signals.

Table 4-3. Code Reply Encodings

CR1	CR0	Transaction
0	0	Reserved
1	0	Successful Memory Transaction
0	1	Memory Wait
1	1	Transaction Fault

The addition of an external pullup resistor is recommended on each reply signal so that, if no external device responds to a transaction, a fault is indicated.

4.3 INTERRUPT AND CONTROL SIGNALS

The following paragraphs describe the signals used by the MC88100 for interrupt and control functions.

4.3.1 Interrupt (INT)

Assertion of the INT input indicates that an external interrupt has been requested. When an interrupt exception is processed, the MC88100 processor freezes its execution context and then proceeds with exception processing using the interrupt exception vector. Software is responsible for saving the context of the processor to memory and for handling all recognized interrupts. Interrupts are sampled on every falling edge of the clock and are recognized and processed when no internal exception is pending and when interrupts are enabled in the PSR.

4.3.2 Phase Lock Enable (PLLEN)

The PLLEN signal controls the internal phase lock circuit that synchronizes the internal clocks to the CLK signal. This signal is asserted during reset to select phase locking. Refer to **5.4 RESET TIMING AND PHASE LOCKING** for specific details.

4.3.3 Reset ($\overline{\text{RST}}$)

The $\overline{\text{RST}}$ signal is used to perform an orderly restart of the processor, bringing it to a known state and beginning program execution at address $0 (the reset vector). When reset

is asserted, all pipeline valid bits and certain internal registers are initialized. When $\overline{RST}$ is negated, the reset vector is fetched from memory, with execution beginning in supervisor mode. Refer to **5.4 RESET TIMING AND PHASE LOCKING**, for more information on the operation of the reset signal and to **SECTION 6 EXCEPTIONS** for information on reset exception processing.

4.3.4 Error (ERR)

This signal is asserted when a bus comparator error occurs, indicating that the MC88100 detected either a P bus mismatch when operating in checker mode or detected an output drive error when operating in master mode. This signal is used in systems implementing a master/checker application, which is described in **4.3.5 P Bus Checker Enable (PCE)**.

4

4.3.5 P Bus Checker Enable (PCE)

The PCE signal is used in systems incorporating two or more redundant MC88100s. In this application, two processors are wired together. The master processor (PCE negated) operates normally. The checker processor (PCE asserted) places all of its outputs in the high-impedance state except ERR; all outputs are monitored as inputs. The checker processor performs the same operations as the master processor and compares its internal results with the results read from the high-impedance pins. If a mismatch occurs between the master and checker, the checker asserts ERR. External logic must then determine the appropriate action for the system.

The master processor also checks that the internal value of the signals that it is driving are the same as the external values. The processor makes this test by comparing the signals on the input and output sides of the internal line drivers. If there is an error, the master processor asserts ERR. This feature is useful for determining P bus shorts or timing problems; the internal and external values of a signal may be different when a bus signal is externally shorted.

4.4 POWER AND CLOCK SIGNALS

The following paragraphs describe the clock and power signals used on the MC88100.

4.4.1 Clock (CLK)

The clock input signal generates the internal timing signals for the processor. The processor internal clock is derived from the CLK signal, and is phase locked to minimize the skew between the external and internal signals. Because the CLK signal is driven to other devices in the system (such as CMMU devices), exact timing of internal signals is required to properly synchronize the devices to the P bus. Refer to **SECTION 9 ELECTRICAL CHARACTERISTICS** for specific details on the CLK signal requirements.

4.4.2 Power Signals (V_{CC})

These signals provide the means for routing +5 V to the processor components. Eighteen power signals are provided to the processor component; these signals are interfaced to two separate power buses. The external line drivers are supplied by one bus; all other circuits are supplied by the second bus. This scheme provides more stable power to the internal circuits of the processor, since their power supply is separate from the potentially noisy external line drivers. Refer to Table 4-4 for V_{CC} pin identification for the power buses and **SECTION 10 ORDERING INFORMATION AND MECHANICAL DATA** for full MC88100 pin assignment identification.

Table 4-4. V_{CC} Pin Identification

Internal Logic	External Signals and Buses
C11, K3	C7, C9, D5, D13
M3, M15	F3, F15, H3, H15
P5	P13, R7, R9, R11, K15

4

4.4.3 Ground (GND)

These are the ground pins for the power signals. There are 18 ground pins separated into two separate ground buses, matching the V_{CC} signals. Refer to Table 4-5 for GND pin identification for the power buses and **SECTION 10 ORDERING INFORMATION AND MECHANICAL DATA** for full MC88100 pin assignment identification.

Table 4-5. GND Pin Identification

Internal Logic	External Signals and Buses
L3, C12	C6, C8, C10, E4
J3, N4	E14, G3, G15, J15
N14	L15, R6, R8, R10, R12

4

SECTION 5
BUS OPERATION

The MC88100 features a dual external bus architecture called the processor bus (P bus). The P bus provides a dedicated bus for instruction memory accesses and a dedicated bus for data memory accesses. The P bus signals for the two buses are shown in Figure 5-1.

In a typical MC88100-based system, the processor buses do not interface directly to memory. Instead, each bus is connected to one or more MC88200 cache/memory management units (CMMUs) which communicate with memory. The CMMUs provide address translation caches and a 16K-byte data cache for instructions or data. The CMMUs interface to the system memory and to peripheral devices via the the memory bus (M bus). Instruction mnemonics used in this section can be identified by referring to **SECTION 3 ADDRESSING MODES AND INSTRUCTION SET**.

5.1 BUS CHARACTERISTICS

The P bus is a fully synchronous bus; the bus transfers between the MC88100 and attached MC88200s (or memory) are clocked by the CLK signal. Full 32-bit transfers are supported, with byte and half-word transfer capability available on the data P bus. The peak transfer rate is one word per clock cycle (80 Mbytes per second at 20 MHz). All instructions and data words are aligned on word (modulo 4) address boundaries, precluding the need for the two lowest order address lines and misaligned accesses. On a data read of a byte or half-word operand, the memory system supplies either the required bytes or a full 32-bit word; the processor automatically selects the required byte(s) from the bus. All memory transactions access either the user or supervisor address space.

The MC88100 is the bus master of the P buses and always drives the address buses, the data byte enable (DBE3–DBE0) signals, the code fetch (CFETCH) signal, and the data bus (except for P bus reads). The instruction P bus code signals (C31–C0) and the data P bus data signals (D31–D0) are inputs during read accesses, as are the reply signals for both buses. All MC88200 CMMUs (or memory devices) on the P bus are slaves to the MC88100 processor and drive the data, code, and reply signals accordingly. MC88100 bus transactions are pipelined, which allows the processor to begin a transaction before receiving the result or status of the previous transaction. Since the processor can initiate a new transaction on each clock cycle, the responding devices (or memory system) should monitor the bus signals on each clock cycle and respond to valid transactions accordingly (as the MC88200 does).

Instructions and data bus transactions are not necessarily required by the processor on every clock cycle. The buses insert null transactions during those clock cycles in which a

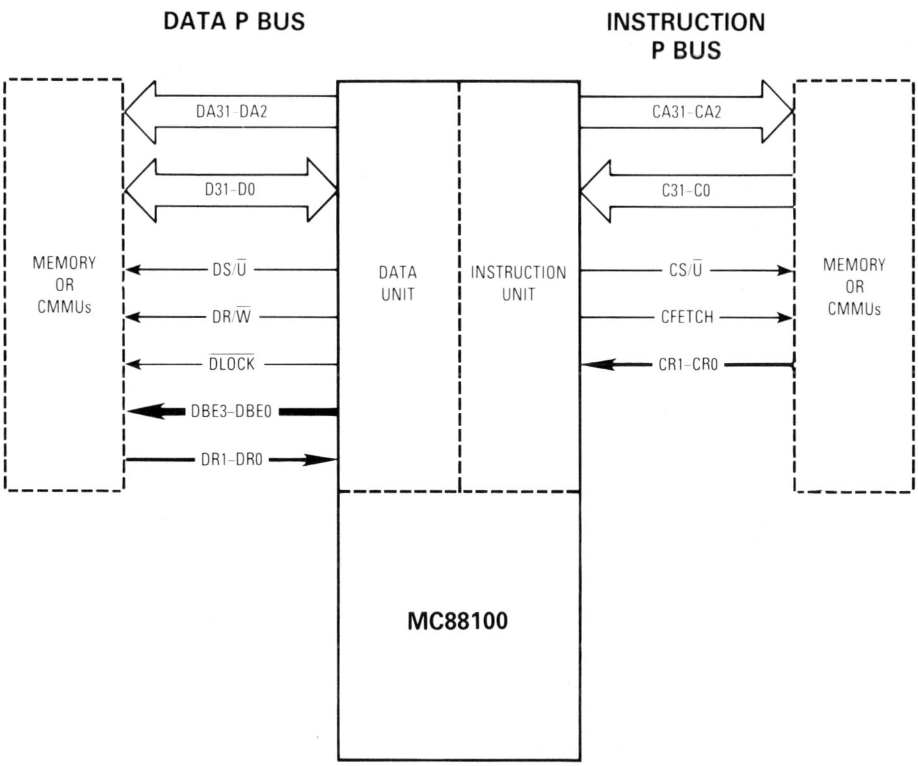

DATA P BUS		INSTRUCTION P BUS	
Signal	**Description**	**Signal**	**Description**
DA31–DA2	Data Address Bus	**CA31–CA2**	Code Address Bus
D31–D0	Data Bus	**C31–C0**	Code Bus
DS/$\overline{U}$	Data Supervisor/User Select	**CS/$\overline{U}$**	Code Supervisor/User Select
DR/$\overline{W}$	Data Read/Write logic high for read, logic low for write		(no corresponding signal)
$\overline{DLOCK}$	Data Bus Lock asserted for bus lock		(no corresponding signal)
DBE3–DBE0	Data Byte Enable Strobes DBE0 ⧫ D7–D0 DBE1 ⧫ D15–D8 DBE2 ⧫ D23–D16 DBE3 ⧫ D31–D24	**CFETCH**	Code Fetch asserted for fetch
DR1–DR0	Data Reply 1 and 0 DR1 DR0 0 0 Reserved 1 0 Success 0 1 Wait 1 1 Fault	**CR1–CR0**	Code Reply 1 and 0 CR1 CR0 0 0 Reserved 1 0 Success 0 1 Wait 1 1 Fault

Figure 5-1. P Bus Signals

transfer is not required. The data (data P bus only) and address lines are driven during a null transaction, but either the DBE3–DBE0 (data P bus) or the CFETCH (instruction P bus) signals are negated. The processor ignores the reply signals for all null transactions.

The P bus input and output signals are synchronous in that all setup and hold times are specified in reference to the clock signal. MC88100 outputs are driven from a clock edge and a maximum delay is specified. In addition, minimum hold times are specified in relation to the clock (see Figure 5-2). The requirements for MC88100 P bus inputs are shown in Figure 5-3. The minimum setup and hold times must be met to guarantee proper device operation.

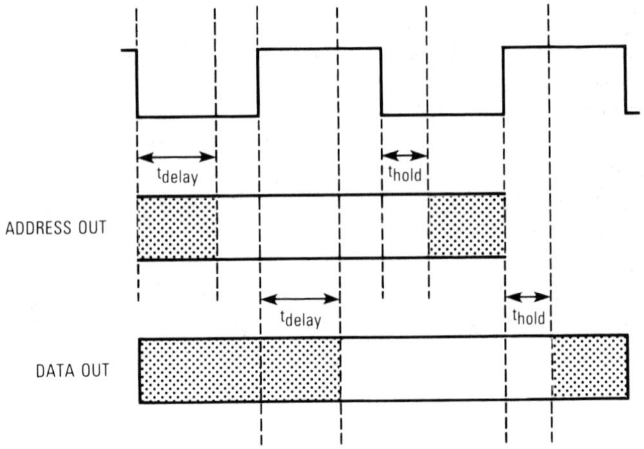

Figure 5-2. Output Signal Relationship to Clock (Example)

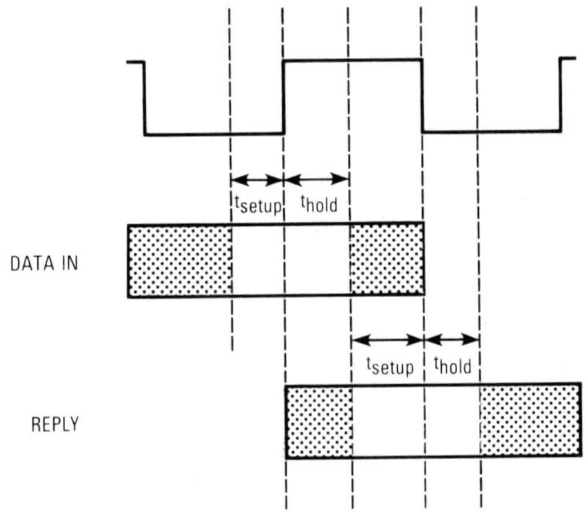

Figure 5-3. Input Signal Requirements (Example)

5

5.2 INSTRUCTION PREFETCH MECHANISM

The instruction unit controls all instruction prefetch operations. The control functions include maintenance of the instruction pointers and instruction decode as well as the generation and interpretation of instruction P bus signals.

Except for three instances described in the following paragraph, the instruction unit attempts to prefetch an instruction on every clock cycle, regardless of the state of the instruction pipeline. If the MC88100 instruction unit pipeline is stalled due to the delay of a data access to memory or an internal delay, the instruction unit repeats the address phase for the next appropriate instruction until the instruction pipeline advances. For repeated accesses due to a stalled processor, the data and reply signals are ignored until the instruction unit advances the pipeline. However, the memory system can not easily predict when the pipeline advances internally, so the system should respond to these repeated accesses appropriately.

5

There are only three instances when the instruction P bus performs null transactions (CFETCH not asserted). One instance immediately follows a processor reset (one null transaction inserted with CFETCH high impedance); the second instance occurs when an instruction pointer that is marked 'not valid' is loaded into the next instruction pointer (NIP) or fetch instruction pointer (FIP) (as a result of an **rte** instruction). The third instance corresponds to the instruction access that is initiated after an instruction memory fault occurs and the exception is taken. Refer to **5.4 RESET TIMING AND PHASE LOCKING** for more information on the transaction following a reset.

5.2.1 Instruction Read Transaction

All instruction memory accesses are read accesses, and one 32-bit instruction is read per access. In systems incorporating an MC88200 on the instruction bus, the instruction is prefetched either from the cache or from the system memory via the MC88200. In systems without an MC88200 for instructions, the processor instruction P bus interfaces directly to memory.

Figure 5-4 shows a flowchart of an instruction read transaction. Figure 5-5 shows the relative timing of the signals that perform the instruction read. To select the appropriate MC88200 CMMU or memory device, a chip-select signal ($\overline{CS}$) is generated by external logic.

P bus transactions have an address phase and a reply phase associated with each access. The address phase of an access is defined by two states: address low (AL), corresponding to the low time of the CLK, and address high (AH), corresponding to the high time of the CLK. Similarly, the reply phase is defined by two states: reply low (RL) and reply high (RH), corresponding to the low time of the CLK and high time of the CLK, respectively, for the reply phase of the transaction.

The code (CA31–CA2), CFETCH, and code supervisor/user select (CS/$\overline{U}$) signals are driven by the falling edge of the processor clock at the beginning of state AL and are set up to

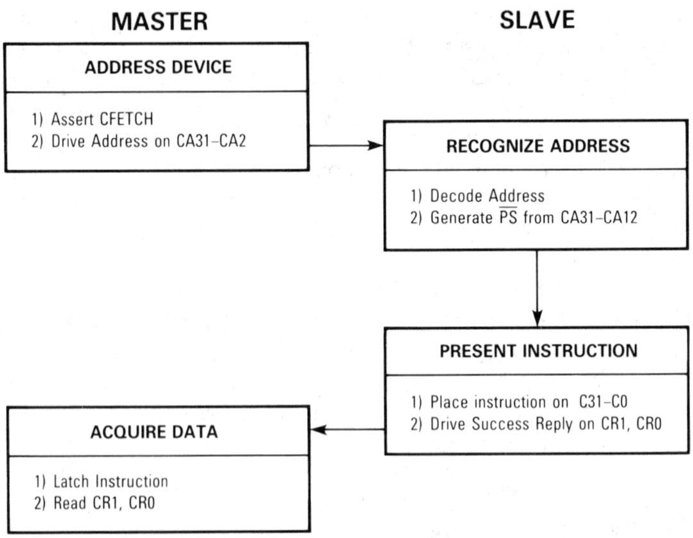

Figure 5-4. Instruction Read Flowchart

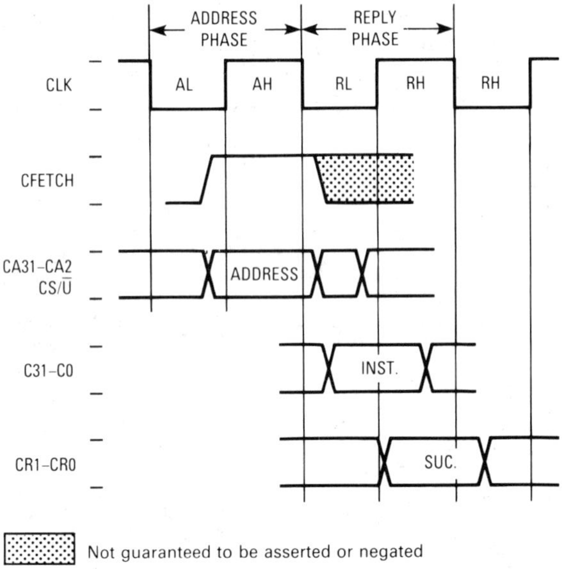

Figure 5-5. Instruction Read Timing

the rising edge at the beginning of AH. The appropriate CMMU or memory device responds to the access by placing the instruction on C31–C0 and by driving the reply signals (CR1–CR0) with the appropriate setup and hold times during the reply phase. Figure 5-1 shows the various encodings of the reply signals.

The reply signals indicate whether or not the bus transaction is successful. If the instruction on C31–C0 is guaranteed to have met the appropriate setup and hold times with respect to the rising edge of the clock of state RH, then the reply during RH should have the 'success' encoding. If the responding device (CMMU or memory) is unable to supply the instruction on the instruction P bus with the required setup time to the rising edge of state RH, then the reply should indicate a 'wait' response. This response causes the instruction unit to ignore C31–C0 and continue driving the next address until a successful or fault encoding is indicated with the reply signals. The responding device can insert as many wait cycles as necessary until the instruction is supplied. Finally, if the memory system can not supply the required instruction (for example, due to a page fault) then the reply signals should indicate 'fault.' This response causes the instruction pointer corresponding to the faulted prefetch to be marked as invalid. If the MC88100 attempts to execute that instruction (i.e., it is not discarded due to a change of program flow), an instruction access exception is generated. An encoding of '00' on the reply signals is reserved and may cause unpredictable behavior in the current implementation.

5

5.2.2 Pipelined Instruction Prefetches

The instruction P bus is pipelined in that the address phase of an access coincides with the reply phase of the previous access. Therefore, the responding device must latch the address and CS/$\overline{U}$ signal information at the beginning of a transaction and qualify the beginning of the next access with the reply for the current transaction. A reply of 'success' for the current access should cause the responding device to update the latched address and begin the next transaction. Figure 5-6 shows an example timing diagram for a read

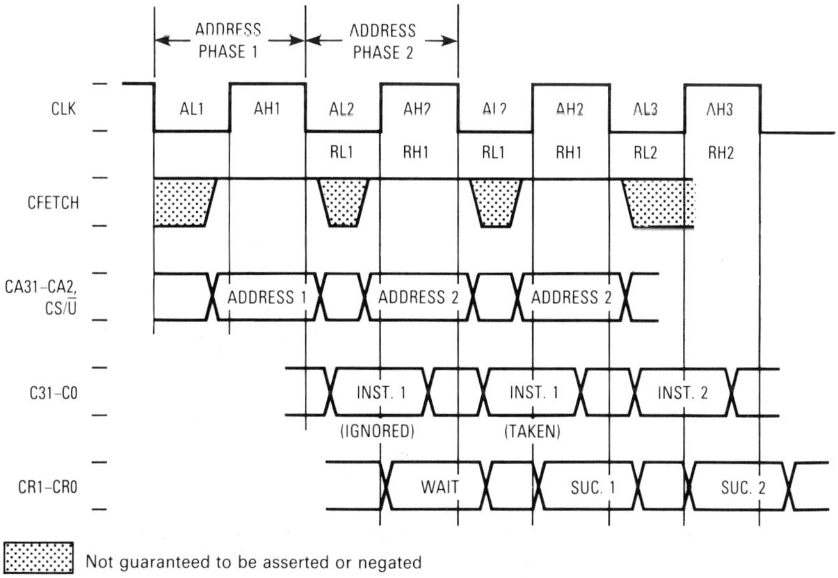

Figure 5-6. Instruction Prefetch with Wait Cycle

cycle with one wait cycle followed by a read access with zero wait cycles. Since the reply for address phase 1 was 'wait', the address phase for the second access is repeated by the MC88100 until the device responds successfully to the first access.

Figure 5-7 shows the relative timing of signals on the instruction P bus when a transaction is initiated but ignored by the instruction unit due to a pipeline stall within the MC88100. The processor ignores the reply and repeats the access until the pipeline advances. The memory system responds to each of these transactions so that the next access can begin as soon as the pipeline advances.

5.2.3 Instruction Memory Faults

When a memory fault occurs for an instruction prefetch, the processor ignores the transaction that follows the faulted one. The memory system should also ignore the access following the fault. The address phase for the next normal processor access immediately follows the faulted-reply phase (see Figure 5-8), and the memory system must respond accordingly. Depending on whether the faulted instruction access is required or not (due to a change in program flow), the MC88100 may then take an instruction access exception.

Figure 5-8 shows the relative timing for the case of an instruction prefetch fault that causes an exception. When an instruction P bus access results in a fault that causes an exception, the next normal transaction is a null transaction. Then the access following the null transaction is the first instruction prefetch from the instruction access exception vector. Refer to **SECTION 6 EXCEPTIONS** for more information on fault exception processing and how the MC88100 supports a demand-paged virtual memory model.

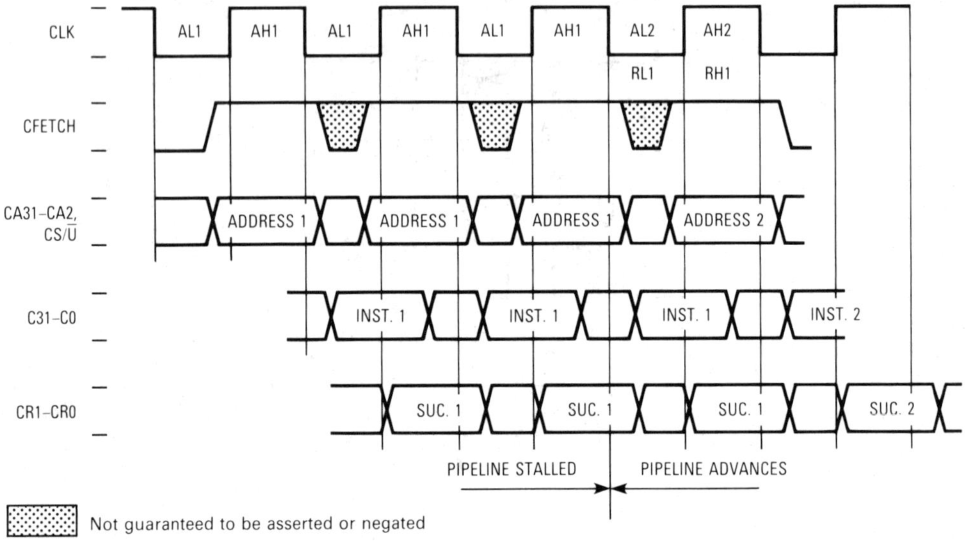

Figure 5-7. Instruction Accesses during Stall

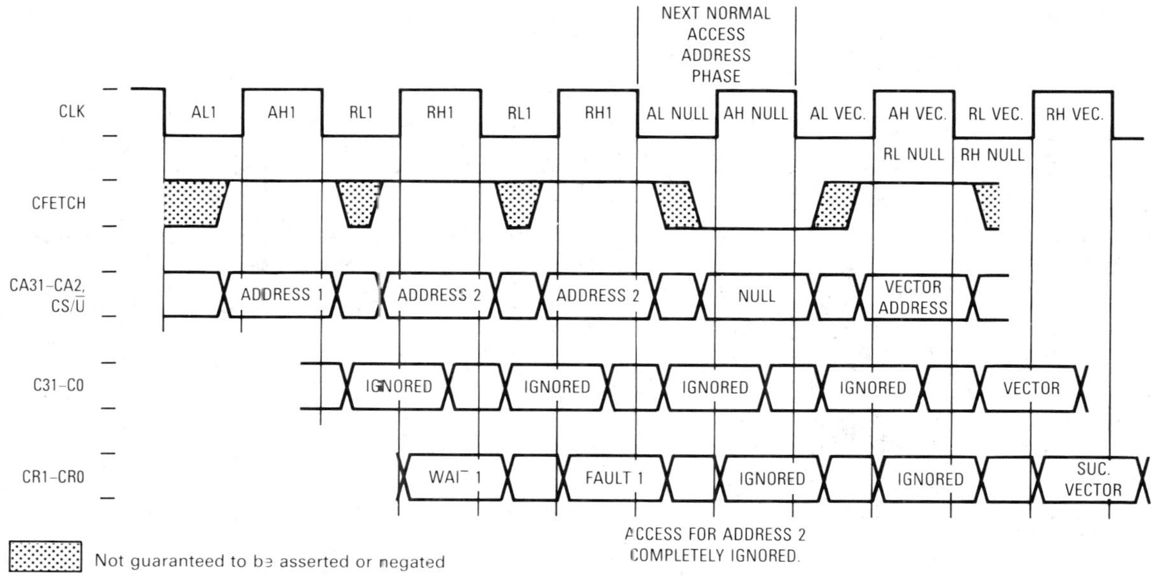

Figure 5-8. Instruction Prefetch Memory Fault — Exception Taken

5

A faulted instruction access that is discarded due to a pipeline flush associated with a change in program flow (i.e., the instruction following the branch is faulted, and delayed branching is not used) does not cause an exception, and normal instruction execution must continue. Therefore, the next normal access is a duplicate of the access 'ignored' after the fault. Figure 5-9 shows the relative timing for an instruction fault that does not cause an exception.

5.3 DATA ACCESS MECHANISM

The data unit controls all data transfers between the processor and MC88200 CMMUs or memory via the data P bus. Data P bus operation is pipelined and similar to the operation of the instruction P bus. However, data transfers can be 8, 16, or 32 bits, memory accesses can be read or write accesses, and memory accesses can be locked for the **xmem** instruction. Therefore, the data P bus incorporates additional signals that control these functions.

The DBE3–DBE0 signals indicate which byte(s) on the data bus (D3–D0) are valid during a data memory transaction. For a data read operation, the upper 30 data address lines select a word in memory, and the asserted byte enable signals indicate which byte(s) within that word are required by the processor. The memory system responds to the read by placing the requested byte(s) on the data P bus corresponding to the asserted byte enable signals. The memory system can supply a complete 32-bit word, and the processor automatically extracts the desired byte(s) from the bus. The processor loads the target register with the proper sign- or zero-extended result. Figure 5-10 shows an example of a byte read operation and the relationship of the byte enable signals to the four bytes on the data bus.

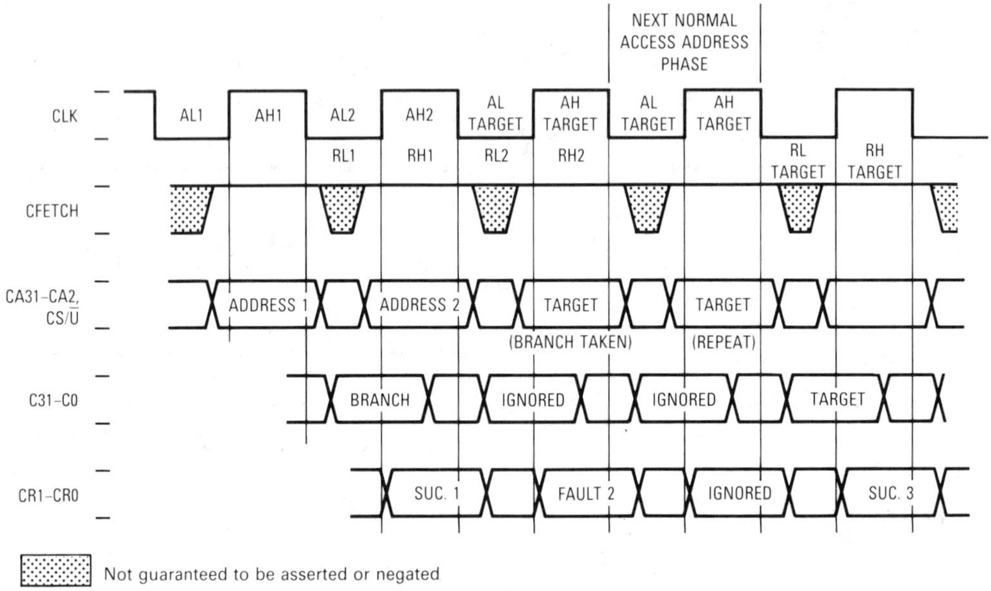

Figure 5-9. Instruction Prefetch Memory Fault — No Exception Taken

During a memory write operation, the byte enable signals indicate which byte(s) in memory should be updated. On a byte write, the MC88100 places the data byte in all four byte positions on the data bus. The byte enable signals indicate the byte in memory where the data is to be stored, and the memory system can extract valid data from any of the four byte positions. Similarly, on the write of a half word, the memory system can extract valid data from either the high-order or low-order half word of the data P bus. Figure 5-11 shows the operation of a byte write transaction.

5.3.1 Data Read Transaction

During a data read transaction, the MC88100 receives a byte, half word, or word from memory. The DBE3–DBE0 signals indicate the size and byte offset of the memory access.

Figure 5-12 shows a flowchart of a data read operation. The $\overline{CS}$ signal is generated by external logic to select the appropriate memory device (e.g., MC88200). Figure 5-13 shows the relative timing of the signals involved in the data read.

5

The data P bus read transactions are very similar to instruction prefetch transactions; the address phase is the clock period identified by states AL and AH, and the reply phase is

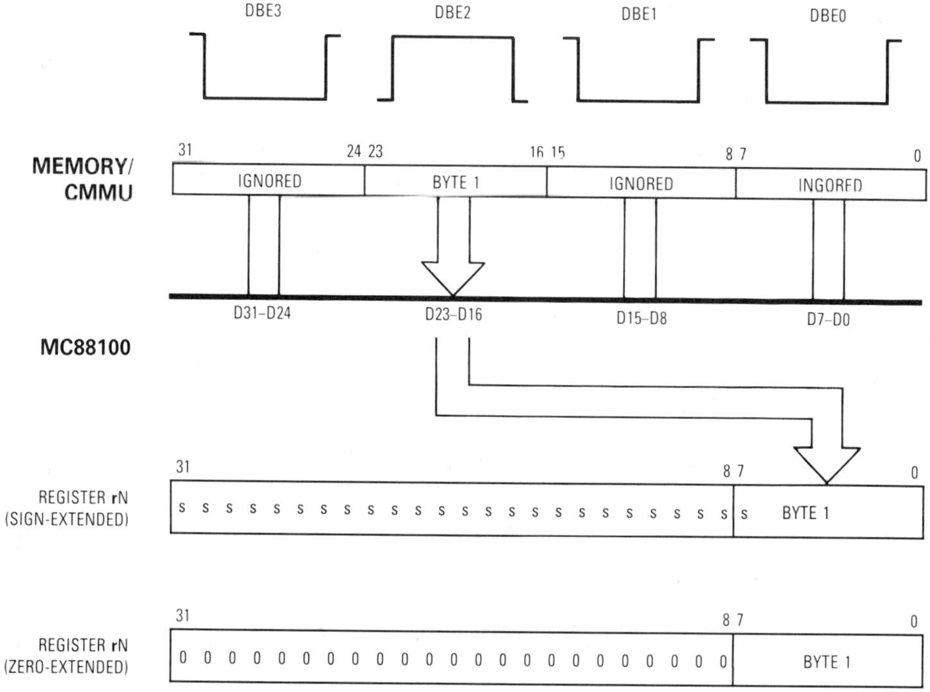

Figure 5-10. Byte Enable Signal Control of Memory Read

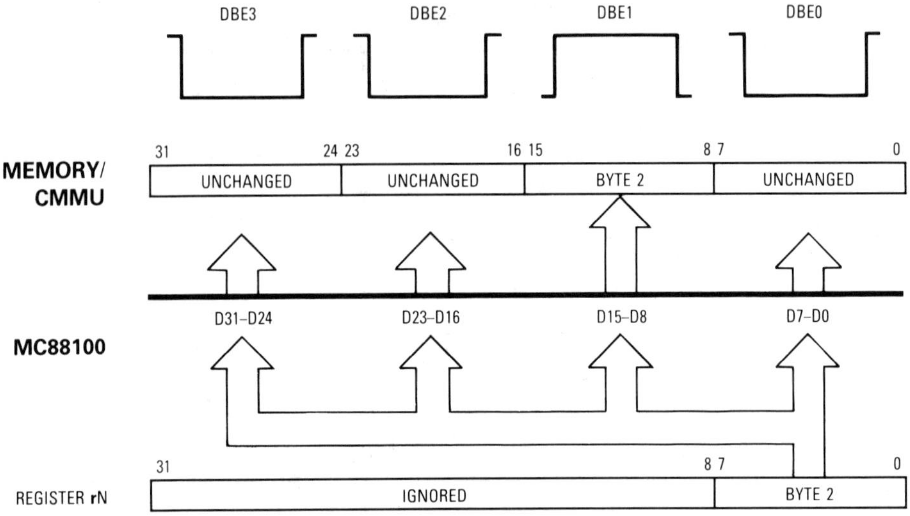

Figure 5-11. Byte Enable Signal Control of Memory Write

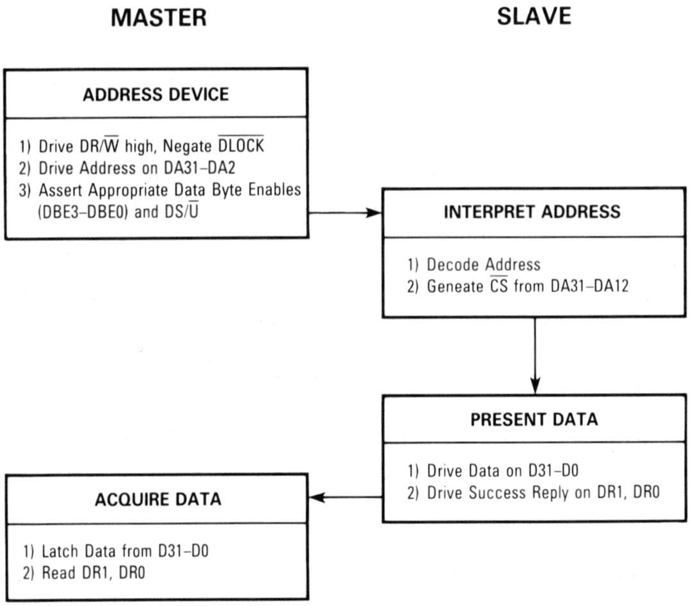

Figure 5-12. Data Read Flowchart

identified by states RL and RH. During the AL state of a read transaction, the DA31–DA2, DBE3–DBE0, and data supervisor/user select (DS/Ū) signals are driven appropriately, and the data read/write (DR/W̄) signal is driven high. All of these signals are set up to the rising

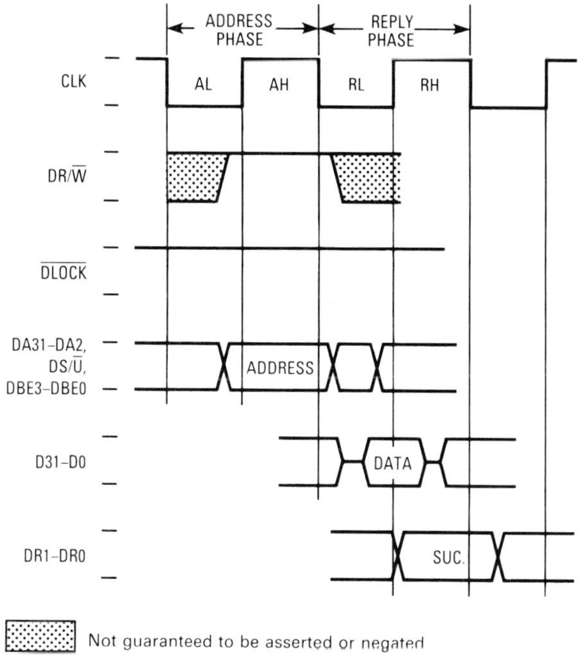

Figure 5-13. Data Read Timing

edge of AH and remain valid through the specified hold time from the falling edge of AH. If possible, the responding device (CMMU or memory) supplies the data on the D31–D0 lines with the required setup and hold times, and also indicates that the transfer was successful with the DR1–DR0 signals.

If the responding device is unable to supply the data appropriately, the reply on DR1–DR0 should indicate a 'wait' response. The data unit then continues to drive the next address until a 'success' or 'fault' encoding is signaled with the reply lines. The responding device can insert as many wait cycles as necessary until the data is supplied.

If the memory system can not supply the required data (e.g., due to a parity error or a page fault) then the reply signals should indicate 'fault.' This causes the MC88100 to initiate exception processing for a data access exception.

5.3.2 Data Write Transaction

During a data write transaction, the MC88100 transfers a byte, half word, or word to memory. The DBE3–DBE0 signals indicate the size and byte offset of the memory access.

Figure 5-14 shows a flowchart of a data write transaction. The $\overline{CS}$ signal is generated by external logic to select the appropriate memory device (e.g., MC88200). Figure 5-15 shows the relative timing of the signals that perform the data write.

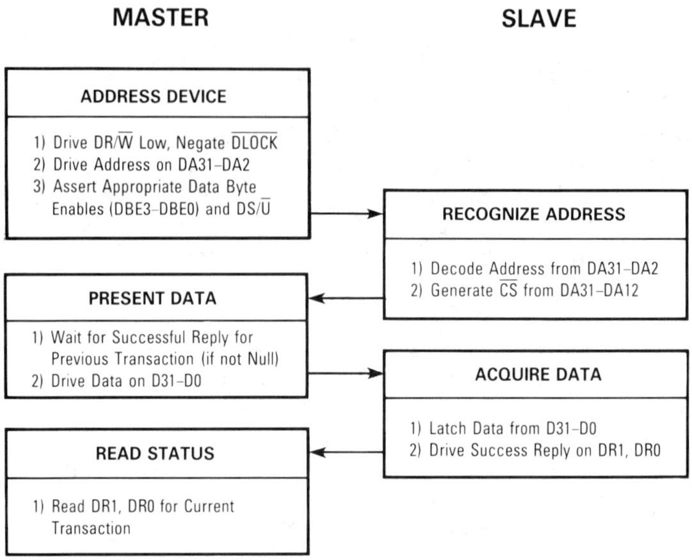

Figure 5-14. Data Write Flowchart

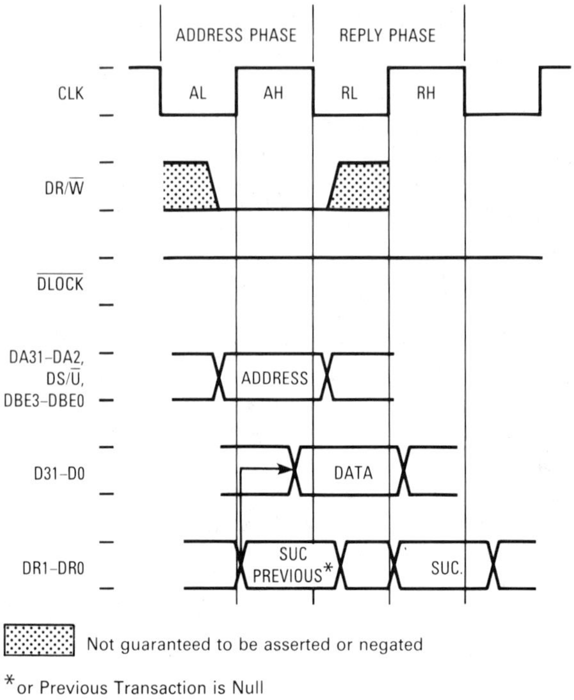

Figure 5-15. Data Write Timing

During a memory write transaction, the MC88100 drives DA31–DA2, DBE3–DBE0, and DS/$\overline{U}$ appropriately; the DR/$\overline{W}$ signal is driven low. All these signals are set up to the rising edge of AH and remain valid through the specified hold time from the falling edge of AH. If the reply for the previous data transaction was 'success' or if the previous transaction is null, the processor then drives the data on D31–D0 so that the data is set up to the falling edge of RL and remains valid through the rising edge of state RL. However, if the reply for the previous transaction was 'wait', the processor does not drive the data signals of the data P bus. Instead, the address phase of the write transaction is repeated until a 'success' is driven for the previous reply. If a 'fault' is signaled for the previous reply, the processor drives the data signals for the current write transaction but ignores the reply.

If possible, the responding device indicates with DR1–DR0 that the current access was successful and latches the data appropriately. Otherwise, the responding device signals a 'wait' response on DR1–DR0, causing the data P bus to repeat the reply phase and drive D31–D0 again with the appropriate setup and hold times with respect to the clock. The responding device can insert as many wait cycles as necessary until the data is latched.

If the system cannot latch the data and complete the access, the DR1–DR0 signals drive a 'fault' encoding, causing the MC88100 to initiate exception processing for a data access exception.

5.3.3 Pipelined Data Accesses

The data P bus is pipelined in the same way as the instruction P bus. The address phase of a memory access can overlap with the reply phase for the previous transaction; the processor may begin a new transaction (and drive a new value on DA31–DA2) even if the initial transaction is extended due to wait replies. Therefore, as with instruction P bus operations, the responding device (or external logic) must latch the value on DA31–DA2 when it is first driven, in case the device requires more than one clock of access time.

The data P bus differs from the instruction P bus in that both read and write operations are performed and the D31–D0 are bidirectional. Therefore, the MC88100 always monitors the reply signals for a transaction before driving the D31–D0 signals for the next transaction. Figure 5-16 shows the relative timing of a data read transaction with one wait cycle followed by a data write transaction. Although the address phase of the write immediately follows the address phase for the read, the data signals are not driven for the write transaction until a successful reply is signaled for the previous access, thus avoiding data bus contention. Figure 5-16 also illustrates a null transaction following the write access.

Figures 5-17 and 5-18 illustrate two other examples of pipelined operations on the data P bus. Figure 5-17 illustrates two successive write transactions (due to two successive store instructions or a store double instruction) with one wait cycle inserted for the first access. Figure 5-18 illustrates the relative timing for a write transaction with one wait cycle followed by one read transaction. Since the timing for the DR/$\overline{W}$ signal is only valid during the address phase of a transaction, it may also require latching by the responding device.

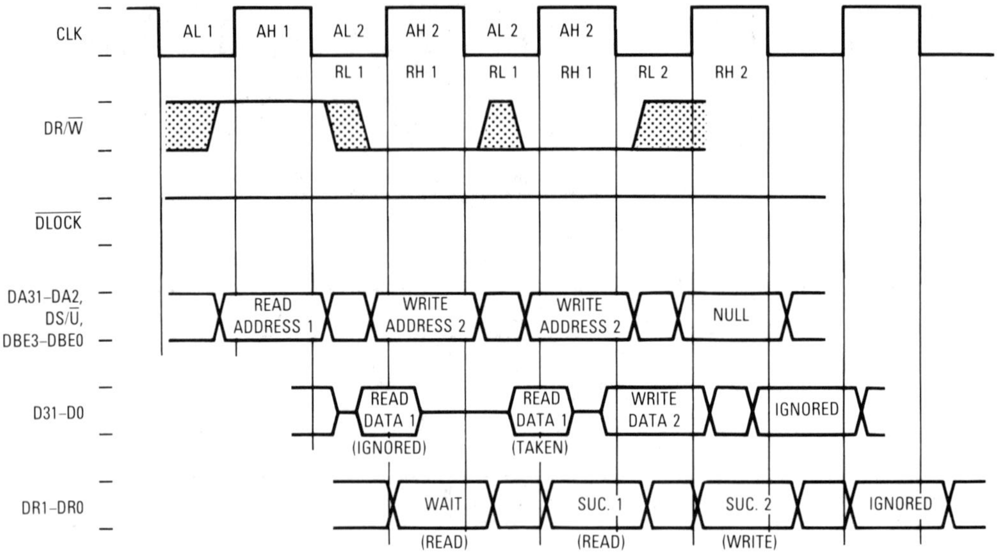

Not guaranteed to be asserted or negated

Figure 5-16. Pipelined Data Accesses (Read, Wait, Write, Null)

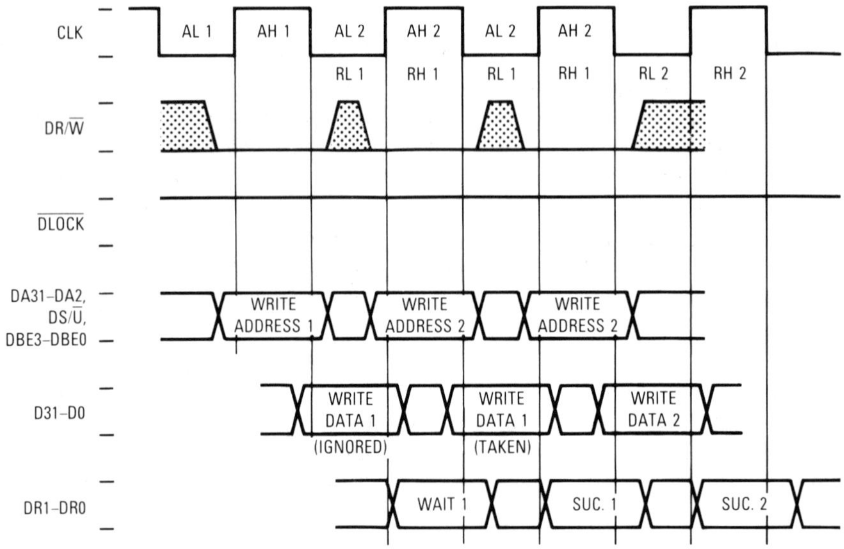

Not guaranteed to be asserted or negated

Figure 5-17. Pipelined Data Accesses (Write, Wait, Write)

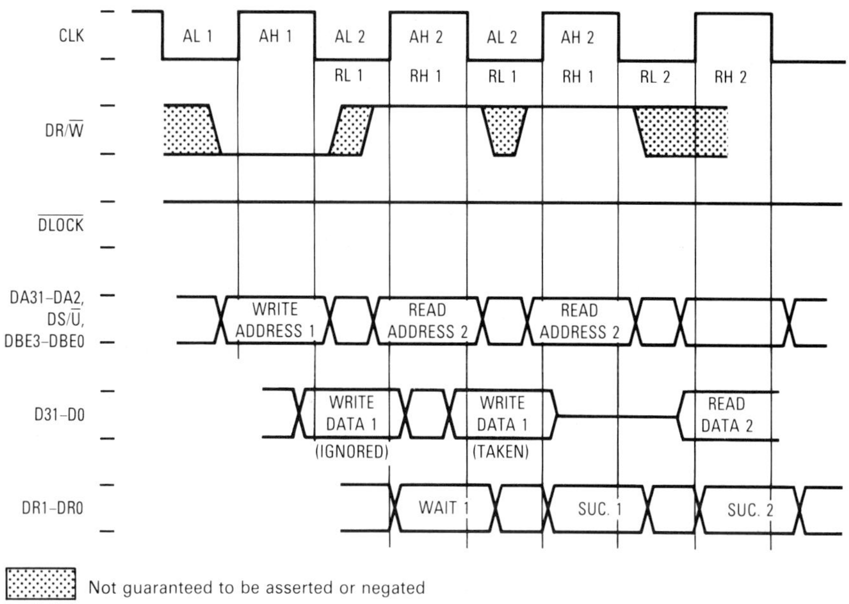

Figure 5-18. Pipelined Data Accesses (Write, Wait, Read)

5.3.4 Locked P Bus Operations

Execution of the **xmem** instruction causes the contents of a general-purpose register to be exchanged with a memory location. To perform this operation, the data unit performs a read transaction from the specified address, immediately followed by a write transaction to that address. The data bus lock ($\overline{DLOCK}$) signal is asserted from the beginning of the address phase of the read transaction (with the same timing as DA31–DA2) and remains asserted through the address phase(s) of the write transaction, regardless of the number of wait cycles in the read. However, $\overline{DLOCK}$ is not asserted during the reply phase(s) of the write transaction. Figure 5-19 shows an example of a locked operation followed by a normal write transaction with one wait cycle in the **xmem** read and one wait cycle in the **xmem** write.

The only way to interrupt a locked operation is to signal a fault for the read transaction via DR1–DR0. Either the read or the write transaction, may be terminated with a fault. A fault response for either the read or the write transaction of a locked operation has the same effect as a fault signaled during normal read or write transactions described in **5.3.5 Data Access Faults**.

When the read transaction of an **xmem** instruction is terminated with a data access exception, the entire **xmem** instruction should be emulated in the exception handler. However, if the write transaction of an **xmem** instruction is terminated with a fault, the software handler may not be able to guarantee that the rest of the program is synchronized with

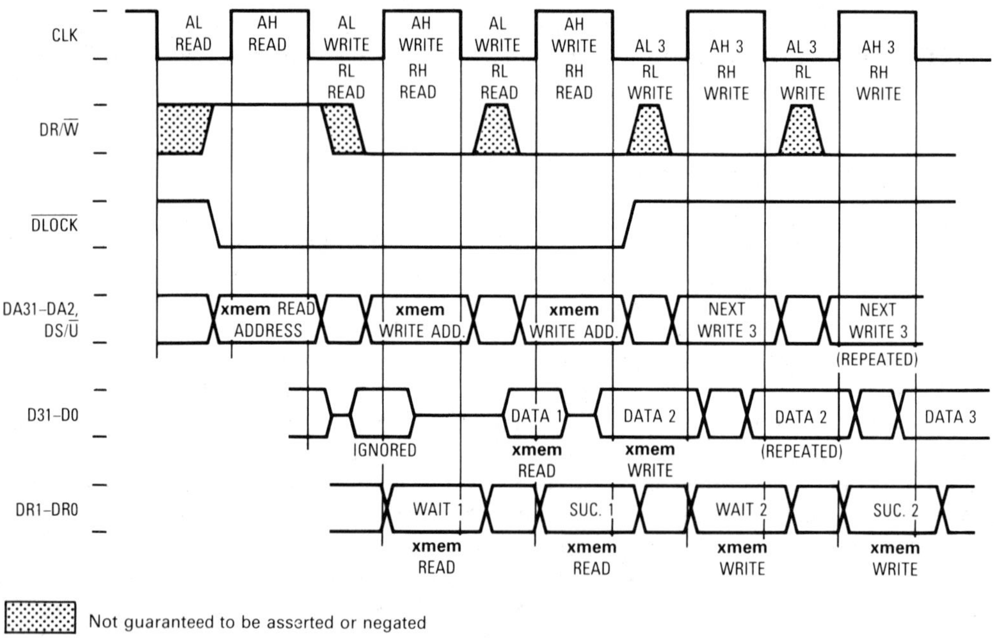

Figure 5-19. Example of Locked Timing (Read, Wait, Write, Wait)

the **xmem**. By the time the write transaction reply phase occurs, the read transaction has already completed, and the general-purpose register has been altered with the data from memory. Therefore, the scoreboard bit for the load operation is cleared, and a subsequent instruction may use the new contents of the register before the **xmem** has been emulated. To prevent this situation from occurring, the programmer can include a trap not taken instruction immediately after the **xmem**. This guarantees that no other instruction can execute before the **xmem** completes the write.

The $\overline{DLOCK}$ signal should be used by the system bus as an indication that the read and write operations should not be interrupted by an alternate bus master. The **xmem** instruction can be used by the processor for semaphore manipulation and, as such, requires indivisible operation between the read and write transactions.

5.3.5 Data Access Faults

When a memory fault occurs during a data access, the processor ignores the transaction that follows the faulted transaction. The memory system should also ignore the access following the fault. When a fault occurs on a data read or write transaction, a data access exception is taken. The next normal data access is generated by the instructions in the exception handler routine.

Figure 5-20 shows the relative timing for the case of a data write access fault. Refer to **SECTION 6 EXCEPTIONS** for more information on fault exception processing and MC88100 support of a demand-paged virtual memory model.

5.4 RESET TIMING AND PHASE LOCKING

The following paragraphs describe the phase locking operations and hardware reset of the MC88100.

5.4.1 Phase-Locked Loop Operation

The MC88100 is designed to operate completely synchronously with other devices in the M88000 system. In this way, all devices communicating on the P bus can make assumptions about the validity of signals with respect to the master clock. The signals can be used by the receiving device as soon as they are valid from the device driving them. To provide a tight tolerance on the relationship between the input clock and the output signals, the internal clock is derived on-chip by a digital phase-locked loop circuit that uses the input clock as its reference. Therefore, fabrication variations between multiple devices do not cause differences in timing delays that might otherwise be induced in the internal clock circuity. The phase-locked loop circuit of the MC88100 is also implemented on the MC88200 CMMU. This allows multiple M88000 devices to reside on the P bus with tightly coupled

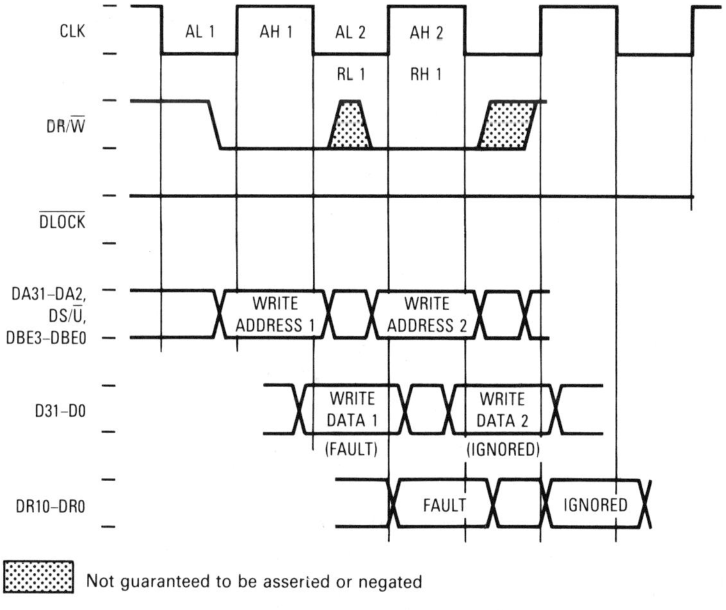

Figure 5-20. Data Fault Timing

timing relationships between them. Since the clock signal is used as a reference for the phase-locked loop, care should be taken in the layout and routing of the clock signal to minimize propagation delays induced by transmission line effects of board traces.

To initialize the phase-locked loop circuit on powerup, the PLLEN signal must be asserted with the appropriate timing in relationship to the $\overline{\text{RST}}$ signal as shown in Figure 5-21 (a). The combination of the $\overline{\text{RST}}$ and PLLEN requirements shown in the figure provide sufficient time for the phase-locked loop to be reset and for the internal clock to phase lock to the external clock on powerup. The PLLEN signal must subsequently remain stable and asserted to guarantee proper phase-locked operation. In addition, these requirements also ensure that the remainder of the MC88100 is properly reset.

NOTE

> Unless the processor is properly phase locked, the AC specifications described in **SECTION 9 ELECTRICAL SPECIFICATIONS** cannot be guaranteed. Nonphase-locked operation is **NOT** recommended.

5.4.2 Reset Operation

To guarantee that the operation of multiple M88000 devices is completely synchronous, the $\overline{\text{RST}}$ and PLLEN signals for all devices in the system must meet the setup and hold times specified in **SECTION 9 ELECTRICAL SPECIFICATIONS** for the same falling edge of the input clock signal (the clock signal must be shared). The same setup and hold time requirements must be met for both the assertion and negation of the $\overline{\text{RST}}$ and PLLEN signals for all devices in the system.

During the time that the $\overline{\text{RST}}$ signal is asserted on powerup, all output signals are placed in the high-impedance state except ERR. The ERR signal is driven low (negated) while the MC88100 is in the reset state. Refer to **SECTION 4 SIGNAL DESCRIPTION** for a list of signal states during processor reset. For detailed information on the state of the processor registers after reset, refer to **SECTION 6 EXCEPTIONS**.

Figure 5-21 (a) shows the timing relationships on the MC88100 P bus for the first instruction prefetch after the negation of reset on powerup. The bus signals remain in the high-impedance state for one clock after $\overline{\text{RST}}$ is detected as negated. The MC88200 CMMU automatically ignores the bus for one clock after the negation of $\overline{\text{RST}}$. In systems that interface an MC88100 directly to memory or peripheral devices, some of the signals may require external circuitry to prevent them from being detected as asserted by the system for that one clock (to make this a null transaction). The first prefetch after the negation of $\overline{\text{RST}}$ is always a read from the reset vector (address $0). No accesses are initiated on the data P bus until the program explicitly requests a data access.

Figure 5-21 (b) shows the timing relationships for a processor reset after the system has powered up and has already been phase locked (warm reset). The only difference between

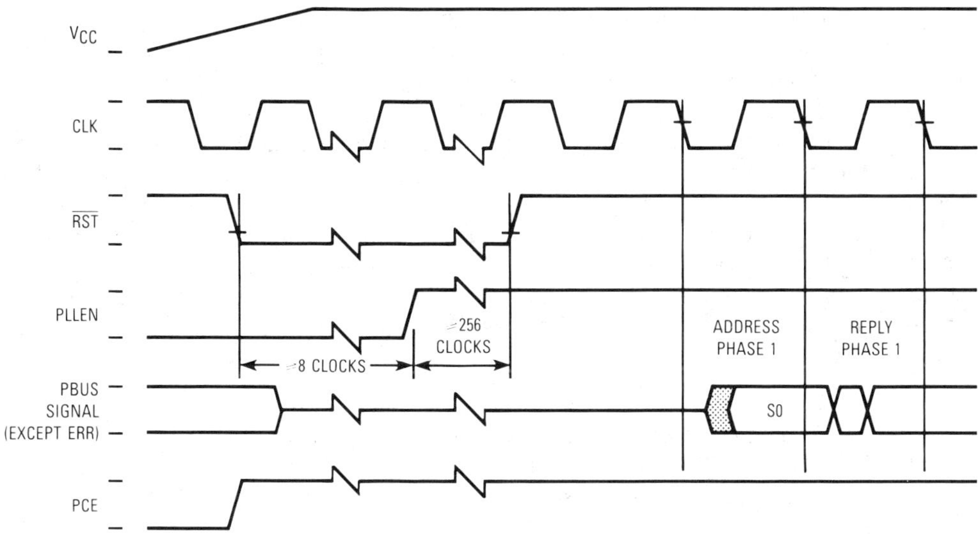

(a) Power-Up Reset

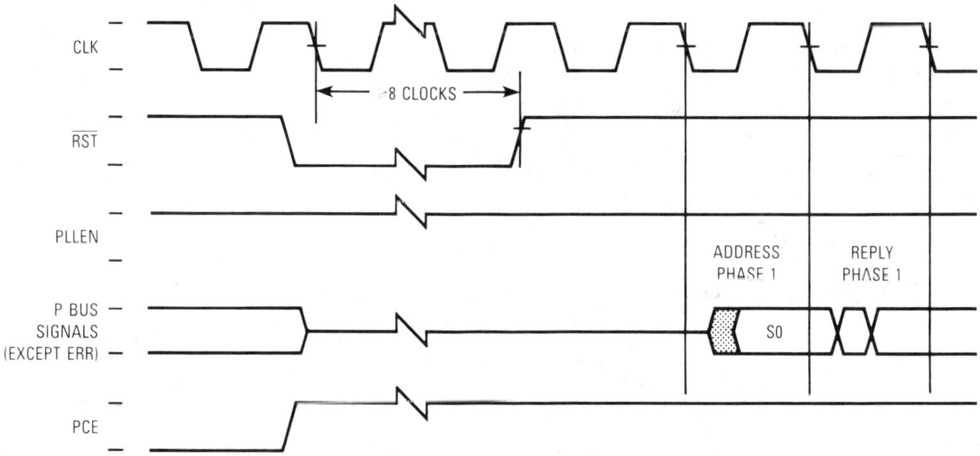

(b) Warm Reset

Figure 5-21. Reset Timing

a warm reset and powerup reset is the assertion length requirements of $\overline{RST}$. Because the phase-locked loop has presumably been properly initialized, $\overline{RST}$ must only be asserted for a minimum of eight clock cycles to ensure a full processor reset. The state of the internal registers and the operation of the buses after the warm reset is the same as that of the powerup reset. The powerup reset sequence Figure 5-21 (a) may also be used for subsequent reset operations.

5.5 P BUS INTERFACE TO MC88200

The MC88200 CMMU provides a P bus interface for communicating with the MC88100 processor and an M bus interface for communicating with memory and the rest of the system. The P bus interfaces of the processor and the CMMU are designed to operate completely synchronously with one another and with little external logic required between them. Up to eight CMMUs can be directly connected to one MC88100: four connected to the instruction P bus and four connected to the data P bus, providing caching and memory management facilities for both instruction and data accesses. The only external logic required for the MC88200 P bus is an address decoder that generates a $\overline{CS}$ signal for each CMMU in the system. Refer to **SECTION 8 APPLICATIONS INFORMATION** for the signal connections for a processor with one CMMU servicing the instruction P bus and one CMMU servicing the data P bus.

5

The MC88200 automatically latches the addresses at the beginning of a P bus transaction and generates the reply signals to the processor with the appropriate timing. The CMMU conforms to the P bus operations initiated by the processor by not latching a new address until a successful or fault reply is driven (by any CMMU) for the previous access. The CMMU also automatically ignores the access that follows a faulted transaction and responds appropriately to the next transaction that begins after the reply phase that signaled 'fault'. Finally, the CMMU (when servicing the data P bus) recognizes the assertion of the $\overline{DLOCK}$ signal from the processor and passes it on to the M bus, ensuring that the read and write accesses generated by an **xmem** instruction are not interrupted by alternate M bus masters.

Refer to *MC88200 Cache/Memory Management Unit User's Manual* for more information on the CMMU functions and the system memory bus.

5

SECTION 6
EXCEPTIONS

This section details the exceptions encountered and processed by the MC88100. The descriptions include the actions performed by the MC88100 to recognize an exception and to resume normal processing after the exception, as well as the operations required from software to handle certain exception conditions. Instruction mnemonics used in this section can be identified by referring to **SECTION 3 ADDRESSING MODES AND INSTRUCTION SET**.

The instruction unit initiates exception processing for all exceptions. However, some exceptions are recognized by the floating-point unit while the integer overflow exception is recognized by the integer unit.

6.1 EXCEPTION OVERVIEW

6

Exceptions occur due to four types of conditions:

- Interrupts, which are signaled externally via the INT input signal
- Externally signaled errors, such as a memory access fault
- Internally recognized errors, such as divide-by-zero
- Trap instructions

The MC88100 begins exception processing at the next instruction boundary after an exception is recognized. The processor freezes the execution context in shadow and exception-time registers (which also precludes other exceptions from occurring), explicitly disables interrupts, and enters the supervisor mode. Additionally, the floating-point unit (FPU) is disabled (and frozen) and the data unit is allowed to complete pending accesses. Instruction execution transfers in an orderly manner to the appropriate exception handler routine, which is defined by the exception vector associated with the particular exception. The exception handler routine is the software that processes the exception condition and restores the processor to normal operation.

6.1.1 Exception Categories

Exceptions fall into two categories: precise and imprecise. With a precise exception, the exact processor context when the exception occurred is available, and the exact cause of the exception is always known. With an imprecise exception, the exact processor context is not known when the exception is processed. The context is not known because concurrent operations have affected the information that comprises the processor context.

Data memory access and floating-point instructions may cause imprecise exceptions. For example, with a floating-point overflow, since the FPU does not save the source operands internally, it does not have a local copy of those operands when the exception is processed. However, the exact context is not needed to recover from the exception condition. With a floating-point overflow, it is sufficient to know the operation in progress and the intermediate result (with the extra precision) in order to recover appropriately.

6.1.2 Shadowing

The instruction unit maintains copies of certain internal registers for use during MC88100 exception processing. The data unit and FPU also maintain copies of internal registers to allow full recovery when exceptions occur. The copies of internal registers are referred to as shadow registers and are updated on every clock cycle when shadowing is enabled.

For shadowing to occur, it must be specifically enabled. Shadowing is enabled when the shadow freeze bit (bit 0) in the processor status register (PSR) is cleared by software (either by writing to the PSR with a **stcr** instruction or by executing an **rte** instruction). The shadow freeze bit is set by hardware when an exception is processed to preserve the processor context. It can be cleared by software after the context is saved (for example, when the context is stored on a stack).

6

The exception-time processor status register (EPSR) is an exception-time register and not a shadow register. The integer unit updates the EPSR only at the time an exception is processed. Figure 6-1 shows all the exception registers for the MC88100.

6.2 EXCEPTION VECTORS AND VECTOR BASE REGISTER (VBR)

Exception vectors are the entry points into the exception handler routines. The MC88100 maintains a vector table consisting of 512 exception vectors on a 4K-byte memory page pointed to by the vector base address in the vector base register (VBR). Each exception and exception vector has a corresponding exception number which is generated by hardware or specified as a 9-bit field in a trap instruction. This number is used as the index into the vector table. Each exception vector is two instructions (eight bytes) long. Table 6-1 lists the exception conditions and their respective exception vectors.

An exception vector contains the first two instructions of an exception handler routine; a common practice is to encode the vector with a branch instruction that uses the **.n** (delayed branch) option. The second instruction can then be the first instruction in the exception handler; this instruction is executed while the branch target is being prefetched.

The VBR is loaded by software, normally during part of the system initialization procedure. It may be modified by software to dynamically specify different pages of exception vectors. However, it is recommended that this register only be modified when exceptions are disabled (the shadow freeze, SFD1, and IND bits of the PSR are set). The lower twelve bits

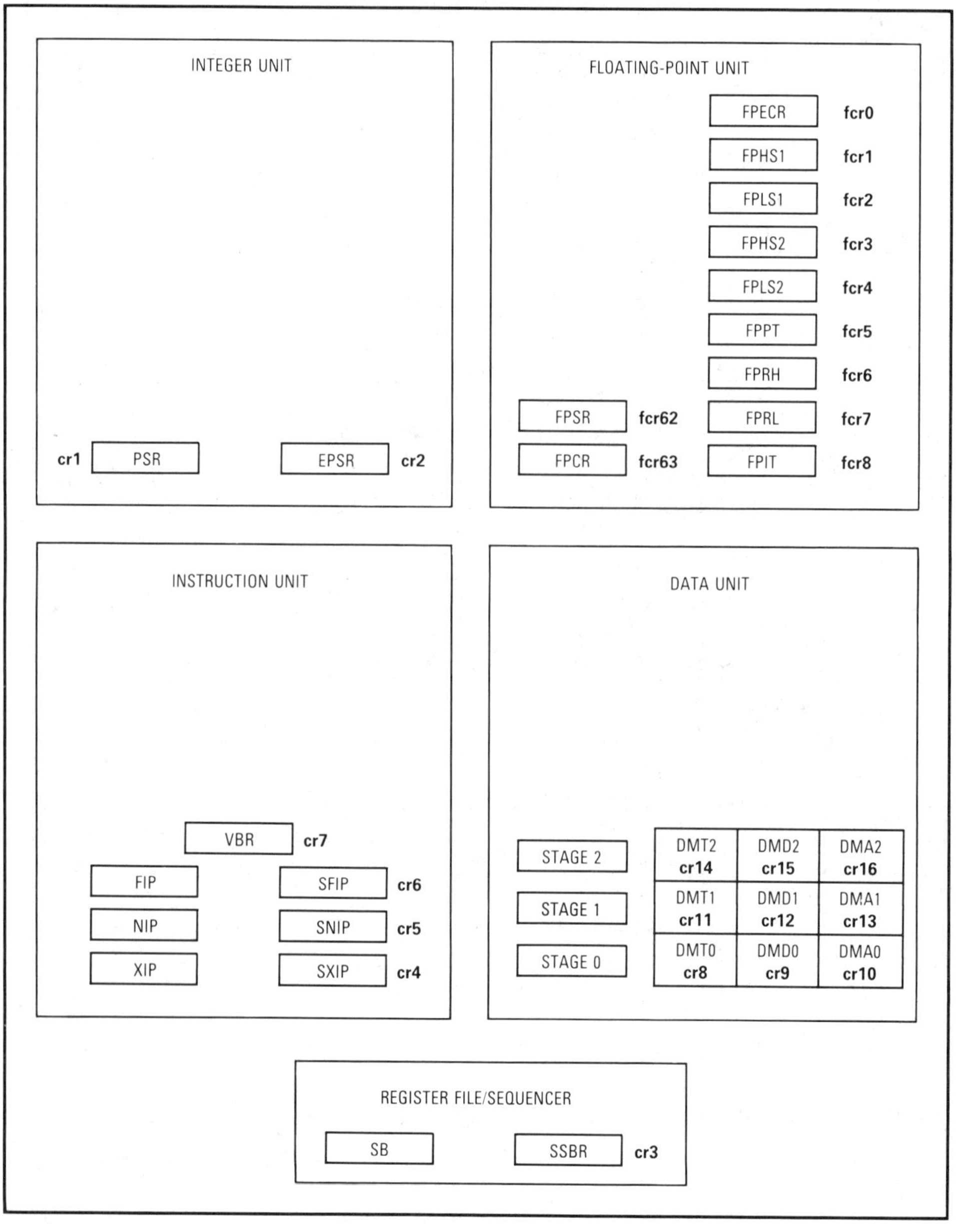

Figure 6-1. Exception-Time and Shadow Registers

Table 6-1. Exception Vectors

Exception Number	Address	Definition
0	0	Reset (the VBR is Cleared Before Vectoring) Exception
1	VBR + $8	Interrupt Exception
2	VBR + $10	Instruction Access Exception
3	VBR + $18	Data Access Exception
4	VBR + $20	Misaligned Access Exception
5	VBR + $28	Unimplemented Opcode Exception
6	VBR + $30	Privilege Violation Exception
7	VBR + $38	Bounds Check Violation Exception
8	VBR + $40	Illegal Integer Divide Exception
9	VBR + $48	Integer Overflow Exception
10	VBR + $50	Error Exception
11–113		Reserved for Supervisor and Future Hardware Use Only
114	VBR + $390	SFU 1 Precise — Floating-Point Precise Exception
115	VBR + $398	SFU 1 Imprecise — Floating-Point Imprecise Exception
116	VBR + $3A0	SFU 2 Precise (see Note) Exception
117	VBR + $3A8	Reserved
118	VBR + $3B0	SFU 3 Precise (see Note) Exception
119	VBR + $3B8	Reserved
120	VBR + $3C0	SFU 4 Precise (see Note) Exception
121	VBR + $3C8	Reserved
122	VBR + $3D0	SFU 5 Precise (see Note) Exception
123	VBR + $3D8	Reserved
124	VBR + $3E0	SFU 6 Precise (see Note) Exception
125	VBR + $3E8	Reserved
126	VBR + $3F0	SFU 7 Precise (see Note) Exception
127	VBR + $3F8	Reserved
128–511		Supervisor Call Exceptions — Reserved for User Definition (Trap Vectors)

NOTE: SFU2 through SFU7 are not implemented. Executing an instruction that is coded for these SFUs causes a precise exception for that SFU.

of the VBR are unused. The VBR is initialized to zero on reset. This register has read/write access.

31 … 12	11											0
VECTOR TABLE BASE ADDRESS	0	0	0	0	0	0	0	0	0	0	0	0

VBR **cr7**

Bits 31–12 — Vector Table Base Address

Bits 11–0 — Reserved

Always contain zero. Not guaranteed to be zeros in future implementations.

Exception vector addresses are formed by concatenating the 20 most significant bits of the VBR with the 9-bit exception vector number, which is generated by hardware or specified as a 9-bit field in trap instructions. This 29-bit value has three zeros appended to form a 32-bit value. Figure 6-2 shows the exception vector address formation.

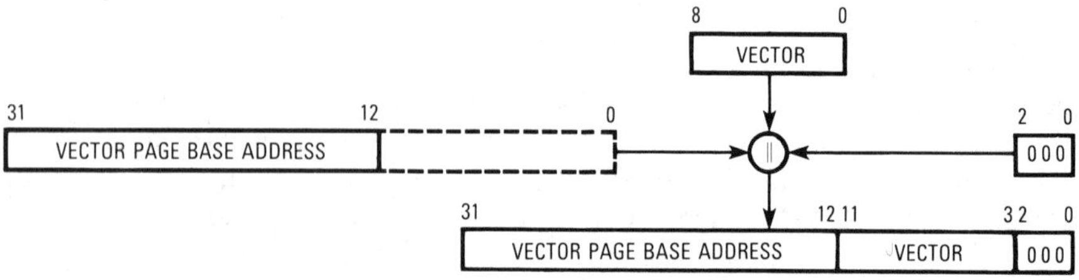

Figure 6.2. Exception Vector Address Formation

6

6.3 EXCEPTION PRIORITY

Due to the concurrent execution units of the MC88100, multiple exceptions can occur at the same time within the processor. When multiple exceptions occur, they are recognized by the processor according to the priority shown in Table 6-2. Exceptions that have the same priority never occur simultaneously.

Table 6-2. Exception Priority

Priority	Exceptions
1	Reset
2	Instruction Access
3	Unimplemented Opcode
4	Privileged Violation
5	Misaligned Access Integer Overflow Illegal Integer Divide Trap Instructions Bounds Check SFU Precise
6	Interrupt
7	SFU Imprecise
8	Data Access

6.4 EXCEPTION PROCESSING

For all exceptions except reset and the error exception, the MC88100 and software handler perform standard procedures for exception processing. These procedures are to recognize the exception, save the processor context, service the exception, and return to normal processing after the exception.

The MC88100 does not automatically save the processor context to memory as part of exception processing; the processor context is stored in appropriate shadow and exception-time registers. Saving the necessary context to memory is the responsibility of the software exception handler.

The processor is in the exception processing state when shadowing is frozen (SFRZ bit of the PSR is set). When the MC88100 is in the exception processing state, it cannot process another exception except for trap instructions. If another exception occurs (other than a trap instruction), the MC88100 takes the error exception, which is a fatal error. In systems requiring nested exceptions, shadowing must be enabled as soon as possible after an exception is recognized to place the processor in the normal state. This allows subsequent exceptions to occur and be processed properly. Shadowing can be enabled as soon as the shadow registers required for handling the exception are saved into general-purpose registers or memory. See **6.10 ERROR EXCEPTION (VECTOR OFFSET $50)** for more information on error exceptions.

6

External interrupts, the misaligned access exception, and the floating-point inexact exception can be masked. When a masked exception occurs, the processor continues to operate in the normal mode and no actions are taken.

Exception processing is performed in three interrelated phases:

1. Exception recognition, during which the processor saves the execution context in shadow registers and changes program flow to the exception handler routine.
2. Exception handling, during which the software corrects the exception condition or performs the function initiated by a trap instruction.
3. Return from exception, during which the processor restores the execution context in effect before the exception occurred, and then resumes execution at the program location before the exception occurred.

The exception handler routine performs specific functions based on the type of exception that occurred. The following paragraphs describe the three interrelated phases.

6.4.1 Exception Recognition

When an exception occurs, the exception-time processor status register (EPSR) is automatically loaded with a copy of the PSR in effect before the PSR is updated with exception

information unless shadowing is frozen. The EPSR has read/write access. The contents of the EPSR are copied back into the PSR by an **rte** instruction. Figure 6-3 shows the logical flow for the exception recognition procedure.

31	30	29	28	27 … 10	9 … 4	3	2	1	0
MODE	BO	SER	C	0 0 0 0 0 0 0 0 0 0 0 0 0 0 0 0 0 0	1 1 1 1 1 1	SFD1	MXM	IND	SFRZ

PSR **cr1**

31	30	29	28	27 … 10	9 … 4	3	2	1	0
*	*	*	*	0 0 0 0 0 0 0 0 0 0 0 0 0 0 0 0 0 0	1 1 1 1 1 1	*	*	*	*

EPSR **cr2**

*Bit setting of PSR at time exception is processed.

When an exception occurs and shadowing is enabled, the processor automatically performs the following actions:

1. Waits until all pending data memory accesses complete or until a data access exception is signaled. If any of the accesses result in a data memory access exception, the memory access exception does not pre-empt the earlier exception. Instead, the valid bit is set in the DMT0 register to notify the exception handler that a data exception has occurred. The exception handler software must check the DMT0 register to determine if this bit is set. If the valid bit is set, the exception handler must correct the data exception (or branch to the data access exception handler) before re-enabling shadowing. The DMT0 register is described in **6.7.3.1 DATA UNIT GENERAL CONTROL REGISTERS**.

   If the initial exception was a data access exception, the processor does not wait for pending data accesses to complete.

   At any time during this exception recognition sequence, instructions requested prior to the exception can be prefetched by the processor. These instructions are discarded, and any code access faults encountered while prefetching these instructions are ignored.

2. Copies the PSR into the EPSR. This saves the PSR value at the time of the exception.
3. Switches the processor into the exception processing state by performing the following actions concurrently:
   - Freeze all shadow registers by setting the shadow freeze bit (bit 0) in the PSR. This saves the contents of the register scoreboard and instruction pipeline at the time of the exception.
   - Disable the FPU by setting the SFU1 disable bit (bit 3) in the PSR. This prevents the FPU from writing results back to the general-purpose registers and from signaling exceptions.
   - Disable interrupts by setting the interrupt disable bit (bit 1) in the PSR.
   - Switch the processor into supervisor mode by setting the MODE bit (bit 31) in the PSR.
   - Clear the register scoreboard so that the exception handler software has access to all general-purpose registers.

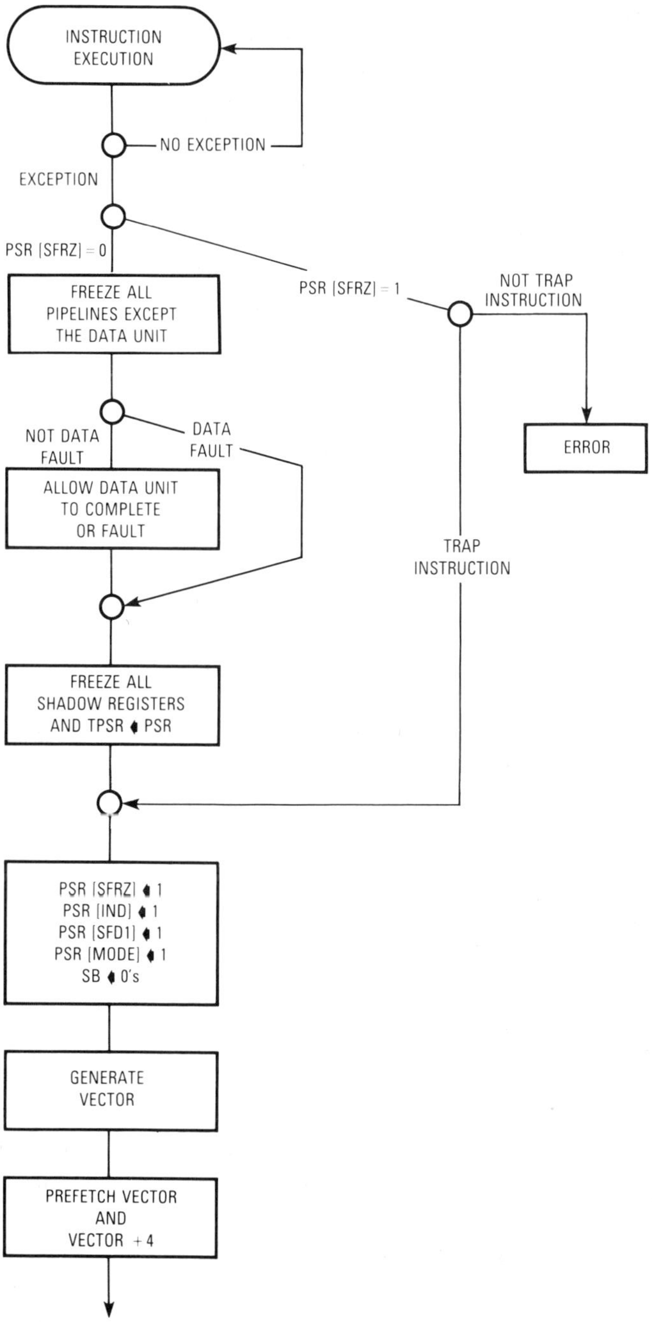

Figure 6-3. Exception Recognition

6

4. Generates the exception vector entry point using the VBR and the vector number. The generated entry point is used to initiate execution of the exception handling software.
5. Prefetches and executes the exception handler instructions while in the exception processing state (shadowing frozen).

Table 6-3 lists the control register states after an exception is recognized, when the MC88100 branches to the appropriate exception handler.

Table 6-3. General Control Register States after an Exception

Register	State
Processor Status Register (PSR)	Bits 31, 3, 1, and 0 set (supervisor mode, FPU and interrupts disabled, shadow registers frozen); all other bits unchanged.
Exception-Time Processor Status Register (EPSR)	Contains the value in the PSR before the exception occurred and after all data unit operations have completed or faulted.
Scoreboard (SB)	Cleared
Shadow Scoreboard (SSBR)	Contains the value in the scoreboard before the exception occurred.
Instruction Pointers (XIP, NIP, FIP)	FIP = exception vector address, V bits in NIP and XIP are cleared
Shadow Instruction Pointers (SXIP, SNIP, SFIP)	Contains XIP, NIP, and FIP values before the exception occurred. Instructions pointed to by the SNIP and SFIP have not been executed. The instruction pointed to by the SXIP may have been aborted or completed, depending on the exception type.
Vector Base Register (VBR)	Unchanged
Data Memory Transaction Registers (DMT0, DMT1, DMT2)	For a data access exception, DMT2, DMT1, DMT0 contain information on the memory transaction in progress. Valid bits are clear if no memory access exception has occurred.
Data Memory Address Registers (DMA0, DMA1, DMA2)	For a data access exception, DMA2, DMA1, DMA0 contain information on the memory transaction in progress. Undefined for all other exceptions.
Data Memory Data Registers (DMD0, DMD1, DMD2)	For a data access exception, DMD2, DMD1, DMD0 contain information only for store operations in progress. Undefined for all other exceptions and conditions.
General-Purpose Registers (**r31–r0**)	Unchanged
Floating-Point Control Registers	FPECR contains information on floating-point exceptions, floating-point precise registers contain information on precise exception, and floating-point imprecise registers contain information on imprecise exceptions; otherwise these are undefined. FPCR and FPSR are unchanged by exception recognition.

6.4.2 Exception Handling

Exception handlers typically process exceptions in one of two ways:

1. Interrupts, the FPU, and shadowing are disabled while the exception handler executes. All information required for exception processing is retained in control registers. This method of handling exceptions removes the need for saving any of the processor context to memory and for restoring the context when the exception condition is

corrected. An **rte** instruction restores the processor context from the control registers at the end of the exception handler routine. If another exception (other than a trap instruction) occurs while shadowing is disabled, the MC88100 takes the error exception.

2. The exception handler software first saves the processor context from the control registers (and possibly the general-purpose registers) to memory. Shadowing is then re-enabled in the exception handler by an **stcr** instruction or an **rte** instruction that clears the SFRZ bit in the PSR, thereby returning the MC88100 to the normal processing state. This allows another exception (a nested exception) to occur while the first exception is being handled. At the end of this type of exception handler routine, the exception handler freezes the shadow registers (with a **stcr** or trap instruction) so they can be reloaded with the saved context from memory. An **rte** instruction then restores the processor context from the exception-time and shadow registers. Refer to **6.4.3.3. UPDATING PSR WITH stcr OR xcr** for more information on software modifications to the PSR.

As stated earlier, the MC88100 allows all pending data unit accesses to complete as part of exception processing. The processor, however, does NOT vector to the data access exception handler if any of these pending accesses results in a fault while processing another exception. Therefore, all exception handlers should check the status of the data-unit shadow registers (mainly the DMT0 register) and handle any pending data access exceptions. Note that this is not required for trap handler because trap instructions synchronize the processor before they execute (ensuring no pending data accesses).

6

6.4.3 Return from Exceptions

When an exception occurs, shadow registers are frozen. The information in the shadow registers is then used to handle the exception as required. When returning to the normal processing state, certain internal registers can be restored from the shadow registers by executing an **rte** instruction.

6.4.3.1 CONTROL REGISTERS RESTORED BY rte. The following paragraphs describe the shadow registers that are restored by the execution of the **rte** instruction (in addition to the EPSR) and how the MC88100 returns to the normal processing state and the original context.

6.4.3.1.1 Shadow Scoreboard Register (SSBR). The SSBR is a 32-bit register that shadows the scoreboard register when the SFRZ bit of the PSR is clear. When an exception occurs, this register contains a copy of the scoreboard register in effect before the scoreboard exception. The contents of this register are copied back into the scoreboard register by an **rte** instruction. Since register **r0** is read-only (constant zero), bit zero of the shadow scoreboard register always contains zero.

The SSBR is not a true shadow register because the entire scoreboard register (SB) is not copied to the SSBR on every clock cycle. Individual bits in the SSBR are set/cleared only when the corresponding bits in the SB are changed. Therefore, after an exception, the SSBR only represents the SB if the contents of the SB and SSBR were equal when the shadow freeze bit in the PSR was cleared. This register has read/write access.

31																															0
r31	**r30**	**r29**	**r28**	**r27**	**r26**	**r25**	**r24**	**r23**	**r22**	**r21**	**r20**	**r19**	**r18**	**r17**	**r16**	**r15**	**r14**	**r13**	**r12**	**r11**	**r10**	**r9**	**r8**	**r7**	**r6**	**r5**	**r4**	**r3**	**r2**	**r1**	**r0**

SSBR **cr3**

NOTE

After an MC88100 reset, the contents of SSBR are not defined. The SSBR must be explicitly cleared before shadowing is enabled. This guarantees that the SSBR reflects the SB when shadowing is enabled.

6.4.3.1.2 Shadow Fetch Instruction Pointer (SFIP). The SFIP is a 32-bit register that shadows the FIP when shadowing is enabled. When a precise exception occurs, the SFIP contains a pointer either to the instruction following the next instruction or to the target of a jump or branch instruction. An **rte** instruction fetches the instruction pointed to by the SNIP and then the instruction pointed to by the SFIP.

The SFIP contains a valid (V) and an exception (E) bit. The V bit can be cleared by software, effectively making the corresponding instruction a no-operation instruction when an **rte** is executed. In this case, the corresponding instruction is not prefetched from memory. If both the V and E bits are set, an **rte** instruction causes the instruction pointed to by the SFIP to generate an instruction access exception when it advances to the NIP, regardless of whether the transaction receives a 'success' or 'fault' reply from the memory system. An **rte** instruction can be made to return to a particular instruction by placing a valid instruction address in the SNIP and the next sequential instruction address in the SFIP (with V bits set and E bits clear). The **rte** resumes execution at the instruction pointed to by the SNIP, then the SFIP. This register has read/write access.

31 … 2	1	0
SHADOW OF FIP	V	E

SFIP **cr6**

Bits 31–2 — Shadow of Fetch Instruction Pointer

V — Valid
- 0 — Fetch instruction is not valid (corresponds to no-operation); ignore E bit.
- 1 — Fetch instruction is valid.

E — Exception
- 0 — Fetch instruction is fetched normally.
- 1 — Force instruction access fault if execution of the instruction is attempted.

6.4.3.1.3 Shadow Next Instruction Pointer (SNIP). The SNIP is a 32-bit shadow register that is updated by processor hardware whenever the NIP is updated and shadowing is enabled. When a precise exception occurs, the SNIP contains a pointer to the next instruction to be executed. An **rte** instruction causes instruction prefetch and execution to resume with the instruction pointed to by the SNIP.

The SNIP contains two bits that indicate the status of the corresponding instruction and that can be used to control instruction execution. The valid (V) bit indicates that the SNIP corresponds to a valid instruction. When the V bit is set, the SNIP contains the address of the instruction that was being decoded when the exception occurred. When the V bit is clear, the instruction is invalid. An instruction can be invalid for three reasons. First, if the instruction pointed to by the SNIP followed a branch or jump instruction, the instruction is invalid if the **.n** option was not specified and the branch is taken. Second, the V bit can be cleared by software, effectively making the instruction corresponding to the NIP stage a no-operation instruction after execution of an **rte** instruction and pre-emptying the instruction prefetch for that stage. Thirdly, the V bit of SNIP is clear if the V bit of FIP is clear, the pipeline advances, and shadowing is enabled.

The exception (E) bit is set when the E bit of the FIP is set, the FIP is updated to NIP, and shadowing is enabled. This bit can also be set by software with a **stcr** or **xcr** instruction. If the E bit and V bit are set and an **rte** instruction is executed, the NIP instruction generates an instruction access exception, regardless of whether the transaction receives a 'success' or 'fault' reply from the memory system. If the V bit is clear, then the NIP is considered to be invalid and a no-operation is performed when the XIP is updated with the NIP information; the E bit is ignored in this case. Also, when the V bit is clear and an **rte** instruction is executed, the instruction corresponding to SNIP is not prefetched. This register has read/write access.

31–2	1	0
SHADOW OF NIP	V	E

SNIP **cr5**

Bits 31–2 — Shadow of Next Instruction Pointer

V — Valid
- 0 — Fetch instruction is not valid so prefetch is not performed (corresponds to no-operation); ignore E bit.
- 1 — Fetch instruction is valid.

E — Exception
- 0 — Next instruction is fetched normally.
- 1 — Force instruction access fault if execution of the instruction is attempted.

6.4.3.1.4 Shadow Execute Instruction Pointer (SXIP). The SXIP is a 32-bit register that is updated by processor hardware whenever the XIP is updated and shadowing is enabled. If an instruction causes a precise exception, the SXIP points to that instruction. If an interrupt or imprecise exception occurs, SXIP points to the last instruction executed by the integer

unit, dispatched to the FPU, or dispatched to the data unit. The processor hardware does not use the SXIP on return from an exception; an **rte** instruction resumes execution at the instruction pointed to by the SNIP.

The SXIP contains two bits that indicate whether or not the instruction was executed. When the valid (V) bit is set, it indicates that the SXIP contains an instruction that was attempting to execute. When the V bit is clear, the instruction was not executed (invalid instruction). The V bit in the SXIP is clear whenever the NIP has the valid bit clear, the NIP is updated to the XIP, and shadowing is enabled.

The exception (E) bit indicates whether or not the instruction was successfully prefetched from memory. The E bit is set when the fetch of the SXIP instruction faulted or when the previous stage (NIP) advanced to XIP with the E bit (and shadowing is enabled) set. The processor sets the exception bit to prevent the execution of a faulted instruction in the pipeline. If the V bit is clear, then the E bit is ignored. MC88100 hardware only sets the E bit of the XIP stage; the E bits of the NIP and FIP stages are not set by the hardware. This register is read only.

31 … 2	1	0
SHADOW OF XIP	V	E

SXIP **cr4**

Bits 31–2 — Shadow of Execute Instruction Pointer

V — Valid
- 0 — Current instruction is not valid; ignore E bit.
- 1 — Current instruction is valid.

E — Exception
- 0 — Current instruction fetched successfully
- 1 — Current instruction not executed due to an instruction access fault

6.4.3.2 rte INSTRUCTION FLOW. After an exception condition has been handled, the **rte** instruction should be executed to exit from the exception handler routine. Figure 6-4 shows the flow for an rte instruction. This instruction restores the processor context from shadow and exception-time registers as follows:

1. The shadow instruction pointers (SNIP and SFIP) are copied to the instruction pointers appropriately, and the corresponding instructions are re-prefetched.
2. The shadow scoreboard (SSBR) is copied to the scoreboard (SB) register.
3. The EPSR is copied to the PSR.
4. Instruction execution resumes after the instruction corresponding to NIP is prefetched.

The instruction pointed to by the SNIP is the first instruction to execute after the return. This instruction is fetched from memory again since the instruction pipeline was cleared during exception processing. If the MC88100 enables shadowing as part of the restore of

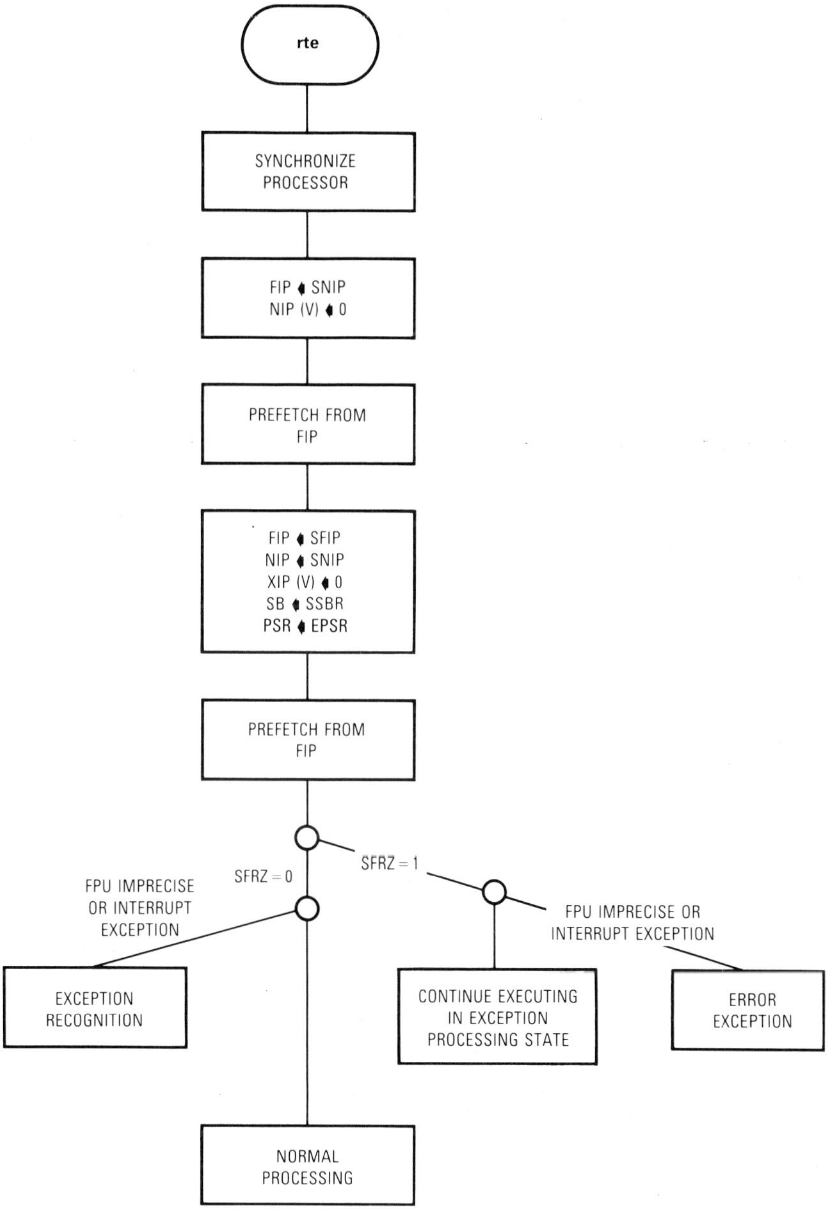

Figure 6-4. rte Instruction Flow

the PSR from the EPSR, the **rte** instruction guarantees that register usage indications are consistent between the SB and SSBR (the SB is guaranteed to match the SSBR because it is restored from the SSBR). Additionally, if the FPU is enabled with the **rte** and there were FPU instructions in progress before the exception, the SB will have the scoreboard bits for the destination registers set appropriately (automatically restored from the SSBR) after execution of the **rte**. The FPU instructions then continue executing. Finally, if the interrupts are enable with the **rte**, a pending interrupt is recognized immediately after the **rte**.

The **rte** instruction also prefetches the next two instructions to be executed after the execution of the **rte** is complete. The next two instructions are guaranteed to be prefetched from the address space specified by the EPSR MODE bit, and the privilege check on the execution of the next two instructions is guaranteed to be based on the EPSR MODE bit.

The **rte** instruction is a flow-control instruction and synchronizes the processor before execution. Therefore, all instructions in the handler are guaranteed to complete before the **rte** begins execution.

6.4.3.3 UPDATING PSR WITH stcr OR xcr. It is recommended that changes to the PSR be made with the execution of an **rte** instruction. An **stcr** or **xcr** instruction can also alter the PSR, but the following effects must be considered. First, for register usage to be correct after an exception is taken, the scoreboard and shadow scoreboard must match before shadowing is re-enabled. This can be accomplished by explicitly clearing the SSBR and by executing a trap (not-taken) instruction to wait for the SB to clear. The trap instruction waits until all scoreboard bits are clear before it executes. At this point, shadowing can be re-enabled.

6

The SSBR and SB do not necessarily match after a processor reset; thus, the SSBR should always be cleared at initialization time. The SSBR can be cleared by executing an **stcr** instruction that stores all zeros to the SSBR.

Secondly, when the FPU is explicitly disabled with a **stcr** or **xcr** instruction, care must be taken to ensure that there are no instructions executed by the FPU currently in progress. Otherwise, the scoreboard bits of the corresponding destination registers will be set, preventing subsequent instructions from accessing these registers. If a subsequent instruction attempts to use one of these registers, the machine will remain in an indefinite scoreboard hold. The prevent this from occuring, a trap or a trap-not-taken instruction should be executed before the **stcr** or **xcr** to ensure that the FPU is disabled only when it is empty.

Thirdly, a trap instruction (can be a trap-not-taken) should be executed immediately before a **stcr** or **xcr** instruction is executed that sets the shadow freeze bit (bit 0) in the PSR. This ensures that instructions in progress that can cause exceptions complete and report the exception before shadowing is frozen.

Fourthly, when a **stcr** or **xcr** instruction that sets the interrupt disable bit (bit 1) is executed, interrupts are disabled following the *subsequent* instruction. Therefore, care must be taken not to freeze shadowing (set the freeze bit) and disable interrupts with the same instruction. Otherwise, an interrupt that is pending at the time that shadowing is frozen may result in the error exception (i.e., interrupt recognized while shadowing is frozen). Combining this

precaution with the precaution for setting the shadow freeze bit described in the preceding paragraph, a recommended procedure for disabling interrupts and freezing shadowing is as follows:

trap-not-taken
stcr to disable interrupts
stcr to freeze shadowing

Alternately, a trap instruction can be executed that branches to a specific code segment that modifies the appropriate shadow and exception registers and then executes an **rte** instruction.

Note that when interrupts are enabled with a **stcr** instruction, there is a delay of one instruction before interrupts are recognized again. However, if interrupts are enabled with an **rte** instruction a pending interrupt is recognized immediately after the **rte**.

Fifth, when the FPU is explicitly enabled (SFD1 bit cleared in the PSR) with an **stcr** or **xcr** instruction, the scoreboard bits corresponding to destination registers of FPU instructions in progress will not be set. Therefore, FPU instructions could overwrite the results of other concurrent operations, and the scoreboard bits for the floating-point instruction will not be set. When the FPU is enabled in this way, it must be empty.

6

Finally, if the MODE bit of the PSR is changed by an **stcr** or **xcr** instruction, two problems can occur with the instructions following the **stcr** or **xcr**. First, the privilege check for the next instruction may not be correct (in the case where the MODE bit is set by the **stcr** or **xcr**). Secondly, the next one or two instructions may have been prefetched from the incorrect address space because the prefetches occurred before the execution of the **stcr** or **xcr**.

6.4.3.4 COMPLETING FPU INSTRUCTIONS IN PROGRESS. The exception processing sequence performed by the MC88100 causes the FPU to be disabled (SFD1 bit of PSR set). This prevents the FPU from writing results back to the register file and from executing new instructions. To allow all FPU instructions in progress to complete within the exception handler, an **rte** can be executed that returns control to a trap-not-taken instruction. The **rte** can restore the SB from the SSBR and can enable the FPU so that all operations complete. The trap-not-taken instruction forces the software to wait for the FPU to complete. This can be performed in supervisor mode.

6.5 INSTRUCTION UNIT EXCEPTIONS

The following paragraphs describe the external interrupt exception and the different types of exceptions that are generated by the instruction unit.

6.5.1 Interrupt Exception (Vector Offset $8)

Interrupts are exceptions generated by the assertion of the INT input signal. Since the MC88100 has only a single interrupt request signal, external hardware must map all external interrupt requests to this signal. Interrupts do not force immediate exception processing;

the INT signal is sampled externally on every falling clock edge, and, if it is asserted, the exception is signaled internally on the next falling edge of the clock. Upon detecting an interrupt exception, the MC88100 performs the standard exception processing as described in **6.4 EXCEPTION PROCESSING**. Because interrupt recognition is voltage-level sensitive (not edge triggered), the interrupting device should keep the interrupt signal asserted until it receives an explicit recognition (normally generated by the interrupt exception handler).

Interrupts can be disabled by setting the IND bit (bit 1) in the PSR. Interrupts should be disabled during exception processing (when shadow registers are frozen). ***If an interrupt occurs while shadowing is frozen and interrupts are enabled, the MC88100 takes the error exception described in* 6.10 ERROR EXCEPTION.**

Typically, systems incorporate an interrupt controller or other hardware that maps multiple external interrupt requests to the INT input. In these systems, the exception handler software acknowledges the interrupt by reading a system interrupt controller (located in the control memory address space in systems that use the MC88200 CMMU devices). The controller can update its interrupt mask and write the vector number of the interrupting device on the data bus. The exception handler uses the vector number to process the interrupt. The vector from the interrupt controller allows the exception handler to incorporate its own vectoring scheme, allowing multiple devices to be serviced through the single interrupt request input. When the interrupt handler finishes execution, the **rte** instruction restores the processor context, the same as with any other exception. When an interrupt is processed, the SXIP points to the last instruction executed or dispatched for execution before the interrupt was recognized.

6

Since interrupts occur in real time, the interrupt latency (time between when the interrupt is signaled and interrupt processing begins) is usually important. The following guidelines provide a method to calculate the interrupt latency, based on the actions performed by the processor to recognize an interrupt.

1. One clock cycle for internal synchronization of the interrupt signal (time between when the interrupt is sampled and any exception processing begins).
2. From zero to four times $maxmem_d$ (longest data memory access latency) cycles for clearing the data unit pipeline. The data unit can have, at most, four outstanding memory accesses, each of which may require the longest memory access time. However, MC88100-based systems normally incorporate MC88200 CMMUs. With the CMMUs, it is probable that all four memory accesses will result in cache hits. If this occurs, then each memory access effectively requires only one clock cycle to finish. Also, the processor normally has less than four outstanding memory accesses, reducing the time required to clear the data unit pipeline.
3. From one cycle to two times $maxmem_i$ (maximum instruction memory access latency) cycles for possibly completing a prefetch already in progress and for prefetching the first instruction in the exception vector. The prefetch in progress is completed in parallel with the data access cycles.
4. One cycle to propagate the instruction through the pipeline and begin instruction decoding.
5. One cycle for instruction execution.

In summary, the worst-case interrupt latency n can be expressed in clock cycles as:

$$3 + \max(4 * maxmem_d, maxmem_i) + maxmem_i$$

6.5.2 Misaligned Access Exception (Vector Offset $20)

Misaligned access exceptions occur when a load, store, or exchange instruction is attempted to a memory address that is not consistent with the size of the access. For example, this exception occurs when a half-word access is attempted to an odd byte address. This exception is a precise exception; the exception condition is detected before the memory access is dispatched to the data unit. When this exception occurs, the SXIP contains the address of the instruction that caused the exception. For a **ld** or **xmem** instruction, the appropriate scoreboard bit is set. The exception handler can emulate the memory access in software or can discard the instruction, as appropriate. This exception also occurs when a double-word access is attempted to an address that is not an even-word boundary.

This exception can be masked by setting the MXM bit (bit 2) in the PSR. If this exception is masked and a misaligned access is attempted, the processor rounds the address *down* to a consistent boundary (for example, a half-word read operation attempted to address $401 returns the half word at location $400).

6

6.5.3 Unimplemented Opcode Exception (Vector Offset $28)

This exception occurs when an instruction with an unimplemented opcode is loaded into the instruction pipeline. Unimplemented SFU instructions do not cause this exception but generate an SFU precise exception. The SXIP points to the instruction that caused the exception. The exception handler can fetch, decode, and process this instruction, thereby emulating unimplemented opcodes in software. If instruction emulation is not needed, the handler can discard the instruction or perform other appropriate processing.

6.5.4 Privilege Violation Exception (Vector Offset $30)

A privilege violation occurs when software attempts to perform a privileged operation while in user mode. Privilege violations occur under three conditions:

1. Accessing a control register other than the FPCR or FPSR while in the user mode.
2. Using the **.usr** option while in the user mode. (This is for virtural machine support.)
3. Specifying exception vectors 0–127 in a trap instruction while in user mode.

When a privilege violation occurs, the instruction that caused the exception is pointed to by the SXIP. The privileged operation is not performed. For load and **xmem** instructions that result in privilege violations (due to inappropriate use of **.usr** option), the corresponding scoreboard bits are set and must be cleared by the exception handler.

6.5.5 Trap Instructions tcnd, tb1, tb0 Exceptions (Vector Offset $400-$7F8)

Trap instructions are MC88100 instructions that explicitly cause the MC88100 to complete execution of all previous instructions and to begin exception processing. When a trap

instruction executes, the MC88100 performs the standard exception processing described in **6.4.1 Exception Recognition**. When the exception handler software finishes, an **rte** (that enables shadowing in the PSR) instruction returns the MC88100 processor to the normal state described in **6.4.3 Return from Exceptions**.

The MC88100 includes four trap instructions: the **tbnd, tb1, tb0**, and **tcnd** instruction. The **tbnd** instruction is described in **6.5.6 Bounds Check Violation**. The **tcnd, tb1**, and **tb0** instructions can initiate any exception handler by specifying the appropriate vector number (see Table 6-1). Vectors 0–127 can only be accessed in supervisor mode. The **tcnd, tb1**, and **tb0** instructions do not begin execution until all scoreboard bits are clear and all data memory operations are completed. This condition applies regardless of whether or not the trap is taken.

Trap instructions that are executed while shadowing is frozen do not cause the error exception. When a trap instruction is executed while shadowing is frozen, the PSR is updated as it is with other exception conditions, and program execution continues at the location specified by the instruction. However, none of the exception-time or shadow registers are modified.

6.5.6 Bounds-Check Violation Exception (Vector Offset $38)

This exception occurs when the **tbnd** instruction detects a value that is out of bounds. The instruction specifies the limit that must be met; if the tested value falls outside of that limit (out of bounds), the trap is taken. The SXIP points to the **tbnd** instruction. The bounds test is an unsigned comparison.

6

6.6 INTEGER OVERFLOW EXCEPTION (VECTOR OFFSET $48)

The integer overflow exception occurs when the result of a signed integer arithmetic instruction cannot be represented as a 32-bit signed number. The SXIP points to the instruction that caused the exception. The destination register and carry bit are unchanged by an instruction that causes an integer overflow exception.

6.7 MEMORY ACCESS EXCEPTIONS

Memory access exceptions occur when a data memory access or an instruction prefetch fails to complete normally. These exceptions, which are generated by the MC88200 CMMU or other hardware, are signaled as a fault encoding on the reply signals during the reply phase of a memory transaction. Memory access exceptions can occur under the following conditions:

1. A load, store, **xmem**, or instruction prefetch operation was issued to an address that is not valid in the current address space (nonexistent address fault).
2. A load, store, or instruction prefetch operation was issued to a segment or page in a virtual memory system that does not reside in main memory and must be read from disk (segment or page fault).

3. A load, store, or instruction prefetch operation was issued by software with insufficient rights (privilege or write protection violation).
4. Problems were detected by error-detection hardware (bus error).

6.7.1 Instruction Access Exception (Vector Offset $10)

Instruction access exceptions occur when an attempt is made to execute an instruction and the corresponding prefetch to instruction memory resulted in a fault reply on the instruction P bus reply signals (CR1–CR0). The instruction access exception occurs when execution of the faulted instruction is attempted. The XIP points to the instruction that caused the exception, and this is reflected in the SXIP. The memory system must provide a status register or other means of indicating the reason that the exception occurred. The MC88200 CMMU includes a local status register, which the exception handler must read to determine the cause of the exception in systems with an MC88200 residing on the instruction P bus.

An instruction access exception is recognized in the following way:

1. The FIP contains the address of the instruction being fetched from memory, which is the fetch that will cause the exception.
2. The value in the FIP propagates to the NIP after the transaction has been initiated (but before the reply is received). When the fault reply is received on the P bus reply signals (CR1–CR0), an internal flag is set that prevents the MC88100 from executing the instruction.
3. The value in the NIP propagates to the XIP. The MC88100 now sets the E bit in the XIP, recognizes the exception, and begins exception processing as described in **6.4.1 Exception Recognition**. The SXIP contains the address of the instruction that caused the exception, while the SNIP and SFIP contain the addresses of the two following instructions. If the V bit of the XIP is cleared, the fault is ignored.

The exception handler must determine the cause of the exception and then optionally retry the instruction fetch. The retry is performed by "backing up" and restarting the instruction pipeline. Specifically, the exception handler

1. Saves the execution context from the control registers into memory. This context should include the EPSR and the three shadow instruction pointers (SXIP, SNIP, and SFIP).
2. Once the context is saved, enables shadowing by clearing the SFRZ bit (bit 0) in the PSR.
3. Determines and corrects the cause of the exception. For example, if the exception was caused by a page fault, the requested memory page must be read in from memory. If the exception was caused by a privilege violation or a nonexistent memory fault, the exception handler may abort the instruction fetch and the task that attempted it.
4. Clears the E bits in the SXIP and SNIP copied to memory. The SFIP is not needed to restart the instruction pipeline.
5. Freezes shadowing by setting the SFRZ bit (bit 0) in the PSR.

6

6. Restores the saved context by:
   a. Copying the EPSR saved in memory to the EPSR.
   b. Copying the SXIP saved in memory to the SNIP control register (i.e., back up the XIP to the NIP).
   c. Copying the SNIP saved in memory to the SFIP control register (i.e., back up the NIP to the XIP).
7. Executes an **rte** instruction to return control to the task that encountered the exception. The instructions pointed to by the SNIP and SFIP are prefetched from memory again; the SXIP is discarded. The instruction prefetches should now return valid instructions without exceptions.

6.7.2 Instruction Tracing

Instruction tracing is a valuable method of debugging programs. Tracing permits the MC88100 execution state to be examined after execution of each instruction if necessary. The instruction access exception can be used to implement an instruction tracing mechanism. As stated above, an instruction access exception is recognized when the MC88100 encounters an XIP with the E bit set. Software can cause this exception by setting the E bit in either the FIP or the NIP, which propagates to the XIP. To enable instruction tracing, the software must

1. Trap so that the instruction pipeline is reflected in the shadow registers (SXIP, SNIP, and SFIP). The trap instruction is effectively a program breakpoint. At this point, the software can save the execution context to memory and enable shadowing to perform typical debugger functions such as displaying memory, etc. The debugger software should enable shadowing; however, the instruction pipeline must not be corrupted. The pipeline should be saved to memory or to general-purpose registers.
2. Set the E bit in the saved SFIP. This forces an instruction access exception when processing is restored to normal operation. If SNIP points to a trap instruction or a branch/jump instruction that does not use delayed branching, the value of the E bit in SFIP is ignored (because the V bit of SNIP is cleared when the instruction propagates to the NIP stage), and the instruction corresponding to the SNIP must be emulated in software.
3. Freeze shadowing and copy the values of SNIP and SFIP saved in memory to the SNIP and SFIP control registers, respectively.
4. Execute an **rte** instruction. The MC88100 fetches the instructions addressed by the SNIP and SFIP. The instruction corresponding to the SNIP executes, but the instruction corresponding to the FIP causes an instruction access exception (since the E bit was set). This instruction is not yet executed.
5. The instruction access exception handler software can now perform any debug operations. To return to normal operations, the exception handler performs the same actions as described in **6.7.1 Instruction Access Exception**. If single-instruction execution is to be performed, the exception handler should set the E bit in the saved SNIP since the saved SNIP is copied to the SFIP before returning from the exception. Setting the E bit in the SFIP allows one instruction (SNIP) to execute, and then the exception occurs again.
6. Because instructions residing in the delay slot of a branch, jump, or a trap-taken instruction are never executed (i.e., the V bit for instruction is cleared in the NIP stage), the 'trace' handler may need to check the opcode of the current instruction and take

6

appropriate action in case no delayed branching is used. The following instructions must be emulated in software in this case: **bsr**, **jsr**, **bb0**, **bb1**, **bcnd**, **jmp**, **tbnd**, **tb0** **tb1**, **tcnd**, and **rte**.

6.7.3 Data Access Exception (Vector Offset $18)

Data access exceptions are recoverable imprecise exceptions; none of the shadow instruction pointers are guaranteed to point to the instruction that caused the exception, but this information is not required to recover from the exception. The exception is caused by a fault reply on the data P bus reply signals (DR1–DR0). The exact cause of the exception is not stored in the MC88100; the memory subsystem must provide a status register or other means of indicating the cause of the exception, if necessary. The MC88200 CMMU includes a local status register, which the exception handler must read to determine the cause of the exception in systems using an MC88200 on the data P bus.

Aside from the cause of the exception, all pertinent information about a data access fault is stored in the memory access shadow registers (accessed as general control registers). There are three sets of shadow registers corresponding to the three stages in the data unit pipeline. When a data access exception occurs, the data corresponding to each memory access in the data unit pipeline is latched into the memory access shadow registers. The first set of data unit control registers (DMx0) contains the information about the access that caused the exception (corresponding to stage 0 of the data unit pipeline). The second set of the data unit registers (DMx1) contain information on the next memory access (stage 1 of the data unit pipeline), which may be a separate access (i.e., a subsequent **ld**, **st**, or load access of an **xmem** instruction), the second part of a double-word load or store, or the second access (store) of an **xmem** instruction. The address phase of this access initiated, but the access was aborted by the memory subsystem due to the previous exception. The third set (DMx2) corresponds to the information in stage 2 of the data unit pipeline. This memory transaction has not begun. Again, this may be a separate access, part of a double-word load or store, or onc of the accesses of an **xmem** instruction.

When an **rte** instruction is executed, the data unit control registers are not restored, and the operations are not retried; thus, the exception handler software must retry all of the memory accesses in progress (or abort them if appropriate). To retry the memory accesses, the exception handler emulates the instruction using the saved information. In addition, the shadow scoreboard bits corresponding to pending data accesses must be cleared when the instruction(s) are emulated. An **rte** instruction is used to return from the exception.

6.7.3.1 DATA UNIT GENERAL CONTROL REGISTERS.

The DMTx (data memory transaction) registers contain the information about the memory access in the data unit when an exception occurs. Table 6-4 lists the data unit control registers. The following text details the information contained in the transaction registers, and Table 6-5 summarizes the bit values.

31–16	15	14	13	12	11–7	6	5	4	3	2	1	0
0 0 0 0 0 0 0 0 0 0 0 0 0 0 0 0	BO	DAS	DOUB1	LOCK	DREG	SD	EN3	EN2	EN1	EN0	WRITE	VALID

DMT0, DMT1, and DMT2 **cr8, cr11**, and **cr14**

SD = SIGNED

Table 6-4. Data Unit Control Registers

Register Number	Acronym	Name
cr8	DMT0	Transaction Register #0
cr9	DMD0	Data Register #0
cr10	DMA0	Address Register #0
cr11	DMT1	Transaction Register #1
cr12	DMD1	Data Register #1
cr13	DMA1	Address Register #1
cr14	DMT2	Transaction Register #2
cr15	DMD2	Data Register #2
cr16	DMA2	Address Register #2

Table 6-5. Data Memory Transaction Register Bit Uses

Data Unit Transaction Register Bits				Actions and Options for Synthesizing Load, Store, and Exchange Memory Instructions
BO (Bit 15)				If BO does not match the current value in the PSR, the PSR bit must be changed to match BO for emulating the faulted instruction.
DAS (Bit 14)				If DAS = 0, use the **.usr** option for the instruction. If DAS = 1, access in supervisor mode.
DOUB1 (Bit 13)				All synthesized load and store instructions can be single word (or less); the **.d** option is not needed.
LOCK (Bit 12)				If LOCK = 0, the transaction is not a part of an **xmem** instruction. If LOCK = 1, the two transactions must be combined into an **xmem** instruction.
DREG (Bits 11–7)				Used to place the data from a load or **xmem** instruction into the proper general-purpose register before returning from the exception handler. (Not used for store operations)
SIGNED (Bit 6)				If SIGNED = 0, the byte or half word is zero extended. If SIGNED = 1, the byte or half word is sign extended. Not used for word, double, and store operations.
Byte Enable (Bits 5–2)				
EN3	EN2	EN1	EN0	
0	0	0	1	Use address of LSB in data address register and **.b** option.
0	0	1	0	Use address of LMB in data address register and **.b** option.
0	0	1	1	Use address of LSH in data address register and **.h** option.
0	1	0	0	Use address of UMB in data address register and **.b** option.
1	0	0	0	Use address of MSB in data address register and **.b** option.
1	1	0	0	Use address of MSB in data address register and **.h** option.
1	1	1	1	User word address in data address register, no option.
WRITE (Bit 1)				WRITE = 0, retry load instruction if LOCKBAR = 1. WRITE = 1, retry store instruction if LOCKBAR = 1.
VALID (Bit 0)				VALID = 0, no pending memory transaction in this stage. VALID = 1, construct a load, store, or exchange memory instruction.

LSB – Least Signifcant Byte
LMB = Lower Middle Byte
LSH = Least Significant Half
UMB = Upper Middle Byte
MSB = Most Significant Byte
MSH = Most Significant Half

6

BO — Byte Ordering

Normally, the byte order has not changed when the exception handler begins execution. If the BO bit is different from the setting in the PSR, then the PSR bit must be changed before the memory accesses are performed by the exception handler.

0 — Big Endian
1 — Little Endian

DAS — Data Address Space

Since the exception handler executes in supervisor mode, the **.usr** option must be encoded in the synthesized instructions that access user memory.

0 — User Address Space
1 — Supervisor Address Space

DOUB1 — Double Word

This bit is set if the access is the first access in a double-word transaction (or the load portion of an **xmem** operation). When this bit is set, the following stage in the data unit pipeline is the second access of the double-word transaction. For a **ld.d** or **st.d** instruction residing in stage 2 in the pipeline, the second access has not entered the pipeline but always involves the 'next word' in memory and the next consecutive general-purpose register. The 'next word' address depends on the byte ordering; the 'next word' address should be generated by inverting the lowest order address bit (A2) The second access of an **xmem** instruction is always a store of the same register to the same address. When retrying the instructions, two single-word load or store instructions can be generated instead of one double-word load or store, but in the case of an **xmem**, it must be performed as an **xmem**.

6

LOCK — Bus Lock

This bit is set if the P bus lock signal ($\overline{DLOCK}$) is asserted, wich occurs only if the transaction is a part of an **xmem** instruction. In the two accesses of the **xmem** instruction, the load is followed by the store; if the transaction in this register is a load and LOCK is set, the next memory access must be a store with the same address and destination register. The corresponding DMDx register contains the data for storage. If the load access is in stage 2 of the pipeline, then the store access will not yet be in the pipeline. However, the DMD2 register contains the data to be stored in this case.

DREG — Destination Register

These bits indicate the destination register for the memory access. For a load or exchange operation, the data read from memory should be loaded into this register. For a store or exchange operation, this field is undefined. The corresponding DMDx register contains the data for storage.

SIGNED — Sign-Extended Bit

This bit is set if the data for a load operation should be sign extended; if clear, the data for a load operation should be zero extended. This bit is valid only for byte and half-word accesses.

EN3–EN0 — Byte Enable Bits

These bits are set to indicate which byte(s) are to be accessed by the instruction. For a byte instruction (**.b** option), one of these four enables is set; for a half-word instruction (**.h** option), bits EN3 and EN2 or EN1 and EN0 are set. For a word or double-word access, all of the enables are set. The value of the enables must be encoded to form the two least significant bits of the memory address (see Table 6-5).

WRITE — Read/Write Transaction Bit

If the transaction is not an **xmem** (LOCK is set), then the value of WRITE indicates whether the memory access instruction was an **ld** instruction (read) or an **st** instruction (write). If LOCK is clear, then the value of WRITE indicates whether the transaction is the read or write access of an **xmem** instruction.

0 — Read
1 — Write

VALID — Valid Transaction Bit

This bit indicates whether or not the transaction is valid. If this bit is clear, then the entire transaction (stage of the pipeline) can be ignored. If this bit is set, then the transaction represented in the pipeline was a valid memory transaction in progress and must be recovered (or aborted) by the exception handler.

Each stage in the memory pipeline has a corresponding data and address register. When the DMTx register indicates that the transaction was a store (**st** or **xmem** instruction), then the corresponding DMDx register contains the data to be stored. The corresponding DMAx registers contain the effective logical address generated by the instruction.

Data in the data unit shadow register (DMD2–DMD0) is only valid if the corresponding transaction is a valid store operation. Therefore, when operating in the master/checker mode, the programmer should store these registers to memory only when the pipeline stage is for a valid store operation.

31 … 0
DATA

DMD0, DMD1, AND DMD2 — **cr**9, **cr**12, and **cr**15

31 … 2	1	0
ADDRESS	0	0

DMA0, DMA1, AND DMA 2 — **cr**10, **cr**13, and **cr**16

6.7.3.2 DATA ACCESS EXCEPTION RECOVERY. The data access exception handler should only be entered if the valid bit is set for stage 0 of the pipeline. The exception handler must first repair the cause of the fault. Then each stage must be examined for pending transactions; pending transactions must be retried by the exception handler before returning from the exception. If a fault occurs while retrying the transactions, it is properly nested.

To process a data access exception, the data access exception handler normally performs the following steps (see Figure 6-5):

1. Saves the execution context from the control registers into memory. This context should include the the EPSR, the shadow instruction pointers, the SSBR, and the appropriate data unit control registers.

2. Once the context is saved, enables shadowing by clearing the SFRZ bit (bit 0) in the PSR.

3. Determines and corrects the cause of the exception. For example, if the exception was caused by a page fault, the requested memory page must be read in from memory. If the exception was caused by a privilege violation, a write protection violation, or a nonexistent memory fault, the exception handler may abort the memory transaction that caused the exception (and the task that attempted it). Otherwise, the exception handler must retry the pending memory transactions that were in the data unit pipeline.

4. Emulates the memory access instructions in the pipeline using the information in the saved memory access registers. As listed above, the transaction registers contain the information needed for recreating the instruction. The data for storage (DMDx) must be loaded when applicable into a general-purpose register. The effective logical address (DMAx) must be loaded into another general-purpose register (the original address operands are not needed). If the operation is a byte or half-word transaction, address bits 1 and 0 must be inserted appropriately into the general-purpose register containing the address.

   The instructions that emulate pending memory transactions can use the indexed form of addressing with **r0** as one of the source operands or the immediate index form. The instructions can use the general-purpose register containing the effective logical address (loaded above) as one source operand and **r0** (which contains 0) as the other operand or an immediate value of zero for the other operand. Therefore, the effective logical address indexed by zero results in the required effective address. When a load or **xmem** instruction is emulated, the appropriate bits of the SSBR (possibly saved in memory as part of the context) must also be cleared. Step 4 should be repeated for all valid data unit instructions in progress.

5. Freezes shadowing by setting the SFRZ bit (bit 0) in the PSR and restores the saved EPSR and shadow instruction pointers to their corresponding control registers. Shadowing must be frozen for the shadow registers to be loaded without corruption.

6. Executes an **rte** instruction to return control to the task that encountered the exception. The instructions pointed to by the SNIP and SFIP are fetched from memory again; the value in the SXIP is discarded.

Figure 6-5 shows the general flow of a data access exception handler.

Figure 6-6 shows how pending transactions should be handled, and Figure 6-7 shows an example of how load and store instructions can be emulated in the data access exception handler. Instructions can be emulated in software by table lookup. Each store, load, and

xmem in the table operates on a fixed supervisor register, and the result is moved into the proper place in the user register file. If the user's byte ordering differs from the supervisor's byte ordering, the supervisor temporarily must change its byte ordering.

NOTE

The values shown in italics in the figures refer to the copies of these registers saved in memory for the exception.

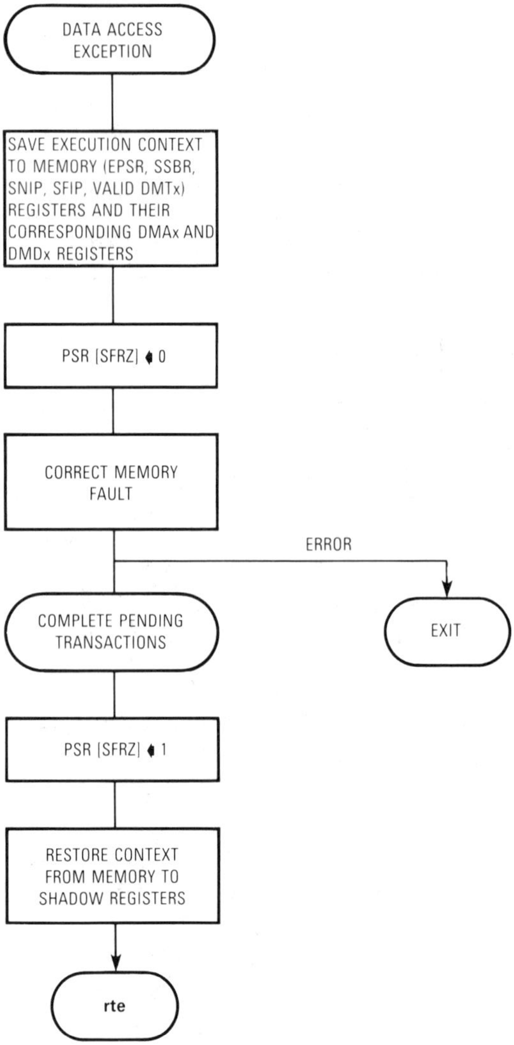

Figure 6-5. Data Access Exception

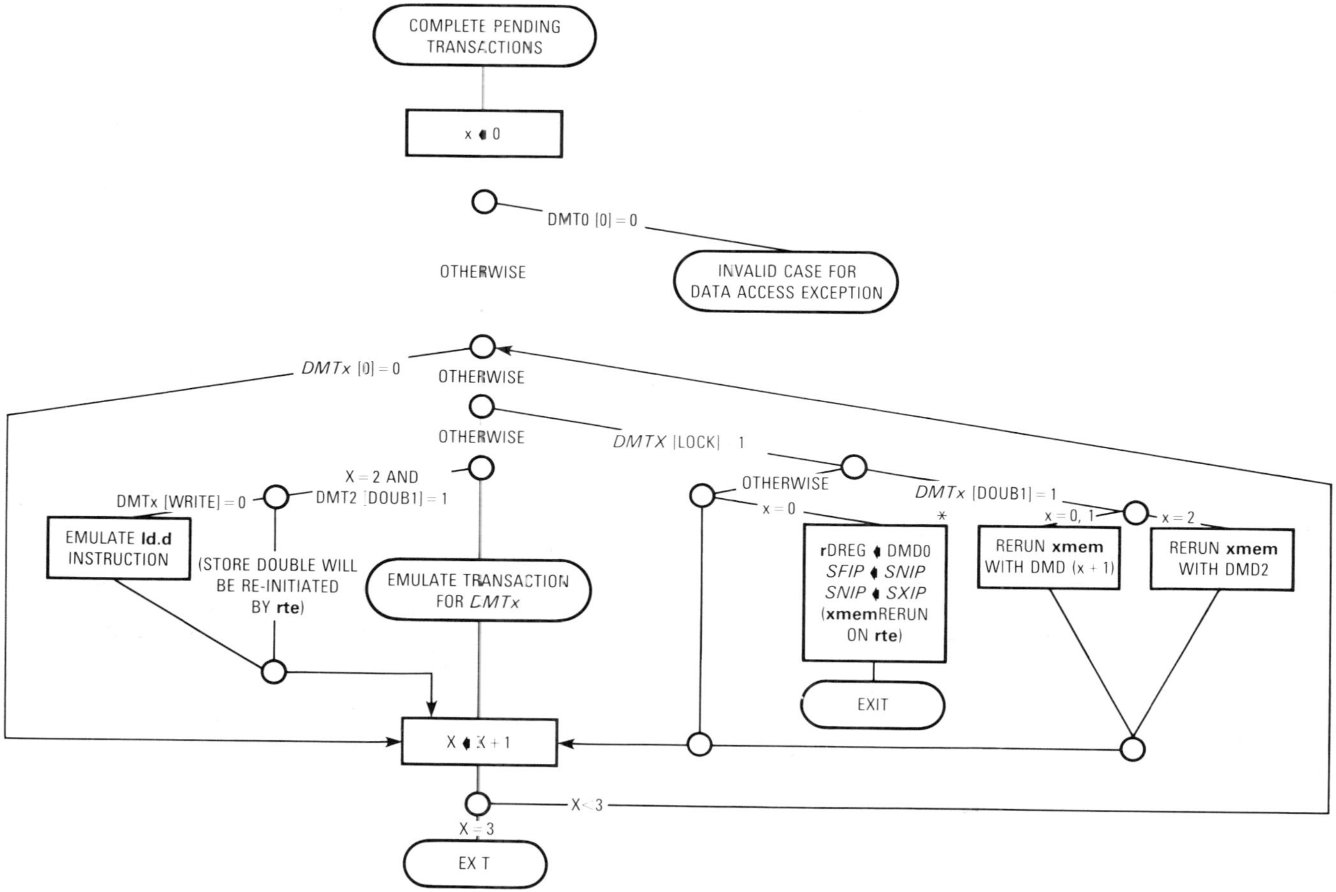

*This step recovers a fault on the store operation of an **xmem** only if the processor is guaranteed to be synchronized (i.e., **xmem** instruction followed by a trap); otherwise, this case is unrecoverable.

Figure 6-6. Complete Transaction Flow

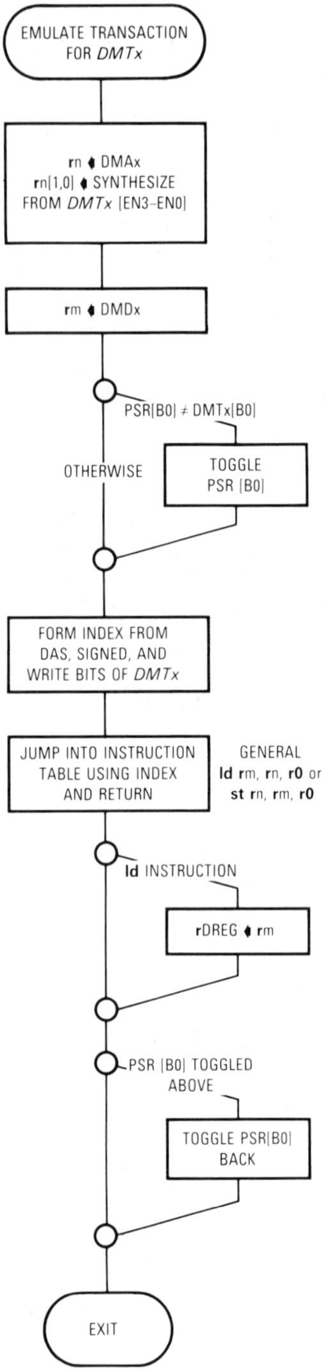

Figure 6-7. Emulate Transaction DMTx Flow

6

If an imprecise exception occurs while in the middle of issuing a store double instruction, the first half of the store double may be seen by the memory system before the exception is recognized. When returning from the exception, the entire store double will be re-executed. The first half of the store double may get sent to the memory system multiple times. Store double should not be used for I/O devices. ***Both store and load doubles are not guaranteed to be atomic operations in any way.***

Some additional considerations apply to the **xmem** instruction (see Figure 6-6). This instruction results in two separate memory accesses, a load followed by a store. Depending on the system hardware, the exception may occur on either of these accesses, or an exception may occur while the two **xmem** accesses are in other stages of the data unit pipeline.

If the load access of the **xmem** instruction is at stage 0 (caused the exception) or stage 1 (aborted when the fault occurred), the store access follows the load access in the pipeline, and the entire **xmem** can be rerun in the handler.

If the system hardware allows the store access of an **xmem** instruction to fault, the software must ensure that the MC88100 is synchronized following the **xmem**, in order to recover from this condition. When the store access of an **xmem** is in stage 0 (determined by DMT0[LOCK] set and DMT0[DOUB1] clear), the load completed successfully but the store encountered the exception. The **xmem** instruction must then be recreated from the stage 0 registers (DMT0, DMD0, and DMA0), and the load access of the **xmem** instruction must be repeated. The instruction pointers can be used to back up the instruction pipeline so that the **rte** instruction causes the **xmem** to execute again from the beginning. If the **xmem** instruction was followed by a trap instruction, the SXIP is guaranteed to point to the **xmem** instruction. Otherwise, this condition is unrecoverable.

If the exception occurs while the load access is in stage 2, then the store access is not in the pipeline. However, all of the information needed to reconstruct the **xmem** instruction can be taken from the stage 2 registers (DMT2, DMD2, and DMA2).

6.8 FPU EXCEPTION PROCESSING

The FPU generates precise and imprecise exceptions. The exception types and actions are governed by the IEEE 754 standard. The floating-point exceptions use two exception vectors, one for precise and one for imprecise.

When a floating-point precise or imprecise exception occurs, the instruction unit saves the execution context (instruction pointers, scoreboard, etc.) to the shadow and exception-time registers, and then branches to the appropriate exception vector. In addition, the specific information needed for handling the exception is stored in the FPU control registers.

The information in the FPU control registers pertains only to the instruction that caused the exception. As part of exception processing, the MC88100 disables the FPU and purges the instruction that caused the exception from the FPU pipelines. All other FPU instructions in progress remain in the FPU and are frozen.

The MC88100 requires software support to comply with the IEEE 754 standard because the floating-point exception handlers are responsible for performing the default operation when an exception occurs. More detailed information about the default operations for exceptions can be found in the IEEE 754 standard.

Users can supply exception handlers that replace or pre-empt the Motorola-supplied exception handlers. Each exception handler must correct or otherwise process the exception condition, again in conformance with the IEEE 754 standard.

The MC88100 branches to the precise or imprecise exception handler for a variety of conditions. Not all of these conditions are exceptions according to the IEEE 754 standard, but the MC88100 completes the operation in the exception handler software. An example of an operation completed in software is arithmetic operations with infinity.

6.8.1 FPU Exception Processing Registers

The FPU contains 11 control registers. Registers **fcr0–fcr8** contain exception information such as the exception type, the source operands and results, and the instruction that caused the exception. These registers are accessible only in supervisor mode. Registers **fcr62** and **fcr63** are used to enable user-supplied exception handler software and to report exception causes in user mode. These two registers are not privileged; they can be accessed in supervisor or user mode. Table 6-6 shows the FPU control registers.

Table 6-6. Floating-Point Control Registers

Register Number	Acronym	Name
fcr0	FPECR	Floating-Point Exception Cause Register
fcr1	FPHS1	FP Source 1 Operand High Register
fcr2	FPLS1	FP Source 1 Operand Low Register
fcr3	FPHS2	FP Source 2 Operand High Register
fcr4	FPLS2	FP Source 2 Operand Low Register
fcr5	FPPT	FP Precise Operation Type Register
fcr6	FPRH	FP Results High Register
fcr7	FPRL	FP Results Low Register
fcr8	FPIT	FP Imprecise Operation Type Register
fcr62	FPSR	FP User Status Register
fcr63	FPCR	FP User Control Register

The **fcr6–fcr8** registers are only valid for imprecise exceptions; **fcr1–fcr5** are only valid for precise and integer-divide error exceptions. As with the general control registers, reserved fields return zeros on reads and are not affected by writes.

6.8.1.1 FLOATING-POINT EXCEPTION CAUSE REGISTER (FPECR). This register is updated by the MC88100 to indicate the cause of a floating-point exception. Bits 7–3 correspond to the precise exceptions, and bits 2–0 correspond to the imprecise exceptions. When a precise exception occurs, bits 2–0 are undefined. When an exception occurs, more than one bit may be set. If FUNIMP is set, all other FPECR bits are undefined. This register has read/write access. The FPECR is configured by hardware to indicate the exception that occurred.

31–8	7	6	5	4	3	2	1	0
0 0 0 0 0 0 0 0 0 0 0 0 0 0 0 0 0 0 0 0 0 0 0 0	FIOV	FUNIMP	FPRV	FROP	FDVZ	FUNF	FOVF	FINX

FPECR **fcr0**

Bits 31–8 — Reserved
Always contain zero; not guaranteed to be zeros in future implementations.

FIOV — Floating-Point Integer Overflow
When set, the precise exception was caused by a conversion to integer overflow.

FUNIMP — Floating-Point Unimplemented
When set, the precise exception was caused by an unimplemented floating-point instruction.

FPRV — Floating-Point Privilege Violation
When set, the precise exception was caused by a privilege violation of a floating-point instruction. This occurs during user-mode accesses to any floating-point control register except the FPSR and FPCR.

FROP — Floating-Point Reserved Operand
When set, the precise exception was caused by floating-point reserved operand check logic (infinity, NAN, or denormalized).

FDVZ — Floating-Point Divide-by-Zero
When set, the precise exception was caused by floating-point divide-by-zero.

FUNF — Floating-Point Underflow
When set, the imprecise exception was caused by floating-point underflow. This bit is undefined for precise exceptions.

FOVF — Floating-Point Overflow
When set, the imprecise exception was caused by floating-point overflow. This bit is undefined for precise exceptions.

FINX — Floating-Point Inexact
When set, the floating-point inexact condition existed for the result that caused an exception. This bit may be set even if the exception was caused by overflow or underflow. This bit is undefined for precise exceptions.

When a precise exception is caused by accessing the FPU while it is disabled, the FPECR does not contain valid information.

6.8.1.2 FLOATING-POINT STATUS REGISTER (FPSR). This register indicates the types of IEEE 754 exceptions that occurred in the FPU. This register is set by software to indicate the exception that occurred (except for the inexact bit, which can be set by hardware or software). Bits in this register are set by the default software operation (in Motorola's exception handlers). This register can be accessed by user exception handler software. This register has read/write access.

31 … 5	4	3	2	1	0
0 0 0 0 0 0 0 0 0 0 0 0 0 0 0 0 0 0 0 0 0 0 0 0 0 0 0	AFINV	AFDVZ	AFUNF	AFOVF	AFINX

FPSR **fcr62**

Bits 31–5 — Reserved
Always contain zero; not guaranteed to be zeros in future implementations.

AFINV — Accumulated Invalid Operation Flag
Set by software when an IEEE 754 invalid operation exception occurs. Cleared explicitly by software.

AFDVZ — Accumulated Divide-by-Zero Flag
Set by software when an IEEE 754 divide-by-zero exception occurs and the user exception handler is disabled. Cleared explicitly by software.

AFUNF — Accumulated Underflow Flag
Set by software when an IEEE 754 underflow exception occurs. Cleared explicitly by software.

AFOVF — Accumulated Overflow Flag
Set by software when IEEE 754 overflow exception occurs. Cleared explicitly by software.

AFINX — Accumulated Inexact Flag
Set by the MC88100 when an IEEE 754 inexact exception occurs and the user exception handler is disabled. This bit may also be set by software. Cleared explicitly by software.

NOTE

AFINX is the only bit set by either the hardware or software. All other bits are set only by software exception handlers.

6.8.1.3 FLOATING-POINT CONTROL REGISTER (FPCR). This register is used to specify the desired rounding mode and to specify which floating-point exceptions the user-supplied exception handlers are to process. This register has read/write access. This register is set by software to enable user exception handler routines.

31 … 15	15 14	13 … 5	4	3	2	1	0
0 0 0 0 0 0 0 0 0 0 0 0 0 0 0 0	RM	0 0 0 0 0 0 0 0 0	EFINV	EFDVZ	EFUNF	EFOVF	EFINX

FPCR **fcr63**

Bits 31–16, 13–5 — Reserved

Always contain zero; not guaranteed to be zeros in future implementations.

RM — Rounding Mode

- 00 — Round to nearest
- 01 — Round toward zero
- 10 — Round toward negative infinity
- 11 — Round toward positive infinity

EFINV — Enable Invalid Operation Handler

- 0 — Disable invalid operation user exception handler
- 1 — Enable invalid operation user exception handler

EFDVZ — Enable Divide-by-Zero Handler

- 0 — Disable divide-by-zero user exception handler
- 1 — Enable divide-by-zero user exception handler

EFUNF — Enable Underflow Handler

- 0 — Disable underflow user exception handler
- 1 — Enable underflow user exception handler

EFOVF — Enable Overflow Handler

- 0 — Disable overflow user exception handler
- 1 — Enable overflow user exception handler

EFINX — Enable Inexact Handler

If EFINX is clear, the MC88100 performs the default exception handling without vectoring.

- 0 — Disable inexact user exception handler
- 1 — Enable inexact user exception handler

NOTE

EFINX and RM are the only bits used by the hardware. All other bits are used only by software exception handlers.

6.8.1.4 FLOATING-POINT SOURCE 1 OPERAND HIGH REGISTER (FPHS1). This register contains the sign, exponent, and the high-order 20 bits of a single-precision source 1 operand or the upper word of a double-precision operand. It is undefined for integer values. This register is read only.

31	30 ... 20	19 ... 0
SIGN	EXPONENT	HIGH-ORDER 20 BITS OF MANTISSA

FPHS1 **fcr1**

Bit 31 — Source 1 Operand Sign Bit
This field is undefined for an integer-divide error exception.

Bits 30–20 — Exponent
The source 1 operand exponent (for single-precision operands, the exponent is sign extended). This field is undefined for an integer-divide error exception.

Bits 19–0 — Mantissa
High-order 20 bits of the mantissa, excluding the hidden bit. This field contains all zeros for an integer-divide error exception.

6.8.1.5 FLOATING-POINT SOURCE 1 OPERAND LOW REGISTER (FPLS1). This register contains the three low-order bits of a single-precision source 1 operand, the low-order word of a double-precision source 1 operand, or the integer operand for integer divide instructions when a floating-point precise exception occurs. This register is read only.

31 ... 0
LOW-ORDER BITS OF MANTISSA OR INTEGER OPERAND

Bits 31–0 — Low-Order Bits of Manitissa or Integer Operand
For double-precision operands, the low-order 32 bits of the source 1 operand. For single-precision operands, the low-order 3 bits of the source 1 operand followed by 29 trailing zeros. For integers, the 32-bit source 1 integer.

6.8.1.6 FLOATING-POINT SOURCE 2 OPERAND HIGH REGISTER (FPHS2). This register contains the sign, exponent, and the high-order 20 bits of a single-precision source 2 operand or the upper word of a double-precision operand. It is undefined for integer values. This register is read only.

31	30 ... 20	19 ... 0
SIGN	EXPONENT	HIGH-ORDER 20 BITS OF MANTISSA

FPHS2 **fcr3**

Bit 31 — Source 2 Operand Sign Bit
This field is undefined for integer operand.

Bits 30–20 — Exponent
The source 2 operand exponent (for single-precision operands, the exponent is sign-extended); undefined for integer operand.

Bits 19–0 — Mantissa
High-order 20 bits of the mantissa excluding the hidden bit; undefined for integer operand.

6.8.1.7 FLOATING-POINT SOURCE 2 OPERAND LOW REGISTER (FPLS2). This register contains the three low-order bits of a single-precision source 2 operand, the low-order word of a double-precision source 2 operand, or the integer operand for integer divide and convert instructions when a floating-point precise exception occurs. This register is read only.

6

31 — 0
LOW-ORDER BITS OF MANTISSA OR INTEGER OPERAND

FPLS2 **fcr4**

Bits 31–0 — Low-order Bits of Mantissa or Integer Operand
For double-precision operands, the low-order 32 bits of the source 2 operand. For single-precision operands, the low-order 3 bits of the source 2 operand followed by 29 trailing zeros. For integer operation, the 32-bit source 2 integer.

6.8.1.8 FLOATING-POINT PRECISE OPERATION TYPE REGISTER (FPPT). This register contains opcode and destination register number for the floating-point instruction that caused the exception. FPPT is undefined for integer multiply instructions. This register is read only.

31 — 16	15 — 5	4 — 0
0 0 0 0 0 0 0 0 0 0 0 0 0 0 0 0	OPERATION	DEST

FPPT **fcr5**

Bits 31–16 — Reserved
Always contain zero; not guaranteed to be zeros in future implementations.

Bits 15–5 — Operation

Bits 15–5 of the instruction that caused the exception. This includes a 5-bit opcode and three 2-bit size fields. The upper bit of each size field is cleared. The size fields are:

Bits 10–9 — Source 1 Operand Size
- 00 — Single precision
- 01 — Double precision

Bits 8–7 — Source 2 Operand Size
- 00 — Single precision
- 01 — Double precision

Bits 6–5 — Destination Size
- 00 — Single precision
- 01 — Double precision

Bits 4–0 — Destination

The destination register number.

6.8.1.9 FLOATING-POINT IMPRECISE OPERATION TYPE REGISTER (FPIT). This register contains information on the instruction that caused an imprecise exception and indicates which user-supplied exception handlers were enabled (by software) when the instruction was initiated. This register is read only.

31–20	19–16	15–11	10	9	8	7	6	5	4–0
RESEXP	0 0 0 0	OPCODE	DESTSIZ	EFINV	EFDVZ	EFUNF	EFOVR	EFINX	DEST

FPIT **fcr8**

RESEXP — Result Exponent

The 12-bit result exponent formed by taking the 8-bit (single-precision) or the 11-bit (double-precision) exponent, then complementing and extending the most significant bit to 12 bits. This representation of the exponent is equivalent to the unbiased exponent minus one. Refer to **SECTION 2 PROGRAMMING MODEL** for floating-point representations.

Bits 19–16 — Reserved

Always contain zero; not guaranteed to be zeros in future implementations.

OPCODE — The 5-bit operation code, bits 15-11 of the instruction.

DESTSIZ — Destination Size

The value of this bit is determined from bit 5 of the instruction.
- 0 — Single-precision destination operand
- 1 — Double-precision destination operand

EFINV — Enable Invalid Operation Handler
- 0 — Invalid operation user exception handler disabled
- 1 — Invalid operation user exception handler enabled
- (Taken from the FPCR at the time the instruction is initiated)

EFDVZ — Enable Divide-by-Zero Handler
- 0 — Divide-by-zero user exception handler disabled
- 1 — Divide-by-zero user exception handler enabled
- (Taken from the FPCR at the time the instruction is initiated)

EFUNF — Enable Underflow Handler
- 0 — Underflow user exception handler disabled
- 1 — Underflow user exception handler enabled
- (Taken from the FPCR at the time the instruction is initiated)

EFOVF — Enable Overflow Handler
- 0 — Overflow user exception handler disabled
- 1 — Overflow user exception handler enabled
- (Taken from the FPCR at the time the instruction is initiated)

EFINX — Enable Inexact Handler
- 0 — Inexact user exception handler disabled
- 1 — Inexact user exception handler enabled
- (Taken from the FPCR at the time the instruction is initiated)

DEST — Destination Register Number

6.8.1.10 FLOATING-POINT RESULT HIGH REGISTER (FPRH). This register contains status information and the high-order 21 bits (including the hidden bit) of the partial result that was computed at the time of the exception. An exception handler may use the contents of the FPRH and FPRL registers to generate a result. For example, in the case of an underflow, the value in the FPRH and FPRL registers may be modified to a value that can be represented by the MC88100. This register is read only.

31	30 29	28	27	26	25	24			21	20 0
SIGN	RNDMODE	GUARD	ROUND	STICKY	ADDONE	0	0	0	0	HIGH-ORDER BITS OF MANTISSA

FPRH **fcr6**

SIGN — Result Sign

RNDMODE — Rounding Mode Used for this Result:
- 00 — Round to nearest
- 01 — Round towards zero
- 10 — Round towards negative infinity
- 11 — Round towards positive infinity
- (Taken from the FPCR at the time the instruction is initiated)

GUARD — Guard Bit for the Result

ROUND — Round Bit for the Result

STICKY — Sticky Bit for the Result

ADDONE — Add One
Set if the result mantissa was rounded by logically adding one

Bits 24–21 — Reserved
Always contain zero; not guaranteed to be zeros in future implementations.

Bits 20–0 — High-Order Bits of Mantissa
The high-order 21 bits of the result mantissa (including the hidden bit). If the result is an integer, these bits are invalid.

6.8.1.11 FLOATING-POINT RESULT LOW REGISTER (FPRL). This register contains the low-order 32 bits of the partial result that was computed at the time of the exception. An exception handler may use the contents of the FPRH and FPRL registers to generate a result. For example, in the case of an overflow, the value in the FPRH and FPRL registers may be truncated to a value that can be represented by the MC88100. This register is read only.

31–0
LOW-ORDER BITS OF MANTISSA

Bits 31–0 — Low-Order Bits of Mantissa (DP)
For a double-precision result, the low-order 32 bits of the result. For integers and precise exceptions, it is undefined.

31	30	29	28–0
			UNDEFINED

Bits 31–29 — Low-Order Bits of Mantissa (SP)
For single-precision result, the low-order three bits of the result; the remaining 29 bits of this register are undefined. For integers and precise exceptions, it is undefined.

6.8.2 Floating-Point Exception Processing Effects

A bit is set in the FPECR whenever the MC88100 branches to a floating-point exception vector due to an exception condition. The MC88100 then checks the corresponding bit in the FPCR to see if a user handler is enabled. The relationship of the bits in these registers is defined by the IEEE 754 standard and is shown in Figure 6-8.

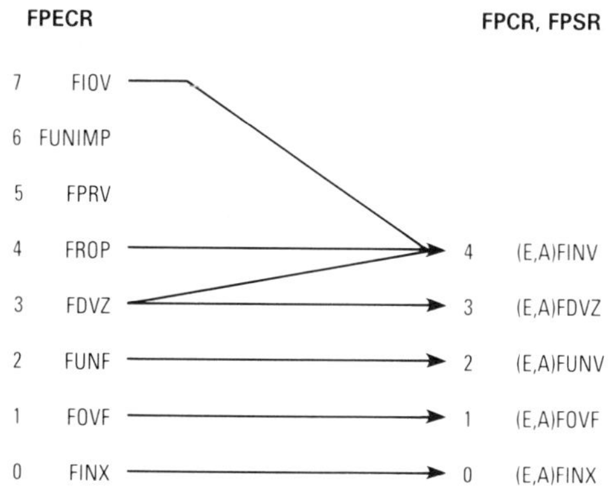

Figure 6-8. Floating-point Exception Register Bit Relationships

When a floating-point exception occurs, the FPU performs the following actions:

1. Signals the instruction unit that the exception occurred.
2. Sets the appropriate bit in the FPECR to indicate the exception type.
3. Sets the SFUD1 bit in the PSR, which disables the FPU and freezes the floating-point execution pipelines. When the execution pipelines are frozen, the internal registers are frozen. The information saved within the FPU as part of the context depends on whether the exception is precise or imprecise.
4. The floating-point instruction that caused the exception is removed from the FPU pipeline.

Once the instruction unit is signaled and recognizes the exception, the integer unit performs the standard exception processing. The exact cause of the exception is determined when the exception handler reads the FPECR.

When the FPU is frozen, the control registers can be read or written, but no floating-point instructions (except **fldcr**, **fstcr**, and **fxcr**) can be executed. However, only the instruction that caused the exception is affected by the exception. When the FPU is restarted (at the end of exception processing by an **rte** instruction), the instructions in the pipeline resume execution. The instruction that caused the exception must be completed (or discarded) by software. Scoreboard bits for destination registers of an instruction that causes a floating-point exception may be set, and the handler must clear them appropriately.

6.8.3 Integer-Divide Error Exception

This exception occurs when the divisor of a **div** or **divu** instruction is zero or when either operand is negative in a **div** instruction. The SXIP points to the instruction that caused the exception. The destination register is not changed, but the scoreboard bit is set for the destination register.

Integer divide instructions are performed by the FPU. When an integer-divide error exception occurs, floating-point control registers **fcr2**, **fcr4**, and **fcr5** contain information pertinent to the integer-divide error exception. Registers **fcr2** and **fcr4** contain the source operands, and **fcr5** contains the destination register number. The source operands can be examined by the exception handler to determine the cause of the exception (zero divisor or negative operand). The data in **fcr5** can be used to clear the destination register scoreboard bit. The opcode in **fcr5** can not determine which instruction (**div** or **divu**) caused the exception.

6.8.4 Floating-Point Precise Exceptions (Vector Offset $390)

The following paragraphs provide information on each of the conditions that cause a floating-point precise exception. In all of the cases, the scoreboard bit(s) for the destination register(s) are set before the exception is recognized. The exception handler must clear those bits as part of exception handling; since the instruction that caused the precise exception is not executed, no result will be written to the general-purpose registers.

6.8.4.1 FPU DISABLED. This exception occurs when the FPU is disabled and an instruction is dispatched to the FPU. The unit is disabled when SFD1 (bit 3) bit of the PSR is set. The instructions executed by the FPU include all floating-point arithmetic and convert instructions and the integer multiply and divide instructions.

6

When this exception occurs, the FPECR does **not** contain valid information. The exception handler must test the SFD1 (bit 3) of the value saved in EPSR to determine if the FPU was disabled. If this bit is set, then the exception occurred because the FPU was disabled. If this bit is clear, then the exception handler should read FPECR to determine the cause of the exception.

6.8.4.2 FLOATING-POINT INTEGER CONVERSION OVERFLOW. This exception occurs when a conversion to integer is attempted for a floating-point number that **may** be too large in magnitude after rounding to be represented as an integer. Overflow occurs when the floating-point exponent is greater than or equal to 30 since rounding may cause overflow. The exception handler must determine if overflow will really occur. If not, the correct result should be placed in the destination. If the operation results in a true overflow, then the operation is considered invalid by the IEEE standard. The largest-magnitude positive integer that can be represented by the MC88100 is $2^{31}-1$; the largest-magnitude negative integer that can be represented by the MC88100 is -2^{31}.

This exception causes the FIOV bit (bit 7) of the FPECR to be set by the hardware. The EFINV bit (bit 4) of the FPCR must be set by software to enable the user exception handler (if supplied). If this exception handler is not enabled, software sets the AFINV bit (bit 4) of the FPSR, and a NAN is written to the destination. This exception, the floating-point reserved operand exception, and the floating-point divide-by-zero exception all use the same bit in the FPCR and FPSR to indicate an invalid operation; the bits in the FPECR can be used to determine which exception occurred.

6.8.4.3 FLOATING-POINT UNIMPLEMENTED OPCODE. This exception is caused by an attempt to execute an unimplemented instruction in the floating-point opcode class. This allows unimplemented functions, such as the trigonometric functions, to be emulated in software. If the instruction is truly an invalid operation, the exception handler can discard the instruction or otherwise process the exception.

When this exception occurs, the FUNIMP bit (bit 6) of the FPECR is set by hardware. The unimplemented instruction has no effect on the scoreboard. There is no user exception handler for this exception.

6.8.4.4 FLOATING-POINT PRIVILEGE VIOLATION. This exception occurs when a **fldcr**, **fstcr**, or **fxcr** instruction is executed while the processor is in user mode, and the addressed register is not the FPSR or FPCR. When this exception occurs, the FPRV bit (bit 4) in the FPECR is set by hardware. There is no user exception handler for this exception.

6.8.4.5 FLOATING-POINT RESERVED OPERAND. This exception occurs when a reserved operand is detected.

6

This exception causes the FROP bit (bit 4) of the FPECR to be set by the hardware. The handling of this exception depends on the exact operands and operation. The default exception handler provides results for most operations performed on reserved operands, in accordance with the IEEE standard. The exception allows processing of IEEE reserved operands (infinity, NAN, denorm) by the exception handler. If the operation is invalid according to the IEEE standard, then the user exception handler is invoked (if supplied). The EFINV bit (bit 4) of the FPCR must be set by software to enable the user exception handler. Regardless of whether the user exception handler is supplied or enabled, the AFINV bit (bit 4) of the FPSR is set by the default operation.

This exception, the floating-point integer conversion overflow exception, and the floating-point divide-by-zero exception all use the same bit in the FPCR and FPSR to signal an invalid operation.

6.8.4.6 FLOATING-POINT DIVIDE-BY-ZERO. This exception occurs when division by zero is detected. When this exception occurs, the FDVZ bit (bit 3) of the FPECR is set by hardware. The bits used in the FPCR and FPSR depend on the value of the divisor. If the divisor is zero (i.e., 0/0), then the EFINV bit (bit 4) of the FPCR must be set by software to enable the user exception handler (if supplied). Regardless of whether this exception handler is enabled, the AFINV bit (bit 4) of the FPSR will be set by software when the exception occurs. If the numerator is non-zero, then the EFDVZ bit (bit 3) of the FPCR must be set by software to enable the user exception handler (if supplied). Regardless of whether this exception handler is not enabled, the AFDVZ bit (bit 3) of the FPSR is set by the default operation.

6.8.5 Floating-Point Imprecise Exceptions (Vector Offset $398)

The following paragraphs provide information on each of the conditions that cause a floating-point imprecise exception. After an imprecise exception occurs, the scoreboard bit for the second register of a double-precision result remains set. The scoreboard bit for a single-precision result and for the first register of a double-precision result are cleared, and the destination register is overwritten.

6.8.5.1 FLOATING-POINT UNDERFLOW. This exception occurs when the result of a floating-point operation is too small to be represented as a normalized floating-point number ("tinniness"). The processor takes the floating-point imprecise exception and sets FUNF (bit 2) in the FPECR. The expanded exponent, the result mantissa, sign, and exponent, and the instruction opcode are available in FPU control registers when this exception occurs.

How the exception handler processes the exception depends on the setting of the EFUNF bit (bit 2) in the FPCR. If the EFUNF bit is set, then control passes to the underflow user handler routine. If the EFUNF bit is not set (no user handler routine), then the default handler checks for loss of accuracy. Loss of accuracy occurs either when the hardware detects that significant bits were lost due to rounding (inexact result) or when software detects that significant bits were lost when the result is denormalized (denormalization loss). If a loss of accuracy exists, AFUNF (bit 2) and AFINX (bit 0) in the FPSR are set, then the exception handler checks if a user handler is available for the inexact exception (bit 0 in the FPCR set). If there is, then control passes to the inexact exception user handler. Finally, if there is no underflow user exception handler and there is no loss of accuracy or if there is loss of accuracy but no inexact exception handler, then the exception handler performs the default operation, writing the denormalized result to the destination register. Once the result is generated, the default exception handler performs an **rte** instruction to return the processor to normal operation.

Figure 6-9 illustrates the exception handling algorithm for the floating-point underflow exception.

6.8.5.2 FLOATING-POINT OVERFLOW. This exception indicates that the rounded result of a floating-point calculation exceeds the magnitude of the largest finite number that can be represented in the destination format. The processor takes the floating-point imprecise exception and sets the FOVF bit (bit 1) in the FPECR. The expanded exponent, the sign, and the mantissa of the result and the instruction opcode are available in the FPU control registers.

How the exception handler processes this exception depends on the setting of the EFOVF bit (bit 1) in the FPCR. If the EFOVF bit is set, then control passes to the user handler routine. If the EFOVF bit is not set (no user handler routine), then the AFOVF bit (bit 1) is set in the FPSR, and the exception handler checks if there is a user handler for the inexact exception (bit 0 in the FPCR set). If there is a user exception handler, then control passes

6

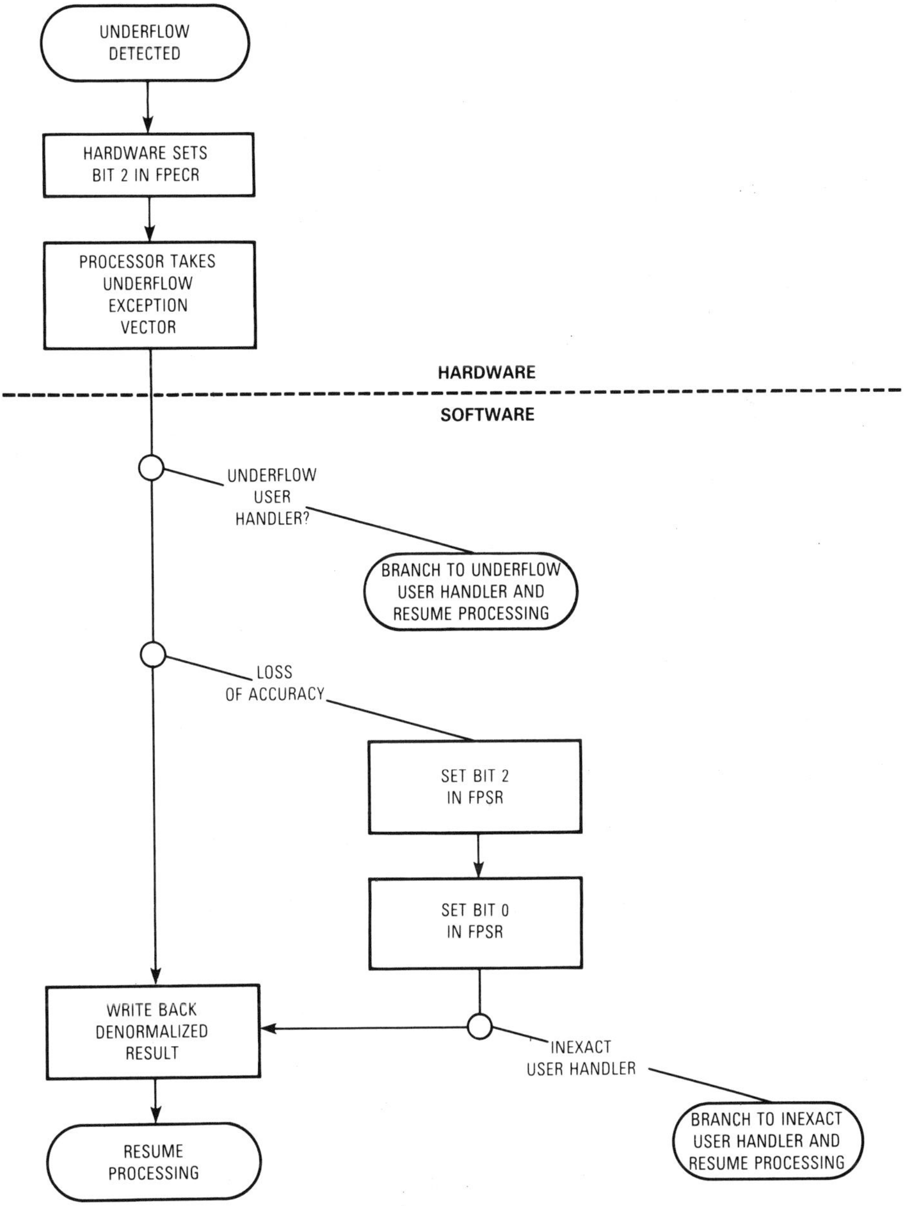

Figure 6-9. Floating-Point Underflow Algorithm

to it. If there is not, then the AFINX bit (bit 0) is set in the FPSR and the exception is ignored. The exception handler performs the default operation, writing the properly signed, largest finite number or infinity, depending on the rounding mode in effect.

Figure 6-10 illustrates the exception handling algorithm for the floating-point overflow exception.

6.8.5.3 FLOATING-POINT INEXACT.

This exception occurs when rounding the result of a calculation to the destination format has caused a loss of accuracy to occur. That is, digits were lost when the result was rounded. The result of the operation, the guard, round, and sticky bits, and whether or not the result was rounded by adding one are available in the FPU control registers. If significant bits will be lost in the result when an underflow exception occurs, the inexact exception also occurs. If an overflow exception occurs and the overflow user exception handler enable bit is not set, the inexact exception is taken.

When this exception is signaled by the FPU, the processor checks the value of the EFINX bit (bit 0) in the FPCR. If EFINX is set, then the floating-point imprecise exception is taken, and bit 0 of the FPECR is set by hardware. If EFINX is clear, then exception processing does not occur, but the AFINX bit (bit 0) is set in the FPSR. EFINX is set or cleared by software, meaning that the floating-point inexact exception can be enabled or disabled by software. This is the only floating-point exception that is enabled under hardware control.

6

The floating-point inexact exception bits also have a bearing on the underflow and overflow exceptions, as described in the previous paragraphs and illustrations.

6.8.6 FPU Control Register Summary

When a floating-point exception occurs, the FPU control registers take on defined values or enter specific states. Table 6-7 lists the control register states after an exception is recognized when the MC88100 branches to the exception handler.

6.9 RESET (VECTOR OFFSET $0)

Processor reset is a special exception case that occurs when the $\overline{\text{RST}}$ signal is detected as asserted. Reset exception processing forces the MC88100 into a predefined initial state. No pending exceptions or partially executed instructions are retained. The VBR is cleared, and the PSR and bus signals enter predefined states.

The exception vector for reset is vector zero, which resides at logical memory address zero because the VBR is forced to zero. The $\overline{\text{RST}}$ signal cannot be masked.

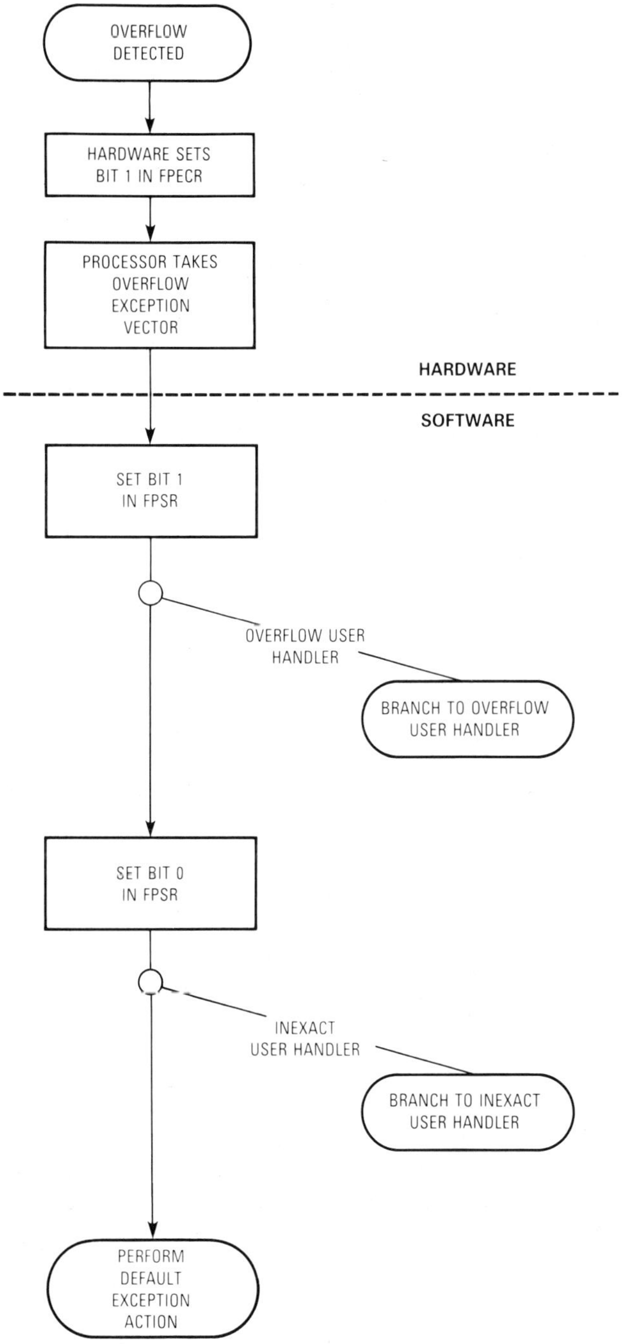

Figure 6-10. Floating-Point Overflow Exception Handling

Table 6-7. FPU Control Register States after an Exception

Register	State
Floating-Point Exception Cause Register	Bit(s) set to indicate which exception occurred; all other bits clear. If multiple bits are set, they are prioritized from 7 to 0.
Floating-Point Source Operand Registers	For precise exceptions, this register contains the source operands of the instruction that caused the exception. For imprecise exceptions, these registers are undefined.
Floating-Point Precise Operation Type Register	For precise exceptions, this register contains the opcode, size fields, and destination register number of the instruction that caused the exception. For imprecise exceptions, this register is undefined.
Floating-Point Imprecise Control Register	For imprecise exceptions, this register contains the opcode, destination size and register number, result exponent, and user exception handler information. For precise exceptions, this register is undefined.
Floating-Point Result Registers	For imprecise exceptions, these registers contain the partial result and information on the rounding used on the result. For precise exceptions, these registers are undefined.
Floating-Point User Status and User Control Registers	Contain the values in effect before the exception occurred.

Table 6-8 shows the contents of the MC88100 registers after reset. The general-purpose registers and the shadow scoreboard are not initialized; the shadow scoreboard must be cleared by the reset handler routine.

Table 6-8. Register States After Reset

Register	State
Processor Status Register	Bit 31 set, bits 9–0 set, all others cleared ($800003FF)
Trap PSR	Undefined
Scoreboard	Cleared
Shadow Scoreboard	Undefined
Instruction Pointers	FIP = reset vector address (physical address 0); V bits in NIP and XIP are cleared.
Shadow Instruction Pointers	Undefined
Vector Base Register	Cleared
Data Memory Transaction Registers	Bit 0 clear (no-op pattern); remaining bits are undefined.
Data Memory Address Registers	Undefined
Memory Data Registers	Undefined
General-Purpose Registers	Undefined
Internal Temporary Registers	Undefined
FPU Control Registers	FPECR, FPCR, FPSR cleared; all others undefined.

6.10 ERROR EXCEPTION (VECTOR OFFSET $50)

The error exception occurs when shadowing is frozen (SFRZ bit set in PSR) and an exception other than a trap instruction occurs. When shadowing is frozen, the shadow registers do

not contain valid data because they are not updated from the time that they were frozen. Shadowing is only frozen by the MC88100 when an exception occurs, so the error exception usually occurs when the MC88100 has not finished processing a first exception and a second exception occurs (catastrophic condition). The error exception provides the means to terminate processing when catastrophic situations are encountered.

Since the shadow registers are not updated when shadowing is frozen, the processor context needed for recovering from an error exception is not available. Therefore, the exception handler for the error exception should halt the processor or initiate a reset operation. The error handler routine can initialize the processor and resume execution at address $0. Alternately, external circuitry can perform a reset operation.

The error exception also occurs when the MC88100 encounters a fault while fetching an exception vector. (i.e., an exception vector could not be fetched). If the error exception vector then cannot be fetched successfully (e.g., memory error on the vector table page), then the error exception cannot be taken. This situation causes the MC88100 to loop on fetching the error exception vector. This loop can only be exited by a processor reset.

To eliminate error exceptions, the exception handlers for all other exceptions should either execute without exception (including interrupts, which should be masked) or they should enable shadowing. The processor must not encounter an exception during the time that shadowing is frozen (i.e., the vector table and the beginning of all exception handlers should be locked into main memory and should always be accessible). **6.4 EXCEPTION PROCESSING** describes how shadowing may be enabled in an exception handler.

SECTION 7
INSTRUCTION EXECUTION TIMING

This section describes the instruction execution time for the MC88100 instructions and the factors that affect the timing. The execution and operation times are presented as guidelines, because exact timing of all possible circumstances cannot be listed. This guideline approach is used since exact execution time, either instruction or operation, is highly dependent on memory speed and other variables in the system. Refer to **7.1 GENERAL TIMING CONSIDERATIONS** for list of guidelines. The remainder of this section describes the detailed timing information for instruction prefetches and then the execution times for all instructions through their respective execution units. Example timings are included for exception processing, scoreboard holds, writeback priorities, and processor stalls due to wait cycles on the buses. An example of instruction arrangement, which shows concurrent execution and various register dependencies, is provided to illustrate some timing interactions. Refer to **SECTION 5 BUS OPERATIONS** for more information regarding bus operation timing. Instruction mnemonics used in this section can be identified by referring to **SECTION 3 ADDRESSING MODES AND INSTRUCTION SET**.

7.1 GENERAL TIMING CONSIDERATIONS

The MC88100 is designed to minimize average instruction execution time. Logical, bit field, and most integer instructions execute in one clock period. Other instructions, such as the integer multiply and divide instructions require more than one clock period. These types of instructions can effectively realize single-cycle execution by using the various features of the MC88100, such as pipelining and feed forwarding. In general, instruction execution is accomplished in four parts (see Figure 7-1): prefetch, decode, execute, and writeback. The instruction prefetch time consists of the address and reply phases on the instruction P bus to fetch the instruction from program space. The prefetch time is not included in the instruction execution timing tables and can be calculated separately (see **7.3 INSTRUCTION PREFETCH TIMING**). The decode time is overlapped with the reply phase of the prefetch and usually does not contribute to overall latency. The total instruction execution time corresponds to the execution phase. The writeback time is the time required to return results to the register file and does not contribute to overall execution time if writeback slots are available when required (some instructions do not require a writeback). Instructions are prefetched and executed concurrently with previous instructions, which produces an overlap period (see Figure 7-1) that is measured in clock periods. This overlap decreases the overall execution time for a sequence of instructions.

The following general guidelines should be used when programming to implement code scheduling that produces the most efficient software for the MC88100 processor. The main

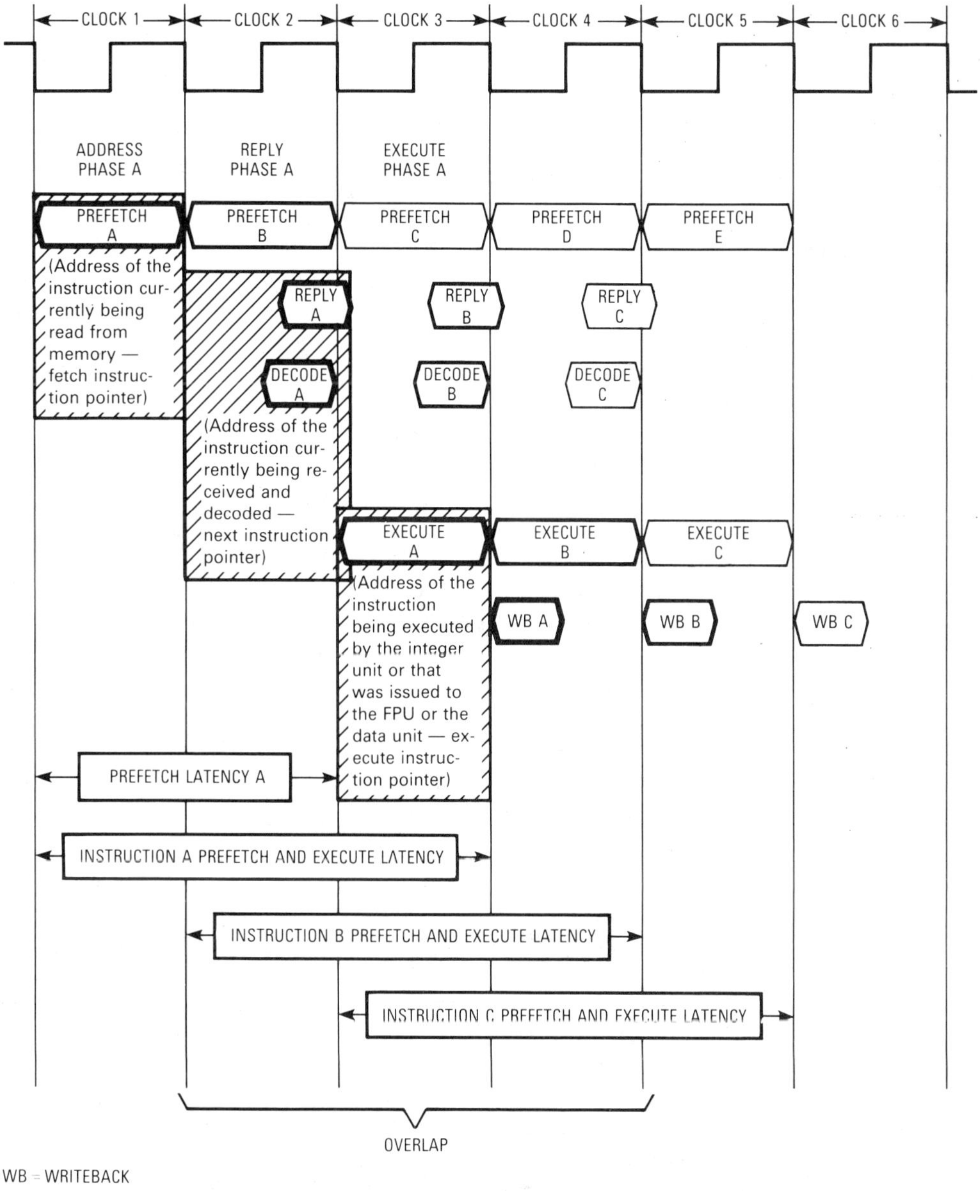

Figure 7-1. Instruction Prefetch and Execute Timing

objective when optimizing software for maximum efficiency is to avoid stalling the instruction unit pipeline. The remainder of this section is dedicated to explaining the reasons for following these guidelines, providing more detailed information on the meaning of certain dependencies, and optimizing performance.

1. Minimize register dependencies between multicycle instructions and subsequent instructions that use their results. Total execution latency must be used as the minimum amount of time from the dispatch of the multicycle instructions until the time a subsequent instruction that uses the result should be dispatched. In general, execute load and FPU instructions for as many clock periods as possible before their results are required.
2. Consecutive data-unit instructions should be scheduled in groups of three or less. If wait cycles are inserted by the responding memory device, the instruction pipeline can continue execution of other instructions.
3. Delayed branching should be used as often as possible. This can be maximized by implementing conditional branch loops such as counting down to zero and checking the value of the count with the **bcnd** instruction. If a useful instruction within the loop cannot be placed in the delay slot, the first instruction at the target address could be moved to the delay slot.
4. Do not follow **ld.d** and **xmem** instructions with a data-unit instruction as this causes the instruction pipeline to stall for one clock.
5. Double-times-double multiply instructions followed by other floating-point instructions should be spaced by at least two other nonfloating-point instructions.
6. Divide instructions should not be immediately followed by other nonmultiply FPU instructions. These types of operations should be spaced by at least 34, 26, and 55 clock periods for single-precision, integer, and double-precision divide results, respectively.
7. Critical-time loops should schedule the writeback slots so that instructions that waive the writeback slot are strategically mixed with instructions that require a deferred writeback.

NOTE

To maximize performance, the hardware should be designed to minimize wait cycles on both the instruction P bus and the data P bus.

7.2 CONCURRENT EXECUTION

The concurrent execution units and the multiple bus design of the MC88100 can perform up to five types of operations in parallel, which allows the performance to approach single-cycle execution. These operations are:

- Access program memory
- Execute an arithmetic, logical, or bit-field instruction
- Access data memory
- Execute nonmultiply floating-point instructions or an integer divide instruction
- Execute floating-point or integer multiply instructions

Figure 7-2 shows an example timing diagram in which all units are operating in parallel. In addition, the floating-point, data, and instruction units are pipelined and capable of completing an operation in every clock period. These units are staged as follows:

- Each of the five floating-point add pipeline stages can contain a floating-point add, subtract, or convert instruction.
- The six-stage floating-point multiplication pipeline may contain up to six multiplication instructions.
- Each of the three data memory unit stages may contain a data access instruction.
- The instruction unit's prefetch mechanism maintains two outstanding code accesses.

Knowledge about the operation of these stages can be utilized by code-scheduling software to fully exploit the high level of hardware execution concurrency, thus maximizing MC88100 instruction throughput.

7.3 INSTRUCTION PREFETCH TIMING

7

As described in **SECTION 5 BUS OPERATIONS**, the instruction unit of the MC88100 prefetches instructions in advance of their execution (via the instruction P bus) and executes flow-control instructions. The instruction unit maintains three instruction pointers: the execute instruction pointer (XIP), which contains the address of the instruction most recently dispatched for execution, the next instruction pointer (NIP), and the fetch instruction pointer (FIP), which correspond to the next two instructions in the instruction stream. The instruction P bus is a pipelined bus and processes the reply phase of one access (corresponding to the NIP) simultaneously with the address phase for the next access (which corresponds to FIP). When a change of flow occurs (e.g., a branch is taken), the NIP and FIP are updated appropriately, and instructions are prefetched from the appropriate target address.

7.3.1 Effective Prefetch Time and Prefetch Latency

The prefetch time for an instruction can be calculated as the total number of clocks from the beginning of the address phase for an instruction access to the end of the reply phase ('prefetch latency' period) for the prefetch (see Figure 7-1). This time is two clocks in a no-wait-cycle environment. However, two accesses are in different stages of prefetch at any given time, and they overlap by one clock, making the 'effective prefetch time' for each access in a sequence only one clock. Therefore, as an arbitrary convention, the address phase of a prefetch is depicted as the 'prefetch' cycle in the figures for this section. Even though the reply phase is also part of the prefetch, it occurs simultaneously with the address phase of the next access, and the second clock is counted as the first clock for the next access. This convention also clearly shows the beginning of an instruction prefetch.

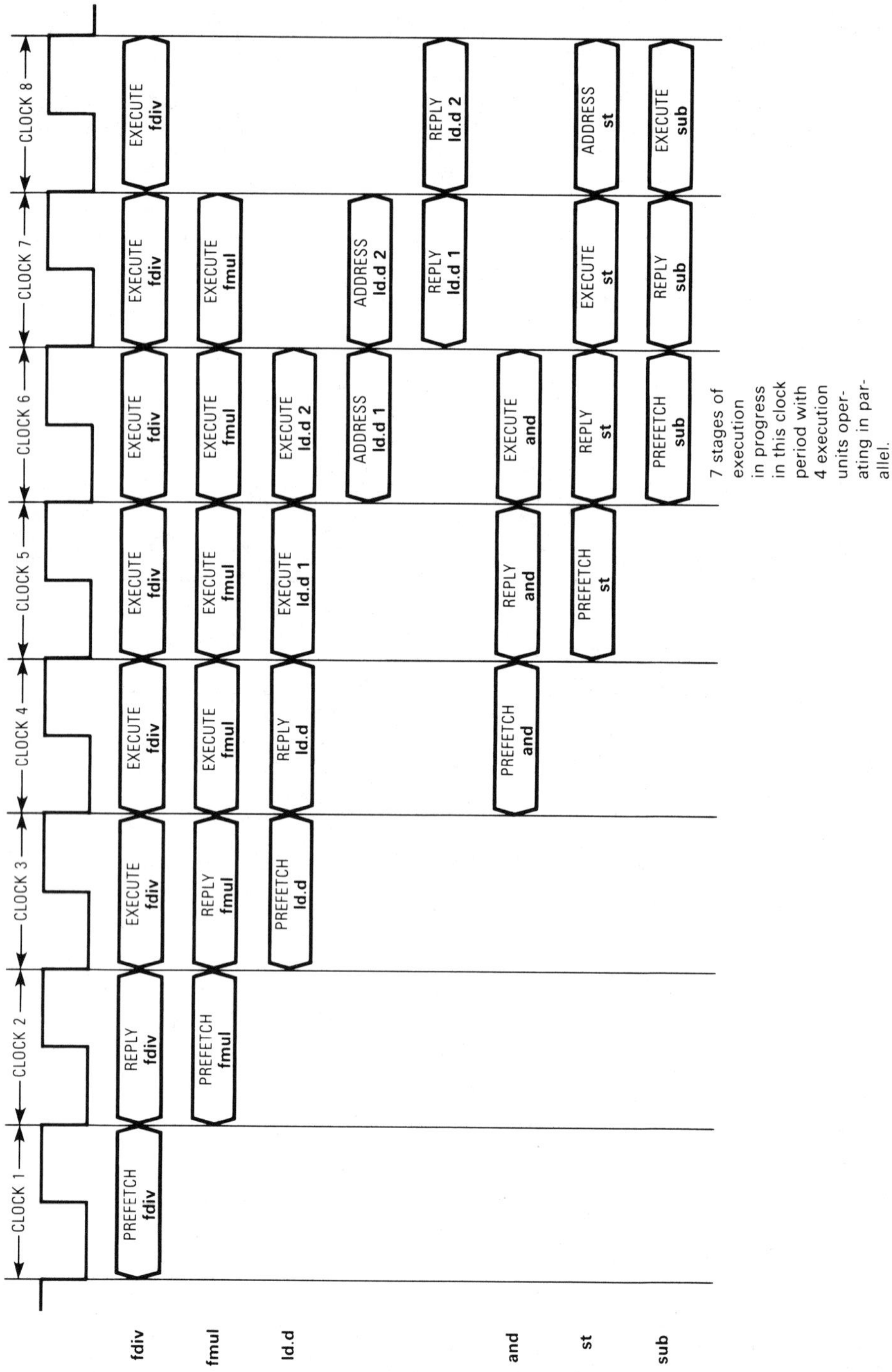

Figure 7-2. Concurrent Execution Example

7

7.3.2 Effects of Instruction P Bus Wait Cycles

Wait cycles in instruction P bus accesses are counted as occurring in the reply phase of the corresponding access. Therefore, as wait cycles are inserted, they are simply added to the one clock of address phase time for a particular prefetch (see Figure 7-3). In Figure 7-3, the effective prefetch time for instruction A is two clocks; whereas, the effective prefetch time for instruction B is only one clock, even though the address phase for B is repeated twice. It is the execution of instruction A that is delayed by the wait cycle, and the prefetch of instruction B does not cause any additional delay. Table 7-1 summarizes the various instruction prefetch times for all MC88100 instructions.

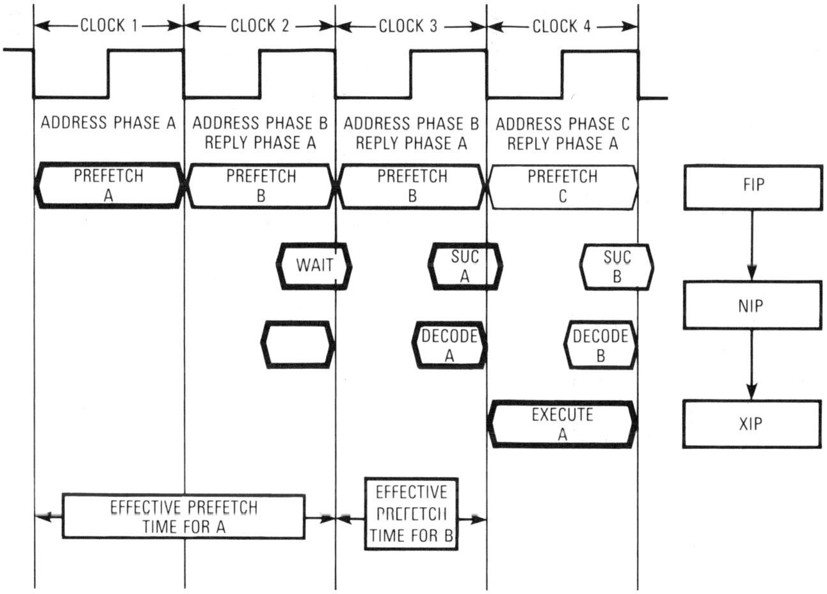

Figure 7-3. Instruction Unit Pipeline (Example)

Table 7-1. Instruction Prefetch Time Summary

Effective Prefetch Time	Prefetch Latency
1 Clock + number of waits	2 Clocks + number of waits

7.3.3 Instruction Decode

All instructions are decoded during the reply phase of the prefetch. For most instructions at the end of the decode time, the scoreboard bits for the source and destination registers are checked. They must all be clear before the instruction is dispatched to the appropriate

execution unit for immediate execution. For floating-point instructions that specify double-precision results, the processor checks the scoreboard bits of both destination registers (**rD** and **rD** + 1) while the instruction is in the decode stage (or both decode stages as in the case of double-precision source operands). If one or more double-precision source operands are specified, the availability of the source operands is checked one at a time (one register checked during each decode stage). For the **st.d** instruction, the scoreboard bits for both the sources and destinations are checked one at a time (the first source and destination are checked during the first decode stage and the second source and destination are checked during the second decode stage).

If the instruction to be executed is a multicycle instruction that can alter the contents of a general-purpose register, the appropriate bits in the scoreboard register (corresponding to the destination register) are set in the clock period after the last stage of instruction decode.

NOTE

The instruction execution times listed throughout the remainder of this section do not include the one clock of effective prefetch time, since it is nearly always overlapped by the execution of other instructions.

7.4 EXECUTION UNIT TIMINGS

After instructions are prefetched, they are either executed by the instruction unit (for the case of flow-control instructions) or dispatched to another on-chip execution unit. The following paragraphs describe the execution of instructions within the four execution units (integer, data, floating-point, and instruction units).

7.4.1 Integer-Unit Instruction Execution

The integer unit instructions, which are the simplest of the MC88100 instruction set, execute in one clock period. Table 7-2 lists the instructions executed by the integer unit and explicitly defines the execution time for each of these instructions as one clock. Figure 7-4 shows the sequencing for a series of integer unit instructions. The writeback time for updating the destination register is not included in the execution time listed because the writeback occurs in parallel with the execution of other instructions and causes no perceivable delay. The **ldcr**, **stcr**, **xcr**, **fldcr**, **fstcr**, and **fxcr** instructions operate entirely within the integer unit and do not initiate any memory accesses. The **stcr** and **fstcr** instructions waive the writeback slot, and the processor can pass it on to another execution unit requesting a writeback slot at that time.

The instructions executed by the integer unit include the integer arithmetic, bit-field, logical, and load/store/exchange control register instructions. The integer multiply and divide (**mul**, **div**, and **divu**) instructions are executed by the FPU and are not listed in Table 7-2. Refer to **7.4.3.2 FPU INSTRUCTION TIMING** for information on these instructions.

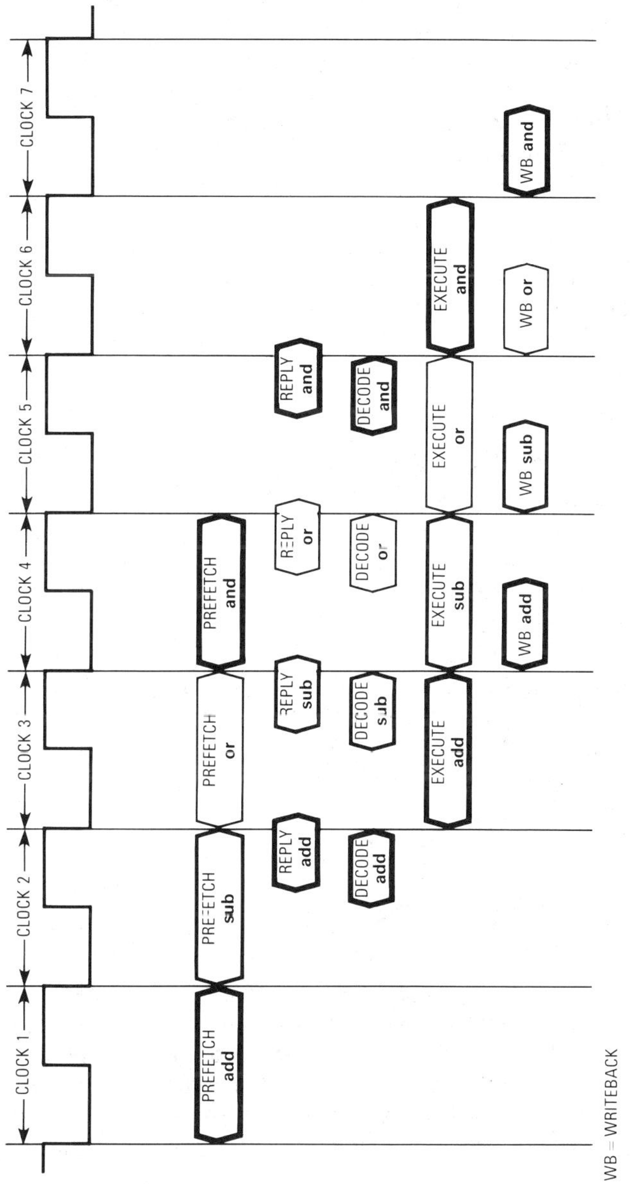

Figure 7-4. Integer-Unit Instruction Execution

Table 7-2. Integer, Bit-Field, Logical, and Control-Register Instruction Execution Timing in Clock Periods

Instruction	Execution Time
Integer	
add	1
addu	1
cmp	1
sub	1
subu	1
Bit Field	
clr	1
ext	1
extu	1
ff0	1
ff1	1
mak	1
rot	1
set	1

Instruction	Execution Time
Logical	
and	1
mask	1
or	1
xor	1
Control Register	
fldcr	1
fstcr	1*
fxcr	1
ldcr	1
stcr	1*
xcr	1

*No writeback slot required for these instructions.

7.4.2 Data Unit Operation

The data unit pipeline has three stages and executes all load, store, and exchange instructions to and from memory. As described in **SECTION 5 BUS OPERATIONS**, the data P bus performs all external data accesses. The data P bus is pipelined like the instruction P bus and can process the address phase of an access simultaneously with the reply phase for the previous access. The three pipeline stages are numbered 2, 1, and 0, and data memory transactions sequence through the stages in that order (2, 1, and then 0).

Stage 2 of the data unit is the address calculation stage and is considered the 'execute' stage for all data unit instructions. Stage 1 of the data unit contains the instruction in the address phase, and stage 0 contains the instruction in the reply phase on the data P bus. Stages 0 and 1 have latches associated with them (referred to as primary and secondary writeback latches, respectively) that can store the results of load operations that are initiated but that cannot writeback to the register file because other instructions are using the destination bus at the time required by the data unit. Figures 7-5 and 7-6 show examples of the data-unit pipeline execution.

The total time required to perform a data unit access is three clock periods, one clock for each stage, assuming no-wait-cycle bus operation. However, as with instruction prefetch operations, the effective execution time is only one clock in many cases because three overlapping operations can be in progress at any one time. Table 7-3 shows the effective execute time for the memory access instructions.

Memory load and exchange instructions set the scoreboard bit for the destination register during the execute phase of the operation. Therefore, the total time to perform the operation may impact average instruction timing. The 'latency' for the execution of a load instruction

7

Table 7-3. Load, Store, and Exchange Memory Instruction Execution Time in Clock Periods

Instruction	Effective Execution Time	Minimum Access Latency
ld.b	1	3+CW
ld.bu	1	3+CW
ld.h	1	3+CW
ld.hu	1	3+CW
ld	1	3+CW
lda	1	No Access
ld.d	1**	4+CW***
st	1	3+CW
st.b	1	3+CW
st.h	1	3+CW
st.d	2*	4+CW***
xmem.b #	1**	4+CW***
xmem #	1**	4+CW***

\# These instructions synchronize the processor so that all previous instructions must complete before the **xmem** executes.
* Includes automatic stall of instruction pipeline.
** Causes data unit to be busy for an additional clock so add one more clock to this number if instruction is followed by another data unit instuction.
*** CW is the total number of wait cycles for both bus transactions.
CW = Number of wait cycles during reply phase on data bus.

7

is the delay from the time the instruction is decoded until the results are available to a subsequent instruction. The latency for a store instruction is the total number of clocks it takes the access to complete.

Although store and **lda** instructions do not return results and do not set the scoreboard bits, they do make use of the writeback phase. The writeback used by store and **lda** instructions follows the execute cycle for address calculation. This is the time in which the source data is fetched from the register file. Because the fetch occurs on the internal destination bus (D bus), no other instruction can write back to the register file at this time.

Memory load and exchange instructions do not use the writeback slot immediately after the execute clock(s); therefore, that writeback slot is available for other execution units. However, these instructions request a writeback slot when the memory access(es) are complete.

7.4.2.1 TOTAL ACCESS LATENCY. The total access latency is dependent on the availability of the processor resources (the data unit pipeline, access to a writeback slot, etc.)

and the number of wait cycles incurred in the reply phases of other accesses as well as the required data access. The pipeline latency can be described as follows:

$$\text{Data Access Latency} = 3 + CW + BW + AW \text{ clocks}$$

where CW, BW, and AW are the wait cycles associated with accesses already in the data pipeline (BW and AW) and the current access (CW). Assuming the data unit pipeline does not stall due to other instructions or causes, the latency is three clocks plus the number of wait cycles incurred by the access as shown in Table 7-3. Data access latency does not include the writeback time for load operations because the writeback may occur simultaneously with the execution of the instruction requiring the result (see **7.5.2 Writeback Priorities and Feed Forwarding**). Figure 7-5 shows the timing associated with memory access latency. Code-scheduling software should consider the access latency for a load operation before issuing an instruction that requires the results from the load.

Wait cycles on the data P bus have four possible effects on total instruction execution. First, they affect the access latency for the execution of the particular instruction with the wait replies. Secondly, they may cause delays in subsequent data unit instructions by causing the data unit pipeline to stall. Thirdly, they may cause the instruction pipeline to stall, delaying the execution of all subsequent instructions. This may occur in the case of a string of data unit instructions awaiting execution when the data unit pipeline is full (three accesses pending) and stalled due to wait cycles on the data P bus. Finally, wait cycles on the data P bus may be an indication that the memory is not responding to the data access quickly. In this case, if instructions are prefetched from the same main memory, prefetches may also be delayed because the long data access prevents the prefetch from accessing the memory when required.

7.4.2.2 MEMORY LOADS, STORES, AND EXCHANGES. Execution time calculations for the **ld.d**, **st.d**, and **xmem** instructions are special cases. Load double (**ld.d**) and **xmem** instructions split into two transactions in the execute phase (stage 2) of the data unit pipeline. Therefore, the effective execute stage time is two clocks if it is followed by another data unit instruction. This creates a stall in the instruction pipeline only if the instruction following the **ld.d** or **xmem** is a data unit instruction. Figure 7-6 shows a timing example of a **ld.d** (A) followed by an **ld.d** (B) instruction. In the sequence shown, **ld.d** (A) causes a stall in the instruction pipeline because **ld.d** (A) resides in stage 2 of the data unit for two clocks. Because the first **ld.d** is still in stage 2, the second **ld.d** cannot advance to the data unit immediately after decode. In addition, the example shows that instruction C is also prevented from advancing to the data unit because the second **ld.d** (B) instruction resides in stage 2 for two clocks. However, if instruction C is not a data unit instruction, the instruction pipeline does not have this additional stall, and instruction C can advance to the appropriate execution unit after decode.

The **st.d** instruction is different from the **ld.d** and **xmem** instructions because it must reside in the decode stage of the instruction pipeline for two clocks. Therefore, it always stalls the instruction pipeline for at least one clock, regardless of the following instruction. Subsequently, the effective execution time for the **st.d** is always two clocks. Additionally, the

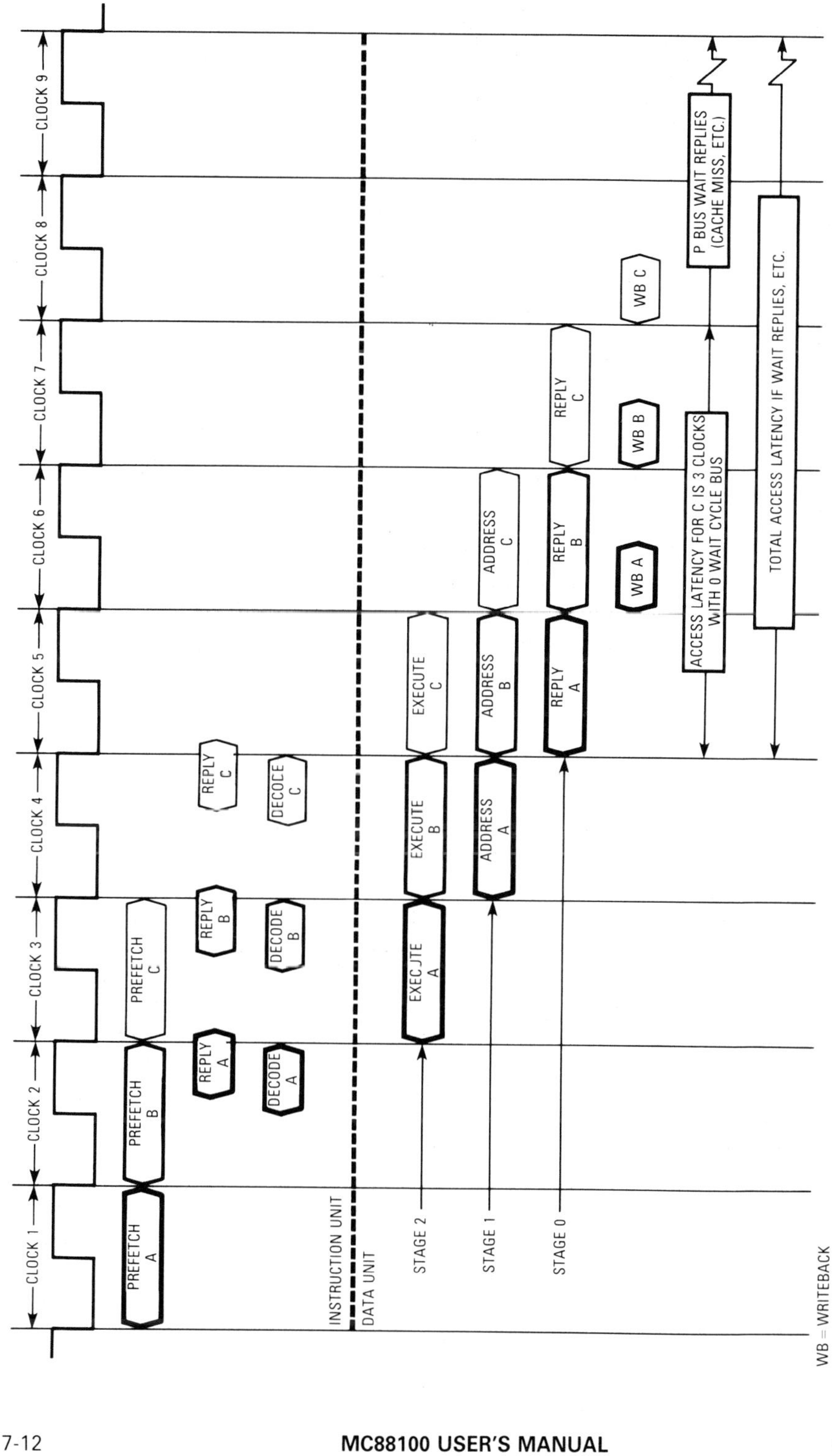

Figure 7-5. P Bus Wait Cycles

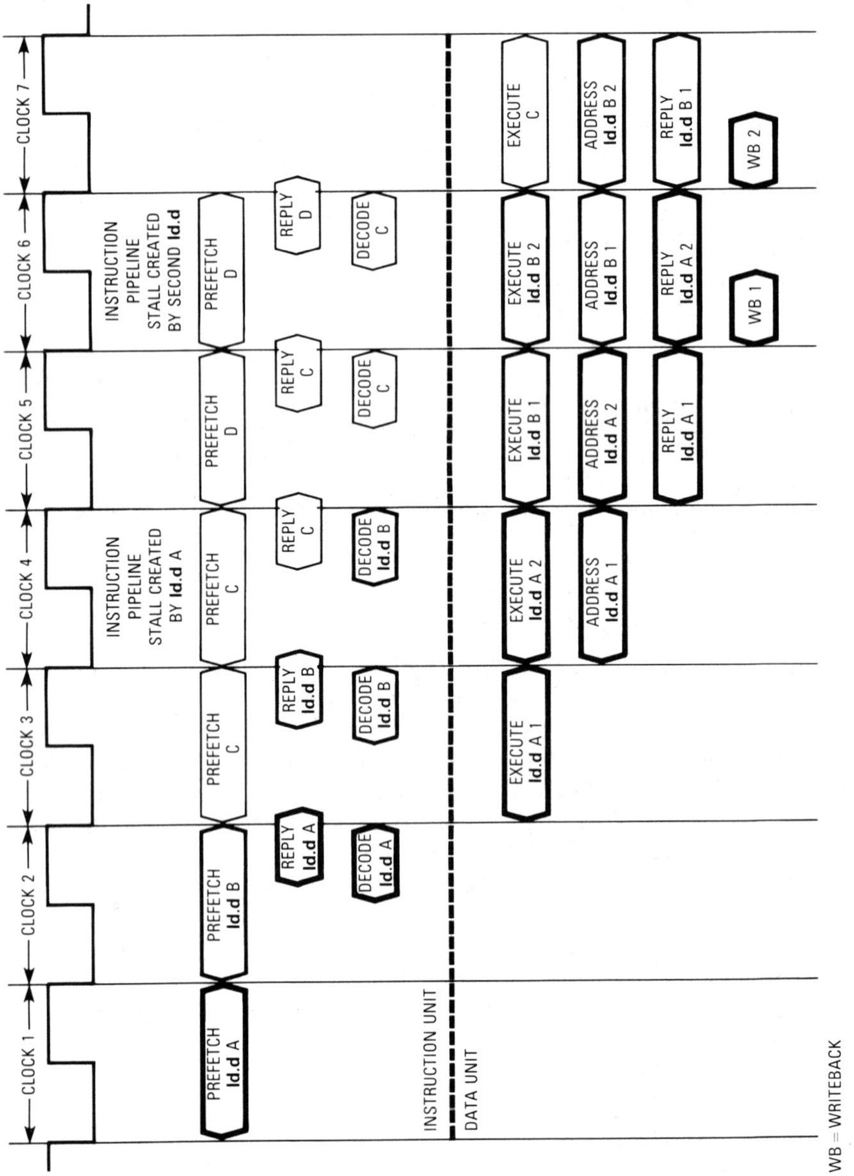

Figure 7-6. ld.d Followed by ld.d Timing (Example)

st.d instructions check the scoreboard bits for the two source registers independently. The first source register scoreboard bit is checked during the first decode clock; the second source register scoreboard bit is checked during the second decode clock. The two halves of the instruction also proceed to the data unit independently. Therefore, the two halves of a **st.d** operation may be separated if the second source register is not available due to a scoreboard hold. In fact, an exception may occur in between the two halves of the store operation, and the handler then must rerun both halves.

Figure 7-7 shows a timing example of a **st.d** followed by a **st** instruction. This example also shows that wait cycles on the data P bus do not necessarily cause additional instruction pipeline stalls. In the example, although the wait cycle causes the data unit to stall, it does not cause additional delay in the execution of instructions A or B, because A and B are not data unit instructions. These instructions can proceed to the appropriate execution unit once the previous instructions have been issued to the data unit.

7.4.3 FPU Instruction Execution

Floating-point instructions require more than one clock period for execution. However, effective single-cycle execution can be realized because of the pipelined architecture of the FPU.

7

A sequence of instructions executed by the FPU that specify single-precision operands (32-bit source and destination) can attain an effective throughput of one instruction per clock period. Instructions that specify one or more double-precision (64-bit) source operands take an additional cycle (in the first stage) to initiate, and can attain a throughput of as little as two clock periods per instruction. Instructions that specify double-precision (64-bit) destinations also require two clock periods to write back to the register file. However, the writeback time is usually not perceivable due to the feed forwarding of the individual 32-bit portions of the result. Although one-to-two clock instruction throughput can be achieved, subsequent instructions that use the results of any multicycle operation must wait until the total execution of the operation is complete.

All instructions executed by the FPU waive the writeback slot that corresponds to the clock period after the first execute clock. Therefore, the writeback slot is available for another execution unit. However, the FPU instructions request a writeback slot when instruction execution is complete.

7.4.3.1 FPU PIPELINE OPERATIONS. The FPU is implemented as two pipelines that share the initial (FP1) and final (FPLAST) stages (see Figure 7-8). Integer and floating-point multiply instructions use the multiply pipeline; all other floating-point instructions and integer divide instructions use the add pipeline. Floating-point instructions sequence through the pipelines at a rate of one clock per stage in most cases. Multiply instructions can operate in parallel with instructions executed by the add pipeline, and up to six multiply operations

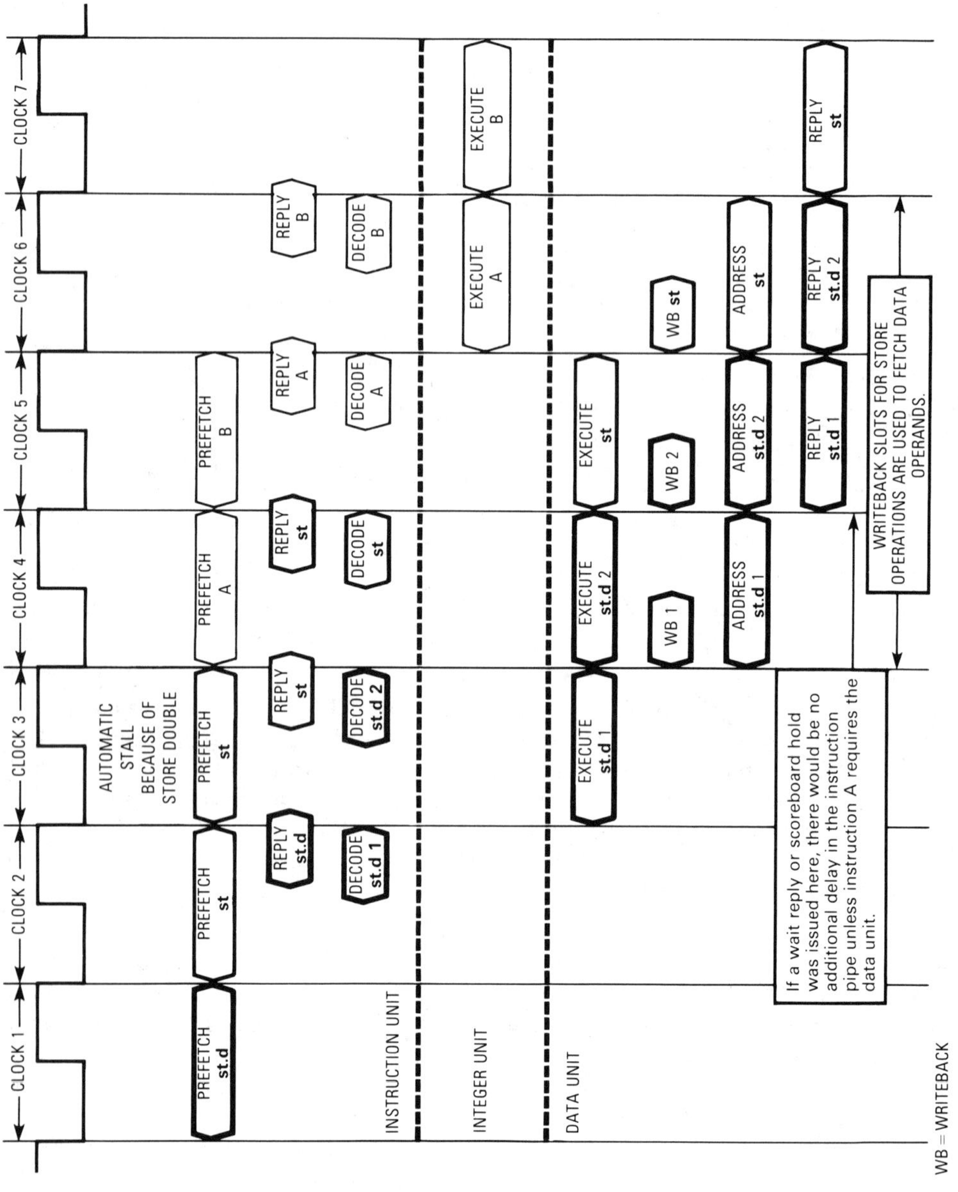

Figure 7-7. Store Double (Followed by Store)

7

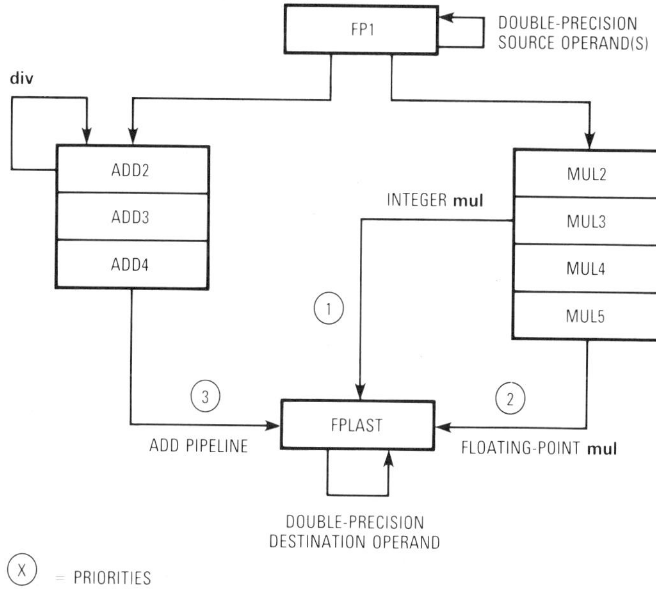

Figure 7-8. FPU Pipeline Stages

7

can be in progress at one time. Alternately, up to five add-pipe floating-point instructions can also execute concurrently.

When a floating-point instruction or integer **mul** or **div** instruction is decoded by the instruction unit, the scoreboard bits for all the sources and all destination registers are checked. When double-precision source operand(s) are specified, the sources are checked one at a time. When the appropriate scoreboard bits are clear, the instruction is loaded into FP1, and the operands are fetched from the register file. During this first execute cycle, the operands are checked for validity and exponents are calculated. Single-precision operands are converted to an internal double-precision format.

If one or both of the source operands are specified as double precision, the instruction remains in FP1 for an additional clock while the second half of the operands are accessed from the register file and additional validity checks are performed (see Figure 7-10). Because the instruction pipeline in the instruction unit maintains the address of the instruction that is being issued to the first execution stage, the instruction unit pipeline can not advance until all source registers specified by a floating-point instruction are available and have been fetched from the register file. Therefore, when double-precision source operands are specified, a one-clock stall is incurred in the instruction pipeline; no other instructions can begin execution while a previous instruction is in the process of fetching source operands. Once all the source registers are fetched, the scoreboard bit(s) for the destination register(s) are set. All precise floating-point exceptions are reported at the end of the one-to-two clock period during which the instruction address resides in the instruction pipeline.

Integer multiply instructions sequence (see Figure 7-8) through stages MUL2 and MUL3 of the multiply pipeline and then proceed to stage FPLAST. The FPLAST stage is shared between all instructions executed by the FPU.

Floating-point multiply instructions sequence (see Figure 7-8) through all four stages of the multiply pipeline. If both the source operands for a floating-point multiply operation are specified as double precision, the floating-point pipeline is also stalled in the FP1 stage for two additional clocks after all source operands are supplied. When the double-times-double multiply instruction is stalled in FP1, no other instructions can be dispatched to the FPU. Figure 7-9 shows the basic timing for a single-precision multiply instruction with a single-precision result. Figure 7-10 shows the equivalent timing for a multiply operation with two double-precision source operands and a double-precision result.

Except for the divide instructions, the sequence through the add pipeline (see Figure 7-8) is the same for all other floating-point unit instructions. The instruction resides in stage FP1 for one or two clocks, depending on the size of the source operands, and then progresses through stages ADD2, ADD3, and ADD4 in one-clock increments. The divide instructions iterate in stage ADD2, and the number of iterations (not including the first clock in stage ADD2) corresponds to 1 + R, where R is the number of bits of precision specified for the result. Therefore, for divides, extra clocks in stage ADD2 equal 1 + R where

R = 24 for a single-precision floating-point result,
R = 32 for a integer result, and
R = 53 for a double-precision floating-point result.

7

While a divide instruction is iterating in stage ADD2, only the add pipeline is stalled. The multiply pipeline can continue to execute instructions. However, if execution of a subsequent add-pipe FPU instruction is attempted, it remains in stage FP1 until the add pipeline advances. This prevents a third floating-point instruction from advancing to the FPU, causing the instruction unit pipeline to stall, and no other instructions may be executed. This type of delay can be avoided by appropriately spacing divide instructions and other instructions that depend on the add pipeline of the FPU.

The FPLAST stage checks for imprecise exceptions caused by floating-point instructions and performs arbitration with the other execution units for a writeback slot to return results to the register file. Because three FPU instructions can be ready to proceed to stage FPLAST at the same time (e.g., **fadd**, integer **mul**, and **fmul**), there is also a priority scheme enforced for the FPLAST stage. The integer multiply path has first priority, followed by the floating-point multiply path, and then the add pipeline (see Figure 7-8).

The writeback for double-precision results requires two cycles through stage FPLAST, one for each register. However, due to feed forwarding, the time through FPLAST does not appear to be greater than one clock except when the result is not used by another floating-point double instruction. The floating-point double instructions can take advantage of feed-forwarding for the second register because they do not use the writeback slot and allow the FPU to receive a writeback slot at that time.

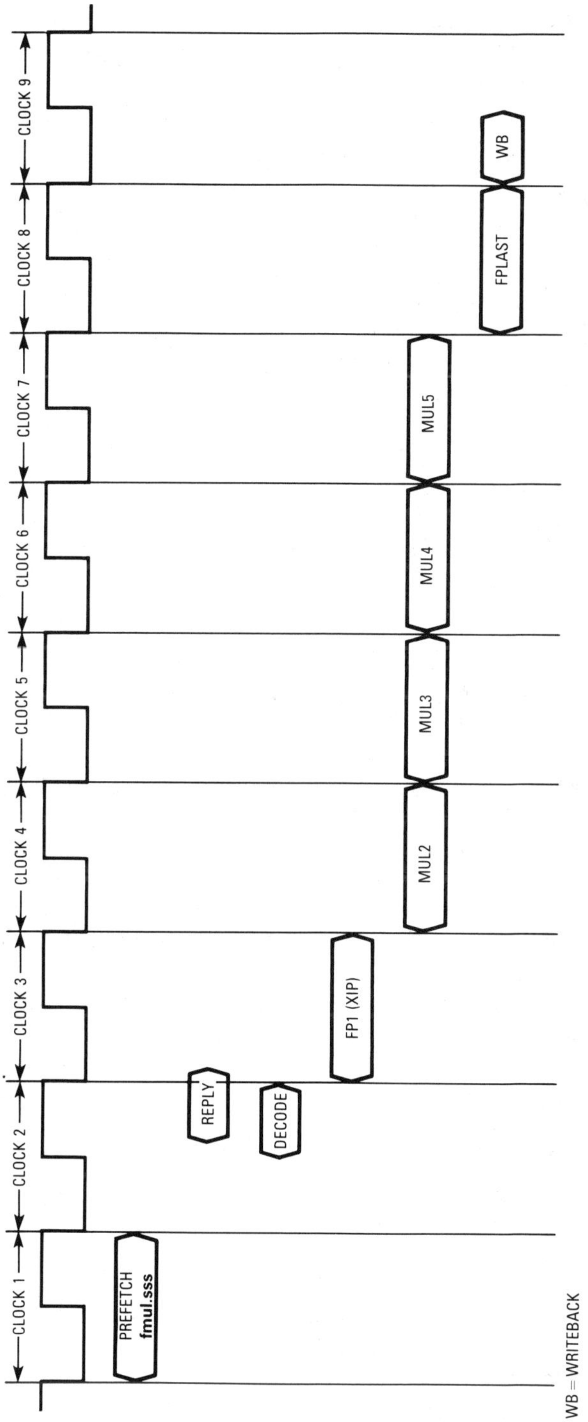

Figure 7-9. FPU Multiply Pipeline

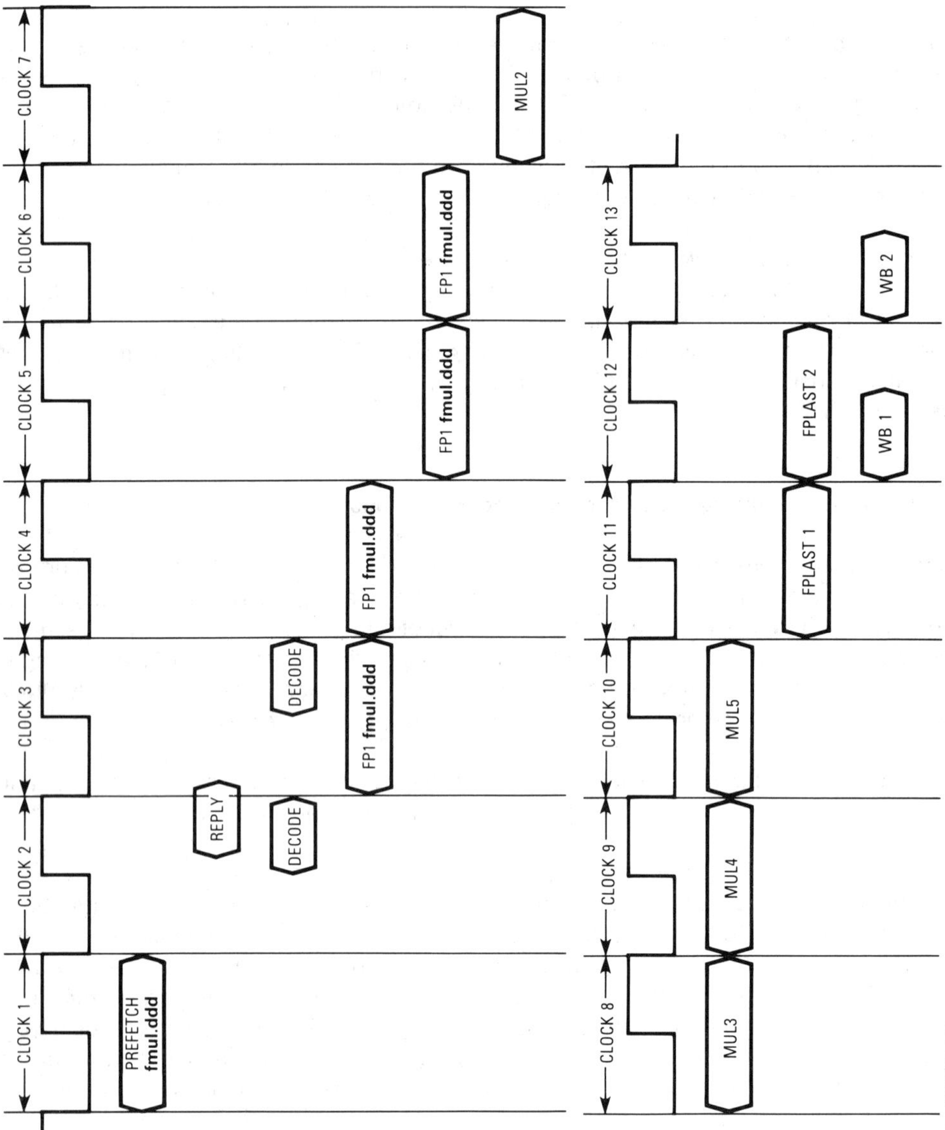

WB = WRITEBACK

Figure 7-10. Double-Precision Multiply

Code-scheduling software can minimize these types of stalls and delays by considering the interdependencies of the floating-point unit pipelines and the other execution units of the MC88100.

7.4.3.2 FPU INSTRUCTION TIMING. In most cases, the timing for a particular code segment of floating-point instructions can be calculated by using the information supplied by the sequencing of instructions through the floating-point pipelines. The summary in Table 7-4 can also be used to calculate instruction execution time. The time listed in the FP1 column corresponds to the amount of delay from the time an FPU instruction is decoded to the time a second FPU instruction can be dispatched to the FPU for execution.

The time in FPLAST is usually not perceived to be greater than one clock; however, the asterisk in the table identifies those instructions that cause two cycles through FPLAST. This second cycle can be seen when a subsequent instruction requires the result that is immediately restored to the second destination register. The total latency column assumes no delays associated with scoreboard holds, writeback priority delays, or pipeline stalls caused by other instructions.

7.4.4 Flow-Control Instruction Execution and Exceptions

7

The instruction unit executes all flow-control instructions by calculating the target address for subsequent instruction execution and appropriately saving the return address for subroutine calls. The **bsr** and **jsr** flow-control instructions save return pointers as a result of their execution and use the writeback slot to update the register file (**r1**) accordingly. However, the writeback time is not included in the execution time because it is not a preceivable delay. All other flow-control instructions waive the writeback slot.

Flow-control instructions are divided into three categories: unconditional, conditional, and trap. Table 7-5 lists the different flow-control instructions and their effective execution times.

When delayed branching is not selected, the unconditional and conditional instructions effectively take two clocks to execute when the branch is taken and one clock when the branch is not taken. For the branch-taken case, the instruction fetched immediately after the branch or jump is not executed, and, although it has already been prefetched, it is discarded. Subsequently, the instruction pipeline is filled with new instructions located at the target address. The following paragraphs provide further explanation on the timing related to branching, delayed branching, and traps processed by the instruction unit.

7.4.4.1 BRANCHING TIMING. Figure 7-11 (a) shows an example code sequence of a conditional branch instruction with no delayed branching followed by an **add** instruction with a **ld** instruction as the target of the branch. Although the **add** instruction is prefetched (before the branch is executed), it is discarded. The example also illustrates the timing

Table 7-6. FPU Instruction Timing Cycles

Instruction	FP1	ADD Pipe	MUL Pipe	FPLAST	Total Latency
fadd.sss	1	3		1	5
fadd.sds, .ssd	2	3		1	6
fadd.dss	1	3		1*	5
fadd.dsd, .dds	2	3		1*	6
fadd.sdd	2	3		1	6
fadd.ddd	2	3		1*	6
fcmp.sss	1	3		1	5
fcmp.sds, .ssd	2	3		1	6
fcmp.sdd	2	3		1	6
		Interations in ADD2			
fdiv.sss	1	3 +25		1	30
fdiv.sds, .ssd	2	3 +25		1	31
fdiv.dss	1	3 +54		1*	59
fdiv.dsd, .dds	2	3 +54		1*	60
fdiv.sdd	2	3 +25		1	31
fdiv.ddd	2	3 +54		1*	60
flt.ss	1	3		1	5
flt.ds	1	3		1*	5
	FP1 Extra (Not in instruction pipe)				
fmul.sss	1 —		4	1	6
fmul.sds, .ssd	2 —		4	1	7
fmul.dss	1 —		4	1*	6
fmul.dsd, .dds	2 —		4	1*	7
fmul.sdd	2 +2		4	1	9
fmul.ddd	2 +2		4	1*	9
fsub.sss	1	3		1	5
fsub.sds, .ssd	2	3		1	6
fsub.dss	1	3		1*	5
fsub.dsd, .dds	2	3		1*	6
fsub.sdd	2	3		1	6
fsub.ddd	2	3		1*	6
int.ss	1	3		1	5
int.sd	2	3		1	6
nint.ss	1	3		1	5
nint.sd	2	3		1	6
trnc.ss	1	3		1	5
trnc.sd	2	3		1	6
		Iterations in ADD2			
div	1	3 +33		1	38
divu	1	3 +33		1	38
mul	1	—	2	1	4

*Add one more clock of effective FPLAST time delay only if the result is used either by a **st.d**, integer instruction, or an instruction that requires the results of a second destination register.

Table 7-5. Flow-Control Instruction Timing in Clock Periods

Instruction	Effective Execution Time	
	Branch/Trap Taken	Branch/Trap Not Taken
Unconditional		
br	2	—
br.n	1	—
bsr	2	—
bsr.n	1	—
jmp	2	—
jmp.n	1	—
jsr	2	—
jsr.n	1	—
Conditional		
bb0	2	1
bb0.n	1	1
bb1	2	1
bb1.n	1	1
bcnd	2	1
bcnd.n	1	1
Trap*		
tb0	3	1
tb1	3	1
tbnd	3	1
tcnd	3	1
rte	3	—
Other Exceptions*	3	—

*The trap instructions, with the exception of **tbnd**, synchronize the processor so that all previous instructions must complete before the trap. Synchronization time must be added to the effective execution time shown in the table.

7

relationship between the execution clocks attributed to the branch instruction and the beginning of the target **ld** instruction prefetch. In reality, these two events do not occur simultaneously as implied in Figure 7-11. The instruction unit performs all address calculations for flow-control instructions during the decode stage for the branch instruction, and the actual execution of the branch occurs in zero clocks. Thus, by the beginning of the next clock (depicted as the first execute phase for the branch), the target address has already been computed, and the address phase for the target instruction prefetch begins. However, no other instructions can be dispatched for execution at this time. This 'dead' clock is therefore attributed as one of the execution clocks for the branch. The second clock for the branch-taken case is caused by the reply phase necessary for the prefetch of the target instruction. Again, no other instruction can be dispatched for execution during this clock if delayed branching is not used.

7.4.4.2 DELAYED BRANCH TIMING. Delayed branching is a feature that can be used for more efficient execution of instruction sequences when branches are taken. Delayed branching (invoked by specifying the **.n** option in a flow-control instruction) instructs the processor to execute the instruction that sequentially follows the branch instruction before the branch target instruction. The next sequential instruction has already been prefetched

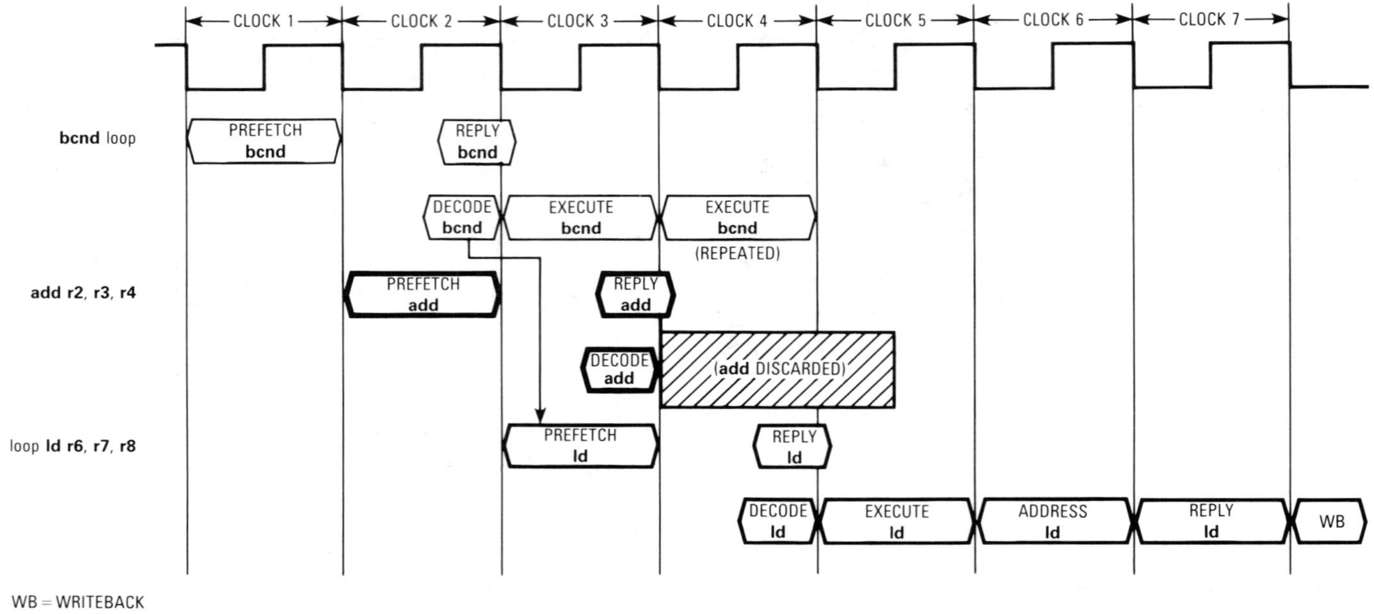

(a) Branch Taken (Delayed Branching — Not Selected)

Figure 7-11. Branch Example (Sheet 1 of 2)

7

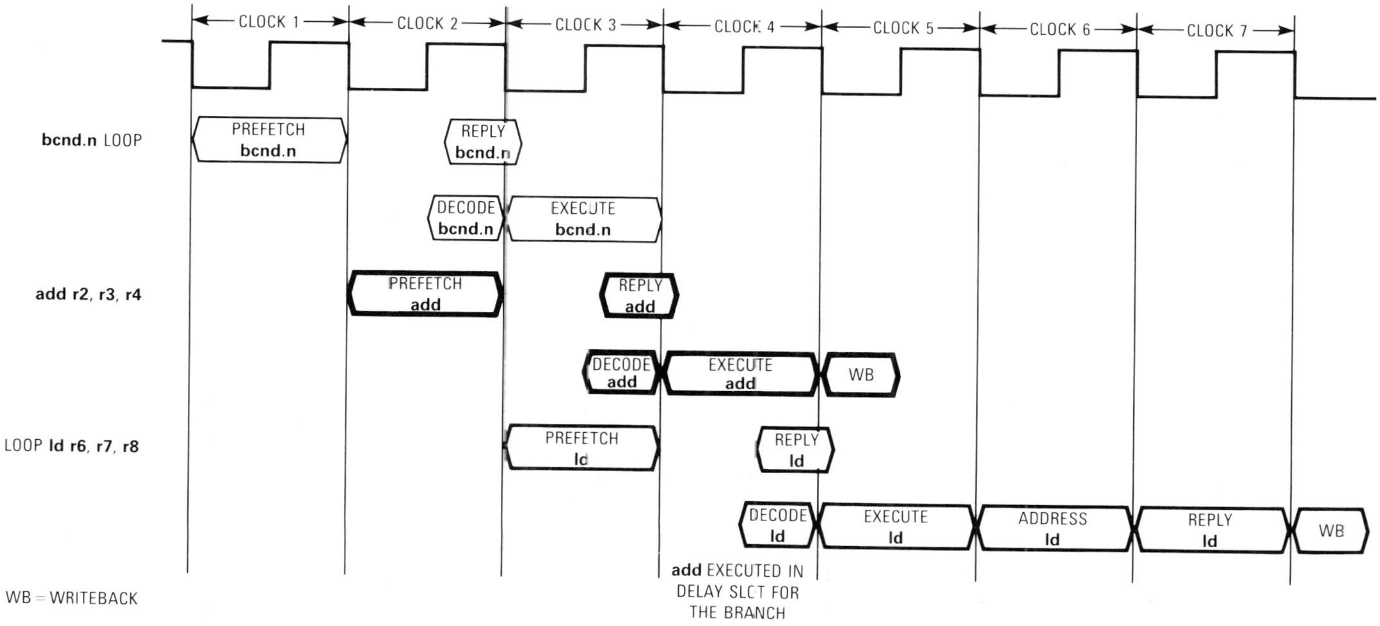

(b) Branch Taken (Delayed Branching — Selected)

Figure 7-11. Branch Example (Sheet 2 of 2)

by the time the branch executes; thus, it can execute while the instruction pipeline is refilled with the instruction at the target address. Figure 7-11 (b) shows the relative timing for an instruction sequence that uses the delayed branch option. The added efficiency afforded by the delayed branch featues is apparent by comparing the two diagrams in Figure 7-11. Figure 7-11 (a) shows that a branch taken with no delayed branching takes two clocks to execute, and Figure 7-11 (b) shows that the delayed branch option allows the **add** instruction (in the delay slot) to execute in one of those clocks. Therefore, the effective execution time for branch instructions that use delayed branching is reduced to one clock, providing the **add** is a useful instruction for the program. This time is the same as that of the branch-not-taken time. The delay slot instruction following a **jsr.n** or **bsr.n** can use the value in **r1** with no scoreboard delay; the value is the result of the subroutine call instruction.

7.4.4.3 TRAP INSTRUCTIONS AND EXCEPTION TIMINGS. The execution timing for trap instructions and other exceptions is listed in Table 7-5; the timing of events relative to the clock is shown in Figure 7-12.

All trap instructions, except the **tbnd**, cause the MC88100 to synchronize its activities (complete execution of all previous instructions) before the execute phase for the trap (this synchronize time is not included in Table 7-5). The execution of the trap-not-taken instructions is similar to that of the branch-not-taken instructions and takes one clock period (not

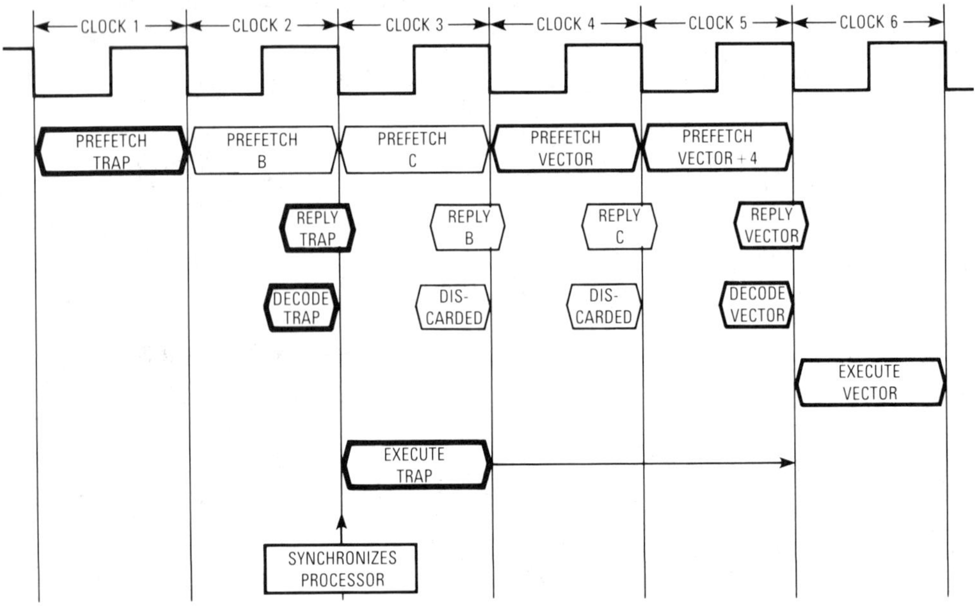

(A) Trap Instruction

Figure 7-12. Trap Instructions and Other Exceptions (Sheet 1 of 2)

7

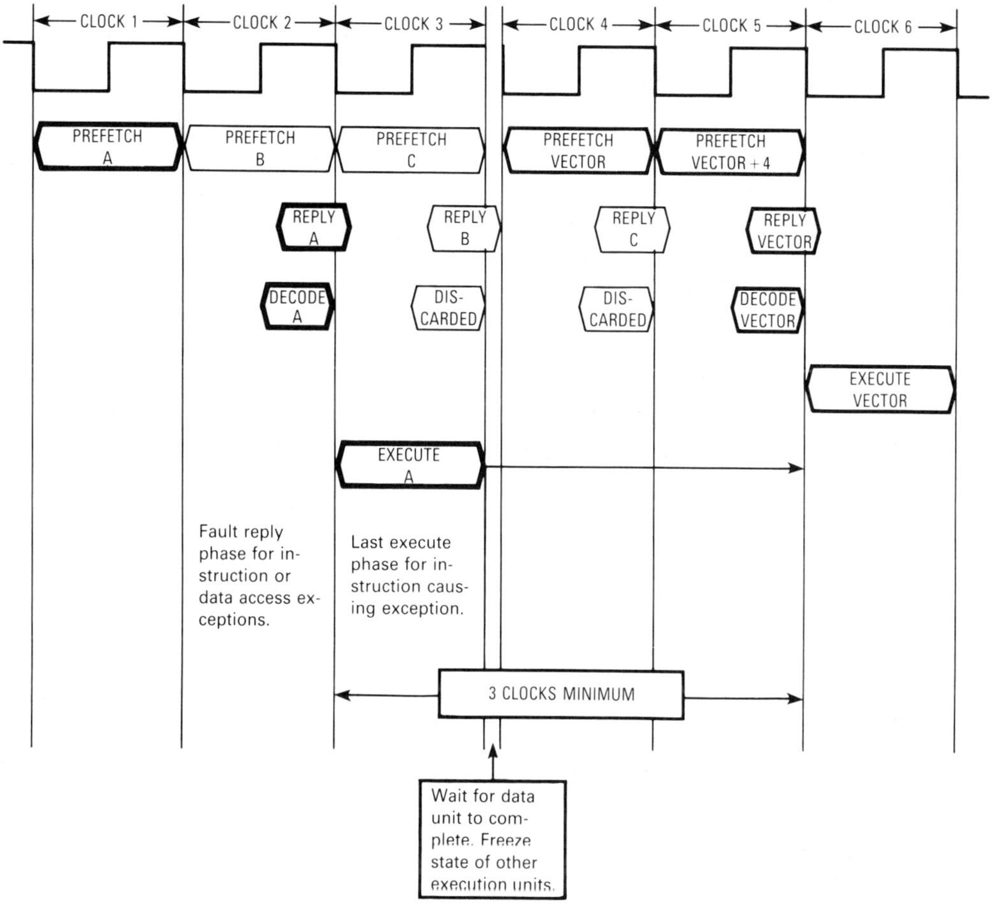

(B) Other Exceptions

Figure 7-12. Trap Instructions and Other Exceptions (Sheet 2 of 2)

including the time to synchronize the processor). The time to execute trap-taken instructions is allocated as three clocks although the vector fetch for the trap begins after one clock of execution for the trap. Similar to the case of branch instructions that do not use delayed branching, the two extra clocks are necessary to refill the instruction pipeline and decode the instruction at the trap vector. Even though the trap instruction is not still executing during these two clocks, no other instructions can be executed. Therefore, the time is attributed to the trap. The two instructions that follow the trap in the instruction stream are not executed and are discarded.

All other exception conditions processed by the MC88100 follow the same relative timing sequence described for the trap instruction. Exception conditions caused by bus access faults take three clocks to process (i.e., three clocks from the end of the fault reply phase and the beginning of the instruction execution at the exception vector). All exceptions freeze the FPU and wait for the data unit to complete pending accesses between clock periods 3 and 4 (see Figure 7-12). When pending accesses are complete (or faulted), the processor freezes the state of the machine, and the vector instruction is prefetched. Exceptions caused by unimplemented instructions are reported during the execute phase for the unimplemented instruction. As in the case of the trap, two more clocks are attributed to the unimplemented instruction timing to account for the prefetch time of the vector instruction. Clock period 3 is the point of reference in Figure 7-12 for floating-point precise/imprecise exceptions as the last phase of execution in FP1 or FPLAST, respectively. Refer to **SECTION 6 EXCEPTIONS** for more detail on processing exceptions and how to handle the FPU when exceptions occur.

7.5 TIMING FACTORS

Certain factors may affect the total execution time of an instruction sequence. These factors include the preceding and following instructions, the residency of operands and instruction words in the caches in the attached cache/memory management units (CMMUs), and the residency of address translations in the address translation cache. Other factors such as scoreboard holds, writeback priorities, wait cycles on the buses, and exceptions determine the total number of clock cycles. The following paragraphs describe scoreboarding, writeback priorities, and wait cycles on the buses.

7.5.1 Scoreboard Effects

Because there are multiple execution units in the MC88100, an operation may require use of the value in a particular general-purpose register that is in the process of being modified by another concurrent operation. Scoreboarding essentially sets an 'in use' bit for each instruction destination register. Subsequent instructions needing this register for either a source or a destination are held in the instruction pipeline decode stage of the instruction unit pipeline (a scoreboard hold) and are not allowed to proceed into the execution stage until this bit is cleared. A scoreboard bit is cleared when the instruction setting the bit has written its result back to the register file, thus providing subsequent operations (possibly on scoreboard hold) with the updated register contents.

Figure 7-13 shows an example of a timing diagram which demonstrates an instruction pipeline stall because of a scoreboard hold. Instruction A requires the contents of the preceding **ld** instruction. During clock period 3, the scoreboard bit is set for the register that is to be altered by the **ld** instruction. During clock periods 4 and 5, instruction A remains in the instruction reply phase (decode) until the scoreboard hold is released; then it enters the execution stage in the appropriate execution unit in clock period 6. Instruction B continues in the address phase (prefetch) until instruction A has entered the execution phase.

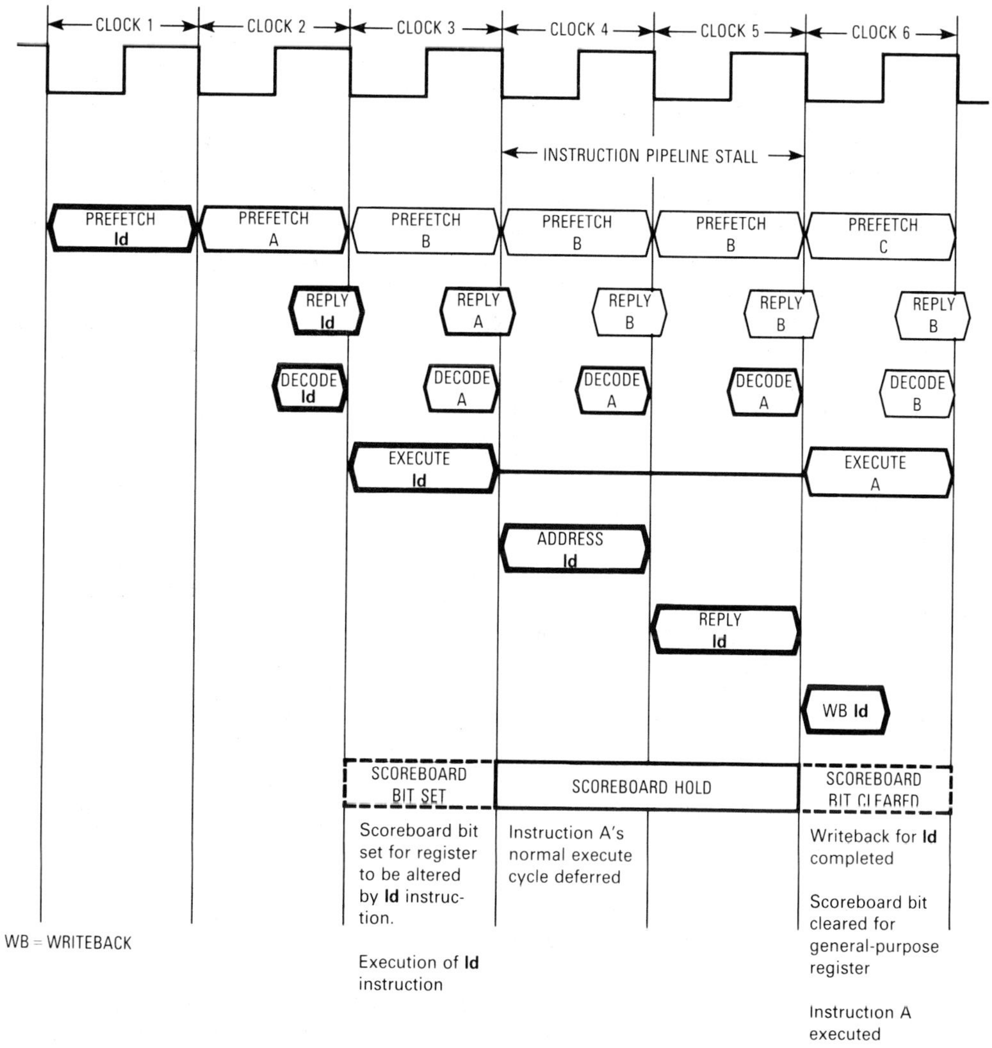

Figure 7-13. Scoreboard Hold — Instruction Pipeline Stall

Register dependencies in sequential instructions have a distinct effect on average instruction timing. A subsequent instruction that is held in the decode stage because of a scoreboard hold stalls the instruction prefetch pipeline until the appropriate registers are available. Overall execution of a code sequence is delayed until the scoreboard hold is released and allows the pipeline to proceed. Although useful work can be accomplished during this delay (floating-point operations or data memory operations already in progress can continue); scoreboard hold may increase execution time for a given code sequence. Figure 7-14 shows a code sequence where instruction A does not require the results of the general-purpose register that is altered by the **Id** instruction. Even though the scoreboard hold

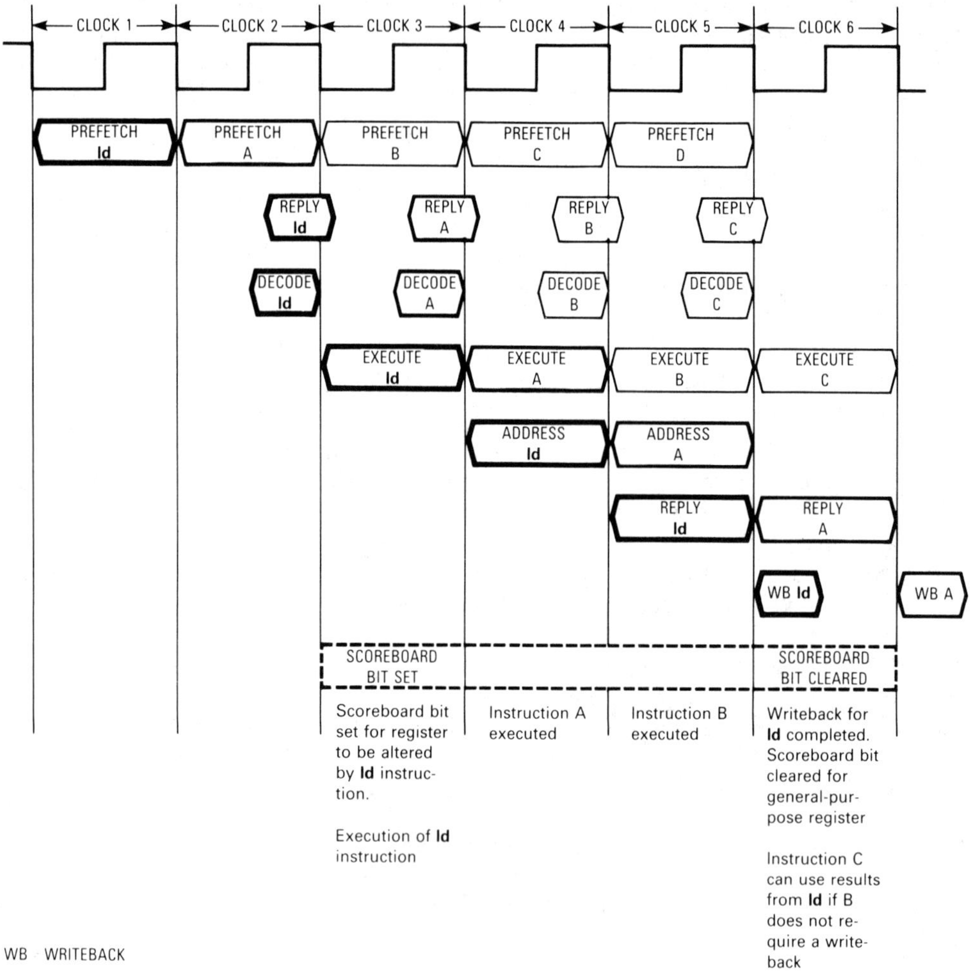

Figure 7-14. Scoreboard Hold — No Instruction Pipeline Stall

begins in clock period 4, instruction A still enters the execution phase at that time. Instruction B may or may not create a stall in the instruction pipeline, depending on whether or not it requires the results of the register that is on scoreboard hold. Code-scheduling software can effectively order operations to minimize the dependencies that lead to scoreboard holds.

7.5.2 Writeback Priorities and Feed Forwarding

All execution units write results to the register file (and store instructions fetch their operands) through the internal D bus. When multiple execution units need to simultaneously

write a result (or fetch a source in case of a store), the sequencer grants a writeback slot to the highest priority execution unit. Instruction completion is delayed if higher priority execution units prevent an execution unit from receiving a writeback slot. The order of priority enforced by the sequencer is as follows:

1. Integer unit, store, **lda**, **jsr**, and **bsr** instructions
2. FPU — integer multiply (from multiply pipeline)
3. FPU — floating-point multiply instructions
4. FPU — add pipeline (floating-point add, subtract, divide, compare, and convert instructions, plus integer divide instructions)
5. Data unit — load instructions

Figure 7-15 shows an example of execution completion that depends on writeback priority. In clock period 1, the FPU and the integer unit complete the execution phase of two instructions. The data unit completes the reply phase for instruction A, instruction B completes its address phase, and instruction C completes its execution phase. By the beginning of clock period 2, all three units have requested a writeback slot. The FPU repeats its last execution phase denoted as FPLAST. The data unit loads the data read for instruction A into a writeback latch that it uses as a holding register and completes the reply phase for instruction B. In clock period 3, the FPU, having the next priority, is granted the writeback slot. Instruction A is allowed to complete its writeback (from the writeback latch) in clock period 4. The secondary writeback latch in the data unit is used to store the results of instruction B until the first writeback latch for instruction A is released. To avoid writeback latch overflow, the data unit does not initiate any new data transactions on the data P bus while there are two outstanding accesses and one of them is awaiting writeback in a writeback slot.

Writeback priorities do not necessarily have any adverse effect on execution timing. However, indirect effects are induced in two ways. First, if an operation is delayed from writing back to its destination register, it may cause a scoreboard hold for a subsequent instruction. Second, an operation not allowed to writeback stalls its pipeline until it is completed.

Figue 7-16 shows an example where the data unit is granted a writeback slot before the integer unit. During clock period 3, the scoreboard bit for general-purpose register **r6** is set. In clock period 5, the execution phase of the **add** instruction is stalled due to the scoreboard hold. During clock period 6, the writeback slot is granted to the **ld** instruction because the **add** instruction requires the results of the **ld** (in **r6**).

Figure 7-16 also shows an example of feed forwarding, which allows execution by the integer unit at the same time the writeback is completed even though both events require the same register. Feed forwarding reduces the number of clock periods that an execution unit must wait to use a register. The D bus is gated to the waiting execution unit over one of the source buses, allowing the new contents of the register to be used while the processor updates the register file. During clock period 6, feed forwarding allows execution of the **add** instruction to overlap in the same clock period as the writeback for the results of the **ld**.

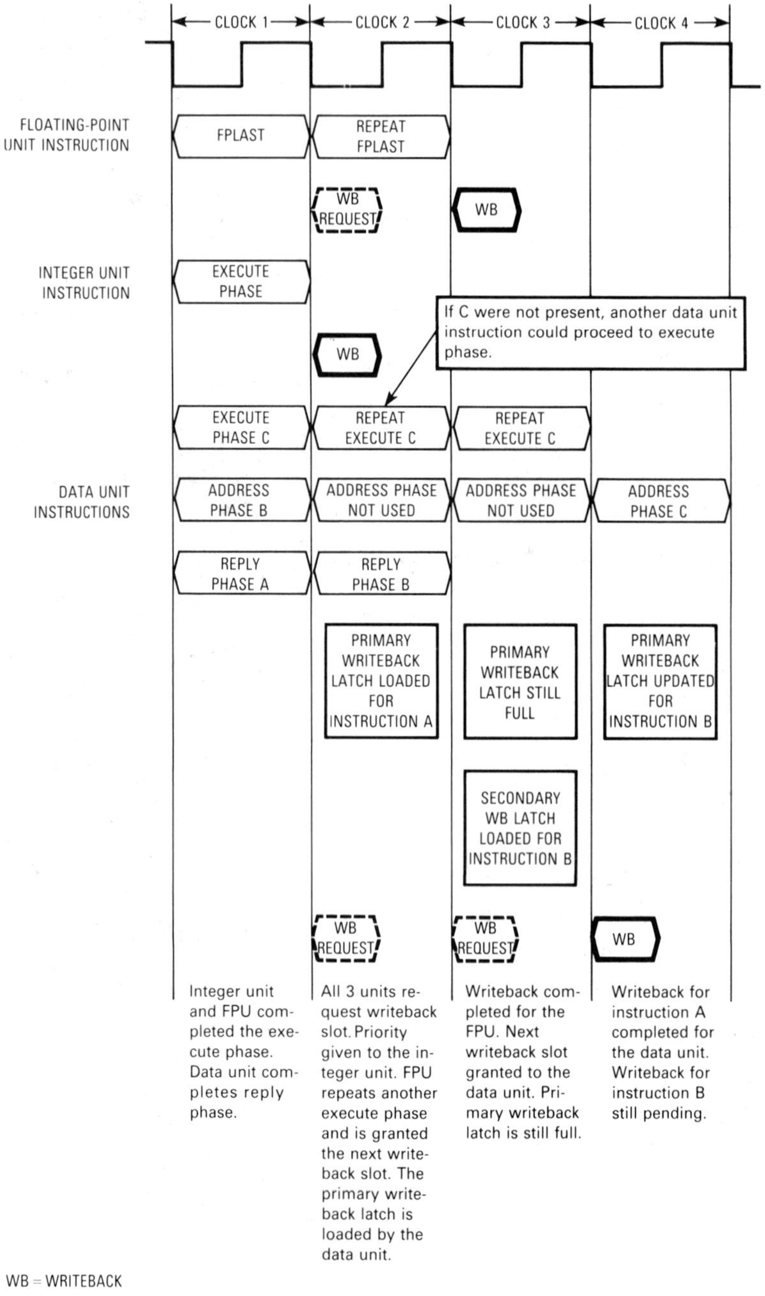

Figure 7-15. Writeback Priority (Example)

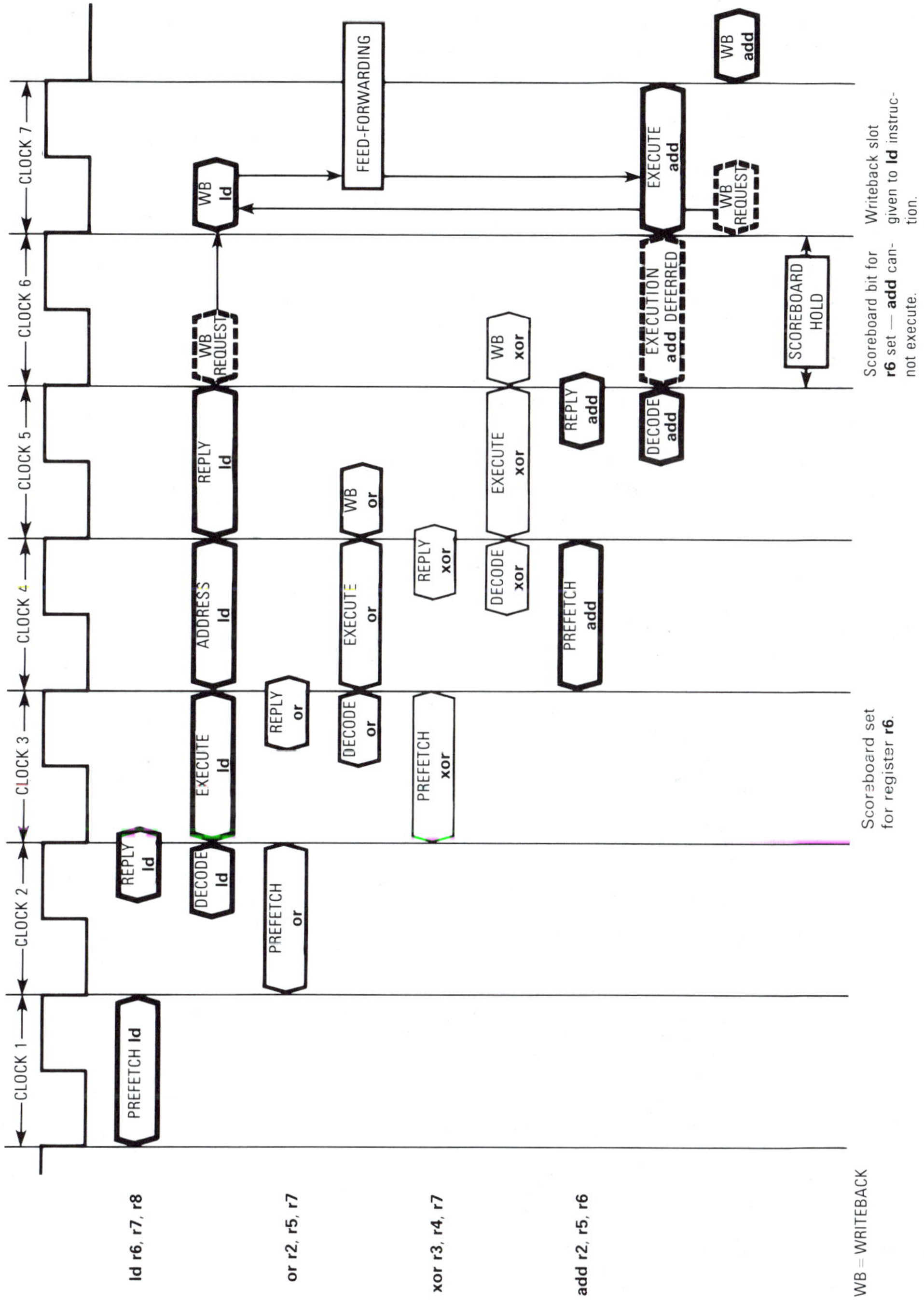

Figure 7-16. Writeback and Feed Forwarding (Example)

7.5.3 Wait Cycles and Pipeline Stalls

Wait responses occur during the reply phase of prefetch or during data accesses when an instruction or a data operand cannot be placed on the data or instruction P bus during the required clock period. The following instruction remains in the address phase until a 'success' reply is received. The responding device can insert as many wait replies as necessary until the instruction or data is supplied. Therefore, the wait reply stalls the instruction or data pipeline in relation to the number of wait replies received.

Pipeline stalls are created when an instruction cannot enter the next stage of execution. Pipeline stalls are induced by wait replies, scoreboard holds, and writeback priorities. Also, certain instructions automatically create pipeline stalls because of the number of clock periods required for execution. Figure 7-17 shows an example of pipeline stalls created by wait cycles, scoreboard holds, and writeback delays. In clock period 2, the prefetch for instruction A has received a wait reply, and the address phase for instruction B must be repeated in the instruction unit pipeline. In clock period 3, a 'success' reply was received, and instruction A enters the execution phase and sets a scoreboard bit in clock period 4. The normal execution phase for instruction B is clock period 5, but it cannot execute because it requires use of the register reserved by instruction A. In clock period 7, the scoreboard bit is released and instruction B enters the execution phase. Because instruction B was delayed in entering the execution phase, instruction C had to repeat its address phase in the instruction unit pipeline.

7.6 EXECUTION EXAMPLE

7

The following assembly language instructions encode (see Figure 7-18) the inner loop of the single-precision Linpack benchmark for execution by the MC88100 processor. It is not intended to illustrate an optimized code schedule — rather, it is provided to illustrate various timing interactions. Instruction prefetch is not shown; however, an instruction-by-instruction explanation is provided in the figure.

7.7 INSTRUCTION SET TIMING SUMMARY

Table 7-6 lists the MC88100 instructions executed by the instruction and integer units and identifies the scoreboard bits checked. Table 7-7 lists the scoreboard bits checked and set by the FPU instructions.

7

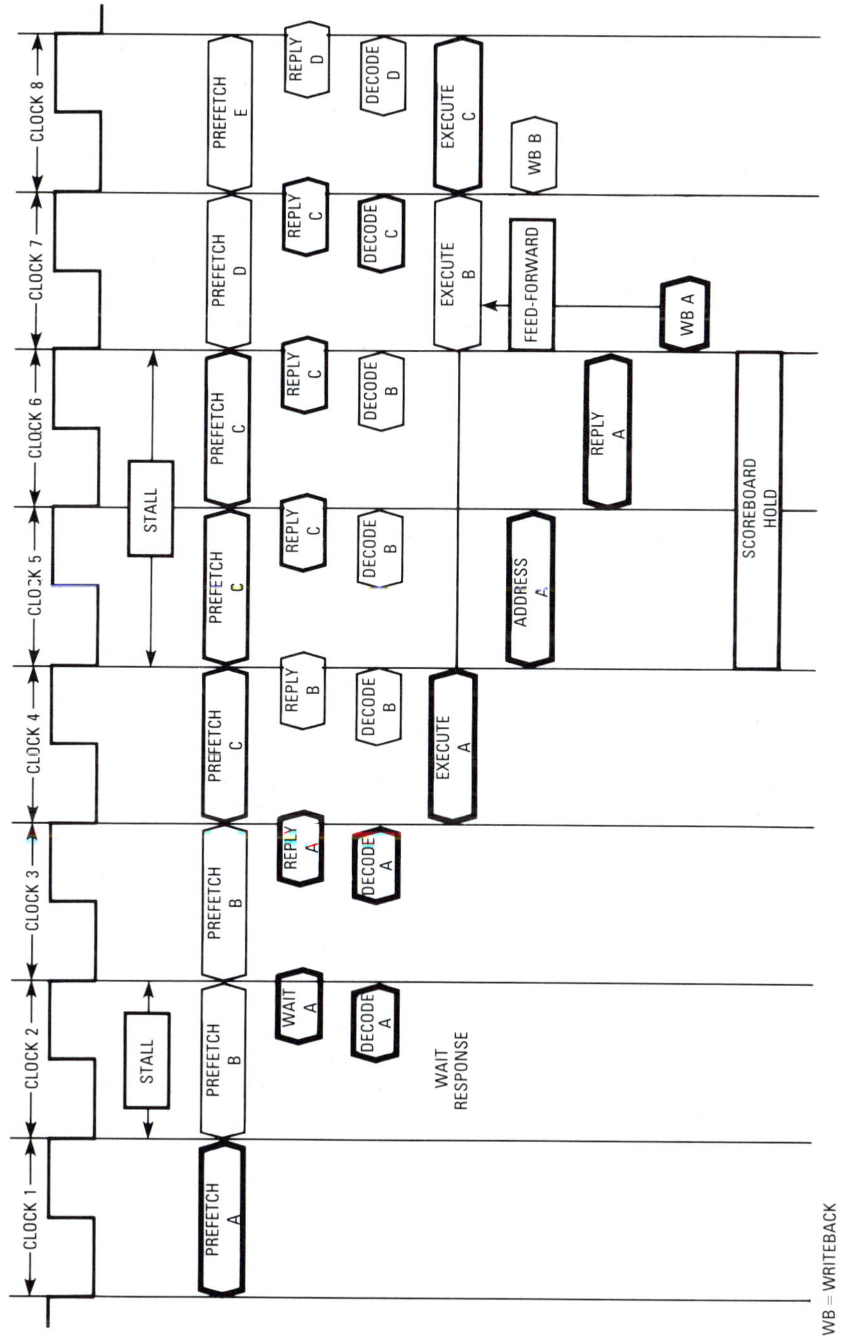

Figure 7-17. Pipeline Stalls (Example)

```
do i = 1,n
  dy(iy) = dy(iy) + da*dx(ix);
  ix = ix + incx;
  iy = iy + incy;

1  loop: ld r12, r3, r8          ;r12 = dx(ix)
2        add r8, r8, r5          ;ix = ix + incx
3        ld r13, r4, r9          ;r13 = dy(iy)
4        fmul.sss r14, r7, r12,  ;r14 = da*dx(ix)
5        add r2, r2, r1          ;i + +
6        cmp r11, r2, r3         ;i = n?
7        fadd.sss r15, r14, r13  ;r15 = dy(iy) + da*dx(ix)
8        add r9, r9, r6          ;iy = iy + incy
9        bb1.n ne, r11, loop     ;do implementation
10       st r15, r4, r9          ;dy(iy) = r15
```

(ff) Feed-Forwarding

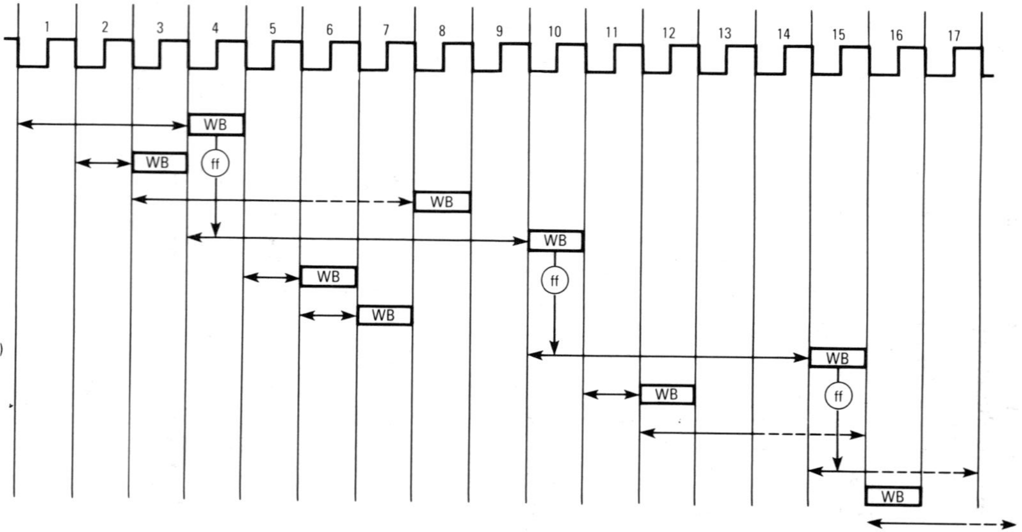

1. **ld** Assumes zero wait cycles, writes to register file during cycle 4 after three cycle pipeline latency. It is followed by parallel operations which give it an effective execution time of one cycle.

2. **add** Single-cycle integer execution.

3. **ld** Assumes zero wait cycles. Because of writeback priorities, it must wait until cycle 8 to writeback.

4. **fmul** Uses feed forwarding of **r12** from first load to begin FPU execution during cycle 4.

5. **add** Single-cycle integer execution in parallel with **fmul**.

6. **cmp** Single-cycle integer execution in parallel with **fmul**.

7. **fadd** Stalled by scoreboard hold until **fmul** completes. At cycle 10, **fmul** results are written into register file and **fadd** operand by feed-forwarding.

8. **add** Single-cycle integer execution.

9. **bb1.n** Delayed branching used. Prefetch of target;**st** scoreboard causes target to be prefetched until store is dispatched.

10. **st** Executed during delay slot of **bb1.n**. Although total access latency is three clocks, target instruction begins execution in cycle 16.

Figure 7-18. Single-Precision Linpack Loop-Clock Cycles

7

Table 7-6. Integer/Instruction Unit Instructions and Scoreboard Summary

Instructions	Scoreboard Checked			Execution Time
	rs1	rs2	rd	
Integer Unit				
add, **addu**, **sub**, **subu** (All Variants)	X	X	X	1
and, **or**, **xor** (All Variants)	X	X	X	1
cmp	X	X	X	1
clr	X	X	X	1
ext, **extu**	X	X	X	1
ff0, **ff1**	X	—	X	1
ldcr	—	—	X	1
mak	X	X	X	1
mask, **mask.u**	X	X	X	1
rot	X	X	X	1
set	X	X	X	1
stcr	X	—	—	1
xcr	X	—	X	1
Instruction Unit				
bb0, **bb1**, **bcnd** (Branch Taken)	X	—	—	2
bb0, **bb1**, **bcnd** (Branch Not Taken)	X	—	—	1
bb0.n, **bb1.n**, **bcnd.n**	X	—	—	1
br	—	—	—	2
br.n	—	—	—	1
bsr	—	—	**r1**	2
bsr.n	—	—	**r1**	1
jmp	X	—	—	2
jmp.n	X	—	—	1
jsr	X	—	**r1**	2
jsr.n	X	—	**r1**	1
rte	—	—	—	3
tb0, **tb1**, **tbnd**, **tcnd** (Trap not Taken)	X	—	—	1
tb0, **tb1**, **tbnd**, **tcnd** (Trap Taken)	X	—	—	3

r1 = the **bsr** and **jsr** implicitly address **r1** for which reservation is checked by means of the scoreboard

7

Table 7-7. FPU Instructions and Scoreboard Summary

Instruction	Scoreboard Checked						Scoreboard Set		FP1		ADD Pipe		MUL Pipe	FPLAST	Total Latency
	rs1	rs1 + 1	rs2	rs2 + 1	rd	rd + 1	rd	rd + 1		FP1 Extra (Not in instruction pipe)		Iterations in ADD2			
fadd.sss, fsub.sss	X	—	X	—	X	—	X	—	1		3			1	5
fadd.ssd, fsub.ssd	X	—	X	X	X	—	X	—	2		3			1	6
fadd.sds, fsub.sds	X	X	X	—	X	—	X	—	2		3			1	6
fadd.sdd, fsub.sdd	X	X	X	X	X	—	X	—	2		3			1	6
fadd.dss, fsub.dss	X	—	X	—	X	X	X	X	1		3			1*	5
fadd.dsd, fsub.dsd	X	—	X	X	X	X	X	X	2		3			1*	6
fadd.dds, fsub.dds	X	X	X	—	X	X	X	X	2		3			1*	6
fadd.ddd, fsub.ddd	X	X	X	X	X	X	X	X	2		3			1*	6
fcmp.sss	X	—	X	—	X	—	X	—	1		3			1	5
fcmp.ssd	X	—	X	X	X	—	X	—	2		3			1	6
fcmp.sds	X	X	X	—	X	—	X	—	2		3			1	6
fcmp.sdd	X	X	X	X	X	—	X	—	2		3			1	6
fdiv.sss	X	—	X	—	X	—	X	—	1		3	+25		1	30
fdiv.ssd	X	—	X	X	X	—	X	—	2		3	+25		1	31
fdiv.sds	X	X	X	—	X	—	X	—	2		3	+25		1	31
fdiv.sdd	X	X	X	X	X	—	X	—	2		3	+25		1	31
fdiv.dss	X	—	X	—	X	X	X	X	1		3	+54		1*	59
fdiv.dsd	X	—	X	X	X	X	X	X	2		3	+54		1*	60
fdiv.dds	X	X	X	—	X	X	X	X	2		3	+54		1*	60
fdiv.ddd	X	X	X	X	X	X	X	X	2		3	+54		1*	60
div, divu	X	—	X	—	X	—	X	—	1		3	+33		1	38
flt.ss	X	—	—	—	X	—	X	—	1		3			1	5
flt.ds	X	—	—	—	X	X	X	X	1		3			1*	5
int.ss, nint.ss, trnc.ss	X	—	—	—	X	—	X	—	1		3			1	5
int.sd, nint.sd, trnc.sd	X	X	—	—	X	X	X	—	2		3			1	6
fmul.sss	X	—	X	—	X	—	X	—	1	—			4	1	6
fmul.ssd	X	—	X	X	X	—	X	—	2	—			4	1	7
fmul.sds	X	X	X	—	X	—	X	—	2	—			4	1*	7
fmul.sdd	X	X	X	X	X	—	X	—	2	+2			4	1	9
fmul.dss	X	—	X	—	X	X	X	X	1	—			4	1*	6
fmul.dsd	X	X	X	—	X	X	X	X	2	—			4	1*	7
fmul.dds	X	—	X	X	X	X	X	X	2	—			4	1*	7
fmul.ddd	X	X	X	X	X	X	X	X	2	+2			4	1*	9
mul	X	—	X	—	X	—	X	—	1	—			2	1	4

*Add one more clock of effective FPLAST time delay only if result used either by a **st.d**, integer instruction, or an instruction that requires the results of second destination register.

7

SECTION 8
APPLICATIONS INFORMATION

This section describes a minimum system configuration, power and ground considerations, master/checker operations and configuration, and synchronization operations. The application information provided in this section has not been tested and is only provided as a guideline.

8.1 CACHE MEMORY MANAGEMENT UNITS

Memory management and caching of both instruction and data operands for the MC88100 are supported by the MC88200 cache/memory management unit (CMMU). The MC88200 includes a high-performance memory management unit that supports demand-paged virtual memory environments. Memory management is "demand" when the programs do not specify required memory areas in advance but request them by accessing logical addresses. The physical memory is paged, meaning that it is divided into blocks of equal size, called page frames. The logical address space is divided into pages of the same size. The operating system assigns pages to page frames as they are required to meet the needs of programs.

The MC88200 also includes a four-way, set-associative, 16K-byte cache memory that is accessed by physical addresses. The cache memory can be used to either store instructions or data operands, depending on the hardware configuration. A basic system implementation uses two MC88200 devices, one for caching instructions and the other for caching data.

8

Figure 8-1 shows a block diagram of a basic system configuration. Two MC88200 CMMUs are used, one for the instruction processor bus (P bus) of the MC88100 and the other for the data P Bus. All system resources such as main memory and I/O devices reside on the multiplexed memory bus (M bus) side of the MC88200s. A common reset signal is provided to ensure that all M88000 devices operate synchronously after a reset operation. The ID initialization block operates in conjunction with the reset circuitry to initialize a unique identification base address for each MC88200. This gives software the ability to communicate with each MC88200 independently. The M bus arbitration block provides the ability for each MC88200 to request and receive ownership of the M bus. The system status interface provides M bus information on bus wait operations, bus errors, retry operations, and burst length control.

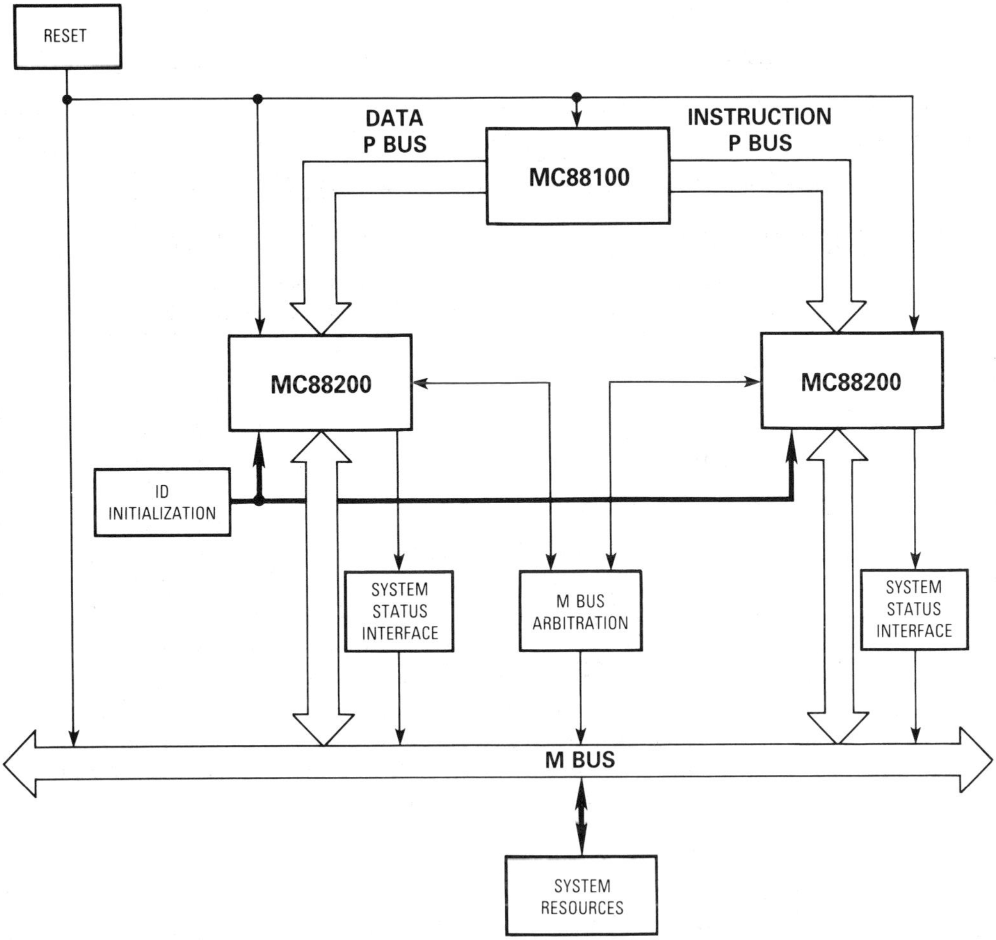

Figure 8-1. Basic System Configuration

8

8.1.1 P Bus Connections

Figure 8-2 shows the connections required to interface two MC88200 CMMUs to the MC88100; one CMMU is connected to the instruction P bus, and the second CMMU is connected to the data P bus. The MC88200 signal names do not necessarily match the signal names of the MC88100 processor since the MC88200 must be capable of operating as either an instruction CMMU or a data CMMU.

The data P bus of the MC88100 is connected to the appropriate signals on the MC88200 (see Figure 8-2) to provide memory management and control caching for data operands. The data P bus of the MC88100 provides addressing information on the data address bus. Only 30 bits of address are needed to access 4 gigabytes of data since an entire 32-bit

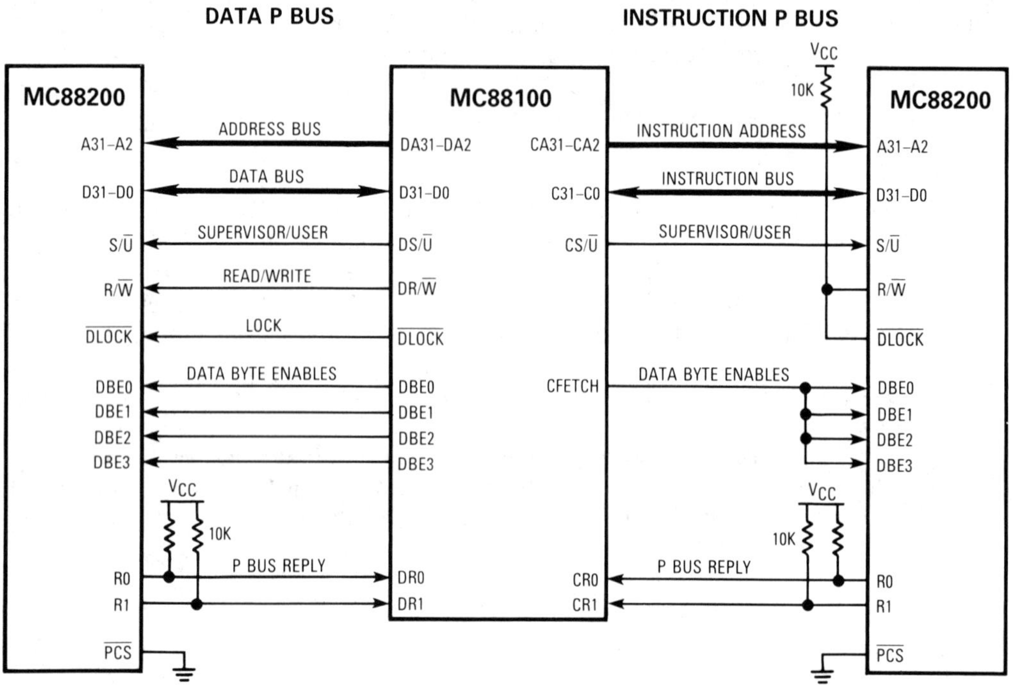

Figure 8-2. P Bus Connection to MC88200's

word of memory is implied for every access. Individual bytes and half words are selected by the data byte enable (DBE3–DBE0) outputs of the MC88100. The data bus provides the 32-bit bidirectional connection for data transfers with the read/write signal (R/$\overline{W}$) indicating the direction of the data transfer. The supervisor/user signal (S/$\overline{U}$) selects between supervisor data and user data accesses while the lock signal works in conjunction with the **xmem** instruction to perform an indivisible load, then store operation. The reply signals indicate wait, fault, and success information for each P bus transaction.

The MC88100 instruction P bus connection to an MC88200 CMMU is similar to the data P bus connection and allows memory management of instruction memory and caching of instruction operands. The instruction P bus is read only, and instructions are supplied via the instruction bus (C31–C0). Therefore, the read/write (R/$\overline{W}$) signal is pulled high through a 10K ohm resistor and indicates to the data drivers of the MC88200 to source instruction information. The supervisor/user signal selects between supervisor instruction memory and user instruction memory. The bus lock ($\overline{BLOCK}$) signal is tied high through a 10K ohm resistor since there are no indivisible instruction P bus load, then store operations. The code fetch (CFETCH) signal on the MC88100 must be connected to all four data byte enable

(DBE3–DBE0) signals on the MC88200 that is used as the instruction CMMU. The MC88200 qualifies each potential access on the instruction P bus with the data byte enable signals and does not recognize an access if all four data byte enable signals are negated (as is the case after a fault occurs on the P bus). Since CFETCH connects to all four DBE signals, buffering of CFETCH may be required when more than one MC88200 is being configured as an instruction CMMU.

The P bus reply signals (DR0, DR1, CR0, and CR1) for both the data P bus and the instruction P bus should be pulled high through 10K ohm resistors (see Figure 8-2). Pulling the reply signals high defaults the response of the P bus to the fault condition. This allows the MC88100 to take a memory access exception if the MC88200 is either not installed in the circuit board or does not respond to a transaction with the appropriate timing.

For this basic system configuration, the P bus chip select ($\overline{\text{PCS}}$) signal is connected to ground for both the data CMMU and the instruction CMMU. The $\overline{\text{PCS}}$ signal is intended to direct a P bus access to a particular MC88200 when more than one MC88200 resides on the instruction P bus or the data P bus. In this basic configuration, $\overline{\text{PCS}}$ is grounded since there is only one data CMMU and one instruction CMMU.

8.1.2 System Status Interface and ID Initialization

Figure 8-3 shows an example of the circuitry that can be used to initialize the identification (ID) base address to each MC88200 and the system status ($\overline{\text{SS3}}$–$\overline{\text{SS0}}$) interface. The ID base address allows system software the ability to access each MC88200 independently. Each register set of the two MC88200 CMMUs shown resides at a different memory-mapped base address. After the reset signal negates, the MC88200 reads the logic levels on the local status (ST3–ST0) pins, the tag monitoring pin (TM0) and the trace pins (TR1–TR0). For this design, the instruction MC88200 ID base address is $FFF7E000, and the data MC88200 ID base address is $FFF7F000.

In addition to initializing the ID base address, the local status pins are also used to interface to the system status signals ($\overline{\text{SS3}}$–$\overline{\text{SS0}}$) of the M bus. The active-high local status (ST3–ST0) signals are wire-NORed through a 74F622 open-collector inverter to connect to the system status signals.

8.1.3 M Bus Arbitration

Figure 8-4 shows a simple M bus arbitration design using one package of two-input NOR gates (74AS02). Bus request (BR) from either MC88200 initiates the arbitration cycle. This signal generates both bus grant (BG) and arbitration busy ($\overline{\text{AB}}$). If both devices request the M bus at the same time, then the instruction MC88200 receives the M bus. Bus acknowledge (BA) is asserted when a device becomes the bus master and is used to generate the bus busy ($\overline{\text{BB}}$) signal. Refer to the *MC88200 User's Manual* for a detailed description of M bus arbitration.

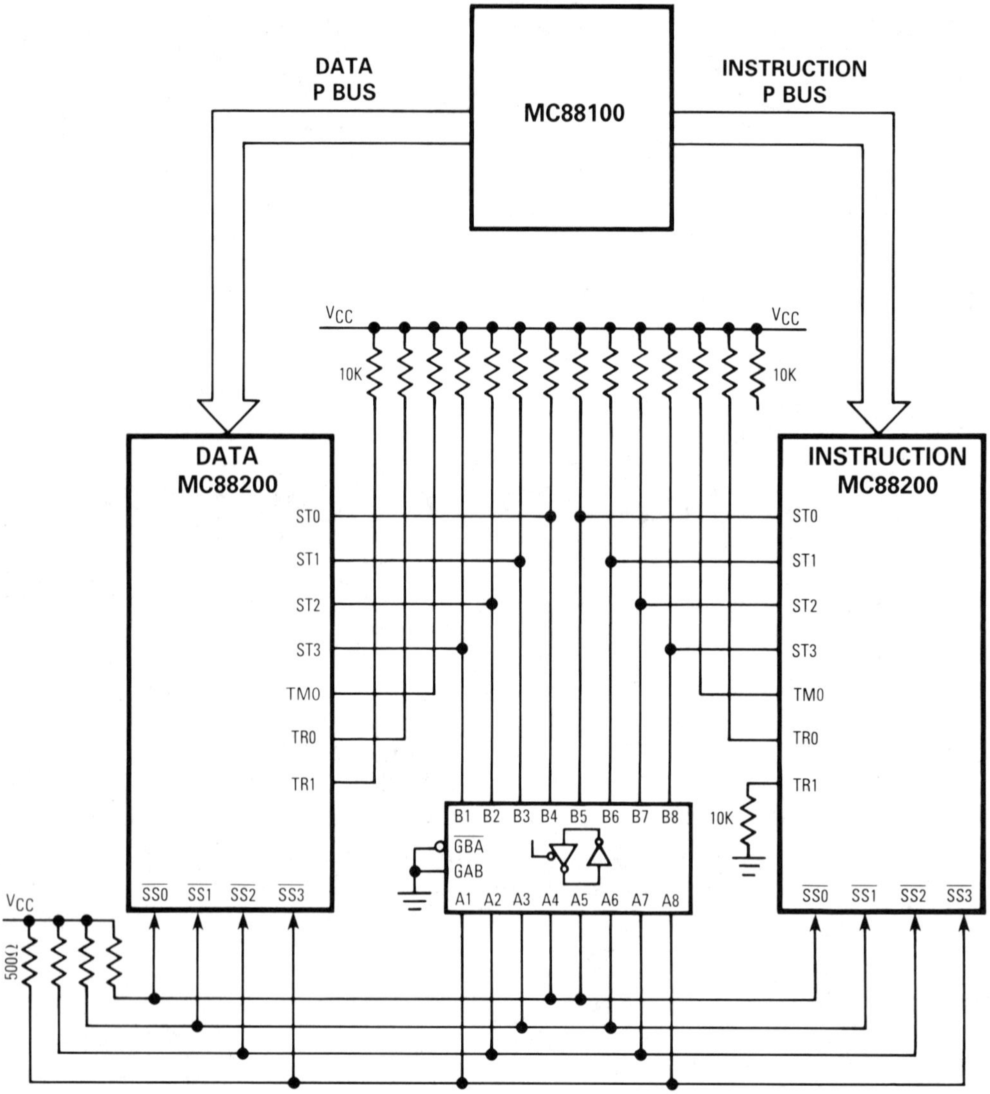

Figure 8-3. System Status Interface and ID Initialization

8.1.4 Reset Circuits

Figure 8-5 shows an example reset circuit which can be used to generate the reset ($\overline{RST}$) and phase lock loop enable (PLLEN) signals to the MC88100 and MC88200s. Three separate reset (RST3–RST1) and phase lock loop enable (PLLEN3–PLLEN1) signals are generated, which allows a separate signal connection to each M88000 device in the basic system

8

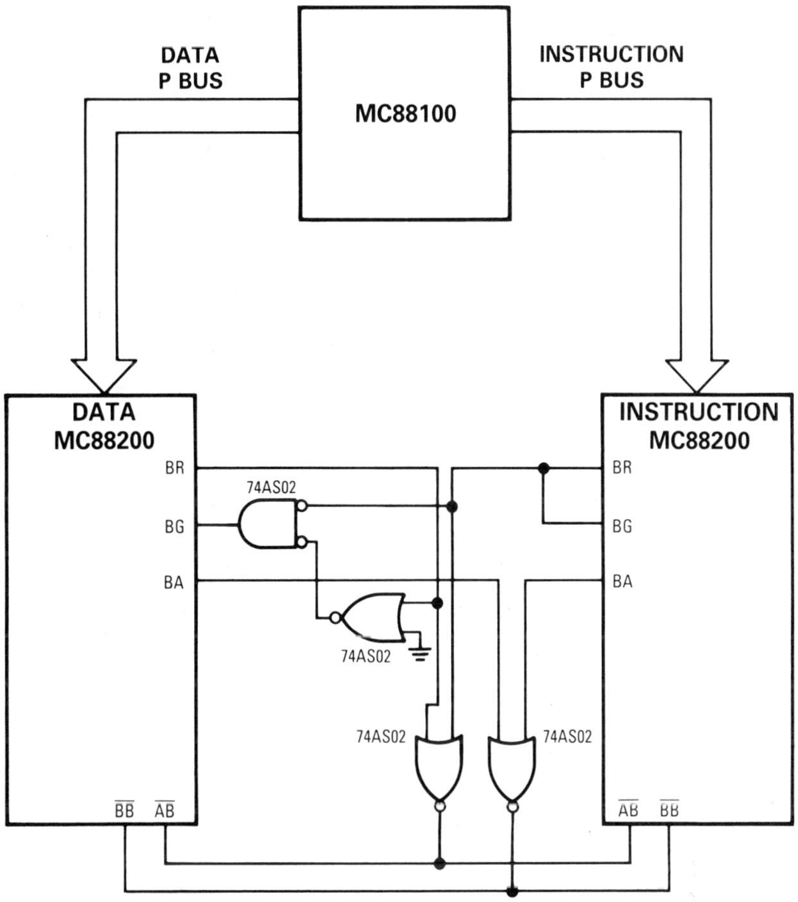

Figure 8-4. M Bus Arbitration

configuration. This prevents capacitive overloading of any one signal. In addition to generating the $\overline{RST}$ and PLLEN signals during powerup operations, the circuit is also used to debounce a pushbutton switch for subsequent reset operations.

The LM393 dual-voltage comparator uses a voltage divider network to generate a reference voltage for the negative (–) input, which is used to compare to a resistor-capacitor (RC) voltage ramp-up. The reference voltage used to generate the PLL signal is set at a lower level than the reference voltage used to generate the reset signal. This allows the PLLEN signal to transition to a logic high before the $\overline{RST}$ signal negates. The duration of the reset signal is based on an RC voltage ramp-up time delay through a 200K ohm resistor and a 6.8 microfarad capacitor. The outputs of the LM393 are then synchronized through a 74AS374 D-type flip flop to the M88000 device clock (CLK) signal. Since the transition times of the reset and PLL signals in relation to the system clock signal (CLK) is asynchronous, a

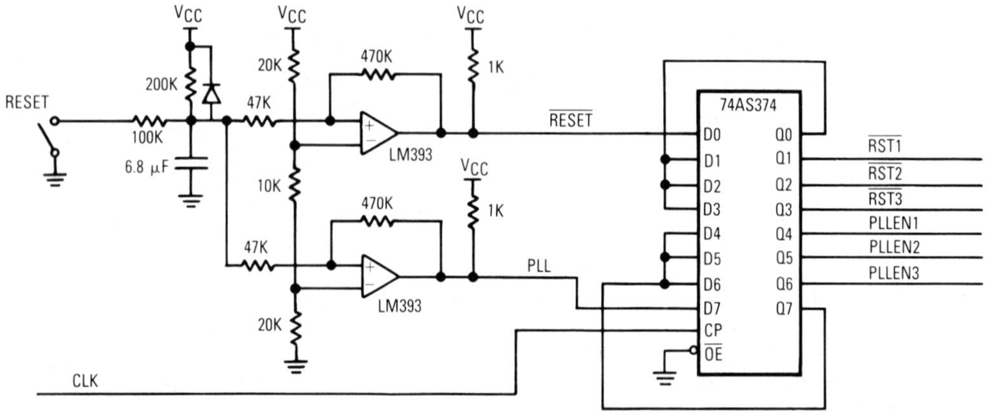

Figure 8-5. Reset Circuit

metastable condition can be induced in the 74AS374. For this reason the $\overline{\text{RESET}}$ and PLL signals are passed through the 74AS374 two times to create a two-stage synchronizer. The first stage, which may go metastable, is allowed to settle out before the second synchronization stage. Synchronization guarantees that all M88000 devices in the system start execution out of the reset condition at the same time.

8.2 POWER AND GROUND CONSIDERATIONS

The MC88100 is fabricated in Motorola's advanced HCMOS process and offers significant reduced power consumption in comparison to an equivalent NMOS circuit. While the use of CMOS for a device reduces power consumption, the high clock speeds of the MC88100 make the characteristics of power supplied to the device quite important. The power supply must be able to supply large amounts of instantaneous current when the MC88100 is switching logic levels for a large number of circuit nodes. These nodes include both the internal logic and the output drivers for both the data P bus and the instruction P bus. The power supply must remain within the rated specification at all times. To meet these requirements, more detailed attention must be given to the power-supply connection to the MC88100 than is required for other devices operating at slower clock rates.

To supply a solid power-supply interface, 18 V_{CC} pins and 18 GND pins are provided. Thirteen V_{CC} and 13 GND pins supply the power to the external signal drivers, and the remaining 5 V_{CC} and 5 GND pins are used by the internal logic and clock generation circuitry. Table 8-1 lists the power and ground pin assignments.

To reduce the amount of noise in the power supplied to the MC88100 and to provide for instantaneous current requirements, common capacitive decoupling techniques should be

Table 8-1. Power and Ground Pin Assignments

Pin Group	V_{CC}	GND
Internal Logic	C11, K3, M3, M15, P5	C12, J3, L3, N4, N14
External Signals Drivers	C7, C9, D5, D13, F3, F15, H3, H15, K15, P13, R7, R9, R11	C6, C8, C10, E4, E14, G3, G15, J15, L15, R6, R8, R10, R12

implemented. While there is no recommended layout for this capacitive decoupling, it is essential that the inductance between these devices and the MC88100 be minimized to provide sufficiently fast response time to satisfy momentary current demands and to maintain a constant supply voltage. It is suggested that a combination of low, middle, and high-frequency high-quality capacitors be placed as close to the MC88100 as possible (for example, a set of 10 microfarad, 0.1 microfarad, and 330 picofarad capacitors in parallel provides filtering for most frequencies prevalent in a digital system). Decoupling capacitors should be placed as close as possible to the power pins of the MC88100. Consideration should be given to the use of undersocket decoupling capacitor arrays or the use of surface mount capacitors attached to the solder side of a printed circuit board. Similar decoupling techniques should also be observed for other VLSI devices in the system.

In addition to the capacitive decoupling of the power supply, care must be taken to ensure a low-impedance connection between all MC88100 V_{CC} and GND pins and the system power-supply planes. Failure to provide connections of sufficient quality between the MC88100 power-supply pins and the system supplies will result in increased assertion delays for external signals, decreased voltage noise margins, and potential errors in internal logic.

8

8.3 MASTER/CHECKER OPERATION

Both the MC88100 processor and the MC88200 CMMU include comparator circuits at the outputs to support fault detection. Applications requiring fault detection can use the error (ERR) signal and the master/checker operating mode. The following paragraphs describe some of the different configurations used with the MC88100 and MC88200.

8.3.1 Comparator Circuits

All output signals of the MC88100 and the MC88200 contain comparator circuits which examine the internal and external state of an active output signal. If a mismatch occurs on any output, then the ERR signal is asserted. Figure 8-6 shows the relative timing from when the comparator circuit detects a mismatch to when the ERR signal is asserted. For the MC88100, the mismatch condition is checked on each rising edge of the clock. If a mismatch is detected, then the ERR signal is asserted off the falling edge of the clock and

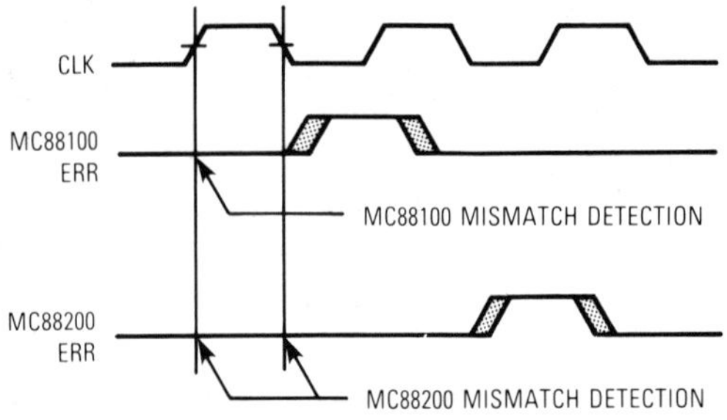

Figure 8-6. Functional Timing of ERR Signal

is valid around the next rising edge of the clock. The MC88200 uses both edges of the clock to drive output signals and therefore needs to check for mismatch conditions on both edges. As an example, the MC88200 P bus data (D31–D0) signals are checked on the rising edge of the clock; the P bus reply signals (R1–R0) are checked on the falling edge. Sampled comparison results from a rising clock edge and a falling clock edge are then collected and evaluated for mismatch conditions on the next rising edge of the clock. The results are used to drive the ERR signal on the next falling edge of the clock, allowing the ERR signal to become valid around the next rising edge.

An external/internal mismatch can occur for two reasons. First, a short or other electrical failure can force the output signal to a single voltage. For example, a bus signal can be shorted to ground. When the component drives a high voltage on the bus, the external signal will be pulled low and a mismatch will occur. The second way is that an external/internal mismatch can occur is in the master/checker mode.

8.3.2 Configurations

The master/checker configuration incorporates redundant components for verification of the results of an active, master component. Two or more M88000 components are wired together on the same bus, pin for pin, except for the ERR signal, the P bus checker enable (PCE) signal, and the M bus checker enable (MCE) signal (MC88200 only). The PCE and MCE signals are used to initiate the checker mode of operation. The PCE signal initiates the P bus checker mode, which disables the P bus output drivers. The MCE signal initiates the M bus checker mode, which disables the M bus output drivers on an MC88200. The checker mode configures the device so that it operates in a redundant configuration using the same input data as the master and compares the results with the master's outputs.

Figure 8-7 shows a basic master/checker configuration using two MC88100 devices. The PCE input initiates the master/checker operation and is sampled on every falling edge of the clock. The PCE signal is low for a master processor and high for a checker processor. When PCE is detected high, the checker processor immediately places all of its output

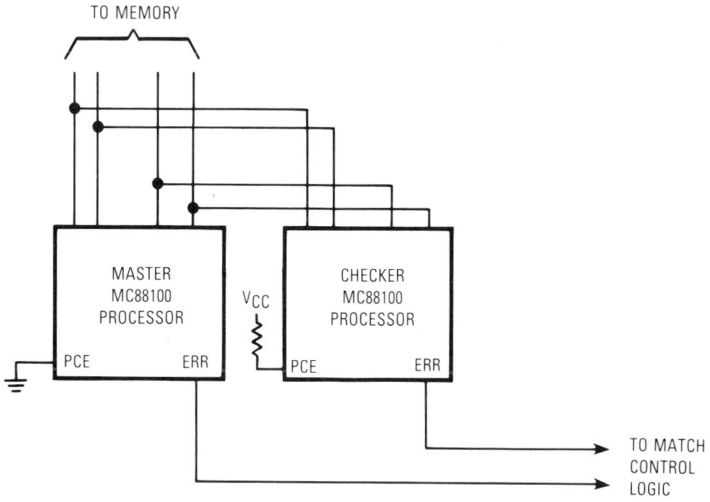

Figure 8-7. Basic Master/Checker Configuration

signals in the high-impedance state. When execution begins (at the reset vector for initialization), both processors fetch and execute the instructions. However, the checker processor does not produce any outputs. It monitors the P bus signals when the master produces its outputs. If the master produces a result (i.e., writes data to memory) that differs from the checker results, then the checker encounters a mismatch error. That is, one or more output signals driven by the master are different from the checker's internal version. The checker processor asserts ERR, and the system hardware and/or software can take appropriate action.

8

The MC88200 has both a PCE and MCE signal, allowing independent configuration of the MC88200 P bus and M bus connections. When sampled high, the MCE signal configures the MC88200 as an M bus checker. As an M bus checker, all M bus output signals, the trace (TR1–TR0) signals, and the tag monitor (TM1–TM0) signals are placed in the high-impedance state. When sampled high, the PCE signal configures the MC88200 as a P bus checker. As a P bus checker, all P bus output signals are placed in the high-impedance state.

8.3.3 Fault Tolerance

Fault tolerance, the ability of a system to correctly execute a specified algorithm regardless of system errors or failures, is directly associated with the concept of redundancy. Components are redundant if they only improve the reliability of a system and do not improve system throughput. Redundant components are needed to compare results to determine fault conditions. The M88000 master/checker operation provides a mechanism to configure redundant components without the need to provide external comparator circuitry for fault detection.

Dynamic redundancy allows the system to actively reorganize around a faulting device to restore normal operation. The four basic steps for reorganizing a system to bypass a faulting component are as follows:

1. Fault Recognition: A fault condition is generated when results produced by redundant components do not match.
2. Fault Isolation: Diagnostics are run to isolate the fault condition to a replaceable part or subunit.
3. Fault Elimination: The system actively reorganizes to eliminate a faulting component by logically enabling redundant hardware.
4. Recovery: Procedures are taken to restore the system to normal operation.

8.3.4 Duplex System

Figure 8-8 shows a duplex system consisting of two M88000 modules on one M bus. Each module contains one MC88100 processor and two MC88200 CMMUs. One module is configured as the master by external match control logic using the MCE signals (MCE3–MCE0). The external match control logic also monitors the ERR signals (E3–E0). When an error is detected, an interrupt is generated to begin fault isolation. The interrupt handler should anticipate that the checker may be out of synchronous operation with the master and

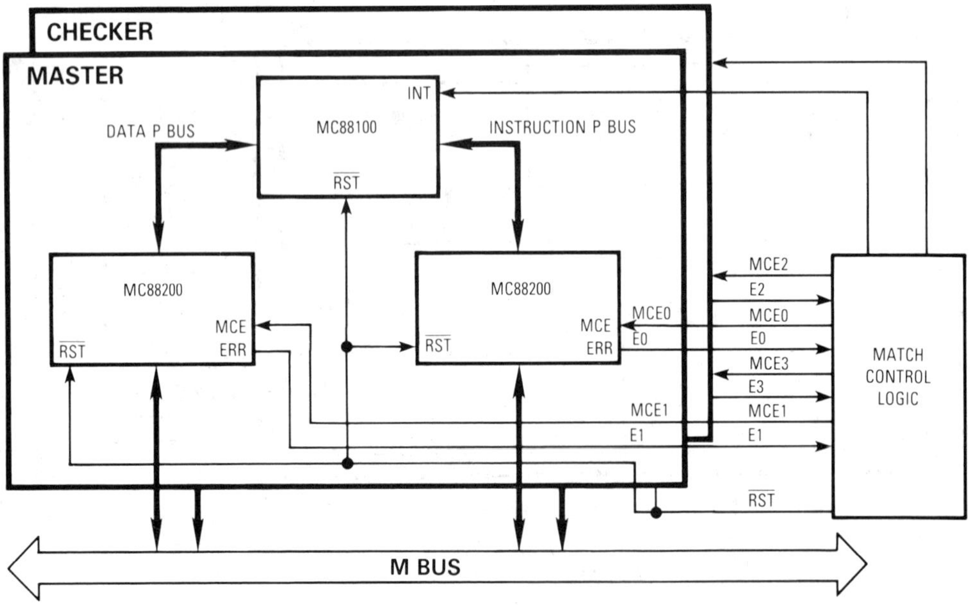

Figure 8-8. Duplex System

8

therefore should save as much state information as possible. If errors continue to be generated, then the external match control logic should generate a warm reset. The warm reset operation only resets the M88000 modules and does not reset any saved state information. The reset software then runs diagnostics to search for fault conditions. Software diagnostics can be run with interrupts disabled to allow the software to verify the results of each diagnostic test without recognition of additional interrupts. If the diagnostics detect a faulty component, the match control logic can reconfigure the master/checker selection by switching the MCE signals and performing another warm reset. Diagnostics are again run and, if they pass, the system is restarted in a simplex mode (only one M88000 module working). The faulting module can then be repaired off-line.

8.3.5 Dynamic Redundant System

Figure 8-9 shows a dynamic hardware redundant system which uses the same M88000 modules as the previous example. This configuration uses three modules in a voting scheme to allow determination of which module is producing the mismatch condition. Each module reports two error signals (two of E5–E0), one for the data MC88200 and one for the instruction MC88200. Table 8-2 lists the error status for each module and has grouped these two possible error conditions into one event. A "1" listed in the table means that at least one error was generated by the corresponding module.

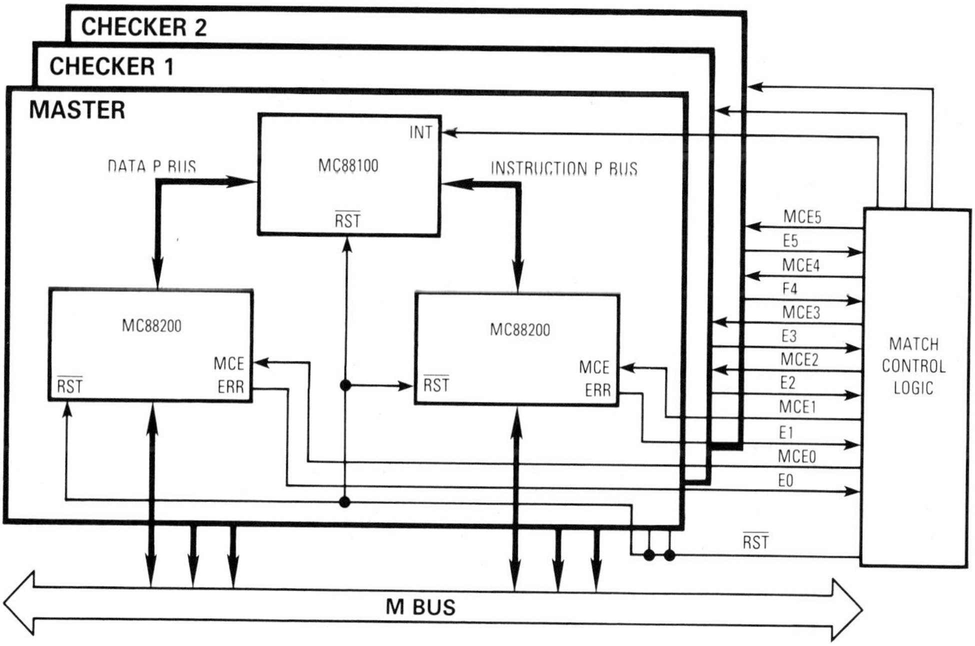

Figure 8-9. Dynamic Hardware Redundancy

Table 8-2. Error Status

Master	Checker 1	Checker 2	Comments
0	0	0	No Errors Reported
0	0	1	Checker 2 Fault Reported
0	1	0	Checker 1 Fault Reported
0	1	1	Master Fault Reported
1	X	X	Bus Fault Reported

Normally, execution proceeds with no errors reported. If one of the checkers reports a fault condition, then an interrupt should be generated. This allows the master to report on the faulting checker and allows diagnostics to be run either on-line or off-line to isolate the faulting condition. If both checkers report a fault, then the master is the faulting component. At this point, the match control logic may try an interrupt to the master to allow the master to save as much context information as possible. The checkers may continue to report errors since they can be out of synchronous operation with the master. If the fault from the master is catastrophic such that interrupts are not recognized, then the match control logic issues a reset and reconfigures the master/checker assignments. Errors reported by the old master are ignored after the reassignment, and the new master reports the status of the old master faulting.

8.3.6 Massive Redunant System

In the previous two examples, the recovery from a faulting master may be incomplete since the reporting of errors does not happen until after the mismatch condition is detected. The faulting master may have acted on corrupt data or written corrupt data to memory before the error reporting process. Total recovery requires the new master to re-execute an entire task or portions of a task to correct corrupt data in memory. To avoid this situation, massive system redundancy may be required. Figure 8-10 shows a massive redundant system where each M88000 computing node is duplicated along with the system bus and the main memory modules (M1 and M2). This configuration essentially duplicates the entire system. Both systems operate in tandem, with only one actually reporting results to I/O devices. Within each M88000 node, each MC88100 and MC88200 are duplicated and run in the master/checker configuration. This generates six ERR signals from each node which the match control logic monitors. When an error is received, the match control logic switches to the alternate system to continue processing. Diagnostics can then be run independently on the faulting system to isolate the error condition.

8.3.7 Multiprocessing System

In addition to using the master/checker mode for fault tolerant applications, it can be used for graceful degradation in a multiprocessing system. Figure 8-11 shows a multiprocessing system where each M88000 node is configured in the master/checker mode. To maximize

8

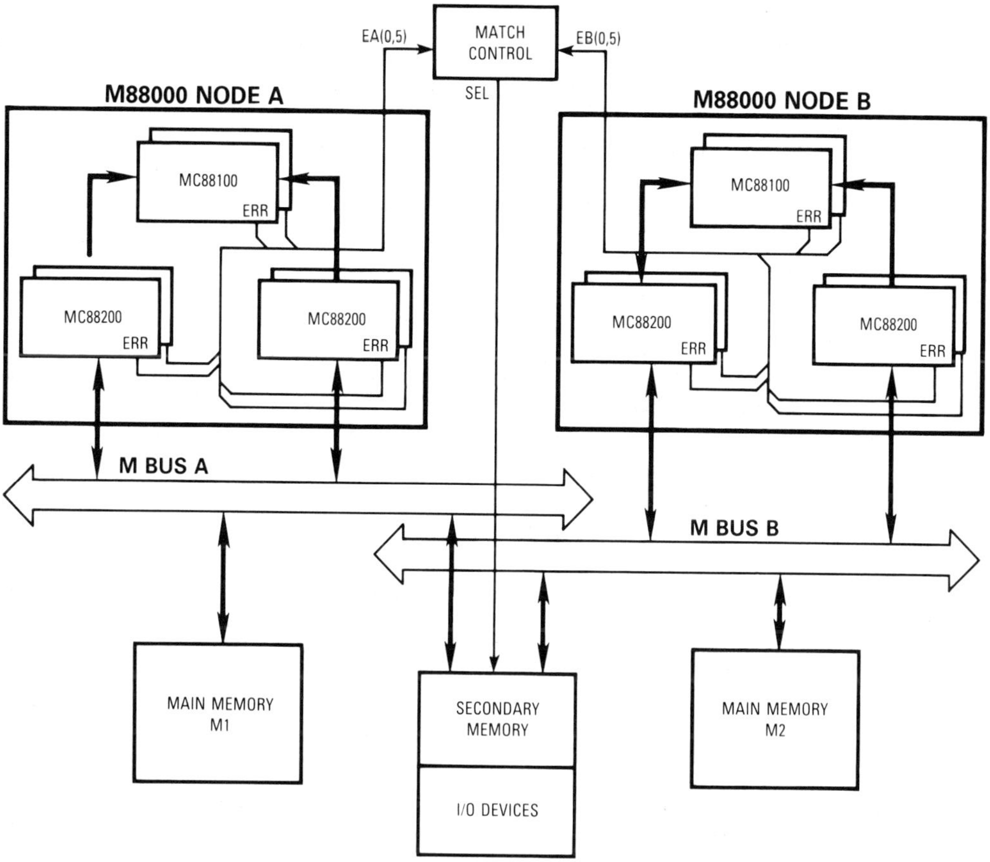

8

Figure 8-10. Massive System Redundancy

system performance, each node can execute a task independently. If a fault condition occurs, the faulting node can be eliminated from the system. The remaining nodes pick up the duties of the faulting node at the expense of reduced system performance.

8.4 SYNCHRONIZATION OPERATIONS

The following paragraphs describe how to implement various synchronization operations on the MC88100 using the **xmem** instruction. Examples of synchronization operations are included, including implementations that use the MC88200 CMMU. Previous knowledge of the CMMU is assumed.

8.4.1 Instruction Definition

The **xmem** instruction provides an uninterruptable combination of a read-write memory access that supports the implementation of various synchronization operations: test and

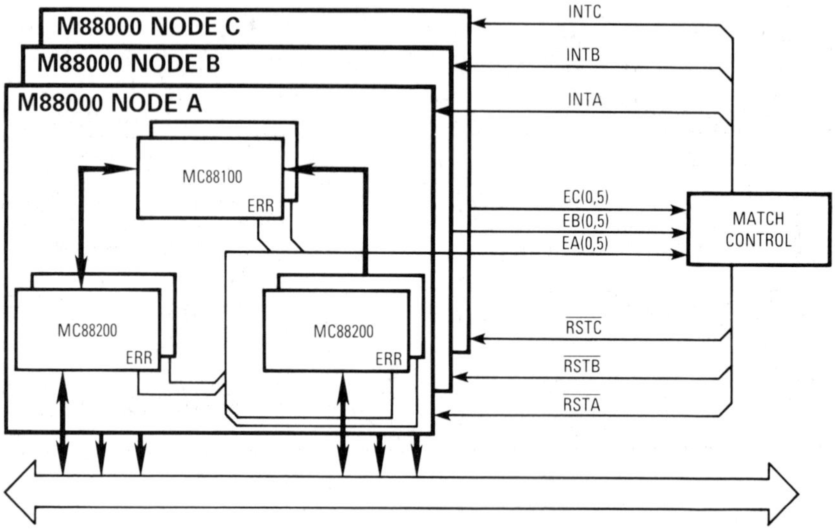

Figure 8-11. Multiprocessing

set, compare and swap, and fetch and add. The memory access is guaranteed to be atomic by an enforced memory bus (M bus) locking protocol. Data coherency protocols implemented by the MC88200 CMMU maintain the atomic memory access in a multiple cache environment and provide very efficient access to synchronization resources.

An **xmem** instruction results in the swap of a destination register and a memory location, shown logically as:

move	temp **r**D
load	**r**D memory location
store	memory location temp

where "temp" is actually a stage of the pipelined data unit (i.e., no general-purpose registers are affected by the instruction except **r**D). The three steps are performed by the processor as an uninterruptable, locked sequence; no exceptions are recognized unless the **xmem** instruction itself encounters an exception (i.e., M bus error or parity error). The processor asserts the data bus lock ($\overline{\text{DLOCK}}$) signal while the **xmem** memory accesses are occurring. This signal must be used by the memory system to block additional bus traffic until both accesses of the **xmem** instruction have completed.

8.4.2 Synchronization Operations

The **xmem** instruction is used to synthesize a wide variety of synchronization operations. Three common operations are examined: test and set, compare and swap, and fetch and add.

8

The semantics of test and set are:

```
test and set unlocked to locked:
  if lock_location = unlocked
    then lock_location ← locked
  else no ← operation
```

The lock_location variable could represent a system semaphore. The data flags "locked" and "unlocked" mean resource not available and resource available, respectively. A process requesting the semaphore-protected resource checks lock_location; if the resource is available (unlocked), then the resource is claimed (locked) by the process. Otherwise, the resource is not available (locked).

This operation can be implemented in MC88100 assembly code. The following sequence demonstrates the general application of **xmem** to a semaphore for protection of a critical resource.

```
                                                 ;lock_location represents a two-
                                                 ;register or register plus immediate
                                                 ;address

spinlock    or       r2,r0,0x0001                ;put the locked flag (= 1) in r2
            xmem     r2,lock_location            ;perform test and set
            bcnd     ne0,r2,spinlock             ;if semaphore not equal unlocked
                                                 ;(defined as zero, repeat
            <critical code>                      ;enter only if semaphore claimed
                   •
                   •
                   •
            st       r0,lock_location            ;clear (unlock) semaphore.
```


This sequence of locking after an active wait period is commonly known as a spinlock. Although simple and effective for enforcing the mutual exclusion of certain global accesses, the spinlock operation can impose system limitations: the "spinning" **xmem** instructions impede other M bus traffic. This degradation appears in a single processor system as delayed instruction fetches. In a multiprocessor environment, the performance degradation is worse because multiple codes attempt synchronization and are stalled in resource contention.

Limitations imposed by bus traffic are substantially reduced in a system that integrates shared snooping caches such as the caches in the MC88200 CMMU. Such caches allow implementation of a test and set variation known as "test and test and set". This is simply a spinlock cycle operating out of a cache instead of operating out of memory. Therefore, bus traffic from "spinning" **xmem** instructions is reduced to only two loads, as shown in the following MC88100 code, plus snooping overhead on global transactions, which may decrease M bus bandwidth.

```
                                                   ;lock_location represents a two-
                                                   ;register or register plus immediate
                                                   ;address

spinlock   ld       r2,lock_location               ;load semaphore into cache
           bcnd     ne0,r2,spinlock                ;spin on cached value
           or       r2,r0,0×0001                   ;put locked value into r2
           xmem     r2,lock_location               ;attempt to claim semaphore
           bcnd     ne0,r2,spinlock                ;if unsuccessful, return to spin
           <critical code>                         ;else enter critical code
                •
                •
                •
           st       r0,lock_location               ;restore semaphore
```

This code exits the cached spin because, when the process owning the resource clears the semaphore, the memory write appears on the M bus. All snooping CMMUs invalidate the semaphore in their caches, thus, this code will experience a cache miss. When the cache miss occurs, the semaphore (now cleared) is read from memory, and the **xmem** instruction is executed to claim the semaphore. If more than one process reads the clear semaphore and tries to claim it, the M bus arbitration priority determines which process gets the semaphore (the one granted the bus for the **xmem** instruction). The MC88200 snooping then ensures that all other cached copies of the semaphore are invalidated when the **xmem** instruction is executed. This entire operation limits the bus traffic to an initial load, a load after cache invalidation from a snoop bit, an **xmem** instruction load and store, and a store to restore the semaphore.

8

The test and set semaphore operation serializes certain global accesses using a memory location that contains simple flags such as "available" and "unavailable". The compare and swap and fetch and add operations, however, must manipulate dynamic data such as counters and pointers. Accesses to these types of global resources must be serialized to ensure proper results, and are therefore constructed using the established test and set (or test and test and set) protection. The exclusiveness of compare and swap, fetch and add, or any other desired operation may be enforced by defining the applicable code as critical and limiting its access to the semaphore owner. The critical code section shown in the previous assembly language sequences will be replaced with the code needed to synthesize a particular synchronization operation. For example, the semantics of compare and swap are as follows:

```
temp ⇐ mem_location
  if register 1 = temp
    mem_location ⇐ register 2
  else register 1 ⇐ temp
```

where mem_location is the address of the protected global resource. The "critical code" that implements the compare and swap operation can be written as follows:

```
                                            ;mem_location represents a two-
                                            ;register or register plus immediate
                                            ;address

          <begin critical code>
             ld      r2,mem_location        ;load resource
             cmp     r4,r1,r2               ;compare to r1 contents
             bb1     3,r4,reg               ;branch if not equal
             st      r2,mem_location        ;else update memory
reg:         or      r1,r0,r3               ;update register
          <end critical code>
```

This portion is then surrounded by the test and set code.

The semantics of the fetch and add operation are as follows:

temp ← mem_location
mem_location ← temp + increment

where "increment" is an increment added to the fetched location. The "critical code" that implements the fetch and add operation can be written as follows:

```
                                            ;mem_location represents a two-
                                            ;register or register plus immediate
                                            ;address

          <begin critical operation>
             ld      r1,mem_location        ;load resource
             add     r1,r1,0×0003           ;increment by 3 (arbitrary value)
             st      r1,mem_location        ;return new value to memory
```

If data caching is used, proper global coherency must be enforced as with the MC88200. Additional discussions of coherency protocols and locked (**xmem**) accesses are provided in the *MC88200 User's Manual*.

8

SECTION 9
ELECTRICAL CHARACTERISTICS

9.1 MAXIMUM RATINGS

Rating	Symbol	Value	Unit
Supply Voltage	V_{CC}	−0.3 to +7.0	V
Input Voltage	V_{in}	−0.3 to +7.0	V
Operating Temperature Range	T_A	0 to 70	°C
Storage Temperature Range	T_{stg}	−55 to +150	°C

This device contains protective circuitry against damage due to high static voltages or electrical fields; however, it is advised that normal precautions be taken to avoid application of any voltages higher than maximum-rated voltages to this high-impedance circuit. Reliability of operation is enhanced if unused inputs are tied to an appropriate logic voltage level (e.g., either GND or V_{CC}).

9.2 THERMAL CHARACTERISTICS — PGA PACKAGE

Characteristic	Symbol	Value	Rating
Thermal Resistance — Ceramic			°C/W
Junction to Ambient	θ_{JA}	25	
Junction to Case	θ_{JC}	10*	

*Estimated

9.3 POWER CONSIDERATIONS

The average chip-junction temperature, T_J, in °C can be obtained from:

$$T_J = T_A + (P_D \cdot \theta_{JA}) \quad (1)$$

where:

T_A = Ambient Temperature, °C
θ_{JA} = Package Thermal Resistance, Junction-to-Ambient, °C/W
P_D = $P_{INT} + P_{I/O}$
P_{INT} = $I_{CC} \times V_{CC}$, Watts — Chip Internal Power
$P_{I/O}$ = Power Dissipation on Input and Output Pins — User Determined

For most applications $P_{I/O} < P_{INT}$ and can be neglected.

The following is an approximate relationship between P_D and T_J (if $P_{I/O}$ is neglected):

$$P_D = K \div (T_J + 273°C) \quad (2)$$

Solving equations (1) and (2) for K gives:

$$K = P_D \cdot (T_A + 273°C) + \theta_{JA} \cdot P_D^2 \quad (3)$$

where K is a constant pertaining to the particular part. K can be determined from equation (3) by measuring P_D (at equilibrium) for a known T_A. Using this value of K, the values of P_D and T_J can be obtained by solving equations (1) and (2) iteratively for any value of T_A.

9

The total thermal resistance of a package (θ_{JA}) can be separated into two components, θ_{JC} and θ_{CA}, representing the barrier to heat flow from the semiconductor junction to the package (case) surface (θ_{JC}) and from the case to the outside ambient (θ_{CA}). These terms are related by the equation:

$$\theta_{JA} = \theta_{JC} + \theta_{CA} \tag{4}$$

θ_{JC} is device related and cannot be influenced by the user. However, θ_{CA} is user dependent and can be minimized by such thermal management techniques as heat sinks, ambient air cooling, and thermal convention. Thus, good thermal management on the part of the user can significantly reduce θ_{CA} so that θ_{JA} approximately equals θ_{JC}. Substitution of θ_{JC} for θ_{JA} in equation (1) will result in a lower semiconductor junction temperature.

Values for thermal resistance presented in this document, unless estimated, were derived using the procedure described in Motorola Reliability Report 7843, "Thermal Resistance Measurement Method for MC68XX Microcomponent Devices," and are provided for design purposes only. Thermal measurements are complex and dependent on procedure and setup. User-derived values for thermal resistance may differ.

9.4 DC ELECTRICAL CHARACTERISTICS (V_{CC} = 5.0 Vdc ± 5%; GND = 0 Vdc; T_A = 0 to 70 C)

Characteristic	Symbol	Min	Max	Unit
Clock Low Voltage	V_{CL}	−0.3	0.2 V_{CC}	V
Clock High Voltage	V_{CH}	0.8 V_{CC}	V_{CC} + 0.3	V
Input Low Voltage (All Inputs Except CLK)	V_{IL}	−0.3	0.8	V
Input High Voltage (All Inputs Except CLK)	V_{IH}	2.0	V_{CC} + 0.3	V
Output Low Voltage @ 8 mA I_{OL}	V_{OL}	—	0.5	V
Output High Voltage @ −4 mA I_{OH}	V_{OH}	2.4	—	V
Input Leakage Current	I_{in}	—	10	μA
High-Impedance Leakage Current	I_{TSI}	—	20	μA
Typical Power Dissipation (T_A = 0°C)	P_D	—	1.5	W
Input Capacitance (V_{in} = 0 V, T_A = 25°C, f = 1 MHz)	C_i	—	15	pF
Output Capacitance (V_{in} = 0 V, T_A = 25°C, f = 1 MHz)	C_o	—	15	pF
Output Load Capacitance	C_L	—	70	pF
AC Output Delay Derating (See Note 1)	C_{LD}	—	1	ns 25 pF

NOTE 1: Only applies when exceeding the specified output load capacitance (C_L). Absolute output load capacitance must be less than or equal to 120 pF per output for correct device operation.

9.5 AC ELECTRICAL SPECIFICATIONS — CLOCK INPUT (see Figure 9-1)

Num	Characteristic	20 MHz		25 MHz		Unit
		Min	Max	Min	Max	
	Frequency of Operation (See Note 1)	16.67	20	20	25	MHz
1	Clock Cycle Time (Measured at 0.5 V_{CC})	50	60	40	50	ns
2, 3	Clock Pulse Width (Measured at 0.5 V_{CC})	(CT* ÷ 2) − 1	(CT* ÷ 2) + 1	(CT* ÷ 2) − 1	(CT* ÷ 2) + 1	ns
4	Clock Rise Time (0.2 V_{CC} to 0.8 V_{CC})	—	5	—	4	ns
5	Clock Fall Time (0.8 V_{CC} to 0.2 V_{CC})	—	5	—	4	ns

*CT = Cycle Time

NOTE 1: The PLLEN and $\overline{RST}$ signals must be asserted as specified (phase-locked operation). Otherwise, correct device operation cannot be guaranteed.

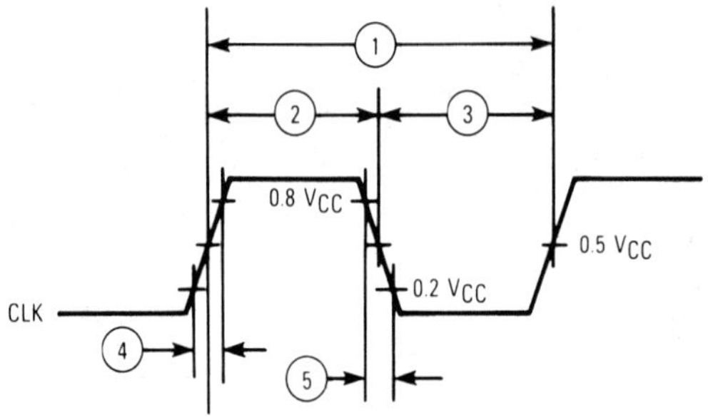

Figure 9-1. Clock Input Timing Diagram

9

9.6 P BUS AC SPECIFICATIONS (see Figure 9-2)

Num	Characteristic	20 MHz		25 MHz		Unit
		Min	Max	Min	Max	
7	CLK Falling to DAxx, DS/$\overline{U}$, $\overline{DLOCK}$, DR/$\overline{W}$, DBEx Valid	—	20	—	16	ns
8	CLK Falling to DAxx, DS/$\overline{U}$, $\overline{DLOCK}$, DR/$\overline{W}$, DBEx V Invalid (Output Hold)	5	—	4	—	ns
9	Later of CLK Rising or Success Reply (DR1/DR0 = 10) Valid to Write Data (Dxx) Valid	—	20	—	16	ns
10	CLK Rising to Write Data (Dxx) Invalid (Output Hold)	5	—	4	—	ns
11	DRx Valid to CLK Falling (Input Setup)	25	—	20	—	ns
12	CLK Falling to DRx Invalid (Input Hold)	3	—	2	—	ns
13	CLK Falling to CAxx, CS/$\overline{U}$, CFETCH Valid	—	20	—	16	ns
14	CLK Falling to CAxx, CS/$\overline{U}$, CFETCH Invalid (Output Hold)	5	—	4	—	ns
15	Read Data (Cxx, Dxx) Valid to CLK Rising (Input Setup)	3	—	2	—	ns
16	CLK Rising to Read Data (Cxx, Dxx) Invalid (Input Hold)	3	—	2	—	ns
17	CRx Valid to CLK Falling (Input Setup)	25	—	20	—	ns
18	CLK Falling to CRx Invalid (Input Hold)	3	—	2	—	ns
20	CLK Rising to Data (Dxx) High-Impedance (Write Followed by Read)	—	8	—	6	ns
21	Later of CLK Rising or Success or Fault Reply (DR1/DR0 = 10) Valid to Data Bus Low-Impedance (see Note 2)	10	—	8	—	ns
22	Data Bus Low-Impedance to Write Data Valid	—	10	—	8	ns
23	CLK Falling to ERR Valid	—	10	—	8	ns
24	CLK Rising to ERR Negated	5	15	4	12	ns

NOTES:

1. CLK Rising/Falling measured from the 0.5 V_{CC} threshold level.
2. This specification provides the time needed for the MC88100 to gate data onto the data bus when a write cycle follows a read cycle.

9.7 MISCELLANEOUS SIGNAL AC SPECIFICATIONS (see Figure 9-3)

Num	Characteristic	20 MHz		25 MHz		Unit
		Min	Max	Min	Max	
25	RST, PLLEN, INT Input Transition Time	—	10	—	10	ns
26	$\overline{RST}$, PCE, INT Valid to Clock Falling (Input Setup) (see Note)	10	25	8	20	ns
27	Clock Falling to P Bus Driven	0	—	0	—	ns

NOTE: This specification is required only to guarantee synchronous operation with other M88000 components. PCE may only transition during reset.

Figures 9-2 and 9-3 are found on a foldout page at the back of this document.

9.8 AC ELECTRICAL SPECIFICATIONS DEFINITIONS

The AC specifications presented consist of output delays, input setup and hold times, and signal skew times. All signals are specified relative to an appropriate edge of the M88000 clock input and, possibly, relative to one or more other signals.

The measurement of the AC specifications is defined by the waveforms in Figure 9-4. To test the parameters guaranteed by Motorola, inputs must be driven to the voltage levels specified in Figure 9-4. Outputs of the M88000 are specified with minimum and/or maximum limits, as appropriate, and are measured as shown. Inputs to the M88000 are specified with minimum and, as appropriate, maximum setup and hold times and are measured as shown. Finally, the measurements for signal-to-signal specifications are also shown.

Note that the testing levels used to verify conformance of the M88000 to the AC specifications does not affect the guaranteed DC operation of the device as specified in the DC electrical characteristics.

9

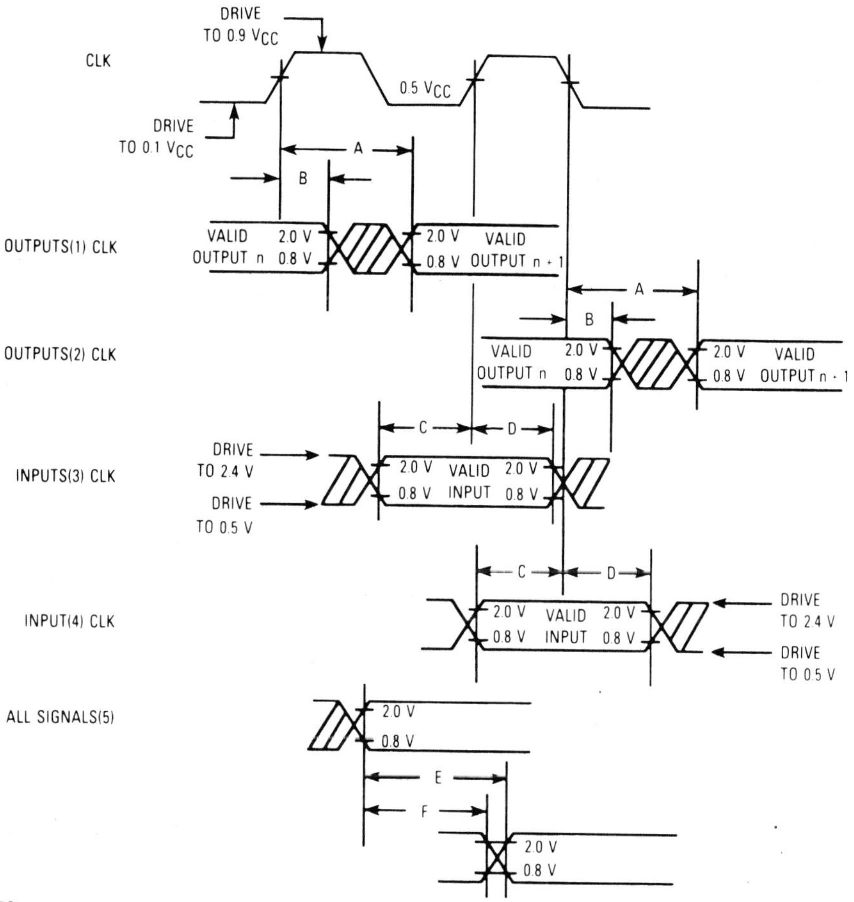

NOTES:

1. This output timing is applicable to all parameters specified relative to the rising edge of the clock.
2. This output timing is applicable to all parameters specified relative to the falling edge of the clock.
3. This input timing is applicable to all parameters specified relative to the rising edge of the clock.
4. This input timing is applicable to all parameters specified relative to the falling edge of the clock.
5. This timing is applicable to all parameters specified relative to the assertion negation of another signal.

LEGEND:

A Maximum output delay specification.
B Minimum output hold time.
C Minimum input setup time specification.
D Minimum input hold time specification.
E Signal valid to signal valid specification (maximum or minimum).
F Signal valid to signal invalid specification (maximum or minimum).

Figure 9-4. Drive Levels and Test Points for AC Specifications

SECTION 10
ORDERING INFORMATION AND MECHANICAL DATA

This section contains the pin assignments and package dimensions diagrams for the MC88100, and also information is provided to be used as a guide when ordering.

10.1 ORDERING INFORMATION

The following table provides ordering information pertaining to the package type, frequency, temperature, and Motorola order number for the MC88100.

Package Type	Frequency (MHz)	Temperature	Order Number
Ceramic Package RC Suffix	20.0 25.0	0°C to 70°C 0°C to 70°C	MC88100RC20 MC88100RC25

10

10.2 PIN ASSIGNMENTS

The MC88100 is available in an 180-pin package. The following figure shows the pin assignment for the MC88100. Pin grouping for power and ground are also listed.

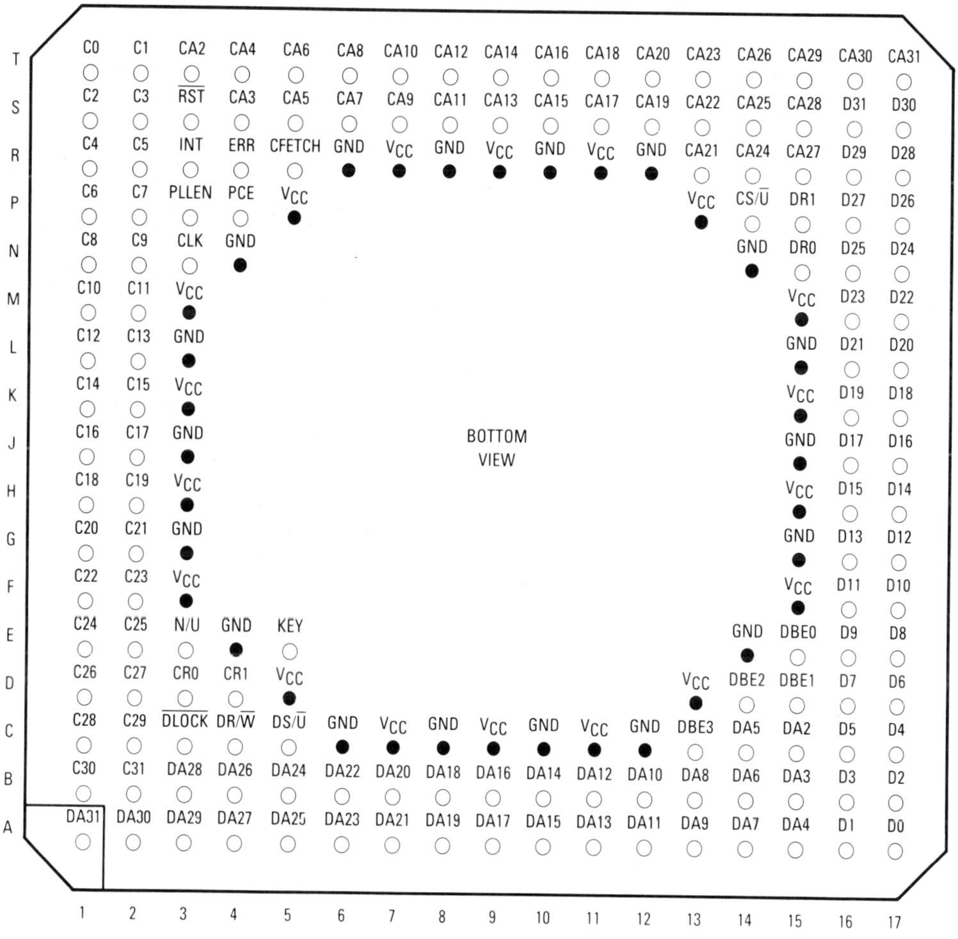

10

N/U = Not Usable

Note: The "KEY" pin is an alignment key with no internal connection.

Pin Group	V_{CC}	GND
Internal Logic	C11, K3, M3, M15, P5	L3, C12, J3, N4, N14
External Signals and Buses	C7, C9, D5, D13, F3, F15, H3, H15, K15, P13, R7, R9, R11	C6, C8, C10, E4, E14, G3, G15, J15, L15, R6, R8, R10, R12

10.3 MECHANICAL DATA

The following figure provides the package dimensions for the MC88100.

RC SUFFIX
CERAMIC PACKAGE
CASE 823-01

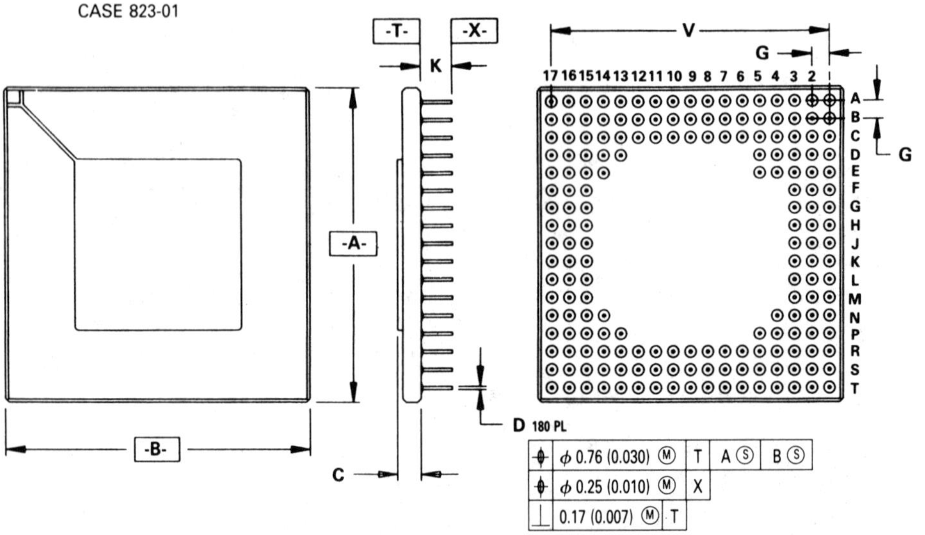

NOTES:
1. DIMENSIONING AND TOLERANCING PER ANSI Y14.5M, 1982.
2. CONTROLLING DIMENSION: INCH.

	MILLIMETERS		INCHES	
DIM	MIN	MAX	MIN	MAX
A	44.20	45.21	1.740	1.780
B	44.20	45.21	1.740	1.780
C	3.05	3.86	0.120	0.152
D	0.41	0.50	0.016	0.020
G	2.54 BSC		0.100 BSC	
K	4.07	5.08	0.160	0.200
V	40.64 BSC		1.600 BSC	

10

GLOSSARY

BATC: See **Block Address Translation Cache**.

Big Endian: A byte-ordering method in memory where the address n of a word corresponds to the most significant byte. In an addressed memory word, the bytes are ordered (left to right) 0, 1, 2, and 3, with 0 being the most significant byte. See **Little Endian**.

Block Address Translation Cache (BATC): A small cache memory in the MC88200 CMMU used for address translation. The BATC contains eight programmable entries for translating 512K-byte logical addresses into 512K-byte physical addresses. Two other BATC entries are hardwired for translating addresses in the control memory space.

Cache: Small, high-speed memory containing recently accessed data and/or instructions.

Checker Mode: An operating mode of both the MC88100 processor and the MC88200 CMMU. Checker mode is used in system configurations with parallel, redundant components, where at least one component is the master; i.e., that component performs the meaningful processing. The checker component never drives the bus(es), but it executes all instructions, functions, etc. and monitors all signals as inputs. If the checker finds a mismatch between its calculated result and the result of the master, an error is signaled. See **Master Mode**.

CMMU: Acronym for the MC88200 Cache/Memory Management Unit.

Context: The internal state of the processor that defines the current execution. The context includes the contents of the various execution pipelines and the state of the register file.

Control Register:

1. An MC88100 register that controls processor execution, provides processor status, or holds context information during an exception. The MC88100 contains two sets of control registers, one associated with the integer unit and one associated with the floating-point unit.

2. An MC88200 register that controls component execution and provides status, that provides BATC load ports, or that provides cache diagnostic information.

Data Unit: The functional unit in the MC88100 processor responsible for data memory accesses.

Delayed Branching: A scheme by which a branch instruction completes execution after the next sequential instruction. This scheme is used to reduce pipeline delays. When the branch instruction is encountered, it is decoded and the target address calculation begins. Then, the next sequential instruction executes while the address calculation completes since it was already decoded in the pipeline. This instruction normally completes at the time that the branch target instruction has been fetched so no processor time is wasted.

Destination Register: The general-purpose register that receives the result of a data manipulation or load instruction. If the instruction produces a double word or double-precision floating-point result, then there are two adjacent destination registers (n and n + 1). Register 0 is hardwired to contain the constant zero, so a write to **r0** is a no-op and the result is lost.

Displacement: The offset of a field, register, data word, or instruction from a given base address.

Exception: An unusual or error condition encountered by the processor or the CMMU that results in special processing. Exceptions for the processor can be caused by arithmetic overflow or underflow, privilege violations, and other conditions; for the CMMU, they can be caused by bus errors and privilege violations, among other conditions. When exceptions occur, the processor stops the current execution and transfers control to the appropriate exception handler. When the CMMU encounters an exception condition, it stops processing and signals the processor that an exception occurred. Exceptions also occur when trap instructions are executed by the processor.

Exception Handler: A software routine that executes when an exception occurs. Normally, the exception handler will correct the condition that caused the exception, or perform some other meaningful task (such as aborting the program that caused the exception). Exception handlers are defined by a two-word exception vector which is branched to automatically when an exception occurs.

Exception-Time Register: A control register that is loaded by hardware when an exception occurs. The data loaded into the register is either part of the execution context or is significant to the exception. See **Shadow Register**.

Execute Instruction Pointer (XIP): The internal register containing the logical address of instruction currently being executed. Conceptually, the executing instruction is "in" the integer unit, the floating-point unit, or the data unit being executed (although the MC88100 does not physically move the instruction to the execution unit).

G

Fault: A logical memory error that causes an exception. Faults are caused by invalid memory descriptors or protection violations, both situations that can be corrected by software.

Feed Forward: An MC88100 feature that reduces the number of clock cycles that an execution unit must wait to use a register. When the source register of the current instruction is the same as the destination register of the previous instruction, the result of the previous instruction is routed to the current instruction at the same time that

is written to the register file. With feed forward, the destination bus is gated to the waiting execution unit over the appropriate source bus, saving the cycles which would be used for the write and read. Without feed forward, the second instruction must wait for the register to be written, then must read the register.

Fetch Instruction Pointer (FIP): The internal register containing the logical address of the instruction currently being read from memory. Once the instruction is fetched, the FIP is transferred to the next instruction pointer (NIP) as the instruction is decoded.

Floating-Point Unit: The functional unit in the MC88100 processor responsible for executing all floating-point instructions plus integer multiply and divide instructions.

General-Purpose Register: Any of the 32 registers in the MC88100 register file. These registers provide the source operands and destination results for all MC88100 data manipulation instructions. Load instructions move data from memory to registers, and store instructions move data from registers to memory.

Harvard Architecture: A computer design featuring separate memory access ports for instructions and data. The MC88100 implements a full Harvard architecture: there is one instruction port and one data port, and each port has separate address and data (instruction) lines.

IEEE 754: A standard written by the Institute of Electrical and Electronics Engineers that defines operations of binary floating-point arithmetic and representations of binary floating-point numbers. The MC88100 implements a subset of the IEEE 754 floating-point operations. This standard is also approved by the American National Standards Institute (ANSI).

Immediate: An instruction operand encoded into the 32-bit instruction. Operands may also be stored in registers or may be in memory for load and exchange instructions.

Integer Unit: The functional unit in the MC88100 processor responsible for executing all instructions except floating point, integer multiply and divide, and memory access instructions.

Internal Registers: Four registers in the MC88100 that are not directly available by software. The registers are the three instruction pointers (XIP, NIP, and FIP) and the scoreboard register.

Instruction Unit: The functional unit in the MC88100 processor that fetches all instructions from memory and performs the initial stages of instruction decoding. The instruction unit also performs some branch address calculations.

Interrupt: An external signal that causes the MC88100 to suspend current execution and take a predefined exception.

Little Endian: A byte-ordering method in memory where the address n of a word corresponds to the least significant byte. In an addressed memory word, the bytes are ordered (left to right) 3, 2, 1, 0, with 3 being the most significant byte. See **Big Endian**.

G

M Bus: The interface between the MC88200 and system memory. The M bus provides 32-bit multiplexed address and data signals with parity protection, control signals with parity protection, and arbitration signals. See **P Bus**.

Master Mode: The normal operating mode of the MC88100 processor and the MC88200 CMMU. In systems with parallel, redundant components, the master components perform meaningful processing, while other components ("checkers") provide redundant error checking. See **Checker Mode**.

Next Instruction Pointer (NIP): The internal register containing the logical address of the instruction currently being decoded. Once the instruction is decoded, it is dispatched to an execution unit, and the NIP is transferred to the execute instruction pointer (XIP).

Overflow: An error condition that occurs during arithmetic operations when the result cannot be stored accurately in the destination register(s). For example, if two 32-bit numbers are added, the sum may require 33 bits due to carry. Since the 32-bit registers of the MC88100 cannot represent this sum, an overflow condition occurs. The MC88100 takes an arithmetic overflow exception (integer operations) or a floating-point imprecise exception (floating-point operations) when an overflow occurs. Overflows only occur on signed add and subtract instructions (**add**, **fadd**, **sub**, **fsub**).

P Bus: The interface between the MC88100 processor and memory MC88200 CMMU. The P bus provides dedicated 32-bit address and data signals plus control signals. There is one P bus for data transfers and one P bus for instruction transfers. See **M Bus**.

Page: A 4K-byte area of memory, aligned on a 4K byte boundary.

Page Address Translation Cache (PATC): A cache memory in the MC88200 CMMU used for address translation. The PATC contains 56 entires for translating 4K-byte logical page addresses into 4K-byte physical page addresses. The PATC entries are loaded and updated automatically by the MC88200 hardware.

Pipelining: A technique that breaks instruction execution into distinct steps so that multiple steps can be performed at the same time. Instruction execution is broken into three stages: fetch, decode, and execute. While one instruction is executing, the next instruction is being decoded, and the next is being fetched from memory. The three instruction pointers (XIP, NIP, and FIP) correspond to the three stages in the pipeline. The execute step in instruction execution may also be pipelined; data memory accesses, floating-point operations, and integer multiplies and divides are all performed in parallel with other instruction execution.

Register File: The functional unit in the MC88100 processor that contains the 32 general-purpose registers. These registers provide source operands and/or result destinations for all MC88100 instructions.

Scaled Indexing: A memory access with the address adjusted to the size of the access. For example, words are aligned on modulo 4 address boundaries; a scaled access to a word has the offset shifted left by two bits. The two least significant bits are filled with zeros, making the offset a modulo 4 value. See **Unscaled Indexing**.

G

Scoreboard: An internal register that tracks which general-purpose registers are currently in use. When an execution unit reserves a register as a destination register, then the corresponding bit in the scoreboard is set. Other units check the scoreboard bit to determine if the register is in use or available.

Sequencer: The functional unit in the MC88100 processor that controls register reads and writes, exception recognition, and program flow.

SFU: See **Special Function Unit**.

Shadow Register: Any of the MC88100 control registers that maintain a copy of the internal registers. There are shadow registers for each instruction pointer (FIP, NIP, and XIP), for the scoreboard, for each stage of the data unit pipeline, and for certain floating-point registers. On each clock cycle, the shadow registers are updated to reflect the contents of the internal register that they shadow. See **Exception-Time Register**.

Source 1 Register: A general-purpose register that provides one of the operands for an instruction. This register is specified by a 5-bit field in a fixed location in the MC88100 instructions.

Source 2 Register: A general-purpose register that provides the second or the only operand for an instruction. Instructions with only one source operand use the Source 2 register to supply that operand. This register is specified by a 5-bit field in a fixed location in the MC88100 instructions.

Special Function Unit (SFU): A special-purpose execution unit in the MC88100. An SFU executes instructions concurrently with other SFUs and with the integer, data, and instruction units.

Supervisor Mode: The privileged operating state of the MC88100. In supervisor mode, software can access all control registers and can access the supervisor memory space, among other privileged operations. See **User Mode**.

Underflow: An error condition that occurs during arithmetic operations when the result cannot be represented accurately in the destination register. For example, underflow can happen if two floating-point fractions are multiplied and the result is a single-precision number. The result may require a larger exponent and/or mantissa than the single-precision format makes available. In other words, the result is too small to be represented accurately.

Unscaled Indexing: An indexed memory access to or from an address formed by addition. See **Scaled Indexing**.

User Mode: The unprivileged operating state of the MC88100. In user mode, software can only access certain control registers and can only access user memory space. No privileged operations can be performed. See **Supervisor Mode**.

VBR: See **Vector Base Register**.

Vector: Two contiguous memory words that contain instructions for handling an exception, trap instruction, or other special condition. Normally, a vector contains a branch or jump instruction that passes control to a proper handling routine.

Vector Base Register (VBR): An MC88100 control register that points to the beginning of a memory page containing vectors. All software vectors are accessed by adding an offset to the vector base register; the offset is encoded in the instruction. Hardware vectors are accessed through the VBR by hardware.

Writeback Slot: The time period provided by the sequencer for the integer unit, data unit, and floating-point unit to write results to the register file.

XIP: See **Execute Instruction Pointer**.

G

INDEX

I

— F —

— G —

— I —

I

I

— J —

— L —

— M —

— N —

— P —

— R —

— S —

— T —

— U —

— V —

— W —

I

6-21 In **6.7.2 Instruction Tracing**, item 5, the third sentence should read: "Additionally, if single-instruction execution is to be performed, the exception handler should set the E bit in the saved SNIP since the saved SNIP is copied to the SFIP as part of the instruction access exception handler before returning from the exception."

6-23 In Table 6-5 Data Memory Transaction Register Bit Uses, the Actions and Options for Synthesizing Load, Store, and Exchange Memory Instructions for the WRITE bit (bit 1) is dependent on the LOCK bit, not LOCKBAR. The word LOCKBAR should be replaced by LOCK.

6-24 The first sentence in the DOUB1 description should be modified to delete the information in parenthesis, "(or the load portion of an **xmem** operation)". Also, the following sentences should replace the second to the last sentence in the same paragraph: "The **xmem** instruction is also a two-stage instruction, where the first part is the load from memory to a register and the second part is a store from the same register to the same address in memory. However, for this instruction, DOUB1 is not set in the DMTx register, but the same information can be obtained by looking at the LOCK and WRITE bits in the same register."

6-24 In the paragraph describing the LOCK bit, the word "wich" is misspelled. It should be "which".

6-31 Delete the second paragraph of the page. Then, add the following paragraphs at the end of **6.8 FPU EXCEPTION PROCESSING**:

Users can supply exception handlers that replace or pre-empt the Motorola-supplied (default) exception handlers. Each user exception handler can provide a result to be used instead of the one that would be generated by the default exception handler. The user exception handlers are enabled by setting the enable bits of the FPCR.

The floating-point exception handling software envelope provides two functions: a managing routine and exception handling code. The managing routine looks at the exception and sets up the environment for a call to either the Motorola-supplied exception handler or user-supplied exception handler. While the same managing routine is used, one or the other exception handler is used depending on whether or not the enable bit is set in the FPCR.

The default exception handlers return with a result and with the appropriate accumulative status bit(s) in the FPSR set according to the IEEE 754 standard. However, the floating-point exception handling software envelope will not set the appropriate accumulative status bit(s) in the FPSR before calling the user exception handler. Since the bit(s) is accumulative, it may still be set from a previous operation.

6-41 Replace section **6.8.4.2 FLOATING-POINT INTEGER CONVERSION OVERFLOW** with the following three paragraphs:

This exception occurs when a conversion to integer is attempted for a floating-point number that **may** be too large in magnitude after rounding to be represented as an integer. This exception occurs when the floating-point exponent is greater than or equal to 30, since rounding may cause overflow. The exception handler must determine if overflow will really occur. The largest-magnitude positive integer that can be represented by the MC88100 is $2^{31}-1$; the largest-magnitude negative integer that can be represented by the MC88100 is -2^{31}. This exception causes the FIOV bit (bit 7) of the FPECR to be set by the hardware and the precise exception vector to be taken.

How the exception handler processes the exception depends on whether or not the floating-point number can be represented as a 32-bit integer. If it can, then the exception handler determines whether or not there is a loss of accuracy. If there is no loss of accuracy, then the valid result is written to the destination register and normal processing resumes. If

6-16 **6.4.3.4 COMPLETING FPU INSTRUCTIONS IN PROGRESS** should be rewritten as follows:

The exception processing sequence performed by the MC88100 causes the FPU to be disabled (SFD1 bit of PSR is set), which prevents the FPU from writing results back to the register file and from executing new instructions. An exception handler performing a task swap should not save the context of the first task without allowing all FPU operations to complete; otherwise, the results of the FPU operations of the first task will be lost.

To allow all FPU instructions in progress to complete within the exception handler, an **rte** can be executed that returns control to a trap-not-taken instruction (i.e., **tb1 0,r0,0**). The **rte** causes the exception time and shadow registers to be restored into the appropriate execution units and pipelines so that all FPU operations complete. The trap-not-taken instruction forces the software to wait for the FPU to complete.

The location of the trap-not-taken instruction is within the current exception handler and requires supervisor mode if the designated vector number is 0 - 127. The EPSR and shadow instruction pointers (SXIP, SNIP, SFIP) should be saved before modifying them to execute the trap-not-taken instruction. The EPSR needs to enable the FPU (clear the SFD1 bit) and set the supervisor mode (MODE bit). The shadow instruction pointers need to point to the location of the trap-not-taken instruction. The easiest way to do this is to clear the Valid (V) bit in both the SXIP and SNIP. The SFIP should be loaded with the address of the trap-not-taken instruction. In addition, the Exception (E) bit of the SFIP should be cleared and the V bit set. Once the EPSR and shadow instruction pointers are modified, the **rte** is executed. The rest of the exception handler code is located after the trap-not-taken instruction since the trap-not-taken does not generate another exception. An example is in the following listing:

```
exception_task_swap:
  ;
  xcr    r24,cr19              ; cr19 points to the context save area for this task
  st     r1,r24,0              ; save current r1 value
  ldcr   r1,cr2                ; get EPSR value
  st     r1,r24,(34*4)         ; save current EPSR
  or.u   r1,r1,0x8000          ; set the MODE bit
  and    r1,r1,0xfff7          ; clear the SFD1 bit
  stcr   r1,cr2                ; restore modified EPSR
  ldcr   r1,cr4                ; get SXIP
  st     r1,r24,(36*4)         ; save current SXIP
  stcr   r0,cr2                ; clear the Valld bit
  ldcr   r1,cr5                ; get SNIP
  st     r1,r24,(37*4)         ; save current SNIP
  stcr   r0,cr5                ; clear the Valid bit
  ldcr   r1,cr6                ; get SFIP
  st     r1,r24,(38*4)         ; save current SFIP
  or.u   r1,r0,trap_not_taken  ; init address for rte
  or     r1,r1,trap_not_taken
  or     r1,r1,0x2             ; set Valid bit and clear Exception bit
  stcr   r1,cr6                ; initialize SFIP to trap_not_taken
  or     r0,r0,r0              ; no-op instruction
  rte    ; go execute trap_not_taken
trap_not_taken:
  tb1    0,r0,0                ; trap is never taken since r0 is always zero
  ;
  ; The rest of the exception handler would now appear below
```

AF807929